Bridging Eight Decades

Bridging Eight Decades

My Life Story—A Memoir and More

Harold E. Kieler

To order additional copies of this book, contact:
Xlibris Corporation
1-888-795-4274
www.Xlibris.com
Orders@Xlibris.com
24002

Dedicated

To Lorine, in gratitude for
fifty unspeakably good years
of fun, faith and love,
patience and joy

To our sons
and their families
BEN
Angela and "Little Ben," Alison, and Michael
BILL
Paula and Naomi
PAUL
Janet, Anika, and Solomon Li Kieler

To our heirs yet unborn

Contents

Acknowledgements

As a novice, I owe appreciation to more people than I can name for assisting me in the adventure of this writing. To all who gave me encouragement and assistance, I am deeply grateful.

For helping me to begin, and for encouraging me along the way, I acknowledge the Shepherd Center of East Wichita housed in The East Heights United Methodist Church and especially its Memoir Writing Class. My first teacher there was Glenn W. Fisher, who was then followed by Edith Coe. Without Glenn and Edith this Memoir would have never come into being. Without my wife Lorine's patience, tolerance, and consultative skills it never would have happened.

I am especially indebted to all three of these persons, Glenn, Edith, and Lorine, for reading almost all the manuscript, aiding in problem identification and providing good counsel. I did not always follow their advice, and I sometimes revised portions of the manuscript without consultation after they had seen it. Therefore, they cannot be held accountable for grammatical and spelling errors, for typos and stylistic difficulties.

I am a near computer illiterate. I shall be eternally grateful to John and Linda Flakes of UNIQUELY US!, Computer Consultants, for assisting me in so many ways.

Again, my appreciation to all the friends and family who nudged and encouraged.

Forward

Throughout time, family memories and spiritual truths have been passed from generation to generation through the ancient art of storytelling or by what is called "oral tradition." This was an easy and natural process. In nomadic and primitive times, the evening campfire as well as the day's activities served to keep family and tribal memories alive. Even as cultures and civilizations evolved, several generations might live under the same roof or families would live in close proximity to one another. Passing the stories on was still easy.

Sad to say, in more recent time, families have increasingly drifted apart from one another living not only in scattered corners of their native land, but in scattered areas of the world. We are losing the old customs of preserving and transmitting family memories.

These pages represent one small effort on my part to keep alive what Philip Geeves had called "the most perishable of inheritances."

Chapter 1

IN THE BEGINNING

"In the beginning God created . . ." are the familiar opening words of affirmation in the Judeo-Christian Bible, and I find it interesting to ponder my own beginnings.

It must have been that I was conceived when my parents were cuddling and became passionate and sexually intimate on a cold winter's night in mid-January, 1929. Through the mysterious and marvelous workings of nature and of nature's God, my life began. A little fetus grew and was nurtured in my mother's womb until that fullness of time when there was a natural viability for me to exist as a human being. Then at last, if I may paraphrase a few sentences from the memoirs of Wayne Karlowski, an older colleague of mine, though I was not aware of the day or date, nor that I was missing the beauty of the glorious October world in Kansas, though I felt very secure and safe there in my mother's womb, I felt an urge to get out! The divine urge that accompanies all birthing was saying to me, "Go on little child of mine and do not be afraid—the world out there is for you. It's good and it's bad, but it's been prepared to be your home for a span of time. Go!" So I entered into my life on Planet Earth at St. Elizabeth Hospital in Hutchinson, Kansas, the United States of America, in the Western and Northern Hemispheres of Planet Earth in this Universe. This is where I first saw the light of Earth. I cannot remember it though, nor did I hear my mother's cry of pain as she released me, nor my father's joy when he first saw that God had given him a son. Another Kieler child was here! A new generation had been started.

Keeping with custom, my parents soon sent an announcement of my birth to family and close friends. We can no longer find the original text but the "jist of it" was:

Who?   Harold Eugene Kieler
What?   A boy born to Fred Albert and Blanche Harriet Kieler
Where?   In St. Elizabeth, Hutchinson, Kansas
When?   October 14, 1929
Why?   Because this was the place my parents lived after they were married. You'll learn more about them as this story unfolds.
How?   A Dr. J. C. Butler delivered me.
And the Day I Was Born? What was it like?

Herbert Hoover was President of the United States of America. The main headline on the front page of the *Hutchinson News* was "ATHLETICS WIN CHAMPIONSHIP"—referring to baseball's World Series with the article describing a dramatic ninth inning rally in which the Philadelphia Athletics of the American League won the world championship of baseball by defeating the Chicago Cubs of the National League 3 to 2. Other main headlines on the front page were:
"CHINA FACING FRESH BURST OF CIVIL WAR"
"SOVIET AIRMEN MAY ATTEMPT ATLANTIC HOP"

> "Safe in Seattle, Washington, after a hazardous flight from Moscow, four Russian aviators today disclosed that they were considering a trans-Atlantic flight as a sequel to this undertaking thus making a complete round-the-world flight."

"SANTA FE TO EXTEND LINES IN SOUTHWEST U. S.—

380 miles of new track to serve farming areas untouched by RRs."

"FRANCE ACTING TO PROTECT HER SOUTHERN FRONTIER—Larger Sum Spent Closing the Gate From Italy than on German Frontier"

"FOX WOULD HAVE TALKIES IN EVERY CHURCH, SCHOOL"

The article referred to a program for the expenditure of three million dollars during the next 25 years to put talking motion pictures in every schoolroom, church, and home. The announcement was made by Mr. William Fox in celebration of his entry 25 years before into the motion picture business.

"EINSTEIN TO TAKE PART IN EDISON CELEBRATION IN DETROIT"

"Albert Einstein, German physicist, will have a part in the celebration to be staged in Dearborn next Monday in honor of Thomas Edison. He will speak into a microphone from a Berlin Studio to Dearborn where his words will be re-broadcast."

"WEATHER"

Fair tonight and Tuesday; not much change in temperature.
Noon temp 72F Minimum 49F Yesterday's Max. 81F
Roads: Wichita—foggy; rough to good roads
Ottawa—clear; rough roads

Dodge City—foggy; rough to good roads
Hutchinson—clearing; roads good

Other pages of the local paper on the day I was born went like this:

Page 2—Advertisements

Page 3—Local News reporting things like the appointment of Methodist Pastors, Funerals, Scouting, "A Case of Poison Booze Hits Workman Who is Hospitalized," "10 Arrests by Police Was the Week-end Toll of Demon Liquor in Hutchinson"

Page 8—The Woman's Page reporting society news, club news, church notes, etc.

Page 9—More Local and Kansas News including news of business, farming, and letters to the editor

Page 10—Sports and Movies including these ads: 10 cents for admission to the

IRIS Theater to see the movie "Blue Satin"
ROYAL theater: Al Jolson musical "Say It With Song"
15 to 35 cents matinees; 35-50 cents evenings
(Lower price in the Balcony)

Page 12—Economic News "No Enthusiasm In Stock Market" Main trend upward following 2 day holiday, but soft spots are to be found"

The rest of the paper was filled with advertisements. Here are some of the advertisements the week I was born:

CURTIS STORE SALE: Single blankets for children 89 cents; part wool double blankets $3.50; Woman's Dress Coat with silk lining fur trimmed $25; boys' knee length ribbed underwear, 50 cents; men's work sox 10 cents.

PEGUES-WRIGHT CO: Home Frocks (dresses) from $1.95 up to $ 3.95.

GOOD DENTISTRY: An upper or lower plate of false teeth, $17.50.

BUICK "MARQUETTE" auto: $965 to $1,035.

GROCERIES:

Rice 3.5 lbs.—-25 cents	Coffee 50 cents /pound
Raisins 2 lbs.—17 cents	Swiss steak 30 cents/pound
48 pounds flour—$1.59	Picnic Hams 19 cents/pound
Bushel of Apples $1.59	
3 lbs. grapes 25 cents	"Redi-Sliced" Bread.

Chapter 2

I WAS BORN . . .
THE STOCK MARKET CRASHED!

I was born. The stock market crashed. The month was October 1929. I was born October 14, 1929. Five days later the stock market crash of 1929 began with impulsive selling of stocks in epidemic proportions. Five more days, by October 24, the Wall Street market hit bottom. The financial boom of the 1920s lay shattered on the floor of the New York Stock Exchange. Millions of Americans had lost their life savings. So I've often jokingly said, I was born and this was the beginning of what American historians call the Great American Depression—a period of great unemployment and massive poverty which was to last a decade. But this was not a joking matter for most Americans living in the nineteen thirties. Many people, especially in the larger cities, were unable to find jobs and could barely find food enough for their survival.

People often ask one another, "What is the earliest memory you have in your life?" I'm not able to identify "the" earliest memory, but I have a cluster of early memories pertaining to "The Depression" as we called it and to the "Dust Bowl." Many of these memories are from listening to adults, usually my own relatives, passionately discussing the pros and cons of the programs of President Franklin D. Roosevelt who followed President Hoover in office. People were so desperate to meet their various physical and social needs that the nation was moved to implement social welfare programs similar to those which Western European nations had adopted decades earlier. The Social Security Act of 1935 was one of these. Some citizens felt very positive about these programs. Others were very critical of them. Discussion never ceased. In spite of the help Social Security gave people, millions of able-bodied citizens still faced social and financial disaster.

Starting in 1933 "Relief" or monetary handouts was paid to help people. President Roosevelt, like many others, felt this demeaned people and destroyed the human spirit so he issued an executive order establishing a Works Progress Administration or "WPA" to take the place of "Relief." Some criticized the WPA as being "just another form of relief—'made-up' work" rather than "real work." WPA was one of the largest public works program ever undertaken by any nation at that time. There were people who felt it was modeled too much on the programs of communist nations. These "public works" built dams, parks, schools, airports, roads, and bridges and also employed professionals to work in their own fields of art, music, writing, and to decorate public buildings, create and perform music, catalogue such things as graveyards, write history, etc. Another criticism that people had of the WPA was that at best it employed less than half of those who were jobless. I remember times our family would drive around looking at "WPA projects." Everyone was quick to express an opinion about how good or not so good these public works were.

The CCC—Civilian Conservation Corp—was another of Roosevelt's programs. In contrast to the public works of the WPA, the work of the CCC was the restoration of the nation's natural resources. This program took unemployed young families off the streets by enrolling the head of the family. The enrollee was paid $25/month and provided with food, lodging, and a uniform. The program was administered by Army officers. There were 3 million enrollees across the nation. Those who looked down on the program called its enrollees by derisive names such as "Roosevelt's Tree Army" and "Soil Soldiers."

Another cause of the Depression, beyond the stock market crash in 1929, was the "Dust Bowl" of the 1930s. This was a time of great drought and wind whipped dust storms. The Dust Bowl was triggered not only by the drought, but by economic excesses. Soaring grain prices following World War I tempted farmers to plow up 100,000s of thousands of acres of native prairie in Western Kansas and in adjoining states to the south, west and north of Kansas. This newly broken ground was to plant larger acreages of cash crops—grain and row crops. When rains failed in the thirties, the prevailing winds (similar in velocity to those over the open ocean) whipped up the top soil turning it into "black blizzards" with devastating consequences in states near and far. I remember street lights being turned on at mid-day in Hutchinson because the dust clouds made it so dark. Margaret Kieler, my second cousin who taught school in Mullinville, Kansas talked about these blizzards bring a mid-day darkness blacker than night. She told how people hung wet towels and sheets around doors and windows to prevent dust from invading their homes. Farms failed. Then businesses supported by agriculture failed.

John Steinbeck's novel, *The Gapes of Wrath*, portrayed the exodus of people from the Great Plains and the social consequences of this. By the mid-thirties the more social and technical aid programs of the Civilian Conservation Corps and the Soil Conservation Service were codified by Congress. The CCC planted millions of trees lining roadsides and farm property lines to help stop blowing soil. With the return of normal precipitation in 1940, Kansas and the rest of the Great Plains region once again became the nation's "breadbasket."

Even in the midst of the Depression and the Dust Bowl many Kansas people could still eke out some kind of small garden and raise at least a few animals or fowls for their own use as food. Our family was fortunate in many ways. While the "mind set" of the Depression marked all of us who lived or grew up during it, my

Dad was never without work. My relatives were always close enough to the land, if not actually on a farm, that they could "get by" even in financial hard times raising their own food and sharing with one another in the family. I still picture the times we got together as an extended family. Everybody brought something to share with the others—fresh garden products, fresh meat, home-canned and home baked foods. Even though specifics of my very young years may be lost to my conscious memory, I remember the times of economic struggle and the prevailing feeling of everyone that "we must conserve and preserve what we have of our perishable resources."

Other kinds of pictures in my mind from early childhood relate to food and related items and deliveries to our home. I can visualize moments when I was standing at our front window, looking outdoors, waiting and watching for certain people to come along our street—the milkman, the iceman, the mailman, the trash collector, an occasional farmer peddling his produce, a Fuller Brush salesman or an Avon Lady.

Milk was delivered to our front door in an assortment of returnable glass bottles (pints, quarts, gallons, etc.) none of which were ever thrown away. These bottles had coin-like waxed cardboard lids that snapped inside a little ring-shaped depression at the top. Milk was delivered early in the morning and placed on our front porch. Though one could also order cream, butter, cottage cheese and cheese, most commonly it was simply whole milk which was delivered (they didn't have homogenized milk yet). This meant that the cream always rose to the top of any bottle. You could clearly see the line between just "milk" and "cream" because the cream was a darker richer color. Commonly people would "pour off" the cream and save it for special uses. In the wintertime, if I didn't see the milkman come or if we were forgetful or slow to bring the milk indoors to the Ice Box, the cream at the top might freeze forming a stick-like column pushing the cardboard cap up sometimes as high as two or more inches!

Speaking of ice boxes, this is what we had preceding the electric refrigerators of today. Ice Boxes were literally thickly insulated wood boxes that stood stacked and attached in two layers. The top box was a chest with a lid opening upward so large blocks of ice (25 or 50 pound blocks) could be lowered into the chest. The chest was so designed that the ice-cooled air would settle down into the lower box, which had a door that opened to the front. This was the area where food was placed to be kept cool.

My earliest recollection of ice delivery is that ice came in a horse-drawn wagon. It was delivered two or three times a week by the "iceman" who brought it to the back door, the door leading into the kitchen. He would knock and then proceed to step inside and place the needed amount of ice into the ice box. Before long, though, technology caught up with us and the ice wagons were replaced with ice trucks. Then, by 1940, ice boxes were made obsolete with the introduction of gas or electric refrigerators.

My earliest and most specific childhood memory goes back to when I was less than 4 years old. The time was the latter part of the summer of 1933. I'm sure that my parents must have used baby sitters in the earliest years of my life in order to go out for an evening or a brief period of time although "baby sitters" were not the common part of family life they were the last half of the twentieth century. Moreover, during the Depression people couldn't afford baby sitters. For many people "baby sitting" by members of the extended family and neighbors was still practical. I remember the first time and almost the only occasion when my parents went away and left me behind for an extended period of time. They were going to the worlds fair.

The various cultures and the scientific and technological advances of the world were exhibited (usually every 10 years, later every 5 years, I think) in a World Fair. The setting of these always moved about from country to country and, when in the USA, from city to city. They were not likely to be very close to Kansas, but in 1933 there was to be a World Fair in Chicago, Illinois. My parents wanted to drive from Hutchinson to Chicago to see The Fair. I was really too small to appreciate the fair and they knew I would have trouble traveling that far. I could hardly stand to be in the car when they drove from Hutchinson to visit my maternal grandparents at their farm 6 1/2 miles Northwest of Peabody, Kansas. This drive is less than an hour drive today, but then it was nearly a two-hour trip. Arrangements were made by Mom and Dad to drop me off at my grandparents' farm.

Having never been away from my parents for so long, I didn't know what to think about this. My parents, I'm sure, were concerned that I might be homesick. Whether or not there was collusion in advance I don't know, but when we arrived at grandmother and granddad's farm there was something new that had never been there before—"Sport," a mixed breed collie dog! Needless to say, I was excited and thrilled. The two of us soon became fast friends. Time flew by. There was no homesickness, "no depression," for me. I don't even remember missing my parents although I was glad to see Mom and Dad when they reappeared a week later. But for years, I remembered this week with warm feelings and always looked forward to seeing Sport during our frequent pilgrimages to "the farm."

Chapter 3

214 EAST FOURTEENTH STREET

In the early nineteen thirties, if you had walked up to 214 East Fourteenth in Hutchinson, Kansas, you would have seen a modest but attractive white wooden bungalow type home with window and door screens trimmed in green, matching a neatly manicured dark green lawn. Walk with me in your imagination. Look more closely. You notice that all across the bungalow's front is a covered, but not enclosed, porch with supporting posts made into a wide vine covered trellis at each corner. There's a narrower trellis on each side of the front steps. Across the width of the porch, just in front of it, are flowerbeds filled with a variety of flowers in beautiful bloom. Out behind this bungalow, filling a sizable part of the remaining portion of its small lot, is a freestanding single car garage which matches the house itself. Still, there's room for a small vegetable garden next to the garage. Come back in front again. As you step up to the porch, you are lead directly to the entrance door centered in the front of the house.

Open the front door of the house. You can almost see the entirety of the home where I lived for the first five years of my life. Basically this rectangular plan has just four rooms built over an unfinished basement which doubles as a storage area and tornado shelter. Stepping through the front door, you enter into a living room that runs to the left end of the house. Turn right and you walk through the door of a small bedroom that's mine. Across from the living room is a wall dividing the house front from back. Glance toward the back of the house to your far left. You see an archway leading into a kitchen with space big enough for a small kitchen/dining room table. Glance mostly straight ahead from your place there at the entrance door. As you look through the open door you see the master bedroom used by my parents. In between that bedroom and the kitchen is a small bathroom. Basically what you experience is a small house, modestly furnished but adequate for our family of three and really quite comfortable.

214 East 14th Street, the house in Hutchinson, Kansas, where the author first lived. Photo from the early 1930s.

If memory serves me right, my parents told me they first lived in an apartment house when they were married and mother moved to Hutchinson to join Dad who was already living there. When they felt they could afford it, they purchased this small lot. It was at the northwest corner of Fourteenth and Maple Streets, not far from the growing edge of Hutchinson, surrounded by larger lots and larger homes already developed. It was Blanche and Fred's first real-estate acquisition. By the time I was born, they had built a home, made this "nest," for me.

I don't have many memories from my six years in this house and virtually no memories of its interior decor. What I most remember is that when I was small, I frequently suffered severe stomach upsets! I had numerous occasions when I developed a nausea that turned me inside out! I carry images in my mind of dashing from my room to the bathroom, of mother sitting by my bedside trying to comfort me, and then as I began to finally feel better, sometimes after two or three days of the "dry heaves" and trips to the doctor. I would be delighted to see Mom walking through the door of my room, caring a tray with tea and toast, to nurse me back to health again.

Another joyful image I still see in my mind, as I remember 214 East 14th, is making homemade root beer. I don't know the exact details of this. All I remember is, we made it out-of-doors in the garage instead of in the kitchen. We would use a brand new clean washtub reserved for this purpose. The tub was filled with tap water and then a variety of ingredients such as flavoring tablets, yeast (?), and sugar which were stirred into the water. We'd fill the bottles, which had been washed and sterilized, with homemade root beer, cap them, and store them in the basement where it was cool, opening them when we wanted to enjoy drinking our own root beer.

I also have a few memories of neighbors. There were two families who lived next to us on the west—the Dunns and the Stuckeys. I remember the lady in one of these families worked at the Reno County Court House, which seemed like an important job. I was impressed to have such a neighbor. In the other family, the man was a detective with the Hutchinson Police Department. Their children were older and I never really knew them. Mainly I remember there was a certain mystique about living next door to a detective. Possible that mystique related to the popular comic strip character— "Dick Tracy," who was a detective and a man of adventure.

Across the street to the east of us, second house over, was a big two-story home where Oliver and Mabel Hester lived. They didn't have children, but they knew my parents through church and "fussed" over me in the absence of children of their own. Oliver, a stockbroker, was both friend and financial counselor to my parents. He often traveled to call on clients all over Western and South-central Kansas. Years later when Lorine and I married, he visited us two or three times a year, wherever we lived, and also advised us very helpfully in some of our investments.

I don't have any recollection—good, bad, or indifferent—of the family who lived across the street from us. However, in 1989, when our son Ben was finishing Law School and looking for a firm in which to settle for his first full-time law position, he interviewed with a well known firm of Shamberg, Johnson, and Bergman in Overland Park, Ks. Mr. Shamberg was the senior member of the firm and one of those who interviewed Ben. In the course of the interview, he said something to Ben to the effect, "Kieler, (pause) Kieler, (pause) your name is familiar to me. When I was a boy growing up in Hutchinson, Kansas, there was a man by the name of Fred Kieler who lived across the street from us on East Fourteenth. I always thought the world of him—he was a very nice, a very fine, honest man. Could you be related to him?" Of course Ben's answer was, "That's my grandfather!"

A final memory comes to mind when I think of 214 East Fourteenth. My mother was expecting my little sister, Shirley. Mom and Dad said, "There won't be room here when the baby comes. We're going to have to look for a bigger house." So it was that early in 1935, we made a move to a house just over a block away to make room for Shirley! When moving day came, I left 214 East 14th to go to my Kindergarten class, but when school was over that day, the folks picked me up and brought me home to a new house. What an exciting time for me!

Chapter 4

MY FIRST DAY AT SCHOOL

It was September of 1934, a beautiful autumn day. I was embarking on a totally new venture—an adventure. I really don't remember what I was felt. Had I ever been in that room before? I don't think so. Was I afraid? Filled with apprehension? Or was I filled with excitement? Joy? A sense of anticipation? I'm not sure. Probably my inners were full of some of all these feelings, but one thing is for sure, I firmly griped my dad's hand as I walked toward the little free standing red brick bungalow building adjacent to Northside Grade School at 930 North Maple Street, Hutchinson, Kansas.

This was the day of enrollment for new kindergartners. I wasn't sure what to expect and I was quite sure I wouldn't know another kid there. As Dad and I walked up the steps to enter the door, Dad spotted another man, boy in hand, who was a casual acquaintance. Dad was Treasurer of the Security Elevator Company. This man was the bookkeeper of Kelly Milling Company. Security had sold wheat to Kelly Milling for the past several years. "Hello there, Eff," said Dad. "Looks like you've got a son starting school."

"Sure do," came the reply, "this is my boy Jim."

"Hello. I'm Fred Kieler and this is my son, Harold." My first school friendship was in the making, and Jim and I were to become lifelong friends.

Approaching the teacher's desk, we met her and began to answer the usual questions. Something happened which would soon bring another change to my life. "Your son's full name?"

"Harold Eugene Kieler"

"And the name that Harold Eugene goes by?"

"We just call him 'Gene'."

"My, this is strange—he's the fifth boy today with the name Gene!" Needless to say, within a couple of days my Kindergarten teacher was asking for a conference with several parents. Utter confusion had begun to reign with all five boys answering to the name "Gene." None of the boys wanted to be addressed with two names. The question of the parent-teacher conference was, could she drop using the name Gene for all of the boys who had two names. One boy had been named only Gene so he had to be called Gene, but could she begin using the other name for each of the other four boys?

At that point, after five years of being known as "Gene Kieler" I suddenly was no longer Gene Kieler—I was now "Harold Kieler". To this day, if I hear someone call me "Gene" I know that they have to be a person who has known me, or my family, for more than 70 years. There really aren't this many of these people around any more! In all probability they are a cousin or my sister, Shirley, who are suffering from a momentary slip of the tongue. Or still more likely, it may be my 95 year old Uncle Harold for whom I was named. He's never ever really gotten over calling me Gene.

Chapter 5

THE FARM

If I were to name *one place* that is the source for many of my most cherished feelings and memories it would be the "the farm."

When America was first settled it obviously was not an urbanized place—it was a wilderness that evolved into a vast agricultural land. Only gradually as the population increased and immigration from abroad brought industrialization did this begin to change. Kansas in the first third of the twentieth century was still predominantly a rural state. Even moving in to the 21st Century, it is still in many ways an agricultural state.

My parents were both reared on the farm, as had been their parents. My paternal grandparents, Reuben and Frances Kieler, were deceased before my father ever finished school, but when I was growing up my maternal grandparents, Burt and Jane Taylor were farming 160 acres of Marion County land. This is where my mother grew up. It was northwest of Peabody, Kansas. Dad, until his parents' death, had lived on an 80-acre farm southeast of Peabody. Not surprisingly, our family frequently returned to Peabody and to the farm where mother was raised. It was there that we visited her parents, my grandparents, and had extended family gatherings with her siblings. Once in a while other more distantly related folks would visit there. That became the occasion for special trips to the farm.

Usually, however, we would go to the farm—to Grandmother's and Granddad's—to celebrate Thanksgiving, Christmas, Easter, and Memorial Day. Wheat harvest, central in importance to farm people, was another occasion for visits to the farm along with Independence Day (Fourth of July as we usually called it) unless it conflicted with a late wheat harvest. Sometimes we journeyed to the farm on Labor Day weekend though this holiday didn't hold the significance for farmers that it did for people who worked in manufacturing. In addition to these one or two day visits, from the year that my parents went to the World's Fair (in Chicago) when I spent a week on the farm until I was in my mid-teens, I always went there on my own every summer for an extended stay of one to several weeks.

For me, "going to the farm" became an adventure to which I always looked forward. On one occasion when I was still in grade school, for some reason Mom and Dad were unable to take me for my annual summer visit. They put me on a Trailway Bus, which dropped me off in Peabody. My grandparents met me. Boy, I felt big being able to make this trip on my own. On another occasion they couldn't come to pick me up at the end of my stay. My grandparents put me on the train by myself for the return trip home to Hutchinson. Again, I really felt "grown up" to be able to make the trip by my self. Both with the bus and the train trip, I have to admit I had a bit of apprehension about whether I would recognize and get off at the right stop.

Coupled with the trips to the farm and visits with Taylor relatives, we usually would swing by one or both of two other towns—either Peabody and/or Whitewater—on the way home to Hutchinson. This was for the purpose of visiting with some of the few surviving members of Dad's family. "The Kieler girls" as everyone called them—three unmarried sisters, Annah, Jenny, and Margaret—lived in Peabody for years. They were first cousins of Dad. For the first ten or fifteen years of my life they were still caring for their father in their home. He was my Dad's Uncle "Will" Kieler, my Great Uncle. As early as I can remember, the Kieler girls always seemed to me to be "ancient" but they were Dad's link to his family and to his boyhood community of Peabody so what they had to talk about was interesting although somewhat foreign to me. Living in Whitewater was my father's sister, my Aunt Kate and her husband—Uncle "Friday." She was a great cook. He was a great checkers player and willing to play with me. This was always a fun stop. These visits added another exciting dimension to visiting "the farm."

Land in the United States was divided into sections (one square mile of 640 acres), half sections, quarter sections, and even 80 acres. These were units of ownership, or rental units, which were within a named Township located in "ranges" which were measured from the nearest meridian and latitude lines. These units were used to describe where and how much a person farmed. "The Farm" which Mom's parents farmed was a quarter section of land. They acquired it by purchase in 1903. Just three or four decades earlier, this land had been unbroken prairie and the first settlers were only beginning to arrive. The thought of this makes me realize how young our country is, and how near I live to the beginning of this nation. In Kansas, life on the farm in the 1930's was still relatively primitive compared with today.

The paved road between Hutchinson and Peabody was not an Interstate highway or the modern state highway of today. Roads were simply narrow two lane cement or asphalt (occasionally even brick) pavement just built on top of the ground and around obstacles without benefit of modern engineering and earth moving. They quickly became rough. In town, streets and roads were often bricks laid side by side on beds of sand. The automobiles of that day were not the smooth riding comfortable cars of today. The farm was a "far away place"—rather remote—because although it was only about 55 miles from home it took us nearly two hours to get there. This seemed like an interminable length of time to me.

To make the trip to the farm more acceptable, my mother would always pack a "lunch" for my sister Shirley and me. We couldn't eat it until we got half way to the farm. Halfway was the point marked by passing the cemetery at Halstead. Coming back to Hutchinson, it was the same routine except that grandmother always packed the lunch. This way we always had something to look forward to.

It wasn't just the condition of the cars and the highways that made this such a journey. Once we got to Peabody, there weren't any more paved roads. The next four miles were somewhat "rocked" or "graveled" but not in the best of condition. The final distance of two and half miles was on strictly dirt or heavy clay roads. When there was rain or snow they could become almost impassable. They often turned into deep slippery mud where one could easily slide off the road into the ditch alongside, or simply sink down to the axles of the car so that there was no more traction left! You'd be stuck until you could walk to a farmhouse where they might be willing to pull you out with a team of horses or later on with a tractor. Even after I had a car of my own which would be in 1950s, as a young adult, this happened to me on at least a couple of occasions. Once it happened after I was married when we had our small sons with us.

The farm was an exciting place to be. There were all kinds of animals: work horses (no riding horses on this farm), chickens which produced needed eggs (the surplus of which could be sold for a little cash income), turkeys, ducks, geese, cattle—dairy and beef cattle—hogs or pigs and occasionally a few sheep. All the animals had to be fed morning and night. "Slopping" the hogs twice daily was probably the least favorite job because their pens were terribly smelly and very muddy at times. None of these animals were for a zoo-like exhibit. They were raised both for the sustenance of the farm family and for cash income. Diversified farming was the name of the game in those days.

Food variety and out-of-season fresh fruits and veggies were lacking for the farm families of the thirties, but we always ate well when we ate at the farm. In addition to the abundance of eggs produced by the chickens, their meat could provide us with fried chicken, roasted chicken, or boiled chickens for noodles or for canning. Pan fried chicken remains one of my all time favorite meals. Turkeys, ducks, and geese, were raised in smaller numbers for special occasions when you desired to have meat that wasn't just "everyday meat."

Milk cattle provided both dairy products for consumption by farm people and skim milk for feeding the young animals you were raising. Cream was always saved to be sold as another source of cash income as well as for making butter for your own use. Beef cattle were raised primarily for selling on the open cattle market to those who sold dressed beef to city people, but one or two head of cattle were always reserved for butchering on the farm. The same was true for the hogs. What few sheep were raised (and they weren't raised every year) were mainly for the sale of wool.

We weren't usually present when butchering took place, after fall harvest was over and the weather turned cold, but we were usually invited to come get some fresh meat right after they had butchered. As soon as freezer plants or lockers were developed and became commonplace in small towns, farmers would take most of their meat to town, rent a locker, and keep it there for use throughout the year until next butchering season.

The Farmyard—A painting done from memory by
Virginia Taylor while living in Europe in the 1950s.
The author's grandparents lived in the large white house,
his Uncle and Aunt, Harold and Adele in the small white
(refrigerator car) house to the left.

In addition to these domesticated animals, there was the wildlife of the country—birds, bees (wow, was that honey good!), bugs, jackrabbits and cottontails, squirrels, raccoons and possums, snakes and on and on. There was the seasonal migration of ducks and geese. Many of these could supplement the food supply if one was a good hunter. Once upon a time there had been buffalo, antelope and deer but pioneer white settlers and "market" hunters had caused these to become extinct in Kansas.

Near the farmhouse, in addition to the chicken houses and pens for the domestic animals, was a big vegetable garden and some fruit trees. When I was at the farm at the right time of the year, one of my responsibilities was to help water and weed the garden and pick its produce. I was to dig small little trenches in the garden to water by irrigation. One of my big pleasures was picking mulberries for my grandmother to use (much to my delight!) in baking pies.

When I first started coming to the farm in the 1930s, there were no modern conveniences on the farm—no electricity, no gas or liquefied petroleum for heating, no running water in the city sense. How did we get along on the farm? For lighting we used coal oil lamps (or kerosene) after dark and depended on daylight in the daytime. Obviously, without electricity there could be no electrified refrigeration. In those days, food was home canned in glass jars and stored in the cellar for future months. Meats could also be "cured" by smoking and/or drying and then kept for several months during the winter. Roots like onions, carrots, and beets could be kept in the garden ground as long as possible for storage. Potatoes needed to be dug when mature—not stored or left in the ground—but for the other roots straw could be mounded over the ground to prevent freezing. Eventually the root crops would have to be dug and placed in the cellar. My grandparents' farm also had a hand dug well made by a former owner. It was about three and a half feet in diameter, stone lined, and went down (30 or 40 feet?) to water level. Butter, sweet cream, eggs, and other small perishable foods were put in gallon buckets and lowered on a rope into the well which was cool year around.

When the first settlers in Eastern Kansas came there were a few woods but for the most part open unbroken prairies were the norm for the entire state. Soon, in the eastern to central half of the state, fields and farms were outlined by planting trees suitable to the Great Plains. The most common tree for this purpose was the hedge or Osage orange tree which grew so tangled, thorny and thick that no cattle could get through it. Of course there were other trees—especially cottonwood and locust—that were useful. In fact catalpa groves were planted to raise fence posts and provide firewood for steam engines. One of the many routine farm chores each fall was to trim and cut trees to create a "wood pile" near the farmhouse.

I can still see in my minds eye my grandparents' woodpile. This would supply the wood burning kitchen cook stove with its iron top, which became hot and in turn heated iron frying pans. The cook stove also had an oven attached next to its firebox. This was where pies, cakes, all of the families' bread and other goodies were baked. A couple of freestanding potbellied stoves were used to heat the rest of the house in the winter. Some coal would be purchased in town and used to supplement the wood supply for heating. We wore heavier clothes and had other tricks like taking heated objects (bricks, irons, water bottles, etc.) to bed with us. Still, keeping warm wasn't easy. Eventually, after World War II, wood grew scarce and liquefied petroleum (butane or propane gas) came to the farm to be used for heating.

What about the water supply? First, the roof of the farmhouse had gutters and down spouts connected to a tile lined underground cistern. This was a supply of good rainwater, but in a land that averaged only about 30 inches of rainfall per year it was a limited supply. The cistern was located under the farmhouse kitchen. A hand pump, supplied from the cistern, was attached to the kitchen sink. It provided easy access to a limited amount of water for kitchen use.

The main source of water was well water. A well had been drilled to the level of the underground water. Above it was a windmill. A hand break allowed the windmill to run whenever water was needed to fill a large cement storage tank holding several thousand gallons of water. When the tank was full the windmill wouldn't be left running. Water would be gravity drained from the bottom of the tank into buckets to be taken into the house for general use. It was also piped to stock tanks to water the livestock, and to a 55-gallon drum that sat on top of an outdoor shower house.

Years later water was piped to the house so that household needs were not dependent on rainwater or hand carried water. In the summer time solar heating warmed our showers. In the winter, a once-a-week bath taken in a wash tub (the kind of tub used for the hand washing of clothes) with water heated on the wood cook stove. When water was scarce because of drought or frozen pipes, conservation necessitated that a bath could be taken in water first used for washing clothes.

In the many years before water was piped to the house, the toilet was a two-hole outhouse (as in a shed out-of-doors!). Seats were mighty cold in the winter and always the toilet paper was *anything but soft*. Of course if you felt rich enough you could buy toilet paper in town and have this luxury. Most people—certainly for many years my grandparents—didn't feel they could afford this. They made do with what was available on the farm and what were available were the hard slick nonabsorbent pages torn from old department store and mail order catalogs.

Television hadn't been invented yet, to my knowledge, and wouldn't become a commonplace public media until I was in college—1947-51. Radios were primitive battery powered radios which drew their electricity from batteries charged by wind-generators. In addition to the windmill, which pumped water, many farms also had a device known as wind chargers. It looked like an airplane propeller which was mounted on a tall poll, and it was propelled by the wind. As the propeller turned, it turned a small generating device which charged a bank of batteries somewhat bigger than those of the modern auto. These powered the radio and sometimes a single light bulb.

Each telephone company (usually one per town) had a number of "lines" some of which reached out into the country. Each "line" was connected to and serviced about 8 or 10 farm houses. The electrical impulse came from a dry cell battery in the wooden cabinet which held the phone and its mechanism. The phone at each house had a bell which rang by a hand-turned crank. The bell sent a "signal" or "ring" over the line to every house on that line and to the central operator (either the word "Central" or "Operator" could be used to refer to this person). These rural lines were called party lines. Each party had its own "ring" or "signal" which consisted of a combination of one or more "long" or "short" rings. There was no privacy. Whenever there was a ring on the line any one or everyone could pick up the phone and listen in. In fact, there was even one ring that was called a "general" ring, which was intended to be for everyone. This was used in case of an emergency or a desire to pass the same message on to everyone with out having to do it 8 or 10 times.

Life on the farm in those days, with few mechanized conveniences, with the economic depression of the 1930s, and with wartime scarcities in the early 1940s, was different and was very hard by today's standards. But, it taught us some of life's most valuable lessons—how to adjust to hardship, to get along with less, to make the most of what we had. People were happy for the most part. They enjoyed a life which didn't depend on ease or material wealth. There was a strong sense of community. Neighbors often worked together to help each other. People relied a great deal on their own inner spiritual resources. In everything we learned to work hard, to pay our bills, to enjoy the earth, the world of nature, and to love God. Simplicity, honesty, reliability, responsibility, being industrious, self-reliant, and economical—these were important values instilled in all kids as I was growing up. I think this is a big part of why "the farm" made a big imprint on me. I was enthusiastic and optimistic about life and enjoyed doing just about everything. It seemed whatever I did was what I wanted to do "when I grew up." The farm was always an emotional destination as much or more than a geographical destination.

Chapter 6

THE ONION HOUSE—
302 EAST FIFTEENTH STREET

Did you have a special place near your childhood home where, when you were growing up, you could get out of the house?, away from your parents?, and just be by yourself or maybe hang out with one or more of your special friends? I'll doubt that it was much more original than mine. As a kid I always had a fertile imagination about things to do and how to do them. I was always planning, then building or implementing the plans.

Shortly after my sister was born I began to feel that our new house at 302 East 15th Street, with my new baby sister in it, was getting a little too crowded. Our next door neighbors—the Scotts— had just purchased some new kitchen appliances. The appliances came crated in some big boxes made of wooden frames with cardboard sides. After the appliances were unboxed and taken to the kitchen, the crates were just tossed in the alley out back to await the coming of the trash man who would haul them away.

Without consulting any one, I decided to get my buddy Jim Jung to help me drag these boxes down the alley to our back yard. We could use them to build ourselves a "hang out." Using the wood frame (more than the cardboard, most of which had been torn up in the uncrating process) and using some of Dad's tools, we framed up our structure to the best of our childhood ability even though we were not exactly union carpenters. But then the problem was, we didn't have any privacy. Young boys needed this! We began looking around for the needed siding which didn't seem to be too plentiful. The only thing that caught our attention was Mr. Scott's good sized very lush vegetable garden. In it were several rows of onions as tall as any I'd ever seen—at least 2 1/2 or 3 feet tall. What ever possessed us I don't know, but again, without asking Mr. Scott or consulting anyone else, we proceeded to pull up every last onion from his garden and drape them over our wooden frames to form the needed privacy curtains for our hang out.

Can you believe what kind of "welcome to the neighborhood" we got from the Scotts? Can you imagine the "consultation" that was held that night between my parents and me after Mr. Scott talked to them? Would there have ever been a better laboratory in which a young boy could experiment with learning the fine art of making apologies and amends? My father gave me a good lecture, marched me over to see Mr. Scott, to apologize, and to promise that I'd never bother his garden again. Fortunately the Scott's didn't hold this transgression against either my parents or me.

Chapter 7

LEARNING HOW TO SPELL

"You know," said my dad, "there are lots of people who misspell this word. Instead of writing 'separate' they write 'seperate'. I used to do that," he told me, "until one time my father told me the correct spelling of the word and said for me to just picture the word sepArate with that big 'A' when ever I started to spell it."

What was this all about?

When I was in grade school we always had homework to bring home. Sometimes it was other subjects but mostly homework consisted of the 3 Rs—"reading, 'riting (along with spelling) and 'rithmetic". Both of my parents (as almost all parents with their children) would go over my spelling and my arithmetic (early on arithmetic meant memorizing and practicing the multiplication tables) with me every night Monday through Thursdays. We hardly ever were given assignments to do over the weekend. Dad usually did the spelling and the arithmetic. Mom did the rest of it, although geography was frequently turned into a kind of family game or fun time with everyone quizzing everyone about the names and locations of different places. Spelling and arithmetic assignments were often in the form of drills. For spelling, we would have ten to twenty words a day for our parents to give us orally making sure, by having us write them down, that we could spell them correctly before the teacher's test the next day.

I remember this spelling story very vividly because I repeatedly misspelled that word "separately." Dad must have taken 15 minutes with me on just this one word, telling me his own story about how he learned to spell "separately" correctly. I never was and to this day am still not a great speller, but even now when I hear the word sepArately I can still see that great big A. Dad and Mom both were always *very supportive and encouraging* when it came to my schoolwork as well as to work and life in general.

One of the things I still appreciate about my education at Northside Grade School was that in their own humble way, the teachers sought to give us, regardless of whether it "took" or not, a very holistic and broad education including a global perspective. Part of this came through *The Weekly Reader*—a newspaper written just for kids at their own grade level. But part of the global perspective also came through assignments. For instance, I recall an assignment "Find and interview some one from another country or culture to learn about how they celebrate Christmas in that country. Report your findings back to the class." Dad worked in Wiley Building (a 9 story office building where the offices of the Security Elevator Company for which he worked were located on the seventh floor along with most of the offices and headquarters of Kansas owned and operated grain elevator and brokerage companies). When I brought this assignment home, Dad told me that one of the grain men in the Wiley Building was from Denmark originally. Dad invited me to come up to his office after school if I wanted him to introduce me to the man so I could interview him. This kind of supportive relationship was always a big part of who my dad, Fred A (for Albert) Kieler, was.

Hard work and self-discipline were another prominent pair of Dad's traits both of which rubbed off on me. Dad was born on a farm Southeast of Peabody, Kansas, February 22, 1897. He grew up in a farming culture which became ingrained in him. Events in his life led him away from being a farmer into the farm related grain elevator and storage business. By the time I was born, Dad and Mom were living in Hutchinson, Kansas, where Dad was working for Security Elevator Company, a business owned by the Summers family. Dad started out as a bookkeeper for Security working his way up to being Vice President and Secretary-Treasurer of the corporation by the time he retired. Because the grain business was a seasonal business, an 8 am to 5 pm workday, five days a week was normal only in the wintertime or for half a year. In the Spring, as wheat harvest began in Oklahoma, the hours Dad worked began to expand until by Kansas harvest-time he was working 7 am to 7 pm, six or occasionally six and a half days a week from mid-June to the end of July.

In addition to the hard work of these long hours, Dad always tried to keep himself physically and financially fit. Dad played in a volleyball league at the YMCA. Later he gave up the YMCA and switched to doing early morning calisthenics at home plus a regimen of walking. The Kielers could only afford one car. Perhaps toward retirement Dad might have been able to swing a second car, but that was an unnecessary luxury. All the time I was growing up, except in extreme winter weather, Dad left the car at home for Mom's use and walked to and from work each day. This meant Dad left home earlier and returned home later so while Dad was getting in good exercise we saw even less of him when his hours were long. Some times, when he was working the 12 hour days, Mom or I (or just me after I was of driving age) would pick Dad up in the car at day's end.

Dad's long working hours meant for me less time to spend with Dad. The shortage of time with Dad is also part of my childhood memories. In the summer, other kids were playing ball with their dads. Not me. Of course as I grew older, spending more summer weeks at my grandparents farm, and during my later teen years working on my own or being with my buddies, I didn't miss my dad so much. However Dad did always manage to find time for us to work and play together some.

Dad enjoyed gardening. He always kept a nice looking lawn, beautiful flowerbeds, and had a productive vegetable garden the fruits of which we enjoyed eating. As a youngster I always helped Dad till, plant and weed the vegetable garden learning a great deal in the process and enjoying our time together. This was a fun activity and in the process I observed Dad, started to imitate him and we would talk, share ideas, and I felt him truly to be my friend and companion. Likewise, I might add, I often helped Mom around the house and especially in the kitchen and the same phenomenon was occurring with her.

As I became an older elementary student and a young teenager I did yard work for Dad. My allowance increased proportionate to the amount of help I was to Dad and Mom. When I was little, one of my jobs was weeding dandelions out of our yard. I was paid according to the number of dandelions dug up. Dad and Mom were obviously thrifty people and thrift was another trait was ingrained in us as my sister and I grew up. Piggy banks and other types of savings banks were given to my sister and to me early in our lives. We were encouraged to save, not spend, our money. As our savings banks filled up, savings accounts at the bank were opened in our names and later savings bonds purchased with our money.

Fun wise, one of the activities I most remember doing with Dad was fishing and many times this was an extended family activity. There were ponds around Hutchinson which belonged to Dad's friends. He was able to take me to these for fishing. We particularly enjoyed fishing the Cow Creek stream. Dad even obtained a fishing lease on a section of the creek just for the use of our family, selected friends and the extended family. Occasionally we would fish the Arkansas River or even drive a little further to fish on the Ninnescah River. We fished mostly for catfish although we caught a variety of other local fish most of which were small. The small ones got tossed back, but we cleaned the bigger fish and thoroughly enjoyed the fish fries Mom would prepare from the "keepers."

As part of their own personal program of thrift, savings, and investments, Dad and Mom bought some farmland. When I was very young, they bought a 160-acre farm near Little River, Kansas, and rented it out. Later they sold it and invested in a couple of other farms, each essentially 160-acre farms. One was near Penalosa, Kansas, and the other southeast of Nickerson not far from Hutchinson. We called the latter the "Cow Creek place" because Cow Creek ran through the edge of it. Cow Creek was always a favorite fishing destination. For farming purposes these farms were always rented to area farmers. The house on the Penalosa farm became a rental house. The Cow Creek place had a farmstead on it at one time. When Dad bought it, the three remaining buildings— a very small house, an outhouse, and a barn—were all pretty much in disrepair. Dad had the barn torn down for salvage. One other form of real estate investments my parents entered into was the acquisition of a small (6 units) apartment house in Hutchinson.

There was a period during my late teens and early twenties when Dad picked up on an idea of my Uncle Floyd's, did some work on the old dilapidated house at the Cow Creek place and turned it into a cabin where people could spend the night when fishing or just for an outing. This became another of the cabins which added delight and enjoyment to the life of our extended family. Something of what this meant to us can be sensed from an e-mail I received from my cousin Virginia Taylor Delaval years later. She wrote,

> "I have wonderful memories of your parents . . . .
> Your father was wonderful in hosting so many camping parties out on the farm at the Cow Creek place. To us children, it was a PARTY from beginning to end with varied sodas which Uncle Floyd brought in a bona fide red and white Coke Cola cooler. Barbecued hamburgers and hot dogs were cooked over the fire your father built. We all had the most comfortable accommodations for "camping out" under a roof on a nice clean screened-in porch. Your father always had the place so beautifully prepared with all the grass cut, all the bank lines prepared, food, drink, mosquito repellent, etc. I cannot imagine how anyone could have gone to so much work to make the time so pleasant for everyone. And going down to the creek after dark to "run the bank lines" only by flashlights was an adventure which will always stay with me. I'm sure he was never thanked properly at the time. Your parents were both very generous. I hope that wherever they are now, they are being waited on hand and foot and having the time of their lives."

More good memories of things we did together as a family relate to trips and vacations. Usually these had to wait until after wheat harvest. Then they were squeezed in before the beginning of school, or before fall Milo harvest which was another busy time for Dad. For the first 15 or 16 years of my life, and for Dad and Mom as long as he lived, there were annual late summer trips to visit the Colorado Kielers. Before they had families, Dad's brothers, my uncles, had migrated from Peabody to Northeast Colorado. Now, with their families there were lots of cousins for me to enjoy. On their farms, out on the high plaines, rattlesnakes were abundant. I was warned always to be on the lookout for them. I was bug-eyed when my uncles opened their leftover 3 pound coffee cans filled with rattles cut off the rattlesnakes they'd killed. I felt lucky because they usually gave me a few to take home as souvenirs.

Old gravity style gasoline pump from 1920-30s like those used at filling stations where the author's family "gassed up" on their road trips during his first decade of life. Photo taken at Otis, Colorado, in 2003 by the author.

Travel took two days each way and cars had no air conditioning for those hot Augusts! We would stop overnight in "tourist rooms" along the way. Tourist rooms were sometimes simply an extra room in a home where people would rent to travelers. Sometimes there were a group of small cabins—a precursor of the motels to come later. While in Colorado, we usually got to explore Denver and/or the Rocky Mountains. There were times, especially at high altitudes, when I suffered from motion sickness and really became miserably sick but these episodes never dimmed my appetite for our trips. On the return trips we also explored various parts of Eastern Colorado and Western Kansas.

Two of my most memorable big vacation trips were in 1937, the summer after I finished the third grade and in 1940 after the sixth grade. For the former, we drove all the way to the Pacific Northwest. Following a visit to the Colorado Kielers, we drove through Casper, Wyoming, to Yellowstone National Park, to Portland, Oregon and on to Seattle, Washington. From there we ferried to Victoria, Canada. Returning, we passed through the Cascade Mountains and along the Columbia River. Here we saw huge salmon migrating inland up the fish ladders built to try to preserve their ability to migrate. The ladders were a necessity for the continued existence of the species which was in jeopardy due to the construction of the Grand Coulee Dam. Also, the dam construction was an impressive sight to observe. This was a long and fabulous trip for me. It was a time when my horizons really began to expand.

The latter of these two most memorable trips was a trip to Old Mexico (as we called it to distinguish it from New Mexico). Dad took us in the car all the way to Mexico City! However, because of the capricious way Mexican authorities were known to treat foreign visitors who happened to get involved in traffic accidents, and because of a high winding stretch of mountain highway leading to Mexico City, Dad hired a Mexican driver to drive us from the border to Mexico City. Lots of that trip is only a vague memory now. I still remember though: the poverty and getting car sick going through the mountains; the floating flower gardens in Mexico City and getting "Montezuma's Revenge" while staying in Mexico City; going to see the pyramids but still being sick and only barely being able to lift up my head to look at the pyramids. After we returned to the City, I was finally able to keep down some food and in our hotel I had some of the most delicious cream soups I'd ever tasted. We also made a fascinating trip to the picturesque little silver mining town of Taxco—a trip I'd still enjoy repeating.

World War II, with gasoline and tire rationing, put an end to
these longer trips. During this period the railroads were playing a
major role in the war effort moving massive amounts of freight and
a mass of humanity with whole military units being transported,
hundreds of thousands of servicemen going home on leave and
back to base again, wives visiting training camps, etc. It was very
difficult for ordinary people to get train reservations. In spite of
the difficulty of getting train reservations, because of his connection
with the railroads as a shipper of thousands of cars of grain, Dad
was able to get reservations for our family to take one late summer
trip to Colorado on the Missouri Pacific Railroad. The novelty of
our trip was having a reservation in a Pullman sleeping car with
pull-down beds in a compartment all of our own! And Porters
made up our bed with clean tightly drawn linens! In Geneseo
where we ordinarily would have needed to change trains, we didn't
have to. They simply switched our sleeping car from the train we
were on to our next train.

Immediately after WW II we did take auto trips, again, while I
was still in high school and before I left home for college. Shirley
was too young to take our two big trips, but she was always part of
these. Post World War II trips were to Minnesota, the Ozarks,
Texas and Oklahoma City where we visited both the city sights
and a relative, the Rev. Lloyd Walters (though we might also have
made one trip to see him in Oklahoma City during the War).
Details on the trip to the Alamo in San Antonio and to Corpus
Christi, Texas, have faded but they were exciting trips for me.

Almost everything I ever saw about what my Dad did or said
spoke of *honesty and integrity*. Everyone who knew Dad always
validated this observation. I don't know if it relates specifically to
this character trait but I remember a saying Dad almost always
used when people would ask him "How are you?" His reply was
invariably, "Pretty straight." Only once do I ever remember anything
on the "shady side" about either of my parents. This relates to a
family fun-time during the depression. I was not yet even in school.
We went to see the Night Rodeo at Pretty Prairie, Kansas. Money
was tight I'm sure. I don't know what the cost of admission to the

rodeo was, but I know they thought there was a charge for even small children. Perhaps my parents hadn't anticipated this. The admission gate preceded the parking lot. When we got ready to drive in, the folks had me scoot down on the floorboard of the back seat of the car and proceeded to hide me under a blanket so they could pay only their admissions!

But Dad taught me honesty and responsibility and integrity not only by his own example but in my life too. One time when I was a third or fourth grader, on a Saturday, I went to the school playground with some other kids to play ball. There was a little lull in the action. I got bored, stooped over, picked up some small coin-sized pebbles and started seeing how far I could throw them. In the process, one hit a school window. I mentioned it when I went home so first thing Monday morning Dad went with me to school to tell the principal what I'd done. They discussed the situation together and agreed I should pay the cost of the new window. That was about three dollars as I recall. Dad paid it with the understanding that I would take money out of my savings to repay him.

Dad never got angry or punished me for something like this. He just wanted to be sure that we "made it right" as he would say. However, disobedience was another matter! Parents were to be respected and obeyed. It didn't happen often (it didn't have to!) but if I were to disobey my folks, or lie about things, I could push Dad to the point of corporal punishment. When I was little, or wasn't being too obstinate, this would be a spanking with his hand. Later it could mean he would pull his belt out of his trousers, have me bend over a chair, and he would give me several swats with the belt on my rear end!

Through the years, as an adolescent, I was pretty wild—much more so than I think my folks ever knew. There was at least a normal amount of rebellion and adolescent-parent stress and strain. Over all, though, I had a good positive relationship with Dad. As a small child there was the excitement and the good feelings that came with "horsy" rides on Dad's leg, our wrestling on the floor together, the Eskimo kisses Dad frequently gave, and other forms of play. As I got older, his support was always more verbal and instructional and more by way of privileges than expressed through emotional hugs and kisses. Later on, as a young adult and after, I would embrace, hug, and kiss my dad, but always with a bit of reticence. I think I kind of grew up "like him".

I never knew my grandparents on Dad's side of the family nor did I ever hear him speak much about them. I never really had much understanding or feel for something of a stoical side to dad and the absence of lots of emotion until I discovered within the last year of his life more about his childhood. In 1984 I started work on my genealogy and family history. I asked Dad to write something about his own life—his childhood and family—for me. What he wrote speaks for itself, I think. It speaks volumes about the molding influences on him as a child and the way he grew up into adult life, perhaps influences which spilled over into my life. This is what he wrote:

> "I have very few memories of my early childhood. I cannot remember at what age I was when mother had a stroke. From then until her death she was an invalid. I cannot remember her ever taking care of me—it was always one of my sisters. Mother's speech was badly impaired so that it was hard for any communication between us. My sister Elsie died at age 19 when I was only 3 years old so I have no memories of her or of her death. I barely remember mother's death and funeral (in 1905).
>
> "This left dad, Bessie, Jim, Ben and me at home as Kate was married and Ollie was working for other farmers around the area and Mable was teaching in the Peabody schools and stayed in town most of the time . . . . Bessie did the cooking and house work and I did a few little things and brought in the wood.
>
> "About 1910 Ollie went out to Colorado to homestead some land. He could find no suitable land so he bought a relinquishment from another man and built a sod house on it and lived in the sod house until he "proved up" on the land.

"When Bessie got married, dad took over the cooking but soon shifted this job to me (ca. age 14). Dad's health was failing as he had pernicious anemia. We had to have a hired man help Jim and Ben with the farm work.

"From the time I can remember we went to Sunday School and church at a country church one and a half miles from our home (1/2 mile East and 1 mile South). It was the Fairplay (Methodist) Church, but was usually known as "The Heath Church" because three Heath families were the pillars of the church.

"I remember being in Christmas programs and we always had a live Christmas Tree with real lighted candles on it. How we escaped having a fire I do not know, but there were quite a few fires in the area that started from Christmas candles. Of course this was before the day of the automobile, but we had a two seated carriage that used some times a team of horses and some times only one horse. For a special treat, dad would sometimes go to Peabody to the Lutheran Church to hear their pipe organ.

"Dad's health was getting worse and he was in bed a lot and I would take him his meals and wait on him. One morning in August 1912, about 4:00 AM, dad called me and asked for a drink of fresh water. I went to the well with the best water—about one hundred fifty yards from the house—and brought a pail of water and gave dad a pitcher of it and went back to bed. Then in the morning when I got up and went into his room he was dead.

"Our country school was about one half mile east of our house. I had started school there and had finished eighth grade. Mable wanted me to go "to town school" in Peabody so I rode my horse to Peabody to school. I did not want to go to "town school" so I enrolled in the 8th grade again in Peabody and thought that would finish my schooling at the end of that year. I think that proved to be a good idea for I learned more that year than any other year. By the end of the year, I liked school there and decided to go to high school.

"Since dad had died in August 1912, Jim, Ben, and I and the hired man continued with the farm, but the summer of 1913 was very, very dry so it was decided to sell the farm and have a sale of everything. We did that. Jim got married and moved out to the same area of Colorado where Ollie was. Then Mabel and Jerry insisted that I come and room at their house and go to school. It was a year or two after Jim went to Colorado that Ben moved also to the same area where Ollie and Jim lived.

"Mabel and Jerry were not home for regular meals, but I had a room there and ate about half of my meals with them. Kate and "Friday" lived on a farm 8 miles southeast of Peobody and kept my horse during the school year. When school was out in the spring, I went to work on a farm for a neighbor of Kate and "Friday". I earned $15 per month and my board and room. That fall I went back to stay with Mabel and Jerry and to go to high school. When school was out the next spring, I worked at several jobs on farms and then with another boy, we went "out west" to work in the wheat harvest in header barges. We thought we were going to strike it rich as we would earn $3.00 per day and board and sleep in the hay mow. Well, that was a wet summer and we were out there a little over one month and got to work thirteen days so we earned $39.00. We had ridden out on the Santa Fe to Rush Center and the farmer picked us up there. When we came back I caught the train out to Colorado to visit Jim and Ollie.

"I stayed with Mabel and Jerry again for my last year in high school and played football and basketball on the high school team. There were 13 boys and 13 girls in my high school graduation.

"I signed to teach in Elbing where Annah Kieler was teaching. I got $50.00 per month and paid $18.00 per month for board and room with a very nice family.

"When school was out in the spring of 1917, I went out to work for Ollie and Jim during the summer. But I had signed to teach again at Elbing at $60 per month. Of course, World War I was in progress, and the draft was in effect, but it did not yet include me. When school was out in the spring of 1918, Ed Logan, my high school buddy and debate partner, went with me to Kansas City where we enlisted in the Navy.

"We were sent to Great Lakes training camp and assigned to the radio operator unit for schooling at Harvard University. There was no room for us right away so we did all sorts of detailed work and drilling until there was room for us in the school. This lasted until about December 1 when we went on to Harvard. Of course, the Armistice had been signed November 11, 1918. We both got a five day leave at the end of December so we went by ship from Boston to New York and spent the end of the year and start of the New Year seeing New York City.

"The flue epidemic had started in the fall of 1918 and kept getting worse as the winter came on. We saw them gather up 8 or 10 bodies each morning. Back in Kansas it seemed worst in January and February. My brother Ben and his wife Leona and two children, Mildred and Billie, had come from Colorado to visit and they all got the flue as did Bessie and Kate and "Friday" and their children. Ben, Leone, and Bessie all died in one week and Kate was

not expected to live. I could not come back for the
funerals, but I asked to get an early discharge because
of the situation. I got the discharge and came back
and went to take over things for Kate and "Friday". It
took 2 months before they were able to take care of
things. After they didn't need me, I went to work as
an elevator man at the Peabody Co-Op.

"My work at the CoOp was handling the grain
and loading the cars and selling feed. A year later we
brought in a lot of oats and shipped about 50 (train)
cars of oats. In handling oats, there was a lot of dust,
chaff and dirt. I developed a very bad cough and
after it continued for some time, I went to the doctor.
He told me I had a spot on my lung and had better
get out of the dirt and stay out of it. He recommended
no work for a few weeks. I quit my job and went out
to Colorado Springs and Denver for a few weeks
and got to feeling better. I came back and had the
doctor check me again and he said I was doing fine,
but to stay out of that dirt.

"I then decided to go back to Denver and enroll in
a business college and take bookkeeping and typing. I
did this and went six months while working in a
cafeteria for my meals. After six months business
training, I came back to Peabody and they hired me as
a bookkeeper and assistant manager at the Co-Op. This
worked out fine for I was entirely out of the dirt.

"In the early part of 1924, we had an auditor
come from Hutchinson to audit the books and the
year's work. Everything went smoothly and I
continued working until September when one evening
I got a phone call from Hutchinson. It was the same
man who had made the audit in February. He said
that he had gone to work with the Security Elevator
Company and they were needing a bookkeeper. He
told them that he had never audited a better set of

books than he found at Peabody and they wanted me to come out and talk to them if I wanted to make a change. I told them I was always looking for anything that would make for an advancement.

"Blanche and I came out to see them, and I took the job, starting with Security Elevator on September 28, 1924. Then a year later, on October 11, 1925, we were married.

"I retired in October 1969 after forty five years. Most of those years went fairly smoothly although there were some years in thirties when I worked 80 and 90 hours per week. One year I developed ulcers. In the Fall of 1984, I am enjoying the retirement and reasonably good health."

Though I never explicitly knew many of these things until 1984, I guess many of the experiences, emotions, values, expressed in these words became part of me through what one might call a process of osmosis. My "spelling teacher" taught me a whole lot more than spelling.

Fred and Blanche Kieler—the author's parents.

Chapter 8

MOM

When I was in Grade School all the students frequented a little mom and pop grocery store located just across the street to the northwest from our North Side School. I don't remember the store's name, and it didn't survive the World War II era. While it lasted, it survived not because of the groceries it sold so much as because of its large selection of pop, candy bars and bulk candies and a high sales rate of these items to kids going to and from school. Kids could and sometimes did stop in the morning, at noon and after school. In those days we had a full hour lunch period because there was no school lunch program. We all walked or rode bikes home for lunch. Mom didn't encourage me to patronize the store and we didn't buy groceries there because Dillon & Sons Grocery store, nearer our house, was a fine full line food store (supermarket in twenty-first century terminology) with excellent fresh meats, fruits and vegetables, and a good bakery as well as groceries. But to tell a kid who regularly walked by a candy store not to go in would never jive with the reality of the way kids are wired. Like everyone else in my school, I often stopped by.

My fiscal resources were very limited so there was no danger of my overdosing on candy. Yet temptation in many forms was always present—the prime source for moral failure on my part when I was a grade schooler. Occasionally I'd look around our house for any loose coins I could discover. Once in a while I would examine the coin purse in Mother's handbag when she wasn't around. I'd see if I could snitch a few pennies or a nickel or dime for use in making purchases at the candy store. I don't recall ever being caught at this, but a guilty conscience and a fear of getting caught deterred me from regularly engaging in this kind of pick-pocketing.

One time, when my sweet tooth was particularly active, I was without either "legal or illegal" money. I returned to the candy store after school. Pretending to browse for "shopping purposes", I managed to steal a pocketful of candy. Returning home, I was observed by Mom eating candy from this stash and was immediately given the "third degree." As soon as she realized what I had done, she promptly drove me back to the store and accompanied me inside to confess what I'd done, to return the uneaten candy, and to offer payment for what I had eaten. The proprietress expressed appreciation for my honest retribution and even said I didn't have to pay 'this time' but 'just don't do it again'. After that I never engaged in petty thievery again. Furthermore, I lost a good bit of my appetite for candy in that store.

Like Dad, Mom made sure that I had a good moral upbringing. Mom, like Dad, helped me with schoolwork and drills and she especially encouraged me with my reading. Grade cards, or Report cards as we called them, were issued every six weeks for us to bring home. For each subject, a letter grade was given. They ranged from "A" at the top, "B" above average, "C" for average, to "D" for below average and "F" for failing to meet the minimum standards of learning for that subject. Parents were to examine the cards and discuss them with us, and then sign them to indicate that this had been done. The next day we returned them to the teacher. My parents were always very diligent about this. Both of them, perhaps especially Mom, were very quick to reward me with a few coins for each "A." As a matter of fact, Mom in my eyes was usually the most generous person.

I received from Dad a set monetary allowance each week. I probably got the "going rate" for those days. Because there was no inflation to speak of my allowance in grade school started at about a quarter a week and it never got over fifty cents a week until I was in Junior High School. Mom, however, frequently made little special gifts of money for extra things and she'd sometimes help me out with one of my many collections.

I always observed Mother doing things for people or giving things to them. This included tangible and non-tangible gifts, monetary gifts and other kinds. She would simply try to enrich life for people. Illustrations which stick in my memory include her relationship to her nieces and nephews and people in service rolls. When I was in the third grade, Mom and Dad had my cousin Bernice Kieler (Glahn in marriage), Uncle Jim's daughter from Colorado, come live with us so she could attend Hutchinson Business College following her high school graduation. When she finished Business College, Mom invited her to stay on a while so she could gain needed work experience. Then about the time World War II began, Bernice returned to Colorado.

My cousin Virginia Taylor (de Laval in later years), Uncle Harold's oldest daughter, wrote me in February 2001, sharing memories and saying, "Your mother was always very generous and I remember her bringing me many hand-me-down clothes from Shirley, which I thought were the greatest. Summers, she also invited me to spend a few days at your home in Hutchinson which I thought was a great treat. Do you think that was the beginning of my travel lust? I loved the new experiences of playing croquet in your back yard, and roller skating on your nice smooth cement driveway (something we did not have in the country.)" I also know Mom later took great joy in trying to be a "patron" of sorts for my cousin Warren Taylor, Virginia's brother, when he was in college and beginning to bloom as an artist.

Mom was always one to keep in touch with family and friends, and to encourage them whenever, wherever and however possible. I think I didn't emulate this quality of her life as fully as I should have, but it did "bend this twig" so that in years to come I was to be attracted to another young woman with the same characteristics—Lorine Martin, who was to become my wife.

Throughout the entirety of their lives, Mom and Dad were faithful active members of Trinity Methodist Church, Hutchinson, (now called United Methodist). Mom was especially involved in Women's Society of Christian Service, WSCS for short. This group studied and supported missions of the Methodist Church. A Kansas woman, Garnett Everly, was a missionary in India. Her salary was paid by Trinity Church. Women of the church corresponded regularly with her. I can still picture envelopes with interesting foreign stamps arriving in our mail from Miss Everly. Mom always read them to us at dinner. Once when Garnett was home on furlough, visiting Trinity, she stayed in our home. Partly by way of supporting the people with whom Miss Everly worked, partly because Mom was a collector of many types of interesting things, Mom ordered and had shipped to us from India a piece of furniture. It was a beautiful small table made of an unusual wood, edged with intricate hand carvings, with folding leaves and legs so it could be made small or larger. This was in our home from the mid-nineteen thirties until the mid-nineteen eighties when the folks gave up housekeeping on their own. Now, in the twenty first century, it's a possession of my sister Shirley.

Mom was always one to offer guidance for me and for others. It was always well intentioned and designed to encourage or correct. Sometimes, however, it was offered out of her own rather rigid habit patterns of doing things. She could do this to the point of creating resistance or resentment. When our second son Bill was born, Mom and Dad visited and helped for a few days. In the midst of all the joy and excitement of a new son there was the stress and tension of adapting to a new family member. Mom was in the kitchen helping. She realized shelves and drawers weren't organized the way she would do them. She promptly proceeded to give Lorine a lecture on how she should organize them. Of course this greatly upset Lorine and I could understand. At an early age I learned simply to adapt by letting such lectures go in one ear and out the other and didn't allow them to bug me. This meant, of course, if I wasn't tactful or cooperative, my response often bugged mom.

I could be belligerent and sassy. One time I really angered Mom to the point where she lost control and got very abusive with me. She was wearing high-healed shoes. She proceeded to yank off her shoes and chase me all over the house until she finally caught me. She shoved me down to the floor, beat me relentlessly with a high-healed shoe, though not to the point of drawing blood, and didn't stop until I cried for mercy. Pictures of Mom's rigidities and this losing of control stands out in vivid contrast to all the other memories I have of Mom. Yet I knew that when it came to matters of discipline and learning responsibility, this was a matter of love even if it was "tough love."

I am bending over the kitchen sink with mother standing behind me pouring warm to hot soapy water over my head, scrubbing it and then gently messaging my head with her fingers. She follows this by rinsing my hair with vinegar water. With the water still running across my eyes and down my face, I blindly grope for the towel with which to dry my hair. This is an image of a weekly ritual performed by mother from the time I was a small child until I was nearly out of high school. I hardly knew how to shampoo my own hair when I left for college. It's illustrative of the tender love side of Mom's love and nurture.

Mom was what would be known today as a "stay at home Mom." In this role she was true to the prevailing norm of her day. I truly believe women should have the same freedom and opportunity for self fulfillment, for education and for employment as men. However, I hope every home will always provide for its children the quality of parental nurturing I experienced as a child. I have such a cluster of good memories of doing things with Mom. These revolve around making the home a happy and wholesome place, a place of hospitality for friends, family and sometimes even strangers.

One bitter winter day when we were snowed in and school had been canceled, the mail carriers were still out making their appointed rounds by foot—the norm for those days. Mom had made a big kettle of hot vegetable soup. When our mail carrier came to the house that day, she met him at the door, expressed concern for his well being in the midst of such bad weather, and invited him in for a minute to get warm and have a cup of soup. It was strictly against postal policy for him to accept the offer but he was chilled to the bone. Without hesitation, he took her up on the offer. This kind of hospitality was also always there for all my friends.

I don't think it matters whether it is the man or the woman who plays this role, but I still have so many good feelings from having a "stay at home mom" and so much awareness of children today who are without benefit of this kind of nurture. My feelings are so strong, in fact, that whenever and wherever there are two parents in a home, and it is at all possible for them to do it, my bias is that one of them needs to be at home when children are young—maybe even when they are teen-agers. Old fashioned? Yes, but to be truthful, this is where I am.

During my preschool and elementary school years, I worked with Mom helping with all the housekeeping chores—laundry, vacuuming and dusting, etc. Good memories abound—especially those revolving around the kitchen. When cooking, Mom always had things that I could help with and she made me a partner in her cooking. She taught me how to make certain dishes on my own. Of course I sometimes had to learn from my mistakes. I remember one time when Mom was gone. I decided to help out by fixing Spanish rice for supper. I found her recipe and proceeded to make it. The only thing was, the recipe referred to a certain number of cups of rice (which was cooked). I thought it referred to rice to be cooked. Suddenly, in the middle of my project, I found rice overflowing the cooking kettle and had more than I could take care of or use!

Another thing that Mom did was to teach me how to shop in the grocery store including teaching me how to look for quality and how to compare prices. Even before I was in Junior High, she frequently would give me a shopping list and send me walking to the grocery store to buy the things she needed. She knew about what these things should cost. She would give me enough money to cover the purchases. Almost always it was adequate for what she wanted. Mom's agreement with me was any change left over after I'd had gotten what she'd sent me for I could keep. This meant that I really learned quickly to be a thrifty shopper and not to indulge in impulse buying.

Even as an adult, when I set up keeping house for the first time, in my own apartment in Nashville, Tennessee, Mom made me a little recipe book. It included both a number of simple and easy dishes and many of my favorite dishes. That was something I always appreciated and cherished for many decades. Unfortunately I've now lost it.

If a woman's way to a man's heart is through cooking, Mom was surely good at it. I can't begin to name all her dishes which were my favorites, but they included a juicy pot-roast, great brisket, great meatballs, fried chicken, wonderful made-from-scratch, baked beans and both homemade yeast rolls and cinnamon rolls just to name a few. Mom always had a sweet tooth. I enjoyed her puddings—tapioca, rice, and bread puddings—her oatmeal raisin cookies and, for special occasions, homemade (never store bought) pies and cakes. Her fruit pies were my favorite.

When strawberries or other berries, apples, pears, peaches, cherries were in season we often had fun excursions to roadside stands and out to the country where farmers sold their own produce or where there were "pick and pay" orchards. What wonderful ingredients these made for mom's baking.

My childhood, and the years which followed, were molded by my parents who surrounded me with love and security. I could not have asked for better parents.

Chapter 9

CHRISTMAS MEMORIES

Children are always excited about Christmas and everything sacred and non-sacred which goes with Christmas including the getting and giving of gifts.

One Christmas especially stands out among my childhood memories of Christmases. Our family always thought of Christmas in terms of our extended family when I was growing up. This included not only Mom, Dad, Shirley and me, but also my grandparents, uncles and aunts and cousins. This kind of gathering was the norm until all of us cousins were out of school. After this, we couldn't all always make it home for Christmas. When the extended family gathered, always the gathering was at grandmother and granddads as long as they were living. This meant gathering at "the farm."

Look in with me on the Christmas I'm thinking of. There stands the farmhouse—a large, plain, rectangular white frame two-story home. It's there in that large Living-Dining Room, perhaps 25 or 30 feet long, 18 or 20 feet wide, that we celebrated. Note at the west end of the room there's a narrow table with leaves enough to expand to seat all fourteen of us. The plain white table cloth with grandmother's best china is there—nothing fancy but nicer than her everyday table setting. This is the way the table is always set not only for Christmas but for every major holiday. See us all gather to feast around that table at noon on Christmas day. Grandmother's feast is always bountiful. It may vary from Christmas to Christmas, but as usual today there's a turkey as well as a roast. Then there's a mountain of mashed potatoes and a big bowl of gravy along with dishes containing several fruits and vegetables all of which were home-canned last summer by grandmother from her garden. There's no fresh produce on the table. It doesn't exist this time of year. If you're looking for a salad, it's that red cranberry salad over on the backboard as well the congealed orange-flavored salad with shredded carrots in it. You can smell the fresh baked bread or rolls, can't you? And see, as soon as grandmother set them on the table we began to bathe them in the homemade butter. Of course, later homemade pies will be coming—pumpkin, mince-meat, and a fruit pie. Oh, I almost forgot to call to your attention, over on the side-board, that grandmother has made her once a year English plum pudding which is a special treat.

The big potbellied wood burning stove normally dominates the other end of the room as it stands right there in the center about 3 or 4 feet out from the east wall. Now you notice it has been moved over to the corner of the room. At Christmas time, my grandparents rearrange things to feature in the center where the stove usually sits, a cedar Christmas tree cut from the farm. You don't notice any light on the tree, do you? These won't come until the early 1940's when electricity comes to the farm. But see, there are other decorations—strings of popcorn and cranberries, multicolored chains made from loops of construction paper, and colored ornament balls. Clipped to some of the tree branches are a few little and old candle holders with candles that we can NEVER light because this would be a real fire hazard!

On Christmas Eve, stockings were hung around the room on chairs since there's no fireplace. This morning, Christmas morning, we children rushed into the room see what "our stocking" contained. Fresh fruits are very seasonal and expensive—not an everyday item in either the grocery story or at home. Almost always my grandparents, or someone in the family, buy some fresh fruit for Christmas, so we found in our stockings a selection of apples, oranges, candy and nuts (in their shells waiting for us to shell them). We were delighted by these. There were even a few very small trinkets and other gifts in each of our stockings.

But let me bring you back to the Christmas which stands out in my memory. As we use to celebrate Christmas, under the tree there was always a package from each family group for each child in the extended family. In addition, we all "drew a name from the hat" at Thanksgiving time. Each person would buy a gift for the one whose name they had drawn. We couldn't afford to buy everyone a gift. So in addition to the children's gifts, the remaining gifts under the tree were for those whose name had been drawn. Of course at our individual homes, before or after the extended family's Christmas, parents gave gifts to each of their children and children to their mom and dad, and husband, and wives exchanged gifts.

The Christmas I most remember as so very special was in the late 1930s while I was yet in grade school. Perhaps I was a fourth or fifth grader. There was the Christmas tree, as usual, and all the wrapped gifts underneath it. But there behind the tree, was a large wrapped package perhaps two feet wide, fifteen inches from front to back, and a foot and a half from top to bottom. It struck me as being *very* big—bigger than any Christmas gift I've ever seen or received. Somehow I thought of it as too big to really be a gift. "It must simply be part of the overall decorations in the room," I said to myself. When all the other gifts had been given and received and opened, granddad asked me to look at this package. I thought I had already received all my gifts. I couldn't believe it when I discover this "biggest ever" gift had my name on it! It took a little special coaxing to get me to open it. As I unwrapped the gift, I discovered that it was a box—a hand-crafted wooden tool chest made just for me by my grandfather. Wow! I already had a few tools and had begun to take an interest in woodworking. This was fantastic! But what was so special about that Christmas was not really the size of the gift and certainly not its cost—it was the ambiance of family and love which surrounded it along with the fact that it was a hand-crafted, one of a kind gift, made just for me.

From that day until the fall of 2002 nearly sixty-five years later, I had that tool chest in my possession and continued to use it. Then when we sold our loft, our retreat place where I had most recently used it, I gave the chest to my grandson, Michael Kieler, since he was the only male grandchild. All these many years it gave me pleasure and warm feelings. I know that what first excited me as a child was the sheer size of the gift, but now, looking back over the more than seventy Christmases that I have enjoyed, I see this chest in symbolic terms. As I think of all the perennial changes taking place in our culture, I can't help being mindful of the increasingly materialistic and commercial nature of our Christmas celebrations today. Over the years I have added many more memories to this chest of memories. I can't begin to enumerate them all, but among them are such things as these:

—The time we've taken, in the midst of our Christmas celebrations, to light the advent wreath, to go to church, to read the Christmas story from the Gospel of Luke before we exchange gifts;

—Aunt Elva's box full of jars filled with many kinds of homemade jellies and jams from which each person got to choose one;

—My parents hosting a World War II Russian refugee student, Nicholas Goncharoff, whom I brought home for Christmas while I was a student at the University of Illinois; then later, my parents providing a home and holidays for two years for Alex Janushevich, another Russian refugee being sponsored by their Sunday School class while he attended Hutchinson Junior College for two years; and our extended family including those two young men in their Christmas celebration;

—Lorine and I hosting Daniel Ebong, a Nigerian student studying at Southwestern College, for Christmas two or three Christmases and years later hosting for one or two Christmases his daughter who came to United States to study at her father's College;

—gifts of banana, pumpkin, zucchini breads baked by various family members and other friends for Christmas sharing;

—tree ornaments, pictures, other arts and craft items of all sorts made by our children for their parents and for other people;

—inlaid woods of various kinds and colors crafted by Ben into a beautiful cutting or bread board for his mom and me;

—working on a genealogy which I presented to my Dad as well as to our three sons at Christmas 1984 (eleven months before my father's death) and hearing dad say "this has been the best Christmas ever;"

—in more recent years, the gift of phone calls from other states and countries by family members who couldn't make it home for Christmas;

—the Christmases when "the first gift" was an announcement by Bill and Paula, and later by Paul and Janet that they were expecting a child;

—the times when some of us would say to one another that we have so much that we don't really need any thing more and we'd negotiate to make part of our gift giving a donation to each others favorite charity whether that charity be for an organization committed to caring for the natural world or for the world of orphans and refugees.

All of this is part of what granddad's tool chest really symbolizes to me. It's the presence of family and friends, the unexpected, the sacrificial, the homemade or the hand-crafted, the truly thought filled (thoughtful) relationships and gifts of love that have and still do mean more than anything which the secular and commercial world touts.

Chapter 10

TOYS, GAMES AND COLLECTIONS

In her book *How to Write Your Own Life Story,* Lois Daniel suggests that one way to reach a long way back into one's memory is to write about toys. She says we nearly all have had a favorite toy, or one we disliked, or one that influenced our lives. The remembering of these helps us get in touch with early memories. Even before I think of toys, I think of the fact that as kids we could entertain ourselves for hours playing "hide and go seek" without any toys at all. Nor was any purchase or toy needed to play "drop the handkerchief"—another source of standard entertainment for parties and school recesses. And, there were many other games we enjoyed which required few if any props.

As I think about toys I had in the 1930s, one thing that strikes me is that they were far less sophisticated and usually far simpler than toys for preteen children of today. When I was growing up there were no toy stores as such. Toys were purchased through general merchandise stores such as Montgomery Wards (a chain of stores which we used to call "Monkey Wards") and Sears and Roebuck. These were mail order stores in the beginning. Twice a year (each Spring and Summer, then again in the Fall and Winter) they would issue a mail order catalogue about 10" x 12+" and at least 2" thick filled with pictures and descriptions of all their merchandise with sizes, and prices for each item along with instructions on how to order by mail. One of my favorite pastimes was reading, studying, and fantasizing as I looked through these catalogues and especially through the toy section. This really sublimated the need for huge amounts of toys. I' m sure I had a lot more toys than I can remember, but I also know that I didn't have closets full of toys, as do so many children today.

What comes to mind as early toys I had are a variety of wooden toys. I had stick *horses*. I had ABC *blocks* on which the alphabet was printed in capital letters on one side and in lower case on another side. Then script, capital and lower case, was on two other sides. The numbers were on fifth side and animals on the sixth side. All of this was in a variety of colors making learning fun as well as giving the enjoyment of building all kinds of towers, walls and other structures. *Carved tops* which would spin and allow me to compete with my friends to see whose top would spin the longest before falling over. *Lincoln Logs* and *tinker toys* were great for building things. I enjoyed them immensely. *Pickup sticks* challenged us to pick up from a pile without moving another stick. I attempted to master *yo-yos* but could never quite do it. I dearly loved to play something else made of wood. I could play with these with adult relatives as well as other kids—*checkers*. Finally, I remember well from my grade school days a special kind of *rubber gun*. The gun was homemade, very crudely shaped out of wood into a pistol with barrel and handle. For "ammunition," we would then take old rubber inner tubes salvaged from flat auto tires, cut the tube through its diameter in strips about half an inch wide and use these "giant rubber bands" to stretch over the front of the barrel, pulling them back to stretch them, aiming and then releasing them to "shoot" one another.

Of course we also had things like balls and bats with their related games. Every boy I knew, had a soft ball for playing catch with or to play "Andy Over." In "Andy Over" we would get on opposite sides of a garage or house, shout "Andy Over" and then throw the ball over the roof with the challenge being for the other person to see it in time to get in position to catch it. I don't recall organized "little leagues" for boys or girls softball or baseball. What we frequently did was to gather a group of kids, find an empty lot or a playground when school wasn't in session, and organize a game of "*work up*" with 13 kids more or less. One kid filled each of the nine baseball positions. The others were batters. There really wasn't any score keeping in work-up. The first batter up would try to hit the pitched baseball. If the batter succeeded and got to base safely, the next player would bat. This would continue as long as no one struck out. When any one stuck out, flied out, or got tagged out while running the bases, they lost their chance to be a batter. They would then go to be left fielder and all the fielders would shift one position with the right fielder becoming third baseman and the other basemen shifting over one base. First baseman would become shortstop, the shortstop would become pitcher, the pitcher would become catcher, and finally, the catcher would then join the batters. The object, was to get to be a batter and to stay a batter as long as possible. We could play that game for hours. Every kid had a soft ball and/or a baseball and bat! If we happened to have enough kids to form two full teams, we played regular ball. If we didn't have the full compliment for work-up, we could always improvise. During recess at school there were always enough kids to play teams. I don't remember girls ever playing ball with us.

Lots of boys also had footballs or basketballs. However, I don't recall these being among my childhood toys even though I might play those games when I was at another boy's house.

Another type of toy I remember spending hours playing with was a wagon. Some people had wooden wagons, but in my boyhood in the '30s most wagons were metal wagons and many toys were also metal. There was no such thing as plastic toys. Plastics, I believe, started to develop with World War II when there was a shortage of metal. Metal play trucks and tools and buckets, etc. were among my toys. I could entertain myself using my imagination as I played with these or as I joined playmates and teamed up with them. I also enjoyed roller-skating long before the days of "roller blades" but never as much as tricycling and bicycling.

Like lots of small children I also had a scooter, which I enjoyed. It was a two-wheel platform (one wheel in front and one in back of the platform which was only 3 inches or so above the ground and parallel to it) with an upright handle to hold on. You put one foot on the platform and pushed yourself along with the other foot. It was lots of fun. Eventually scooters went out of fashion. Now, at the beginning of this century they are coming back into vogue for children although some of today's scooters are motorized.

While I was still very young I had a tricycle. I enjoyed riding it up and down the block as well as in our driveway, which had just enough slope toward the street to make it a small hill. I would take care of it like people took care of cars—washing it, greasing it, working on it. One day I decided to "adjust" the handlebars. I proceeded to find one of my dad's wrenches and managed to unscrew and remove the nut that held the handlebars on the post. However when I started to take off the handlebars, they were stuck with rust or something. I couldn't get them off. Since I couldn't get them off I decided just to forget my project so I didn't even bother to put the nut back on. Later I was riding down the sidewalk as fast as I could. All of a sudden the front wheel hit a bump in the sidewalk. That jarred the handlebars off and as they fell forward, since I was leaning on them, I just shot right over the front of my tricycle landing on my nose on the sidewalk. I had a nosebleed and ran home screaming bloody murder. Mom took me to the doctor who got the bleeding stopped. He said I probably had a broken nose but there was really nothing that could be done except just let it heal. It did heal, but I had a very crooked nose. Later on it was discovered that the broken bones had healed so as to obstruct my nasal passages.

When I was in the third grade they decided that I needed surgery to correct this situation. I again went to the hospital where I was born, St. Elizabeth Hospital in Hutchinson. It was a Roman Catholic hospital and our family hospital in my memory was Grace Hospital—a Methodist hospital. I had no recollection of ever being in St. Elizabeth before and I didn't know much about Catholics. It seemed liked a strange place with all those nuns in their habits running around. When I woke up from the operation, everyone was hovered around and very attentive. It seemed that during the surgery I had swallowed my tongue. They had feared I might not survive so now they were frequently checking on me. I had a miserable several days of recuperation with nausea and pain and I wasn't a very happy patient.

Several times a day one of the Sisters would come in and try to cheer me up. On the second or third day one of the Sisters asked me if there was anything I needed or anything she could do for me. I complained about the food—especially about breakfast which never included eggs, one of my favorite breakfast items. She had the kitchen bring me a soft boiled egg right away. From then on breakfast included toast, tea, and a soft boiled egg—favorite comfort food from childhood days. I was so grateful. Ever since that time, I've always had warm and positive feelings toward Catholic nuns.

Although the operation helped my breathing they were unable to totally correct the situation. I would have to wait until after I was fully grown before a second surgery was performed. I didn't have that surgery until a few months after Lorine and I were married. There's no doubt but that my tricycle with related events was one toy which created a great impact on my life.

I remember playing and enjoying three board games as I child—monopoly plus Chinese checkers and regular checkers. Like most kids, I had a sack of marbles and enjoyed playing them with other buddies. But I didn't like playing "for keeps." In the game of marbles we placed one marble in the center of a circle or ring of marbles. Each player, usually two of us, would have a marble called the "shooter." We would take turns shooting the shooter, cradled in the bend of the index of our index finger and flipping it with our thumb. The object was to hit the center marble and knock it out of the ring without hitting any of the marbles forming the circle. If you succeeded in doing this you got to pick up that marble and add to your collection.

Another hobby popular with boys in the period between World Wars I and II was making and playing with lead soldiers. If you were to look down to the foot of the basement stairs in our Fifteenth Street home, you were likely to see me standing there, lighting an old gas stove which Mom kept as an "extra" to use for canning. I would rummage through a box of molding supplies and drag out a dirty looking old aluminum sauce pan, drop in a small bar of lead, and place it over the lighted burner.

After about 15 minutes all the lead would be melted. More rummaging in my box would bring out several little steel blocks about 1" thick, 2" high, and 1 ½" wide. These little boxes were hinged on one side and had a little opening or hole in the top. They were my molds. Open them and you would see on the inside hollowed out shapes of soldiers—one crouching with a rifle to his shoulder, another in standing guard or marching with rifles position, etc. Since there was no workbench, you could see me down on my knees on the unfinished cement basement floor holding a little funnel to the hole in the top of the mold. Very carefully so as not burn myself, I would pour the hot melted lead into the molds. This done, I would leave them to cool or harden. Several hours later, I would return, open the molds, tap out my soldiers, and trim the edges to clean wherever lead had run the little crack between the two halves of the mold. If I broke one of my little miniature soldiers in this process, I could always melt it down again and make it over. Soon after I'd completed removing and finishing the half-dozen new soldiers I'd made for my collection, you'd see me down on the floor on my hands and knees, lining up my soldiers, or hiding them, and in my imagination "fighting a battle."

My parents played bridge a lot so several decks of playing cards were always round our house. I played lots of rummy, as well as other card games—some times with Dad and Mom, often with my buddies. Jim Jung and I played lots of double solitaire.

Bigger toys came along as I joined Boy Scouts somewhere around the third or fourth grade. I got started with most of these things apart from scouts, but some related to my Boy Scout merit badge programs or other scouting activities. For instance, I started collecting stamps and coins, enjoyed these collections tremendously, worked energetically at them and learned a lot through them, but I also earned a merit badge in each of these for my Boy Scout advancements. I continued these interests actively for many years beyond the nineteen thirties.

Another very favorite "toy" of mine was my bicycle—so much so that even though I didn't continue bicycling during most of my adult life, I picked it up again when I retired. I remember the adventures of working on my Bicycling merit badge for scouts. Besides having to learn about bikes and bike safety, etc., we had to do six 25-mile bicycle rides and then a 50-mile ride to earn out merit badge. I worked on the six rides with various scout friends riding half the 25 miles trip out in to the country on highways, then turning around and returning home. For the 50-mile ride a friend and I rode to Sterling, Kansas, 25 miles northwest of Hutchinson. This was a great adventure for us in both the planning and in the riding. I'm not sure how old I was—perhaps 14 or 15 years old. Today most parents would not allow two Junior High boys to pack a lunch, leave town unaccompanied by an adult, to spend the day riding on a highway 50 miles through the country. No one thought much about it in that day. We had a great time. Along the way I had a flat tire. Having no adult accompaniment, no cell phone to call 911 or AAA Road Side Assistance, we managed to fix it with a patch kit we carried and kept going. We took a nice rest break at Nickerson, half way between Hutchinson and Sterling. We stopped there going and coming back. We each spent one of our hard earned dimes each time. A nickel went for pop, and a nickel for a candy bar. When we got to Sterling it was time for our sack lunches. We arrived safely home before suppertime. We may have been tired, but we felt very good about our achievement of the day.

Interestingly, more than 50 years later I rode a bicycle through Sterling again. This second trip was September 14, 1996. After taking up biking again in my retirement, I decided to enter the Autumn Classic 150 Bike Ride to help raise funds for the MS (Multiple Sclerosis) Society of South-central Kansas to benefit national MS research and assist persons locally who were suffering from the disease. We started at Hesston, Kansas and rode roughly 75 miles west and 75 miles north to Lucas, Kansas, in a two-day period, most of it in a cold driving rain. Sterling was about the half waypoint for our first day and we had a hot lunch in the Sterling College dining hall or gym at noontime. It was so good to get in where it was warm and dry. The day was nothing like the beautiful Kansas summer day more than 50 years before, but I warmed to the memories of that first ride into Sterling. Moreover, this retiree managed to survive the weather, endured the ride, and did some good for his fellow human beings. Once again I had similar feelings of pride and accomplishment.

Since that time (as of 2003) I have done 4 or 5 other MS 150 Bike tours raising over $7,500 to benefit MS research and care for local patients. In my retirement, I've also ridden once in the Bike Across Kansas program (riding 450+ miles from the Colorado boarder west of Kanarado, Kansas, to White Cloud, Kansas, where we dipped our front bike tire in the Missouri River. I look forward to repeating this.

Chapter 11

BOYHOOD YEARS

Building a hangout ("the onion house") when we moved to "302 East 15th Street" didn't turn out to be too practical, but that adventure was just the first of many in my boyhood years in Hutchinson. The 1930s were happy years for me. Unlike the last half of the Twentieth Century when people became so mobile that many lost their roots and a sense of stability and groundedness, these things were hallmarks of my life. True, the thirties were years of great economic depression. People around me in Hutchinson held on to the jobs they had if they could, but if they were out of work, instead of packing up and leaving to seek work elsewhere, most stayed put. They did what they could to eke out a living with odd jobs and part-time employment until things got better. At the very least, people were close enough to the soil (literally, emotionally, and in terms of their life experiences) that they could always garden, perhaps raise chickens or animals, and manage to grow food for themselves and their family. People in the thirties learned to make do with what they had. We didn't feel we had to shop or spend money to have fun nor did we feel we needed gourmet, or out of season, foods to eat well!

Northside Grade School was a happy time because teachers were very caring. In my second grade class, Miss Puckett realized there were a few of us who seemed bored with our reading lessons.

She had a conference with the mothers of each us suggesting they buy some science and other books that would be more challenging and she managed to get us involved in a supplemental reading program. Our teachers did lots of things like inviting special guests to our class (sometimes they were parents of our fellow classmates) to enrich class time with new and creative experiences. *Weekly Readers* was a kid's newspaper that became a reading, sharing, and discussion supplement to formal lessons. The majority of kids in my grade were kids with whom I'd been in class year after year. We were friends, we knew each other, we studied together, played together during morning and afternoon recesses and after school, and we shared each other's birthday parties. In short our lives were lived with a real sense of community and continuity.

Spring 1937: Author's 3rd Grade Class at Northside School
Teacher is Miss Puckett.
Front row (l. to r.): Howard Manges; Jim Holland; Bill Spence; _____; Jean Edie; Eddie Vissor; Mary Ann Martin; June Kandy; Jimmie Snyder; Jim Jung; Middle row: George Clay; Eugene Ryan; Don Shank; Derald Ward; _____); Gene Ackerman; Betsy Dillon; _____; Lila Zimmerman; the author/ H.Kieler; Back row: Don Elliott; Dan Upson; Jack Riggs; Don Sweet; Barbara Creel; Bill Zimmerman. At least 19 of these 27 class members continued in school graduating together as members of the Hutch High Class of 1947.

April 1940: Author's 5th Grade Class at Northside School.
Teacher is Miss Hardford.
This is essentially the same class (as previous picture)
three years later. As usual, the teacher has the
Author standing next to her.

There were times when I gave my teachers lots of trouble.
Discipline was part of school—not harsh discipline but strict
rules for behavior which everyone was expected to follow. I can
remember being sent to the coat closet to spend 10 minutes or
so (I think maybe it was less but it seemed this long) in isolation
when I was being very contrary or disrespectful to the teacher
and to rules of the class. Our ultimate threat was being sent to
the Principal's Office. Rumor had it that there was a big wooden
paddle kept there which the Principal would use on you if you
didn't "stay in line." Having made several trips there myself,
I'm not sure that this was true. If it was, it was used very
sparingly and on rare occasions. Mostly the "pressure" of being
sent to the Principal's Office for discipline was enduring a long
wait in the outer office where we could "think things over."
Then we got a "talking to" when the Principal finally called us
in to his or her office. The real threat beyond this was that "if
this happens again, I will have to call your parents." We were
aware that some of our friends came from poorer homes or more
well-to-do homes than we did, but everyone was treated alike.

There was no favoritism and there was little bullying or mean-spirited teasing.

Another thing that helped to develop a sense of community at school was that almost everything like music, art, special talks, films, etc. took place in our own classroom. We had no lunchrooms, commons area, gym, or auditorium. For the occasional all school assembly, classes gathered as groups on one big main floor hallway and sat on the floor or on the stairways coming down from the second floor. This was crowded and uncomfortable and the time or two each semester when we had such assembles our gathering was very brief.

As I recall, school began at either 8 or 8:30 am each day and ended at 4pm, but we were dismissed at 12 Noon for one hour to walk home for lunch and a brief break and then returned by 1 pm. This meant all kids would be coming and going to and from school twice each day. We tended to walk or ride bikes in groups with other classmates who lived in the same general direction from school as did we. This always made for lots of camaraderie. In the process, we visited and could also plan things that we'd like to do together after school or on the next Saturday.

After I was old enough to ride a bike regularly, there were three or four of us—Jimmy Snyder, Jim Jung, Byron Green, and myself who almost always rode bikes together back and forth from school. We walked or rode up and down Maple Street (a street which ran along the west side of both Northside Grade School and my house which was about nine blocks north). Long before we rode bikes, about a half dozen of us boys in the second and third grade usually walked together to school. This was before we discovered girls. The group consisted of my closest buddy, Jim Jung; Don Elliott whose dad was a Funeral Director; Dan Upson, whose dad was the High School basketball coach; Byron Green whose dad may have been a salesman, and I think Jim Sherman and Clarence "Chauncey" Jones. There may have been others. I'm sure the group varied from time to time.

Girls existed when I was kid. There was no enforced segregation. But by and large, girls played as a group and went to school in groups, and boys played and went to school in separate groups.

Co-educational socializing might occur after we got to school and were waiting for the doors to open, or as a bunch of guys and a bunch or girls might pass each other on the way to or from school, or when parents had parties—especially birthday or Halloween parties—for us. Otherwise, the co-ed socializing didn't really begin much until we were in Junior High School.

I have a vivid recollection of us boys doing things outside of school. During Grade School there was a year or two when I organized what we called "The Saturday Morning Club." We didn't have any real purpose except getting together. We got together mostly in the wintertime when it was too cold to play out-of-doors. Our basement was where we met. Ours was basically an unfinished basement, but we walled off one room with old sheets or curtains that hung from the ceiling to form our 'Club Room." We had a membership list made with block letters inked on an ink pad and stamped on sheets of paper. Attendance was taken and recorded with a roll each time. I don't recall we did much else except talk, tell stories, dream dreams, and so on.

Though our Saturday Morning Club was a rather "organized thing," most of my activities were less structured and involved two or three people. My pets included a dog, a cocker spaniel named Ginger whom I enjoyed; gold fish and rabbits. These always involved a joint effort of caring for pets. Sometimes I cared for them, sometimes my little sister did, and always one of my parents was a back-up caregiver.

My friends joined with me when I was involved with wild creatures like pigeons, doves, and garter snakes. Alternating between first one friend and then another, or working with a pair of friends, we would go looking for pigeons or doves—especially pigeons. We could sometimes catch them on the streets. We would search for garter snakes (a rather common, small, harmless snake) which we could find in water meter manholes or under rocks. I would keep and care for these creatures for limited amounts of time in my own backyard cages or "zoo."

My family had certain ritual activities to which I always looked forward. Many a warm summer evening after Dad got home from work and we finished supper, we would take an evening ride in the

car. These often culminated with a stop at the A & W Root Beer
stand where we got curb service to deliver us a nice frosty mug of
root beer. Occasionally, we might wind up with a stop at the Ice
Cream Parlor where you could buy one, two or three scoops of ice
cream on a single cone for a nickel, or later, a dime a scoop. The
most exciting thing about this was the fact that Ice Cream Parlors
then had twenty or thirty flavors to choose from! These family
times were unbelievable great times!

As I got older I joined a Cub Scout Pack followed by a Boy
Scout Troop as did most of my friends. Younger play and "Club"
activities melted away. After Grade School, school friends gradually
began going in different directions for their extra curriculum
activities but there was a bonding which lasted through all our
school years and beyond.

Scouting was either "girl scouting" or "boy scouting" when
I grew up. Boys joined Cub Scouts when we were in the third
or fourth grades and by the time we reached the fifth or sixth
grade we would join a Boy Scout troop. Boy Scout troops were
usually sponsored either by churches or by civic clubs or groups
like the American Legion. The two biggest Boy Scout Troops in
Hutchinson were sponsored by the First Presbyterian Church
(Troop One with A. Lewis Oswald as Scoutmaster) and by my
church, Trinity Methodist (Troop Thirteen with Dick Dadisman
as Scoutmaster).

There was lots of good-natured rivalry and competition between
these two troops. The program of scouting encouraged and taught
a variety of things that kids should learn as they grew up—life
skills, safety and physical fitness, hobbies, cultural and civic
activities, etc. Most of these were usually approached from the
standpoint of a Merit Badge Booklet to be studied. Related to the
study were achievements for each of the skills or activities to be
accomplished in a way which demonstrated mastery of subject or
area of life. A badge to be worn was awarded us when this mastery
was completed. There were adult with whom we worked toward
the goal of earning the Merit Badge.

Scouts wore an official uniform. Pins were attached to the uniform to show a boy's level of achievement as he progressed from Tenderfoot, to Second Class, First Class, Life, Star and finally to the rank of Eagle. Also a Merit Badge Sash would be worn on the uniform. Whenever a merit badge was earned, a little round cloth patch with a related symbol of that skill or activity was awarded. This would be sewn on the sash. All told, I suspect that we had a theoretical possibility of earning perhaps 75 to 100 different merit badges. They cover a range of things such things as Hiking, Bicycling, Camping to First Aid, Swimming, and Life Saving to Bee Keeping; Animal Husbandry, Citizenship, Reading, Art, Photography, Stamp Collecting, Coin Collecting. For each level or rank of achievement, we'd have to earn a certain number of merit badges. Some were specifically "required." We were free to choose other "electives." A minimum of 21 badges, about a third of them required, was needed to become an Eagle Scout. Percentage wise very few boys ever made it to Eagle and I was not one.

Troops had weekly meetings with a variety of activities (such as knot tying; human pymirid building, etc.); talks; time for working on merit badges; and planning for our monthly camp out. The rivalry between the Presbyterian Troop and our Troop at Trinity revolved around such things as: the total number of merit badges earned in the troop for the month; how many boys attended the monthly camp out; the number of boys achieving the rank of Eagle. Scouting was probably the most exciting part of my social life when I was growing up. I earned enough merit badges that I could have been an Eagle Scout but two merit badges required to become an Eagle evaded me—Swimming (including a mile swim) and Life Saving (learning to rescue a drowning person). I never learned to swim with any great proficiency and thus could not pass these two merit badges. However, I thoroughly enjoyed working on merit badges and they contribute to several of my hobbies such as photography, stamp and coin collecting, bicycling—things I have enjoyed either for periods of my life or throughout my entire life.

A phenomenon of the late 20th/early 21st Centuries is the vast number of "Third World" and/or "Urban" children who grow up without the opportunity to have my kind of childhood, without the opportunity to go to school, who are perhaps homeless or orphaned because of AIDS or other diseases, who are children raising children, or who are recruited at a very young age to be in paramilitary groups. Even in the United States of America among families who are well educated and comfortably well off there is the trend of home schooling. This often provides a quality intellectual education with its one on one or very low ratio of students to teacher. On the other hand, it certainly tends to deprive children of the experiences and opportunities which were mine at their age—experiences of give and take with peers, and the opportunity to bond with large numbers of schoolmates. These things develop pride and loyalty to social institutions; they teach coping skills when there are differences and difficulties. Based on my boyhood experience, I believe a classroom with a dozen and a half or more children who represent a microcosm of society, of the world, is a prime place to learn skills of nonviolent and interpersonal relationships, to experience a community and social consciousness which feels optimism, compassion and concern in relationship to others.

Another dimension of my boyhood years was the sense of community which surrounded us. Neighbors knew our names and who we were and they took an interest in us. I can't recall his name now, but there was a man who lived "catty-cornered" southwest from our house. He was a candy salesman. I'll never forget one Friday the 13th. He was cleaning out his garage, preparing to restock his car with a fresh supply of candy samples. He gave me all of the old samples. Wow! From that day on I've always felt that Friday the Thirteenth was my lucky day!

Miss Woolf lived across from us. She seemed old from the moment we moved into our house, but she was a friendly person who loved kids. She was a retired U. S. Army Nurse who served in the Spanish-American War. She lived alone and had no relatives, but she never tired of inviting my sister and me over to her house for cookies with milk or tea and some visiting. Almost all of the neighbors knew us and kept track of us. Within a couple of blocks of our house were several families who had children at Northside. These parents were always looking out after all of us and our parents looked after their kids. It was a good time and a happy time in which I grew up. Would that all the children of the world could have the childhood opportunities and the joys I had.

Chapter 12

ENTREPRENEURING AND OTHER JOBS

In the 1930s and 40s, all residential type lawnmowers were the hand pushed reel type mowers. As I got big enough and strong enough to push the mower and do mowing for my Dad, I also solicited mowing jobs from our neighbors. I wasn't ever really successful in securing lots of these. The ones I did get were more on the occasional basis such as vacation mowing. Possibly my only regular customer was Miss Wolf. Nevertheless, every mowing job I got helped with my goal of increasing my earnings. I came up with lots of ways to earn money.

At a rather early age I began to want to earn a little extra money for myself over and above my allowance. As a kid with a fertile imagination, I was always dreaming up ways to do this. Some of the things I came up with were more successful than others but I always seemed to do pretty well at pocketing a little extra money and of saving part of it so that I could multiply it by earning and compounding interest of my savings.

While still quite young I was always offering to do extra things, beyond the normal expectations, by way of chores and errands for my folks. This is how I came to be paid on a piece work basis for the "number dug" when it came to digging dandelions. I think it may also have been the way I got started grocery shopping for my mother with a chance to keep the change that was left over after the bill was paid.

Working with Dad in his garden and learning about flowers, I became aware of how they formed seeds and how some sent out new runners to multiply. Some flowers like zinnias and columbine were my favorites. It was also easy to harvest their seeds. I quickly came up with the idea of harvesting, packaging and labeling seeds in envelopes and then marketing them door-to-door in the neighborhood. I don't remember how many seasons I did this but I do have some recollection of responsive neighbors.

I must not have received too many rebuffs as I did door-to-door selling of flower seeds and chrysanthemums plants because I applied for and was hired for another door-to-door job that was available even to young elementary kids. This was a magazine delivery boy job. In the 30s the U.S. Postal System was not the primary means of distribution for the magazines people subscribed to. Magazines could be purchased at newsstands as they can today, but when people wanted to receive their magazines at home on a regular week basis, magazine publishers used magazine distributors who in turn hired youngsters to staff delivery routes to do that job. I enjoyed this work. We received a canvas bag with shoulder strap for carrying our magazines and we were paid by the number of magazines delivered. It was pretty good pay—several cents, maybe a nickel a magazine. We could also increase our earnings by selling new subscriptions. I delivered several magazines but the three most popular, as I remember, were a news magazine, *LIFE*; a ladies' magazine, *WOMAN'S HOME COMPANION*; and a youth magazine entitled *BOY'S LIFE. THE SATURDAY EVENING POST* was another of my magazines.

In developing the hobby of stamp collecting I had discovered one way young collectors secured stamps for themselves, in addition to soliciting all their relatives and acquaintances, and trading with friends, was to order stamps *on approval from* stamp dealers. Stamps were mailed on display sheets. People then had a week or ten days to look them over, choose stamps they wanted to purchase and return their payment along with the other stamps. I decided I should become a stamp dealer! I got all the necessary forms, instructions, stationery, etc. and made up my own approval sheets using my duplicate and surplus stamps. I even placed an ad or two in magazines and newspaper want-ads. I got quite excited about all this, enjoyed getting ready, but I never got an order or made a sale.

As a Junior High student I came up with at least two other jobs. With W.W. II agricultural laborers as well as other laborers were in short supply. West of town, on sandy loam next to the Arkansas River, was truck a farm where vegetables and fruits were raised for sale locally and for the Dillon & Sons Grocery warehouse. One farmer had, among other crops, two large asparagus patches. Asparagus grows very fast in the spring and needs to be cut quickly when it's at just the right size. Otherwise, it becomes too large and tough to be good and quits producing. This farmer got the idea of hiring high school and junior high students to come out and cut asparagus after school each day. I'd ride my bike out to the farm, cut asparagus for about 3 hours, and then ride back to home. We alternated harvesting one patch one day, the other patch the next day, from mid-March to Mid-May. This was a really good job. I enjoyed it even if it was a short-term job. I did this two different springs.

My other Junior High job was again strictly entrepreneuring. I raised chickens and eggs. Miss Wolf, the delightful retired Spanish-American War Army nurse who lived across the street, didn't have a large home. It didn't look to be older than the houses surrounding it, but it may have dated back to an agricultural era. Her garage looked older and had a small hen house and chicken pen attached to the back of it. Since many food items were rationed during the War, and I was always seeking new ways of making money, I talked to her about the possibility of using her set-up for raising chickens. Miss Wolf agreed.

With the pen's limited size I could keep less than a dozen and half hens. I wanted young hens. They produced more eggs and made good fryers if I had too many. I promised to "pay her" with all the eggs she could use. Since she was single she didn't need many eggs. It became a real deal for me. The hens would produce a dozen or more eggs daily.

In Dad's grain office they had sample pans of grain for every rail car of wheat, oats, milo and whatever other grains they handled. Once the sale was consummated they discarded the samples. Dad was able to furnish me free of charge most of my chicken feed from discarded grain although I had to buy some "mash" to supplement the hens' diets. I also had to buy a bit of straw to use in the nests or boxes where hens laid their eggs. Every morning I went across the street to open up the hen house to let the chickens out into their pen. Every night I reversed the procedure. Morning and night I also had to feed and water the chickens, clean the pen, and gather eggs. My family got all the eggs we could use and even after Miss Wolf's share, I had enough eggs that I could peddle them to the neighbors and earn pretty good money.

As I write this I find myself wondering if our neighbors ever got tired of seeing me come to their door with my projects. If it weren't for War, I'm sure the neighbors would not have indulged chicken raising in town, but to my knowledge there were never any complaints.

Probably the most significant business I began was one I ran two summers. It began with a bona fide problem. Dad suggested the business to me as a solution to the problem. I've already spoken of the grain samples, which every grain dealer received, for each railroad boxcar of grain they handled. Grain inspectors took these samples from every box car arriving in their rail yards after trains had brought them to Hutchinson from country elevators. The railroads delivered the samples to the grain offices so these dealers could have the State Grain Inspectors weigh, test, and certify the quality of grain. On the basis of this information and after a box car load of grain was either sold to be shipped on somewhere else, or it was decided to put it into the terminal elevator for storage, a new "Bill of Lading" was prepared. The old one had come to the railroad freight offices when the grain arrived. Bills of Lading were the paper work legally describing what the railroad was shipping, to whom, under what tariffs (rates governing shipping charges) along with any other necessary information or instructions. In and around harvest-time there was a terrific volume (hundreds, even thousands per day) of these Bills of Lading to be transmitted to, from, and between the 3 railroads that served Hutchinson and the twenty some grain dealers or brokers located there.

Because of wartime labor shortages, grain dealers and railroads were finding it very difficult to find someone to shuffle all these Bills of Lading between their offices. This was long before the day of Faxes. Dad suggested that I form a "Messenger Service" to do the job. I did this using my bicycle as my means of transportation. I also advertised not only to my primary customers (railroads and grain companies) but also to the community at large. From "the little old ladies" who couldn't get gas for their cars or weren't able to get out, I received calls to mail letters, take telegrams to Western Union or the Postal Union, pickup medicine, etc. For years I had a copy of an article that appeared in the newspaper one day—"New Wartime Business Starts in Hutchinson." It was an article about me and about the important service role I was performing. I felt important and I made excellent adult level money as I worked my tail off and had a great time doing it.

After these two summers, I was old enough to be legally employed by regular employers. Labor was still in short supply. The Hutchinson Navel Air Station needed civilian employees. Dad drove me out to the Navy Base located about six miles south of Hutchinson so I could put in a job application. I was hired and assigned to work in the "Ship's Store" on the base. Ship's Store was the name for a kind of general store selling things to provide for the needs of sailors and officers. It also had a restaurant, a recreation room and a soda fountain. I worked in the soda fountain regularly although occasionally I was assigned to kitchen work such as dish washing or potato peeling (with a machine that did the peeling). I was taught how to make ice cream shakes and malts, Sundaes, Sodas, and different fountain drinks from 'windmill sodas' (just a glass of plain water) to Cherry Cokes and Green Rivers (carbonated water with sugar syrup and lime coloring). I learned to keep a clean fountain and to "secure" or close things up at the end of the day.

I worked full-time two summers. During the school year in-between, I worked part-time as much as I could considering my debate schedule and other activities. This was a great learning experience as I met naval personnel from all over the country, gained new skills and accepted some management responsibilities. And I matured through such things as hearing my boss, Charlie Thierry, a Petty Officer from Pennsylvania, a man of French extraction with family still living in France, spin the tales of a sailor. I had to walk about 3 or 4 blocks to catch the Navy buses or "cattle trailers" to get to work on time for my second shift job (3 p.m. until 11 p.m. and occasionally 12 midnight) and to return home late in the evening.

After the war, the final job I worked while still a high school student was at Black's Drug Store. It was commonplace for drug stores to have Soda Fountains and Lunch Counters. Because I had experience I was able to get this job in the downtown heart of Hutchinson. Much of it consisted of the same type of fountain work I had learned at the Naval Air Station, but I also made sandwiches and prepared plates for the customers at the Lunch Counter. This was strictly a 9 to 4 type job so when there were slack periods I also did a bit of waiting on general drug store customers. Once again every new job brought new experiences.

Maybe I had a bit of luck and good fortune growing up to do the things I did and get the jobs I held, but certainly each one enabled me to build upon the previous job and prepared me for bigger and better things. If there are any young heirs of mine who chance to read these memoirs in years or decades to come, I hope they would not be content to twiddle all their free time away and I would wish them well in entrepreneuring and in the pursuit of jobs.

Chapter 13

GRANDMOTHER

She was weather beaten with the ruddy complexion that came from spending much time out-of-doors tending chickens, turkeys, geese, the garden, and walking to the fields to take lunch or a snack to the men folk working there. Most of her life was lived before farms had electricity or many of the modern conveniences (including hot water!) of the latter part of the twentieth century. She had dishpan hands from the large number of hours time spent in her kitchen where she cooked everything from scratch, washed all her dishes by hand, and did the family's clothes in wash tubs using wash boards for the scrubbing. She was not allergic to hard work.

She was a stocky person, about 5' 2" in height, with coal black hair, until it grayed with age, and she had sparkling dark brown eyes. Except for Sunday and go-to-town occasions, I almost always saw her dressed in flowered print dresses (*NEVER* in jeans or shorts) which she had made with her own hands from flour sacks. It was the merchandising practice of that day to sell most staples like flour and sugar (even sometimes animal feed) in large 50 or 100 pound cloth sacks with printed designs intended to make them useful for recycling into clothing and other household articles.

She was a woman of beauty in the sense that she nearly always had a pleasant appearance about her with a kind and gentle disposition, fun loving in the sense of liking to tease. She was a woman of strong faith, ideals, convictions who radiated an inner strength and beauty. She was my maternal Grandmother, Jane Elizabeth Wurtzel Taylor.

Growing up I enjoyed being Grandmother's helper when I spent time on the farm in the summers. This was doubly true when I was too young to work with the men in the fields and in the barnyard. Out-of-doors I learned to feed the chickens, treat them for mites, gather eggs, and weed and water the big vegetable garden. I also loved the smell and taste of everything that came from Grandmother's kitchen because it was all made from scratch and Grandmother's kitchen repertoire was a bit different from Mother's. Garden fresh was no commercial slogan in those days and *every* meal produced wonderful aromas. Since all our breads, cakes and pies were home baked the smells of baking frequently preceded the supper smells.

Normally grocery shopping happened only once a week—on Saturday which was the day reserved for going to town. There was too much to be done on the farm to go more often. For that reason, however, there were numerous peddlers or door-to-door salesmen who went from farm to farm selling items needed by the "housewives" as they were called then. Tinkers sold pots and pans, sharpened and repaired kitchen items. Fuller Brush salesmen sold brooms, mops, brushes and cleaning supplies of all sorts. The Watkins Salesmen sold kitchen supplies, spices, extracts (vanilla, almond, orange, lemon, maple flavorings, etc.), puddings, gelatins and other items. I always enjoyed hearing the sales pitch and watching to see what Grandma would buy. One thing he sold was called "Junket." It came in tablet form and was dissolved in warm milk and then hardened or stiffened into a soft pudding type of dessert. Junket was always a favorite with me along with tapioca pudding. It was a treat to hear grandmother order junket or tapioca because I knew one of these would soon be coming up for dessert.

Mondays were almost always washday for Grandmother (in fact for almost all homemakers whether on the farm or in town), followed by Tuesdays for ironing. With no mechanized washing machines in the early 1930s, washing was labor intensive. Washday involved me in bringing in wood and helping build fires in the cook stove where tubs of water were heated. Grandmother did the hand scrubbing of clothes on wash boards; we both worked at wringing the clothes with a "wringer" which meant turning a crank that rotated a pair of rubber rollers which squeezed clothes to get them as dry as possible. I'd help hang the clothes out-of-doors on a wire clothes line using wooden clothes pins to keep them there so they wouldn't fall on the ground as they fluttered in the wind and sun. When they were dry we took them down and brought them indoors in wooden bushel baskets. When Grandmother ironed, she had to fire up the cook stove and then place solid cast—iron "irons" on the top to get them hot enough she could iron out the wrinkles.

There was a little rhyme people used to say or sing. It named all the days of the week and the specialized work or events planned for that day. It went somewhat like this: Church on Sunday; wash on Mondays; iron on Tuesdays; mend on Wednesdays; market on Thursdays; bake on Fridays; and clean on Saturdays. This was pretty much Grandmother's routine except Thursday was a cleaning day because almost universally farm families went to shop on Saturday. Saturday, seeing all their friends, was almost like a festival in town.

As already suggested, clothes weren't fancy but everyone had at least one dress outfit to wear for special occasions like going to church on Sundays, going to weddings, funerals, etc. Sunday, the Sabbath Day, literally was a day of rest and recreation. It was *always* honored in the Taylor family. No matter what the circumstances there was no farm work done on Sunday except for absolute essentials like feeding, watering, milking livestock. My grandparents did not even harvest grain on Sunday when it was ripe. Sunday mornings we always went to Peabody to attend worship in their Lutheran Church. I always did this with my grandparents when I was staying at the farm just as surely as I always attended Methodist Sunday School and Worship with my parents when I was home with them. After church it was back to the farm for a special Sunday noon dinner and free time for the remainder of the day—rest, play games out-of-doors or indoors, visiting other people or just visiting at home, reading, and the like.

With one or two exceptions, I can only remember attending a single funeral before I was in college. When I was very young, perhaps 4 or 5 years old, my grandparents had a friend who died. They wanted to attend her funeral. Of course, they couldn't leave me alone on the farm so they took me along with them. It was also their way of introducing me to the realities of life. This was the first time I'd ever seen a dead person. Viewing the body seemed strange and mysterious, yet I don't remember that we ever discussed death much even then or at any other time or place in my upbringing.

Grandmother was always a special person for me as I think most grandparents are for most youngsters. When I made a trip to Kansas with Lorine to introduce her to my family before we married, I made a point of stopping by grandmother's place on the way to Hutchinson. This occurred in 1954 at the end of a hot summer. Lorine and I were dressed informally and as cool as possible since we traveled in my unairconditioned car. We both had on shorts. Shorts weren't normally worn in the days when grandmother was raised or in the days when she raised her children. I thought nothing about it when we visited Grandmother. She received us with perfect hospitality and seemed to enjoy meeting Lorine, her new grand-daughter-in-law to be. An hour and a half later when we arrived in Hutchinson and told mother about our visit with Grand Mom, Mother was horrified that Lorine had been wearing shorts when she met Grandmother. She was sure Grand Mom would not be pleased with such dress. As always though, grandmother handled things in warm, friendly, and special way.

Grandmother did not live many more years but I have two other memories relating to her and to my family. Early in our marriage, one of the gifts Grandma gave my wife surprised and befuddled Lorine who was from Kentucky. The gift was a black wool scarf. Grandmother was a practical kind of person. She was used to facing the harsh, cold elements of Kansas winters and thought this was something Lorine would surely need as a new Kansan.

When we moved to Kansas we had our first-born son, one-year-old Ben. Whenever we visited Grand Mom, she delighted in calling him "Sammy" even though Ben would protest, "that's not my name." It was simply her way, in old age, of having fun with Ben and teasing him. It was just part of who Grandmother was.

Chapter 14

GRANDDAD

The main work of the farm was the making of a life and a living, the rearing of children and the raising of crops. In the 1930s there was a considerable division of labor into "men's work" and "women's work." On the farm this was blurred more than many modern sociologists might make it sound. Farm work involved team work and partnership between husband and wife.

My grandparents practiced diversified farming. One of their main crops was red hard winter wheat (planted one fall, harvested the next summer)—a crop brought to America from Russia by Mennonite farmers. Generally it was a good cash crop. Farmers could also have it milled for their own use as flour although other types or blends of wheat were better suited to baking. Other major crops included row crops like milo and corn. These were good grains to feed livestock along with silage fed in the winter. The silage, or fodder, was the chopped corn and milo stocks. Silage was usually stored in tall cylindrical storage structures called silos; sometimes it was stored in trenches dug in the ground. Milo and corn as a grain was also a cash crop. Some years Granddad raised some oats and barley. Alfalfa hay added diversity for both animal nutrition and some cash income.

Livestock (beef cattle, milk cows, hogs and a few sheep) was an important part of their family income. Most of the beef cattle were sold a farm truck load (5 or 10 head of cattle) at a time at the stockyards in north Wichita. When cattle were ready for market, Granddad would deliver them one day to leave on consignment to be sold to meat packers the next day. Occasionally, if there was reason to sell just one or two animals, they might be taken to a Saturday morning auction in a nearby community. Dairy cows were sold only when they were getting too old to produce milk or when the calf crop produced more heifers than the farm could accommodate.

In the 1920s workhorses played a big part in farm work. Horses were used to pull plows, harrows, drills and corn planters, cultivators (for weeding corn and milo when these crops were still young), mowers, rakes, binders (to bind wheat, oats, and barley into bundles that were shocked by hand, and stood up on-end in teepee-like fashion until thrashed), hay racks and grain wagons. Horses still played a prominent part in farming when I began coming to the farm.

Cream Separator was cranked by hand to separate cream from whole milk. Its multiple parts were disassembled for washing after each usage.

Much work was also done by hand. This included walking fields to hoe weeds and to de-tassel corn rows; following the binder to set up shocks of wheat; shoveling thrashed grain, pitching hay, feeding the horses and cows, milking cows, carrying buckets of milk to the cream separator and cranking it to separate the cream from the milk and washing milk pails and a multitude of little parts from inside the cream separator. The cream could be sold, along with eggs, at "creameries" in town. The whole milk was consumed by people on the farm; skim milk was fed to the calves, cats and dogs.

Apart from the automobile, the first form of farm mechanization was the tractor. When Granddad began using a tractor in the mid-thirties, it gradually began supplanting the horses. By the beginning of World War II horses had completely disappeared. But in the transitional period, Granddad taught me how to harness horses and drive a team. Mostly I drove horses that pulled hayracks or grain wagons. Occasionally I might use the horse drawn cultivator. During the transitional years, some horse drawn equipment was adapted so it could be used by the tractor. At first tractors were used for plowing, harrowing and planting seed with the drill, while horses were still used for things like pulling hay racks and grain wagons. During the war, before I started working summers in Hutchinson, Granddad also taught me to drive a tractor.

Occasionally I did things like plowing. Granddad taught me that to plow straight rows I had to identify a landmark on the horizon dead ahead of me and drive toward it. This learning became a lesson about life. To be successful one has to have a clearly established goal and keep your eye on it.

My grandparents had three children—two boys, Floyd and Harold, and a girl, my mother, Blanche who was between the boys in age. Farm children grow up helping their parents with chores (indoors and out-of-doors) and with all the main farm work. By the time I began coming to the farm, Uncle Floyd was married and living away from the farm, as was my mother. Uncle Harold was in his twenties. He was a bachelor, still living at home, and was moving toward a farming partnership with his dad. When I came to the farm in the summers for an extended stay, I was like a farm child helping with both indoor and outdoor chores and learning farm work.

Each year as I grew older and stronger and matured a bit more, I assumed more and more the role of a farm hand. This made me feel "big." I enjoyed learning and taking responsibility and I enjoyed the out-of-doors. Granddad's role certainly involved the physical labor and the "know how" required to till the land, plant, cultivate and harvest crops as well as the physical labor involved in animal husbandry. Just as Granddad had nurtured his own children in and through farm work, he did the same for me.

Part of the excitement of the farm, for me, was being able to spend time helping both of my grandparents with their respective roles. I was fascinated with each and every piece of farm equipment on granddad's farm. The barn and the small to mid-size drive through grain storage elevator as well as almost every one of the more than a dozen buildings on the farmstead had been made by my grandfather. To construct buildings, operate all the equipment, and maintain and repair it, and do the farming meant a farmer had to be a veritable mechanical genius and a jack-of-all-trades. To work the horses and care for all of the animals on the farm was yet another whole field of endeavor—animal husbandry.

I followed granddad around as he did his work and he taught me about what he was doing. As I grew older, I did chores, operated some of the equipment, followed the binder and shocked wheat, loaded and drove the hayrack, pitched bundles into the threshing machine, drove the grain wagon, fed and occasionally milked the cows as granddad entrusted me with more and more responsibility. It was exciting. However, being a jack-of-all-trades and being able to repair breakdowns, etc. never rubbed off on me. Granddad was not a large man—perhaps 5'6" or 5'8" and a wiry 160 pounds—but he was a big man in my estimation. My admiration of his reservoir of knowledge and talent never wavered.

Granddad built every building but one on the farm. The largest building he built was the barn. The big barn was dim airy place. Barn swallow darted in and out at will. There was no electricity when it was built. Coleman lanterns were used when light was need at night. After electricity first came, a single wire hung down with a light bulb on the end of it, to provide light for early morning and late night milking. The barn had stalls for both horses and milk cows, a tack room and storage areas for tools, grain bins, and then a large hay mow.

Climbing up a ladder to the hay loft to help with the process of horses (or the tractor) pulling ropes on pulleys to hoist slings of alfalfa hay to the top of the hay mow, tripping them one load after another to fill the loft and store hay for the year's needs, then later climbing up the ladder again to grab a pitch fork and toss hay down for the horses and cattle below, was like climbing to heaven.

A similar process was repeated when we filled the 30 or 40' silo with fodder (course livestock food including the leaves, stalks, and sometimes grain coming from the forages). Chopping the silage and blowing it through a large pipe up into the silo was a mechanized rather than a horse powered process. When we were "filling silo", I worked up in the silo with a pitch fork spreading fodder around as evenly as possible and stomping it down to pack in as much as possible.

Most memorable of all work each summer was wheat harvest. Neighbors formed a "thrashing ring" which was a cooperative effort to help each other with thrashing. A farmer would cut and bind bundles of wheat when it was ripe, shock (or stack) it in teepee fashion to dry and remain dry in the field until threshing time. The thrashing ring took turns going from farm to farm to help each of its members with their thrashing. Thrashing required a crew of several men. It involved setting up a thrashing machine and a steam engine, connecting the two with a large heavy belt of twenty or twenty-five feet in length to transmit the engine's power from the flywheel on its side to turn the wheels which operated the various parts and functions within the thrasher. Then it also involved loading the wheat shocks on the horse drawn hay racks, the hay racks from the field to the thrashing site, cutting each bundle's binder twine and pitching the straw with grain heads into the thrashing machine. On the opposite side of the thrashing machine would be a horse drawn box wagon to receive grain machine. When the wagon was filled, it needed either to be hauled to the farm elevator where grain was stored or to the town elevator where it was sold.

Trashing machine, crew, horses, straw pile in background—used for thrashing wheat and other grains in first third of 20th Century.

There would be at least half dozen men in the thrashing ring which gathered to help Granddad and Uncle Harold with threshing. At noon time, all the work would stop for an hour or so for rest and refreshment. Grandmother would have prepared a feast for everyone. It was like one great banquet party as well as a jovial time of talking and telling stories and a few minutes for a nap in the shade. One of the men in the thrashing ring was Elmer Hanneman, a young bachelor farmer. He always use to tease and kid me a lot so I'd do the same with him, but I was so young that I didn't know when to stop. I know I made a nuisance of myself many times. One time, I pushed Elmer a little too far. To get my attention and get me to stop, Elmer grabbed me, picked me up and carried me over to a garden hose which he also picked up. He pushed the end of the hose down into my bib overalls and turned the water on full force. As I got soaking wet I screamed and struggled. I thought I was being killed. No real harm was done because the weather was 100 degrees F and I soon dried out, but I did learn not to make a nuisance of myself. Nothing on the farm ever compared to these thrashing events!

One of the biggest disappointments of my life came one summer at the end of the 1930s. I arrived to spend the summer on the farm and discovered that there was to be no thrashing that summer. Technology had arrived. Granddad and Uncle Harold had purchased a combine. Wheat was now to be harvested without horses or a thrashing ring. Harvest wasn't nearly as much fun. However, at this stage at least three people were still needed—one to drive the tractor which pulled the combine (self-propelled combines were still to come), one person to run the combine adjusting the height of the cutting table to the height of the wheat, and a third person to drive a truck hauling away the wheat. By then Uncle Harold was married and Aunt Adele was often the truck driver. However, I was still able to fill-in on the combine sometimes or do other things to help.

In everything my granddad did, he was hardworking, upright, and sought patiently to give me needed guidance. We were never to be wasteful or be idle when there was work to do. Always, whether I was growing tired hoeing weeds in the cornfield on a hot summer day or whatever, Granddad understood, yet he was strict and sometimes rigid. Usually he was patient, but at times he could be harsh. One of my character learning times was when I got upset at some one—Granddad, I think. I called him or whoever "a fool." Granddad stopped, was very sharp with me. He proceeded to tell me I was never to do that again because "the Bible says that we are to 'call no man a fool'." His stern admonition was enough to put great fear in me and that was the end of that subject. As far as profanity was concerned, this was one thing that was not part of my grandfather's vocabulary. Overall I got the impression that Grand Dad, while he tended to treat me with special consideration, could be and probably had been with his own sons quite harsh in instilling discipline and work habits.

Another event stands out in my memory. It comes from those solar showers we all took to clean up at the end of each work day. At the end of the first day of my first harvest, because I couldn't stand the itchiness of the wheat chaff, I hurried to be the first one to take a shower. This outdoor shower had one 55 gallon drum mounted over the shower. Water was piped to this barrel where the sun heated it all day long. We just turned on a faucet and gravity drained the warm water from the drum onto us as we showered. That shower felt so good. I just stood there and really enjoyed it. By the time I finished and my uncle and granddad came for their showers, all the warm water was used up and the sun wouldn't be back to warm any more before tomorrow. They both had ice cold showers and weren't too happy about it. I got a good reminder of what sharing meant and a strong admonition that there were to be no more showers like that one. Moreover, I was told in the future I was to wait my turn until after Granddad and Uncle Harold had their showers. They also instructed me that when I showered I was to get wet, turn off the spigot, soap up and scrub, and then turn the water back on using only what was necessary to wash off.

By the time I was in high school, I had other summer jobs and wanted to stay near home in Hutchinson, so gradually my summer visits to farm became much shorter and less frequent.

My summer job following my graduation from high school was a four-month job allowing me barely enough time to get to my first semester in college which began October 1 that year. Consequently, I didn't see much of Granddad that summer.

While away at the University of Illinois, letters from home told me that Granddad was beginning to have memory problems. One time when I was home from college, I visited Granddad who was then hospitalized with his "senility" as it was called. This was in the days before Alzheimer's was a recognized disease. That was my last visit with Granddad and, of course, it really couldn't be much of a visit. Then in the Spring of my Senior year, on April 27, 1951, I received word that Granddad had died. Studies and upcoming final examinations combined with the time for which the funeral was set and a lack of any quick easy transportation prevented my making the trip back home from Champaign, Illinois, for Granddad's service. I still carry regret in my inner being that I wasn't able to be there to celebrate his life and share the sorrow of Grandmother, Mother and the rest of the family.

B. L. Taylor family of rural Peabody (ca. 1925)
Left to right: Burt, Blanche (Kieler by marriage)
,Jane, Harold, Floyd
Author's grandparents, mother, and uncles.

Chapter 15

UNCLE FLOYD'S CABIN

Uncle Floyd and Aunt Elva were conscientious workaholics throughout most of their lives. For years their efforts went largely unrewarded. They took so little time to play along the way, that *I remember them for only one thing when it comes to leisure time. But this project became an important part of their life and the life of our extended family.*

Several years after they moved to Wichita, before World War II, they bought a lot on Marion County Lake. Shortly after, Floyd began building a cabin on it. It wasn't that the egg business became so good that Floyd could suddenly afford a second home. In fact, he and Elva were still living in the old house on Seneca when they bought the Marion County Lake lot. But as Floyd was delivering eggs to the aircraft manufacturing plants, he made a discovery. The plants sometimes received parts in huge wooden shipping crates. They had to dispose of those crates and Floyd found he could acquire them for little or nothing, take them apart, and recycle the lumber for use in building his cabin.

Building the cabin was a slow, long, drawn-out process. Uncle Floyd first built a relatively small all purpose rectangular room. He roofed and finished it to serve as a little cabin for "camping out" at Marion County Lake. Floyd did most of the work on its construction by himself. Many weeks he could work only Saturday afternoons on it. However, the whole family chipped in with moral support, helping here and there with construction. Often Floyd's dad, my granddad, came up to assist. Elva and Oleve, their daughter, worked on it some. If Uncle Harold could take time off from the farm he and Adele would come up and help a little. I vaguely remember our family even helping a bit.

Later the small cabin, the all purpose room got expanded. A second room was added on back. Finally, a big screened-in porch was added to the front becoming one of the special features of the cabin. Don and Oleve remember Adel helping with one of these phases of construction while she was pregnant with one of her children.

Marion County Lake, two miles south of the town of Marion, had been a WPA (Works Progress Administration) project during the 1930s depression. After the dam was completed, a little county park and a shelter were built by the WPA and the lake stocked with fish. People began acquiring lots around the lake. Some built big fancy almost house-like cabins on them; some built mid-sized cabins; and, some were very modest little cabins. Floyd and Elva's place was the latter type. During the building of the cabin and, especially when it was finished, the cabin often became the site of our extended family gatherings during summer holidays—Memorial Day, Fourth of July, and Labor Day. Everyone brought covered dishes and we had great picnics. The family would fish, sometimes swim a little, and we enjoyed watching people better off than we sailing their boats or water skiing. These were great times together. Uncle Floyd's Cabin became the first in a series of cabins that members of our extended family enjoyed across the years!

Exactly when the cabin was finally completed I'm not sure. I know it was totally finished and ready for the first night of Don and Oleve's honeymoon, February 19, 1948. Before and afterward, it was the setting for many of my happy memories.

By 1952 Floyd and Elva were ready to give up on their old Seneca Street house. They wanted to build a new one next to it, and raze the old one. To achieve the goal of their new house, Floyd and Elva needed to sell the Marion County cabin and invest the proceeds in their new home. All together there must have been at least a seven year period when Uncle Floyd and his family enjoyed their cabin and generously shared it with their larger family.

Mother had two brothers—my uncles Floyd and Harold Taylor. I never remember a time when Uncle Floyd wasn't married to my Aunt Elva. He always lived away from the farm. I do remember for a long time Uncle Harold was a young bachelor living on the "home place," the farm. Then one time we came for a visit and Uncle Harold was suddenly married to Aunt Adele (Unruh). We often saw both sets of my uncles and aunts at the farm. A couple times a year we would visit Uncle Floyd and Aunt Elva at their home.

A variety of things made Uncle Floyd special for me. Floyd worked and farmed several different places during his lifetime: near Peabody; for a little less than two years near Langdon, Kansas; and for the major portion of his working life in Wichita where Floyd was self-employed in the egg business. He procured, processed and sold chicken eggs. As a child and even in my early teens I had occasional opportunity to participate with Uncle Floyd in the procurement and processing part of his business.

The business was always a small business operated solely by Floyd and Elva but it grew from being very small in its beginning to being a rather large operation for two people during World War II. They started it at the end of 1937 or the beginning of 1938 shortly after moving to Wichita. (They retired sometime in the early 1960s.) Floyd and Elva bought a suburban track of a few acres of land when they left the Langdon farm where he was a tenant. Their new tract of land was located at 5720 N. Seneca, Wichita. At first they eked out almost subsistence—type living. They began raising chickens for themselves. Elva occasionally dressed chickens for people she knew, selling them and the surplus eggs produced by her hens. Floyd would deliver the chickens and eggs.

Because Floyd knew many farmers in the Peabody area where he'd grown up, and his father and brother still lived in that area, he got the idea of expanding egg delivery into a business. He began his business by driving from Wichita to the Peabody area to buy eggs from farmers. They were delighted to sell their eggs directly to him rather than having to take them to town to market. Floyd then returned home where he had set up a place to process the eggs in his garage. He and Elva would wash them as necessary, sort them by size, color, and quality and candle them. Candling is a process of holding the egg to a little hole with a bright light behind it to examine the eggs for cracks, blood specks or other abnormalities. These were either discarded or sold as seconds to bakeries.

Floyd first peddled the eggs door to door in the residential districts of Wichita. As business grew, he began selling exclusively to bakers, restaurants, and the cafeterias which fed the thousands of employees at the large aircraft manufacturing plants during World War II. As the business expanded, Floyd added additional pickup routes in the country and then had to start buying eggs from the cream stations in the small towns within a fifty or seventy mile radius surrounding Wichita. I have in my possession a brief article dated 1960 from the employees' newsletter of the Boeing Company. In it I learned that Uncle Floyd "began delivering eggs to the Boeing cafeterias in 1942, 5 cases at a time. By 1960 he was delivering up to 46 egg cases a week, each case with 30 dozen eggs. This was 26,560 eggs a week . . ." And this is what he sold just this one company. The newsletter also reported that in all those 18 years Floyd never missed a delivery!

During periods I spent on the farm, I got to make "pick up rounds" with Uncle Floyd. Floyd would always stop by his parents' farm early on the day he was picking up eggs. Several times each summer, after checking with Grandmother, he invited me to go with him. I got to spend the whole day just with him—visiting and seeing how he did things. It was a great adventure for me to enjoy the countryside, to hear Floyd visit with others, and to learn so much. I learned a lot about rural life, agriculture, and business. We would talk about family and history. Floyd was an avid reader and my horizons expanded during these trips.

Occasionally, either when Floyd picked me up at the farm or when my folks took me to visit my cousin Oleve and her parents, I would spend two or three days in Wichita at their house. I watched them at work processing the eggs, and even worked with them at the various tasks—especially the candling. Of course, I got to do things with Oleve and play as well.

Work, however, always came before play for Floyd. In many ways, he was a "chip off the old block"—much like granddad. This included being a strict disciplinarian. He was a hard-working no-nonsense kind of person. Sometimes I even felt he was rather harsh—even more so than my Granddad. In her later years, Oleve shared with Lorine and me stories of her childhood which indicated there were times when she was even very afraid of her dad.

Elva, like most women of her time, spent hours in the kitchen cooking everything "from scratch." She was particularly a great baker of pies and cakes and also taught her daughter well. When I was at their house, I spent most of my time with Floyd or playing with Oleve, rather than being in the kitchen but one of my "chores" would be to help dry dishes.

Floyd and Elva were avid gardeners—partly out of necessity to provide for themselves, partly because they just loved growing things. They grew both veggies and flowers and maintained a beautiful yard. Floyd built a green house. They used it both as a place for starting seeds and plants early in the spring and for over-wintering plants at the end of the growing season.

In their retirement Floyd and Elva really developed for several years another business—a hobby business—Cacti. They scoured the country to acquire many varieties to propagated and raise. Beyond their own personal enjoyment of cactus, they sold them as a means of augmenting their retirement income. Even in my adult years, especially after Floyd's retirement when he had a more leisurely pace, I enjoyed going to see the greenhouse and garden. This even became an occasional family activity for Lorine and me with our boys when they were growing up.

In addition to the weeks I spent at the farm each summer, and the days spent with Uncle Floyd "on the road" and at his house "helping" with eggs, part of the joy of my pre-teen years was spending time in the summer with my cousin Oleve. We would set up a tent and campout in the yard at the side of her house. Camping was always fun for me. One thing we did was to make "spearmint chewing gum." Floyd and Elva raised lots of spearmint. Oleve had come up with a recipe for "chewing gum." Of course, it wasn't really gum. I remember something of our production process. We made layers of mint and sugar in a pan or glass dish, then pressed them together with a weight on top and allowed this mixture to set for a day or two. It turned into kind of a gummy substance which we ate more like a candy, but we thought it was great fun to "make our own gum"!

Oleve was active in 4-H and had a variety of projects. One project is still vivid in my mind—Oleve's butterfly project. She had to learn to identify 50 or 100 species of butterflies. Then she would net as many different species as she could find and capture, chloroform them, and mount them on an exhibit board. Oleve had a beautiful museum-like display—perhaps 3' by 6'—which was intriguing and impressive.

Sometimes Oleve and I would work with her mother in the garden. While I've always been partial to vegetable gardens, Aunt Elva grew many kinds of beautiful flowers and I was thoroughly impressed by them. It was neat to work "among" the flowers. Elva was also a great cook as were my grandmother, Aunt Adele, and my mom, but in addition to her cooking and baking, Elva really specialized in making all kinds of jams and jellies! Naturally, if I was there when she was "jamming" I got to taste the fruits of her labors. That added to my enjoyment of being with the Floyd Taylor family.

My most vivid memory of all time spent with Oleve was the time I got sick. It was during a damp cool spell in the summer. Camping out sleeping on the ground probably contributed to it. I developed pleurisy of the diaphragm. I'd never heard of it. None of us knew what it was, but I knew it was excruciatingly painful. Aunt Elva did what she could to help me, but to no avail. I was crying and so miserable she had to phone Mom to come get me. It was not until being treated by our doctor in Hutchinson and some days of convalescence that I got better.

Floyd and Elva worked so hard that they went several years without vacations, seldom taking more than a Saturday afternoon and Sunday off from work. Except for Uncle Floyd's cabin, fun and play were mostly missing from their lives until they retired! That was why the cabin was so important for them. It was their saving grace. However, retirement did bring Floyd and Elva many pleasures—travel, raising cacti in their greenhouse and selling them at garden shows and swap meets, and more. Not only did they begin traveling all over the desert Southwest to find various species of cacti, but they also traveled all over the country. Photography became one of their great enjoyments. For me, and then for my family, seeing their travel slides was another pleasure that came from spending time with Uncle Floyd and Aunt Elva.

Chapter 16

MY FAVORITE UNCLE

In a family where there are two maternal uncles and three paternal uncles it's a little dangerous to single one out as "my favorite uncle," but this is how I feel about Uncle Harold. The reason for this feeling probably has more to do with age, occupation, and proximity than anything else. Of the three Kieler Uncles, Uncle Ben died before I was born. Uncle Jim and Uncle Ollie lived in Colorado. I was lucky to visit them once a year; they never made it back to Kansas. I was much closer in many ways to both Uncle Floyd and Uncle Harold, but Uncle Harold was 14 years younger than Uncle Floyd so he was nearer my age even if he was 21 years older than I. Uncle Harold remained on the family farm to live and work all of his active life. With all the time I spent on the farm in first ten or twelve years of my life, I spent more of my growing-up years with Uncle Harold than with Uncle Floyd. Moreover, Uncle Floyd was a lot like his dad—usually serious and somewhat on the stern side—whereas Uncle Harold was very fun-loving.

I worked on the farm with Uncle Harold as well as with Granddad Taylor learning about farming from both of them. Uncle Harold was a bachelor when I first started spending time on the farm. When there were days or evenings that were free, Uncle Harold might play with me. He took me fishing with him at Marion County Lake.

Author as a boy with his catch of fish after he had been fishing with his Uncle Harold. (Photo taken in front of the railroad refrigerator car converted to a home by his uncle)

Uncle Harold enjoyed music. Sometimes he would play the harmonica. The instrument on which he really thrived was the Banjo. When I was young Harold played his Banjo a lot. Then there was a period he didn't play much. Later on he was at it again. But only occasionally as an adult did I hear Uncle Harold play since he didn't like to perform solo. He liked being in a band and usually played special events or for dances away from home where I didn't get to hear him. The Blues and Country music, with some gospel music and polkas thrown in, were his interest. But for 30 years or so Harold did enjoy making music with his friends. They made up a small group or band which was often invited to play throughout Marion County and surrounding counties.

One of the biggest shocks of my young life was one time when I arrived at the farm only to discover that Uncle Harold was married! His new bride was Adele Unruh—my Aunt Adele. At first I didn't know what to think about this—I had to share Uncle Harold with his wife! But because Aunt Adele was so friendly, warm and fun-loving she very quickly became just as special to me as Uncle Harold.

About the same time that Uncle Harold got married, he bought a used refrigerator rail car from the Santa Fe railroad and had it moved to the farm just about 100 yards south of my grandparents' big old two-story white frame farm house. This was a new idea to me. He partitioned it off into three or four rooms and finished it as a house where he and his new bride first lived. During visits at my Grandparents, I enjoyed being able to leave their house to go spend time visiting at Harold and Adele. As my grandparents got older and I was growing up, I needed a little more "space." I could get this by spending evenings with Uncle Harold and Aunt Adele. The flip side of the coin was also true. My grandparents, needing a little time without me, probably encouraged me to make these visits. Aunt Adele assumed a kind of protective role in relation to me. Before he was married, unlike Granddad, Uncle Harold used to cuss quite a bit. Aunt Adele would call him on the carpet saying that he was setting a bad example for me. It wasn't too long before he cleaned up his language.

Another thing I especially enjoyed about Uncle Harold was learning something about hunting and trapping from him. He wasn't ever what one would call an avid hunter or trapper, nor did I become either an avid or a life long hunter or trapper, but Harold knew something about both. Enough possums, raccoons, muskrats and even an occasional beaver remained in the wild in those days that there were still some fur traders and markets for hides. Trapping was a way a person could supplement his income and/or diet. Occasionally Uncle Harold went trapping in the slough and little ponds in his pasture and perhaps elsewhere. When I was visiting in the winter time, I'd go with him and learned to set traps. Then a day later we'd "run the traps." One time I got so curious about whether we might get something I went down to the pasture by myself to check the traps. One of them had something in it! I didn't even know what it was but I could see that it had a long hairless tail. I went running back up to the house to tell Uncle Harold and the others. When they asked me what it was, I said I didn't know but it looked kind of like a monkey! That got them so curious we all had to go back and find out. It was a possum, of course.

Uncle Harold also taught me how to shoot a rifle and a shotgun. Dad, who also could shoot a little, would sometimes go hunting with us or just engage me in a little target practice. Occasionally ducks landed on the two little pasture ponds but the ponds were so small the ducks didn't frequent them much. When we went duck hunting, we'd dig a little blind to hide in, but I don't remember our ever getting any ducks. Perhaps elsewhere Uncle Harold or Granddad had some success along these lines because I recall one or two Christmases when we had duck and a goose for the table.

Mainly our hunting consisted of simply walking the roads and the hedge rows around the farm looking for squirrels and cottontail rabbits. There were also jack rabbits but since people didn't eat jack rabbits we didn't hunt them ordinarily. Uncle Harold was an experienced hunter, of course, so he did well in getting his game. Occasionally I would get a cottontail, but I don't remember ever personally being successful in getting squirrels. This was something I always wanted to do. When we finished a hunt we picked up our game, took it back to the farm, dressed it and Grandmother or Aunt Adele would fry it. I've always liked rabbit as a meat dish, but squirrel never made much of an impression on me.

Perhaps it was my lack of success in getting squirrels that led Uncle Harold to present me with one of my all time favorite Christmas gifts. One year, Harold took a squirrel which he'd shot to a taxidermist, had it stuffed and mounted on a short piece of tree limb, and wrapped it as a Christmas gift for me. I was totally surprised and thrilled when I opened that package and found this gift! I must have kept that squirrel in my room at home for ten years 'till finally the moths got into it and it had to go.

Several times Harold took me New Year's hunting. Both Jack Rabbits and Cottontails were so plentiful and such a nuisance, so destructive of gardens and row crops, that once a year farmers would gather on New Year's Day for a "rabbit hunt." A hunt would cover an area of about 16 square miles. Farmers met at the school house within the area bring as many of their friends and relatives as they could round up.

Everyone at the school house received instructions about 10 am; then they were sent out to form a giant "circle" along the perimeter of the area to be hunted; at the designated time the hunt began with all the hunters staying within sight of each other, keeping in line, walking, moving toward the center of the circle, firing at every rabbit that jumped up. The younger boys picked up the rabbits that were killed and carried them along. When everyone got so close to the center that they could no longer continue firing their guns without endangering others, the hunt ended. At this point all the rabbits which had been killed and carried along were piled in one gigantic heap.

The hunt really resulted in a massive destruction of the wild rabbits. Although the fur may have been salvaged and the meat sent to a rendering plant, none of the rabbit on New Year's Day was used for human consumption. Each year during November and December in rural communities everywhere you could find handbills posted in public places advertising such hunts. Eventually the time came when people realized that the rabbits were about to become extinct so the hunts were given up.

In 1942, Uncle Harold and Aunt Adele had their first child— Virginia. In the next few years they added two more children to their family—Jane and Warren. I was a teen-ager by the time these three cousins came along so I never really spent time playing with them as I had with Oleve, but I always enjoyed them as small children. The older they became the more I enjoyed them when we got together as a larger family several times a year. About 1970

I was honored, while serving as Pastor of Trinity United Methodist Church, Wichita, to have Jane ask me to perform her wedding when she married Gene O'Neil. I was doubly pleased that they chose to be married in the church I was serving!

The time came in the latter part of the 1940s when my grandparents were aging and needed to retire. They bought a little house in Peabody and moved to town. Uncle Harold and Aunt Adele took over the farm completely. Harold had already begun this process several years earlier. During all of the summers I spent time working on the farm, I always worked simply out of the sheer enjoyment of the out-of-doors, of nature, and of family. Occasionally I was given a bit of allowance or spending money while I was there, but one summer stands out in my mind. By then I was old enough to be of real help as an extra hand for Uncle Harold. At the end of the summer he came to me and told me how much he appreciated my help and handed me $100 cash in an envelope. That money was worth a lot in those days. Wow! Did I feel grown up and rich!

From the time I was a teen-ager, Uncle Harold always related to me on an adult to adult basis. Whether it was during my high school years, college years, years in the Navy, or as a United Methodist Pastor we always visited together about the issues of the day. On some things Uncle Harold would be very conservative. On other things he would be very liberal and broad minded. Always he had an opinion and was anxious to share it. Sometimes he was and still is "just down right opinionated." Still I have enjoyed trading ideas with him and knowing that he would allow the other person his opinions even when he was being opinionated.

Aunt Adele, like Grandma Taylor, was always hard working and busy both as a housewife and with farm chores (caring for the chickens, helping with the livestock). At harvest time, even other times, she also drove a truck and worked in the field. Years after I ceased spending summers on the farm, after I was married, in the fall of 1956 I think, Harold and Adele visited Lorine and me in Nashville. It had always been their custom when they visited family to bring something from the farm to give whether it was garden produce, freshly butchered meat or whatever. For this trip, Adele packed an ice chest and brought to us a freshly dressed turkey she had raised. That was a really nice gift on her part. The only difficulties were: we hadn't been married too long and didn't have a big roaster yet; and, Lorine almost had an "anxiety attacK" having never cooked a turkey in her life and not being quite sure how to go about roasting it! No problem, though. We went out and bought a roaster. I wasn't timid about cooking and Lorine graciously allowed me to stuff and roast the turkey as she has every holiday since.

These memories are a few of many examples of the hard working, yet kind and gentle spirit, of my Uncle and Aunt. When times got very difficult for farmers (in the 1950s or 60s) it was really hard to make a living off the land. Both of them took on additional work along with their farming—they began driving school busses for the Peabody school district. They would bring kids to school early in the morning, return home to work until school was out, then leave their field and house work to pick up the children, deliver the children to their homes, and then return back to their own farm to finish the day's field work or other tasks in which they were engaged. Even when times got better on the farm again, both of them continued driving their bus because they knew that the money they were earning would make a good retirement nest egg.

When retirement came, Harold and Adele began to travel. They especially enjoyed taking tours which the travel company in Hillsboro offered and at times Harold and Adele would join with my parents to do a trip together. As I recall, Harold and Adele and my folks took the Copper Canyon tour in Mexico together at least twice.

Uncle Harold knew how to throw a party! After he and Adele retired, four different times around Labor Day weekend, Harold and Adele invited everyone they knew—all the Taylor family, all the Unruh family, and all their friends and neighbors, more than a hundred people in all—to come out to the farm for a Bar-B-Que followed with a "concert" by the Plainsmen, his band. What fun. This was also great for Lorine and me and sometimes our kids who by then were older. All of us also enjoyed joining with the larger family for a celebration dinner when Harold and Adele celebrated their 50th wedding anniversary.

Not too long after this celebration, Adele was diagnosed with cancer. She put up a brave battle but in the end lost her fight. While Adele was hospitalized, Uncle Harold had a heart attack and ended up undergoing open heart surgery. He too put up a good fight and was fortunate enough to triumph over his heart problems.

Adele and Harold both doctored with the same doctor at Canton. Harold was lost without Adele but he still planned on traveling and making the best of things. One day when he going to a doctor's appointment, Uncle Harold suddenly realized that the doctor's receptionist, who had known both Adele and him, was a widow who enjoyed life just as much as he did. Lorine and I were having the whole Taylor family for Thanksgiving. Uncle Harold wanted to know if he could bring a friend, Yunietta. You can guess the rest of the story. In no time they were married. All of us were tickled to discover that Yunietta was just as caring and accepting as Adele, enjoyed traveling, and made a wonderful companion whom our family has thoroughly enjoyed.

January 3, 2004, Uncle Harold and Yunietta put together another party—a party to celebrate the day after the actual day, the milestone of Harold's 95th Birthday. About 175 people were there—some testimony to how Harold relates to people. And Harold is already saying maybe he will take a year off for his 96th birthday, but that for his 97th birthday he wants of have "a polka party."

Chapter 17

LIBERTY JUNIOR HIGH SCHOOL DAYS

Can you remember one particular period of great anticipation that stands out above all others in your life? In the Spring of my sixth-grade year at Northside Grade School our teacher began to tell about what to expect in Junior High School, to introduce us to algebra, to the writing of papers, generally preparing us for the transition from grade school to Junior High in such a way that I really began to anticipate this transition. We knew that we would join with kids from many grade schools to become part of a much larger school. We would have much more freedom as we chose the different subjects we wanted to study and as we moved from room to room each hour. We would have responsibility for studying on our own. While I had a bit of anxiety about all the changes that I would be experiencing, I was excited to be entering into this "almost adult" world (even if we didn't yet know the meaning of adolescence)! Certainly this still stands out as a period when I was filled with great anticipation.

Early in September of 1941 I walked through the doors of Liberty Junior High School for the first time and *life really began to change for me!*

> I had a "homeroom" with a "homeroom teacher,"
> but I also had many other teachers;

I had hundreds of kids to meet and become
acquainted with;

I had my own locker—a tall, narrow steel compartment
with dozens of others just alike on each side of it,
each with hooks and shelves for the hanging of coats
and the storage of books;

I discovered the opposite sex for the first time—girls
who were attractive, who had magical powers to make
you want to be interested in them.

Among many fine teachers at Liberty, at least three stand out
in my mind to this day. They were wonderful career teachers
nurturing and affirming all of us with patience to endure the typical
adolescent who is constantly flipping back and forth between
childish behavior and responses which are much more mature.
Ross Herron was my science teacher. A quiet, stabilizing kind of
person, Mr. Herron possessed the ability to whet our appetite for
knowledge, to arouse our curiosity, to expand our horizons, to
make science really live for us and to answer (or help us find the
answer to) endless questions.

Vetra Hahn was my homeroom teacher. Miss Hahn taught
sewing or cooking as I recall, subjects which in the unenlightened
early forties were considered "for the girls." She was never one of
my teachers in the sense of a subject that I studied, but as my
homeroom teacher she possessed a genuine interest in each and
every one of us who were in her homeroom class—the class where
we checked in first thing every morning for attendance registration,
receiving special instructions at the beginning of each day and
where we returned once during the day for an hour of study time.
She was very caring and encouraged each student to do his or her
very best. Besides being quality teachers, Ross Herron and Vetra
Hahn both happened to be active members in our family's church—
Trinity Methodist Church. They knew me in church as well as in
school. Faith and learning were intertwined for them and their

interest in those of us from Trinity who happened to attend Liberty
Jr. High School carried back and forth in both directions. In fact,
as years rolled along, even when I moved on to high school, while
I was in college, then in the Navy, and through my years in the
ordained ministry, they continued to have a genuine interest in
me. No wonder they standout in my mind and memory.

So does a third teacher, **Miss Perrill**. I had her for Ninth Grade
English. I'm sure I was one her most frustrating students that year.
Even though she may never have known it, she probably influenced
my life more than any other teacher at Liberty. She didn't just
teach English in a "mechanical" fashion. I had another English
teacher who drilled us endlessly in grammar. Miss Perrill would
try to relate her subject to what was going on in our lives and to
the current events of the day. I know I was a very disruptive student,
always interrupting and arguing about things, challenging her as
to why this or that was important. There were three others in the
class that were just as troublesome as I was. One day when she was
at her wit's end, Miss Perrill told the four of us that if we wanted
to argue so much about things, we needed to learn to do it in a
structured way like the formal fashion of a debate.

I didn't even know the word debate or what it really meant.
She proceeded to explain to us how a formal debate was carried on
as an academic subject. There were teams of two. Each team had a
fixed amount of time to explain a given subject, either affirming a
thesis stating the day's topic or negating it. Taking turns, the
affirmative side would start with one speaker, then the negative
side would have time to make its case, then the other affirmative
speaker could add to the team's position after which the other
speaker for the negative could further contend for his side. Following
this, uninterrupted time would be given to members of both sides
for a formal period of rebuttals in which the facts or the logic or
reasoning of the other side could be questioned or challenged using
other facts, other viewpoints or alternate lines of reasoning. After
this, the debate was ended and a judge would rank the speakers in
terms of their effectiveness and decide which side had made the
best case.

Miss Perrill gave a subject or proposition that we were to debate. Our assignment was to spend our study times and evenings for a couple of days preparing for the debate. Then on the third day, the four of us were to sit (stand when speaking) in front of the class and the debate would ensue! I had never really spoken in a structured way before a group of people. I was uneasy about this. I'd never dealt with matters of logic or formal reasoning and persuasion. The long and short of it was that I learned new skills, new respect for others and for their viewpoints and ideas. I developed confidence in preparing and presenting ideas of my own. By the time Miss Perrill's class was completed, I had greatly matured and I had a new sense of anticipation. When I got to high school I wanted to be on the Debate Team! Miss Perrill (actually Mrs. Perrill for she was a young widow whose husband had been a high school speech, drama and debate teacher) could have taken a strictly punitive way of dealing with those of us who misbehaved in her class but instead she took a positive and creative way of intervening and became a tremendously influential person in the way my life unfolded.

Liberty Junior High School days were good days for me. They gave me a chance to try out things, to test myself, to build relationships, all without experiencing undue pressures. Sports were intramural, not competitive with other schools. I never remember wanting to be a "big athlete" at any point in my life, but I enjoyed it when our gym coach divided the class into two groups and we played basketball or went outside to do track. However, I never felt enough excitement or sense of achievement in these sporting activities to want to go out for any of the big team sports when I got to high school.

During my teen years popular music was more the province of orchestras and bands and vocal groups than it was of solo artists. I don't remember classical music being part of my upbringing in Hutchinson. If the Community Concert series existed in Hutchinson at that time, it was something that my parents either couldn't afford or chose not to attend. Mom and Dad weren't musical and music, popular or classical, really wasn't part of our family life. There was a city band which played weekly in a downtown park during summer and sometimes we attended those concerts. Occasionally, I would listen to classical music on certain radio programs (like "The Firestone Hour"). Somehow though I ended up fantasizing that I might like to take band or orchestra at Liberty. It was my middle year when I gave this a try. When asked what instrument I might enjoy playing, I really had no idea. Bass drums and snare drums always fascinated me whenever I saw a marching or concert band. Likewise, on the rare occasions when I was exposed to a symphony orchestra, timpani drums (or the "kettle drums" as we called them then) seemed to capture my attention. I just blurted out to my band and orchestra teacher, "I want to play the drums." Since there was an opening, they put me in the percussion section. Two problems quickly emerged. I discovered that there were more instruments than just drums in a percussion section and I didn't have much interest in the other instruments. Also, I didn't have much of an ear for music. I couldn't distinguish between notes on the musical scale nor did I have a sufficient sense of timing or rhythm when playing. This seemed to cause the band and orchestra some difficulties! Needless to say, by the end of my first semester in this class I discovered that I didn't have enough musical aptitude to continue in this class.

Dances weren't a huge part of school life but they were part of it. We'd have about three all-school dances each year. Sometimes parents would also host small groups of kids in home recreation rooms or elsewhere for dances. I always remember Mrs. Dillon (of the founding family of the Dillon Food Stores, later acquired by the Kroger Chain) with great fondness. She was Betsy's mother. They lived a block north and a block east of our house. Several of my female classmates lived between us. During the winter of 1942 for several weeks she entertained several teenagers in her home for dance lessons. I felt honored to be one of the group. Somehow though, I just never caught on to dancing. Perhaps I was too self-conscious. Maybe it was that same lack of musical aptitude, of being unable to feel rhythm well and keep musical time. When we had school dances I enjoyed being there because I liked to be part of the group, but I was mostly just a wallflower.

Another memory from Junior High days relates to our "Lyceum Courses." These were a carryover from early pioneer days when the Lyceum was an institution or custom popular for educating people and enhancing their knowledge. They brought to town or school lecturers, discussions, and concerts to augment local community life. Our Lyceum courses took place in all school assemblies several times each year. These special resource programs and persons added a kind of "liberal arts" dimension to our school. We had musical concerts. One of our lectures which I remember was on health. It was given by a Dr. Jerrod, MD, son of our principal. It was on how the human body functioned. What was truly memorable was that fifty years before smoking became a public health issue for the nation and the world, Dr. Jerrod lectured us on the physiology of veins and arteries, on the cardiovascular system, and explained how smoking tended to reduce irreversibly the elasticity of veins and arteries thereby overworking the heart and wearing it out prematurely. Another program was presented by a traveling lecturer from General Electric. His presentation was a fascinating light show. He dealt with things of the future by demonstrating laser beams and flexible conduits which could conduct light beams even around corners! Whoever said school couldn't be interesting?

I wasn't living in horse and buggy days but neither was it commonplace either for teen-agers to have cars or for schools to bus pupils. We would ride our bikes to school. When weather was especially inclement, parents would arrange to drop us off as they drove to work or have a car pool do this. In the ninth grade we had two or three kids who acquired old cars and drove them to school part of the time. I think they were probably under the legal age, but somehow they and/or their parents managed to get by with it. In a way these kids were the envy of the rest of us, but still they were the exception rather than the rule. No doubt about it though, in almost every way, Junior High School fulfilled my great anticipation for it. In fact as well as in name, Liberty Junior High School days were the beginnings of "liberty" for me in my life's journey toward adulthood.

Chapter 18

MY FIRST AIRPLANE RIDE

The biggest source of everyday entertainment for me through all my elementary and junior high school years was "radioing." We had two family radios—one in our living room, one in our kitchen—and I had my own little radio in my bedroom. Television didn't exist yet! Radio stations filled the airways mostly with four basic kinds of programs—news and weather, sporting broadcasts, music, and drama including comedy and adventure. After school and play on ordinary days, kids "radioed." Little did we realize 60 years later we would look back on these days with warm nostalgic memories.

There were weekly adventure programs that I still remember. These include "Jack Armstrong, the All American Boy," "The Lone Ranger" and "The Shadow." The Lone Ranger was a weekly series featuring a cowboy who rode the range on his horse "Silver," with his side kick "Pronto," always doing good for people in distress. The Lone Ranger was forever rescuing people from bandits and other kinds of "bad guys." The Shadow was a mystery series featuring a detective and all kinds of eerie sound effects. Shivers would run up and down my spine when high pitched squeaking doors were heard as the Shadow would try to sneak into a room unnoticed. Without pictures, with everything depending on the audio presentations, these adventures left lots of room for fertile imaginations to work.

Comedy shows which still generate pleasant feelings and smiles on my face included "Fibber McGee and his wife Molly" with his famous overstuffed junk-filled closet. At least once a week everything fell out with a loud long crash when Fibber opened the closet door. Two other comedians were "Red Skeleton," master of just pure stand-up comedy, and "Jack Benny" who was always in dialogue with family and friends. As his conversations went along, Jack Benny portrayed himself as an unbelievable and notorious "tightwad." Jack was also known for his lack of skill in violin playing. He was forever talking himself into positions where he would play the violin and end up making a fool of himself. Another memorable comedy show was "The Chase and Sanborn Hour" featuring Charlie McCarthy (an obnoxious personality in the form of a dummy) with Edgar Bergen (a ventriloquist). Bergen would talk to his puppet and ask him questions, then using his skills as ventriloquist, feed him lines of response that were full of outrageous insults and berating humor.

The Major Bowes "Amateur Hour" was another great source of entertainment. Major Bowes scoured the country to discover ordinary people whom most folk had never heard of but who had some extraordinary talent. A group of these people would perform on his program which also featured an "applause meter" which registered the volume of sound coming from the audience response at the end of each person's performance. As each show ended, the guest who had the highest rating on the applause meter was chosen as the winner. The guest received a large cash prize as well as publicity which often landed that guest on other radio programs and/or live stage performances and sometimes became career launching. I couldn't miss the "Hit Parade," a weekly popular music show which tracked the record sales for songs and played them in a countdown fashion covering the top ten songs for the week.

During the big league baseball season my best buddy, Jimmy Jung, and I frequently got together at one of our houses to listen to the "big league" baseball broadcasts. Jim was an ardent New York Yankees fan, but not me. The Yankees always had one of the best teams in the league, and Jim cheered them on with great gusto. I wanted to root for the underdog so whether it was Kansas City, Chicago, or some other team I cheered with equal enthusiasm for the other side. We loved to torment each other over missed plays and the like as each game progressed. The torment was simply part of the ritual and fun of listening together.

Dad always listened to early morning news (frequently around breakfast time) as well as the 6 p.m. news. If the news came on while we were eating, Dad turned on the kitchen radio and the news became part of our mealtime conversation. Otherwise Dad listened to the news—local, state, national, world—in the living room and some, if not all of us, in the family were likely to join him.

Friday evening, December 5, 1941, I was "radioing"—listening to a hometown program. It was not uncommon for these local programs to try to increase the number of their listeners by having contests of various sorts with the awarding of a variety of prizes. Often the prizes were merchandise connected to the commercials. I don't remember whether that evening the contest was "for the first listener to phone in" or whether it was "for the first listener to give the correct answer" to a trivia type question. I rather think it was the former. At any rate, a contest was announced and the prize was one which I thought was *absolutely fantastic*! It was being awarded by an advertiser—a flight school at the Hutchinson municipal airport—and it was for a free 10 minute airplane ride. Like most folks at that time, I'd never been in an airplane. The usual price of such a ride was beyond my means, and I wasn't likely to talk my folks into paying for such a ride. I jumped at the contest. Low and behold, I won a free airplane ride! I could take the ride any time in the next seven days. I had no inkling that within two days my life and my world would change more than I could possible imagine!

That very weekend on Sunday morning, December 7, my sister
and I along with Mom and Dad went to Trinity Methodist Church
for Sunday School and worship as was the usual custom of our
family. When worship ended, we came home to eat our Sunday
noon meal. Mom almost always had a juicy pot roast with potatoes,
onions, and carrots cooking in the oven while we were at church.
By the time we got home our meal was ready to eat. We were
setting the table and preparing to eat. Although it wasn't his usual
Sunday noon custom, Dad turned on the radio. It had only been
on a few minutes when the program was interrupted with a special
news bulletin. *The United States Naval Base at Pearl Harbor in
Honolulu, Hawaii had just been bombed in a sneak attack by the
Japanese.*

There had been no previous declaration of war or any
announcement of hostilities. Our nation was shocked and angered
beyond description. On that quiet Sunday morning when most
people in Honolulu were still sleeping, four battleships were sunk,
four more disabled. Eleven other ships were also sunk or critically
damaged. 188 naval aircraft were destroyed on the ground at
Hickman Field (the naval air station). 2,300 American service men
and women plus 100 civilians were killed. Three Navy aircraft
carriers which were at sea and managed to escape this devastation,
succeeded in launching fighter planes that shot down 29 Japanese
planes. Simultaneously, the Japanese had launched other raids on
British and American facilities throughout the Pacific. Within 24
hours the entire Western Pacific seemed to belong to the Japanese.

The newscasts on that Pearl Harbor Sunday immediately began
announcing an American response and we heard the words,
"Effective tomorrow, Monday, December 8, all U. S. civilian aircraft
will be grounded!"

Having neither age, maturity nor wisdom to fully understand
the implications of what all these events meant, my big concern
for the moment was, "I've got to go take my free airplane ride
today or I won't get to use my prize!" Whatever else might have
been going through the minds of my parents, they did take me to

the Hutchinson Airport that afternoon and I did get my free and my first airplane ride! It was a thrilling thing for me and it is a great irony that December 7, 1941, is still vividly remembered by me in two ways—as the exciting day when I first rode in an airplane, and as the tragic day when the Japanese bombed Pear Harbor and World War II began for the United States.

Chapter 19

WORLD WAR II THROUGH THE EYES
OF A YOUNG KANSAS TEEN-AGER

Immediately after Pearl Harbor our nation was energized and mobilized. Congress declared war against Japan, Germany, and Italy (the Axis powers). Adolf Hitler, Nazi leader of Germany, had already "annexed" Austria in 1938, and invaded the Czech Republic and Poland in 1939 causing Britain and France to declare war against Germany. In 1940 in a series of bold military actions, Germany swept through most of mainland Europe. United States tried to remain neutral. With Pearl Harbor our country could no longer attempt neutrality. Hitler thought we were defeated and declared war on us December 11. World War II became an overlay for my school years from Pearl Harbor until the end of the war in August 1945. The war effort was something that involved every American of every age, place, rank, and circumstance—not just those in the armed services.

I remember, for instance, there was a great national fear that Pearl Harbor might be followed by bombing raids on the US mainland. Enemy submarines were sighted off both coasts. Every city in the country developed Civil Defense plans which included air raid drills. Every city need to have trained aircraft spotters who could function just the way storm spotters function today. Rank and file citizens were trained to do this. Part of their training was learning to identify aircraft by their silhouette. To facilitate this training endless numbers of precisely accurate model planes had to be made and distributed for spotter training. Through scout and other groups, school kids were recruited to make these models. I was one of them. We were given pictures, paper outlines, and designs plus wooden and other necessary materials and we quickly went to work doing the job which was finished in just a very few months.

Every block in every city had a Block Warden and Assistant Warden. Their main duties were to educate those who lived in each house on preparedness for air raids, and we had drills to practice what we learned. There was advanced preparation such as having a basement location, stocked with essential supplies. People were instructed to go to their shelter when the sirens sounded. Also, people had to be sure that their house looked completely dark, so that the entire block would be completely blacked out. With a total black out in every block there would be no city lights which could be seen from a plane in the sky. I, along with many teen-agers, served as an Assistant Warden. Our main duty was to walk the block and check during air raid drills to be sure that our block was perfectly dark.

The massive, fast-paced military and industrial build-up that became the heart of our early war mobilization effort also impacted us as civilians in many ways. The buildup was costly. The government needed to finance it not only by increased taxes, but by borrowing money. Every citizen was asked to buy government War Bonds sold through local banks and creative Bond Drives. They were sold by their size at maturity which would be 10 years— $25, $50, $100, $500, and $1,000. Because of the war there were fewer goods available in the stores, so many people could engage in this type of savings. Not everyone, however, could easily fork over the money needed to buy a bond ($18.75 bought a $25 bond, etc.) so buying them was made even easier. Even children could participate and were encouraged to do so. War Bond savings stamps were sold at twenty-five cents each. Free booklets for stamps were distributed. When you filled up a book with 75 stamps you could turn it into the bank and get your Savings Bond. Contests of all types were held to see which class, troop, club, etc. could sell the most bonds. Gus Leonida, a Hutchinson businessman, gave a free dinner for anyone purchasing a war bond at his restaurant on Wednesday night.

With massive need for guns, planes, tanks, ships, trucks, etc., metal soon came to be in short supply. Schools were organized to conduct scrap-iron and tin—can drives for the war effort. We kids and our parents would scour the country to find scrap iron, and a mountain of junk could be seen in almost every community before it was hauled to smelting plants. Because of the reallocation of resources to the military, gasoline, tires, foods like meat, butter, sugar and other items were rationed for everyone. Ration coupons were given out at the beginning of a month, and you had to make do with what these coupons would allow you to buy for that period. Some items like new cars were virtually nonexistent during the war.

Many communities in Kansas, and in every state, were like Hutchinson where a military training base (in our case, a US Naval Air Station) sprang up almost over night. Our base was about 5 or 7 miles south, southeast of town. It was built on farm land acquired whether by purchase on a voluntary basis or by the right of eminent domain I don't know. Ironically the land was in the heart of the Amish community which by historic religious tradition was pacifist.

Train loads of naval personnel were soon shipping in. Many were from the East Coast. Some had never been out of their home state or west of the Mississippi River. There were stories circulating in Hutch that some of these people thought they were going to see wild Indians when they stepped off the train. More naval personnel were assigned to the base than the housing could accommodate. Some of the officers had to find housing in town. Hutchinson didn't have that much available housing so people from town offered to rent portions of their homes to those who needed it.

Our family allowed a Navy pilot to live in our unfinished basement. My folks spruced it up a bit but it was nothing very fancy—just an area with a rug and a couple of rocking chairs, an old bed and dresser with a hanging sheet around the area for a bit of privacy, an old shower surrounded by rubber curtain, and an old gas cook stove with a small breakfast table. I don't remember the pilot's name, but I do remember that he was friendly and nice. Many days he left early in the morning and didn't get home again until after supper. He usually ate on the base. While his living accommodations in our basement weren't much, at least he had a comfortable dry place to sleep. In fact, he said he really enjoyed it because it was in a family home. Sometimes, if Mom knew that he would be home in time, she would invite him to have a meal with us. He was of Italian background and from Pennsylvania. One time Mom had spaghetti which he really seemed to enjoy, but I think it made him a bit homesick for his mother's Italian cooking. He offered to write his mother for her spaghetti recipe and Mom said she'd like to have it. When Mom received the recipe and tried it out, I really enjoyed it as did our pilot friend. Unlike Mom's spaghetti, it had a kind of sweet sauce and it was abundantly topped with little button mushrooms. I've been looking for that recipe in Mom's recipes ever since we packed up her things when the folks had to move out of their own home.

In addition to the naval personnel, thousands of civilians worked at the naval base. Mass transportation was nonexistent and couldn't be purchased or constructed. I still picture the system which was devised for people to get back and forth between town and work at the base. A few gray colored school type buses were found and pressed into service. However, there weren't enough of them to meet the need. Lengthy cattle trailers pulled by pickups were converted from their original use into bus-like vehicles with long benches running from front to back on each side. They would start running at 5 a.m. and continue until midnight. They made continuous round trips starting from north 30th and Main Street. They ran straight south to the end of Main Street, over the Arkansas River Bridge into South Hutchinson, down the length of that Main Street and out into the country to the Navy Base. With stops and all, a one-way trip took nearly an hour.

At the same time these things were happening, many people were going off to war. I didn't know many of them personally. I do remember that one young male teacher at school was drafted. My dad, as with the fathers of most of my classmates, was too old to be drafted. I knew that some of my classmates had older brothers who were drafted. Over all, although we would read in the papers about service personnel from Hutchinson being killed, wounded, or listed as "missing in action," the losing of friends or loved ones in war was not something I personally experienced.

As the war progressed in Europe, many Germans were taken as prisoners of war and many of these were transported by the United States to our country for internment. Several of the POW camps were set up in Kansas. One of these was in Peabody, Kansas, not far from Granddad and Grandmother's and Uncle Harold's farm. The camp was actually located right downtown in a large old building that was no longer in use. Many Kansans in Marion County, and in Harvey County just to the west, were of German lineage. Many of these were Mennonite farmers and members of historic peace (pacifist) churches. Perhaps for these reasons, there seemed to be no great fear or controversy about their presence in the community. These prisoners were not even under any heavy or great armed guard. Furthermore, there was a great shortage of labor on the farms during the war and especially so in the harvest seasons. Farmers were permitted to come to the POW camps and hire the prisoners! They would take them to the farm in the morning to work in the harvest or in the fields, have lunch with the family, and then be transported back at the end of the day. In some cases such a friendship developed between farmers and their "prisoner of war" laborers that, in the years following the war, visits were made back and forth across the Atlantic. Although these two groups are now beginning to die out, it still is not unusual to read in the newspapers about these relationships and visits. I was fascinated as a teen-ager and young adult by this paradox—prisoner, yet free to an extent; enemy, yet friendly and helpful. I still think this stands as a symbol of the fact that, even in the midst of war, humanitarian concerns can transcend violence and hostility.

Chapter 20

THE SALT HAWKS

Any observant person who has ever driven the Kansas country side is aware that hawks of many species are a prominent feature of the landscape. They are seen perching on fence posts, in trees and topping telephone poles as well as soaring the skies. Also populating the state are jays—noisy, mischievous and aggressive birds. Because, early in pre-Civil war days, Kansans nosily opposed slavery, or became marauding antislavery guerrillas, "Jay-hawks" or "Jayhawkers" became a 19th Century nickname for Kansans. The name has stuck with the state ever since. It's a nickname that I've always had a sense of pride to be associated with.

Six-hundred feet under my hometown of Hutchinson (below 2 different levels of subterranean water underflows) is a deposit of salt left from prehistoric time. Permian seas partly cut off from the ocean, covering much of what today is known as the Great Plains states, laid down this salt deposit which is 450 to 500 feet thick in many places. These salt deposits are under a number of counties in Central and West Central Kansas. They were discovered in Hutchinson in 1887. Shortly after, they became the basis for one of the town's thriving industries. Growing up in Hutchinson, one was always aware that our town was dubbed by many as "Salt City." It was quite natural that just as "Jayhawks" had become the nickname for the mascot and students at the University of Kansas and for Kansans in general, "Salt Hawks" became the nickname for students at Hutchinson High School.

I made my transition in the summer of 1944 from Liberty Junior High School (presently known in educational circles as "middle school") to Hutchinson High School, and proudly became a Salt Hawk. However, there was much more than school on our minds that summer—on June 6, D-Day of World War II began. This was the invasion day when Allied military forces began their assault to re-take Nazi-occupied Western Europe. England was the launch base. D-Day was the largest sea borne invasion in history involving 2,000 ships plus 4,000 landing craft and 11,000 aircraft. The allies put 155,000 men ashore in France that first day. Thousands upon thousands of Allied personnel were killed. Newspapers, magazines (especially I remember the photo magazine, *Life*), news reels in motion picture theaters, and radio broadcasts were filled with the details of the fighting. Our entire nation was caught up in keeping abreast of in what was taking place. Yet I have to confess that the enormity of the death toll of Americans, not to mention other allied personnel, enemy soldiers and civilians, did not really sink in on me at the time. (We weren't even aware of the holocaust yet. Only when Allied troops moved deep into German territory in 1945 did evidence of this most appalling of all Nazi crimes come to light.) Yes, I was involved in a lot of the emotional impact of it, but it all seemed so surreal. I simply don't recall feeling first hand the pain that so many were experiencing.

German resistance to the invasion was fierce, but by the time High School began in September the Allied air offensive with its massive bombing of Germany finally began to undermine the industrial production behind the German military. We could sense that the Germans were beginning to weaken. The Allies had broken out of Normandy and were racing across France (although the Low Countries and Germany were yet to be invaded). We were developing a much greater sense of hopefulness and optimism than we had during Junior High. The heaviness of the war did not seem to pervade school so much as in the previous three years. In fact before my sophomore year ended, in the spring of 1945, the mood was almost one of euphoria.

Walking up three or four outdoor steps into Hutchinson High School on that September Tuesday following Labor Day (always the first day of school when I lived in Hutchinson), I walked into a large well worn three or four story building filling half a square block at 28 East Seventh Street. Large beautiful Dutch Elm trees shaded it on the South, East, and North sides. With its high ceilings and sheer mass, the building was large enough to create a sense of awe, making me feel overwhelmed. It was a very classical 34 year old well maintained red brick structure although not a particularly inspiring building in my eyes.

A familiar doorway to those of us in the Class of 1947.
This school opened in 1910 and served as the Hutchinson
High School until 1960 when a new high school opened at
13th and Severence. It then became a Junior High and
Middle School until 1983 when it was abandoned.
This sketch was made for the class' 50th Reunion.

Upon entering HHS you didn't stay at ground level. You either went down a half flight of stairs to the first floor level (really a half basement) or you went up a half flight of stairs to the next level. Then there were two more floors above this. The only public high school in Hutchinson, it was filled with more than a thousand students. Our individual class groups varied in size from a dozen students to perhaps an average of 20-25. We had more students in activity classes like Boys' and Girls' Glee Clubs, band, symphony, and gym. Incidentally, although some students looked down on those who played in the symphony, a belated point of pride for many in my class in years to come would be that one of our classmates, Elna Claire Valine, who was a violinist in our school symphony, later went on to play in the Wichita Symphony Orchestra. Eventually she became Principal Second Violinist!

Students were generally well behaved and respectful of teachers. As we moved around in the halls or had free time, students usually related to one another with respect, although at times there was smart-aleck rowdiness and a bit of sexual harassment. Perhaps I was naive, but except for alcohol or tobacco, I don't recall ever having the slightest indication that we had any drug related activity or problems. I hardly even knew about marijuana let alone any other drug. There was some smoking. Most of it was just "experimenting" with the use of cigarettes. Few students, none that I knew personally, smoked more regularly.

For students who wanted to be in organized club-type activities we had a number of different clubs—athletic, science, music, literary, home economics, photography, etc. Some were just for girls, some just for boys, and some were coed. One of the latter clubs was the Perrill Club which encouraged and promoted all types of speech, dramatic and forensic activities. This is the only club in which I participated very fully. Those interested in going out for sports tried out for boys' football, basketball, tennis and track or girls' hockey, basketball, and volleyball. In all competitive activities, our school was one of eight schools in the Ark Valley (named for the Arkansas River) League. The other schools were Newton, El Dorado, Wichita North, Wichita East, Wellington, Winfield and Arkansas City.

My sophomore class, the class of 1947, had 313 graduates. I'm sure we had over 325 students when we began school that fall, but I don't think we had a big problem with drop-outs. I didn't have quite the same sense of anticipation upon entering Hutch High that I had when entering Liberty. Nevertheless, this was an exciting time, full of great expectations. I knew this would be a time for developing many new relationships. Graduating freshmen from Liberty (a school with many students from the economic middle to upper middle class and largely white) and those from Sherman Junior High School (where students from more racially diverse backgrounds and from all economic levels) were merging into one student body. More than half of our sophomore class as well as most of the juniors and seniors were strangers. Perhaps even more significantly, it was a time of metamorphosis, a time when adolescence was coming into full bloom. More than a subject to be studied, the biology of adolescence wasn't a matter of bugs but of hormones and human anatomy! My whole high school experience was a time of experiencing new horizons and establishing independence. It was filled with both idealism and reality checks.

Neither Mom nor Dad were college graduates so they really didn't think of high school as "prep school" for college. My school was entirely different from the high school they had experienced. It was different in student body size, in the multitude of subjects from which classes were chosen, and it had an urban culture versus a rural culture. As a result I got very little counsel, advice or guidance from my parents on school matters. The few "messages from home" that I received pertained largely to matters of manners, attitudes, moral behavior, and other generalities that were not academically related. Mom and Dad never sought to "program me vocationally." Mr. Cole, whom I knew from church and who was a friend of my parents through their church school class, was our High School Counselor. He was a friendly person and I liked him. He was always available whenever I wanted to talk but I received only a minimum of academic guidance from him. What he did do once each year was to give and interpret vocational aptitude tests. I found this helpful and enjoyed thinking about what I might do with my life.

Although I've always felt I received a good education at Hutch High, I was not guided in a direction that prepared me well for college or university studies. For instance, I could have taken or been required to take at least one or two courses in the science department, but overall, I didn't have an interest in taking chemistry or physics. I don't recall taking these subjects at all. Today I feel short changed in this area of my life and regret not having had more science. I did like mathematics so I took a couple of years of algebra and one of geometry, but I wasn't pushed to take more. I thought I'd like to learn to speak Spanish, so I took first year Spanish but I didn't do well in it—in fact I got a D or D minus in that course. I didn't pursue foreign languages any further. I wish I had received more encouragement and help in this direction, and that I had done more with foreign languages. The smaller our world becomes today the stronger grows this regret.

For the most part I liked my teachers and found them to be helpful and encouraging. I took a couple of commerce classes (we call them business classes today). This probably was the one instance of taking classes at the encouragement of my dad. He thought they would stand me in good stead in life, and they did. These classes were a semester of typing and two of bookkeeping. Both subjects were helpful and practical as lifetime skills.

One story stands out in my mind in relationship to Mr. Rinehart, my bookkeeping teacher. I was beginning to experiment with smoking. Perhaps he could smell it on me or sense it. High school basketball games were played in the City of Hutchinson's Convention Center downtown because it had much more seating than our High School Gym and many town people as well as students and parents enjoyed coming to our games. Since this was not a school building, there was not a "no smoking in the halls" policy, but it wasn't allowed in the auditorium around the basketball court. This was fifty years before most public buildings banned smoking. One night during half-time I "sneaked" a smoke out in the halls or lobby. Apparently, Mr. Rinehart saw me. The next day at school, when bookkeeping class ended, he asked me to wait a minute. When everyone was gone, Mr. Rinehart proceeded in a very kind and gentle way to tell me that he had seen me. He said softly, "I know your parents would be disappointed to know you were doing this. I hope you won't do it anymore." There was no criticism, no threat to tell my parents, and the subject never came up again, but he did succeed in getting me to think about it and to slow down my experimental smoking for quite awhile.

Among my most enjoyable courses was an English course which introduced me to literature. The first novel I remember reading was Somerset Maugham's *The Razor's Edge.* History, especially American History, taught by Mr. "Chop" Cairns (a coach and one of the school's most popular teachers) was one of my favorite courses. "Chop" Cairns included in his lessons a look at the legislative track records of different national administrations and the stances of different political parties. Studying under him generated for me an awareness of and an interest in politics. Debate, of course, was more than a course. It was also an extracurricular activity which made it immensely enjoyable. Debate honed my skills in researching subjects. Psychology, taught by Mr. Cole, would go on my "most enjoyable" list.

I gave a brief try going out for tennis but I suffered enough from spring allergies that I didn't stick with the team very long. The one extracurricular activity which I really went for and really excelled in was debate. We researched and prepared during the fall semester. From November through February, our debate teams traveled as far east as Kansas City, Kansas, and as far west as Garden City on Saturdays for debate tournaments. Once or twice annually we hosted tournaments. We debated 25 to 30 teams from Kansas High Schools and sometimes a few from just across the Oklahoma, Nebraska, or Missouri borders.

Our squad consistently did well during my years in high school. In the 1944-45 season we debated the subject "Resolved that the legal voting age of the United States should be reduced to 18." This was a subject I was personally and politically interested in and continued to be until the State of Kansas reduced the voting age to 18. We ranked high in most of our meets that season, but the climax was winning first place in the Ark Valley Debate Tournament.

The 1945-46 season was our most successful season. For the first time in the history of our school we placed first in the Ark

Valley League, the District Tournament, and in the State Tournament! I believe this was the year we had an international topic dealing with what should be the relationship between the United States and the emerging United Nations. However, it may have been when we debated the topic "Resolved that United States should institute universal health care."—a topic which 60 years later is still a matter of national discussion. It was quite a thrill to be part of this triple championship team.

In the 1946-47 season, we debated "Resolved that the United States should have compulsory military service." Although this final debate year was not as successful as the previous years, we still won about 80% of our debates.

Debate really gave me a feeling of being very adult and independent. It gave me the opportunity to travel and to mix with people from a broad spectrum of backgrounds. Our coach couldn't be everywhere all the time during debate tournaments. He gave us our schedules and we were responsible for showing up at the right place at the right time. The trust relationship between coach and students gave us a great sense of affirmation. We usually had up to a half dozen rounds of debate in a tournament. Between debates we might have a free period when we could choose either to engage in more last minute preparation or simply do what ever we wanted to including going "out for a coke." It was neat to have such freedom. Since debate proved to be an arena in which I excelled it was also a means by which I could "prove myself" both to peers and to the adults of my world.

On May 6th, 1945, following several months of horrendous "firebombings," "carpet bombings" or "area bombings" in Germany, our long awaited V-E Day (Victory in Europe) was announced. I'm not even sure whether the Salt Hawks were granted an official holiday by our principal or school board, but our class as well as the junior and senior classes simply bailed out of school that day and hit the streets to celebrate. We piled into cars of friends who had them or who were able to borrow their parents' cars. After cruising the streets, honking horns, waving and shouting, from one end of town to the other, we headed out to the sand hills not far north and north east of Hutchinson. Part of the sand hills was unfenced raw undeveloped land. The sand hills included "motorcycle hill" where young adults and a few daring teen-agers used to ride the steep slippery sandy slopes in daredevil fashion just for the thrill of it. The sand hills were a favorite place to go when we wanted to get away from the watchful eyes of parents and others in authority. One of our classmates, John Oswald, lived on a farm near the sand hills. Their pasture was another favorite party place at times. In the sand hills groups could gather to hike, just to jaw, to enjoy nature, to have a clandestine beer party or a legitimate picnic. Infatuated lovers could find privacy for sweet embraces. Oswald's farm may have been the spot were we ended up on V-E Day. Our celebration was a great day just to forget school, forget the war, to rejoice that it would all be over as soon as we had V—J Day (Victory in Japan), to rejoice that the military would be coming home and that *we wouldn't get drafted* into the armed services.

The summer of 1945 proved to be most eventful and most historic. On August 6 an American B-29 bomber arrived over Hiroshima, Japan, at 8:15 a.m. dropping for the first time ever an Atomic Bomb obliterating the city and killing 80,000 people in one fell swoop! Although stunned by the magnitude of the devastation, I think most Americans were excited to learn that we had such a decisive weapon and felt its use was justified. Within hours President Harry Truman reported our action to the nation saying, "If they (the Japanese) do not now accept our terms, they may expect a rain of ruin from the sky the like of which has never been seen on this earth." Two days later the Soviet Union, which had been one of our allies in the European phase of W.W. II, declared war on Japan. Two more days later, the United States dropped a second atomic bomb—this time on Nagasaki. On August 14 Japan surrendered. On September 2, 1945, U.S. General Douglass MacArthur received the surrender documents aboard the battleship *USS Missouri* in Tokyo Bay.

Although we had one returning veteran, Earl Jamison, who had dropped out of school to join the Navy and who now came back to finish school, with unbelievable speed the memory of World War II began to fade. *Allagaroo 1946,* our school yearbook, was dedicated "to those who gave" and had a picture of our school's military service Honor Roll with its hundreds of names of alumni and an occasional gold star for those who died.

Following the end of World War II, another truly historic moment occurred in 1945. Shortly after my sixteenth birthday, on October 24, 1945 the United Nations was formally established. It resembled the post-World War I League of Nations in some ways only the UN had much broader responsibilities and many more members. As World War II drew to a close, the Allied Nations decided that such a war must never happen again. Representatives of these nations met in San Francisco in April 1945 to work out an organization to help keep world peace. That summer as the war was ending, 50 nations signed the Charter of the United Nations. Since then many more have joined. As of this writing, I believe the UN has nearly 200 members. When John D. Rockefeller Jr. gave money to buy land along the East River bordering New York City, it was decided to locate the main UN headquarters there. From then on, unfortunately, the United Nations became and still is a source of real controversy within the United States. Many Americans have seen it as a threat to our sovereignty and still hold a philosophy that is somewhat isolationist. But I think most Americans believe in the UN and feel that it has played a significant and positive role in world affairs. I am one of these.

My junior and senior years at HHS were typical normal carefree and fun-filled years. They were carefree for me because I didn't have any great academic goals. I didn't even tie together in my mind academic and vocational achievement. My focus was on school plays and concerts, attending athletic events, dating and social occasions such as movies and dances.

Some of our dances were "all school" dances, others just for a single class. Dances were held several times each semester on Friday or Saturday nights. Occasionally we had noontime lunch hour dances. Only one or two dances a year were formals. Most dances were unpretentious and causal—nothing that created a lot of stress.

I danced more than I did in Liberty Junior High, but I attended mostly for the social aspects—just to be together with friends and maybe to flirt with the girls.

Dances were usually held in the school gym. There would be a line of folding chairs set up on opposite sides of the gym. The boys tended to sit on one side and the girls on the other. The gym lights were dimmed. Usually someone put up some decorations for the occasion. Only our formal or semi-formal dances had live music and I think only these dances had an admission charge. Lots of us guys were content to stay on our side of the dance floor unless we just wanted to walk over to visit with some of the girls in general or one in particular. If the music was slow and easy, I would ask a girl to dance. One of the big dance styles at the time was the "jitter bug". That definitely was beyond my ability. I must admit to a bit of envy toward the guys and gals who "jitter bugged" so well. When a jitter bug started, I always headed back to my seat.

Jazz Combos had been popular in the 1930s. Some of the great leaders were Jazz Duke Ellington, Louis Armstrong, and Count Basie. Their "depression era" music still persisted into my teen-age years. To this day, Jazz is still some of my favorite music. By the 1940s these combos were gradually being replaced by a different style of music and orchestra. My Junior High, Senior High, and College years came to be known as the "Big Band Era." Big bands were made up of perhaps twenty musicians (given a small plus or minus).

These orchestras or bands featured whole sections of brass instruments, woodwinds, or rhythm instruments rather than the single instruments of the Jazz Combos. Most big band leaders were known for a particular instrument on which they sometimes played solo parts. Some of the band leaders whom we all loved were Benny Goodman (on the clarinet), Glenn Miller (on the trombone), Guy Lombardo, Harry James (on the trumpet), and Woody Herman. Some of the tunes which I was especially fond of were "Stardust," "Sentimental Journey," "Always," "In the Mood," and "Moonlight Serenade." These were the ones I enjoyed dancing to. Other tunes which were "a little fast" for me but which I thoroughly enjoyed were "String of Pearls," "Tuxedo Junction," and "Wood Choppers Ball."

There were many more bands and great tunes. The old hand-cranked wind-up Victrola or phonograph of the 1930's (like the one standing in my Grandmother's house) had already been replaced before the beginning of WW II. Electric phonographs played 77 rpm records. Instead of the tapes or CDs of today, we bought these records, or even 45 and 16 rpms, when we wanted to have our own music. School dances featured the big band records rather the live bands. Every community had its "small band" versions of the big bands. We drew on small bands for special occasions. The father of Jim Stout, one of my classmates, was leader of one of these. When I hear music from the Big Band era, it stirs my musical memories and brings back the emotions and the relationships of my days as a Salt Hawk.

My sense of independence was enhanced by my sixteenth birthday, October, 1945. Now I was old enough to get a driver's license! There was no such thing as Driver's Education courses in public schools as this time. Parents taught their children to drive. Dad had been taking me out to the country to teach me how to drive where there was little traffic. There were no automatic transmissions. We had to learn to stick shift gears. This was an experience as we slowly let out the clutch trying to prevent the car from suddenly lurching forward.

Our family, most families, had only one car. Most kids in my high school didn't have their own cars. There was never any possibility that I would have a car of my own in high school—it wasn't even a dream. Nor was there any chance I would be driving to school. It was still walk or ride a bike. But since the rationing of gasoline was ended, getting a driver's license meant for dates or special occasions in the evening it was possible for me to ask the folks if I could use the family car. If they didn't have plans of their own, I would often get an affirmative answer. Having wheels truly gave me a sense of freedom and independence. But it was also a perilous time!

People often ask others, "If you were sixteen again, what would you do differently?" This brings on another story from my Salt

Hawk days. It's not one of which I'm proud but which I tell because of its potential significance for my grandchildren or generations yet to be born. Like a number of my peers, I was eager to try my wings of freedom and independence and to "taste of some of the things that adults do." One of those things was to drink alcoholic beverages—usually beer but once in a while distilled liquor. Sometimes we would go the pool hall, play pool, and while there order a few beers. Usually age didn't seem to be a barrier to getting a drink just as in those days there was no *enforced* limit as to when young people could buy cigarettes. Occasionally someone whose parents drank would sneak something out of their house for us to drink when we got together.

After we had our driver's license and could get access to a car, we would sometimes use cars as an opportunity to rendezvous with others and have a drinking party. Although I didn't frequently engage in this behavior I did from time to time. I can remember getting our family car on more than one occasion, putting a washtub in its trunk, driving by to pick up buddies, going to a grocery store to buy crushed ice, and going on to a liquor store to buy a case (24 bottles) of beer to put on ice in the tub, and then heading out to some secluded place in the country for a drinking party.

I've shivered many times since then with the realization that when we got ready to head home, I as the driver (sometimes other guys as a driver) had consumed enough beer that I didn't have all my senses about me. How fortunate that I never had an accident! How fortunate that none of my buddies ever had an accident. How fortunate no one with whom we were involved, or whom we encountered while driving, was ever killed or maimed. In retrospect, I really consider myself lucky that I made it through these years. Although alcoholic beverages are more regulated today, this kind of behavior still happens. Too many times every year, one reads in the papers about teenagers having fatal accidents while under influence of alcohol and innocent people becoming their victims.

To this day the "what might have been" at these parties and binges haunts me. It was not that my parents knew or condoned or were indifferent. In fact one time when I had been out in someone else's car, and I came home late and had been drinking, Dad did discover me and took me to task with harsh words, a slap to the face when I talked back, and some restrictions in the coming month. Most of the time I was deceiving them and got by with it. But *if I were sixteen again all of this is something I would not repeat.*

We've had High School class reunions every five years. Almost always, one of my classmates will come up to remind me of my wild days, slap me on the back and laugh as he says, "Kieler, how did you ever become a minister?"

I was part of a great Salt Hawk class. A large percentage went on to college. Most of those who did not go on to college excelled in whatever they did. Of those who went on to college, our class produced many teachers, engineers, and other professionals. Byron Batthauer became a NASA pilot. Dorla Jane Abbott has been recognized as an outstanding leader in social work.

I think more than a normal number of classmates became doctors and dentists. One of those who became a physician was Ron Linscheid who became an Orthopedic Surgeon at the Mayo Clinic. He became one of if not "the" world's foremost authority in the field of hand and wrist surgery. He is known not only for his understanding of ligaments, his skills as a diagnostician and surgeon, but also for his development of artificial wrists and joints and his training of hand surgeons around the world. Ron may have been our most famous classmate, but there were others who were well known for their achievements. My whole class was special in many ways.

Chapter 21

INFLUENTIAL PEOPLE

Many young people can be more profoundly and positively influenced by an adult friend from beyond their family circle than from their pears—some person of good character, a good listener, understanding, supportive and affirming. I had such a friend—John Crutcher.

John was a Hutchinson native who, following his graduation from college, entered the U. S. Navy in World War II. Commissioned an Ensign in the United States Naval Reserve, John served as assigned, was promoted to Lieutenant Junior Grade (JG) and then to full Lieutenant. At the war's end, John returned home to enter business. When a Naval Reserve Unit was established in Hutchinson a few months after the war, John also became its Commanding Officer.

John was one of those community-minded citizens who volunteered to serve as a debate judge for the public schools whenever they were hosting district or area-wide debate tournaments. It was in this context that I met John and fell into a conversation about the previous year's debate topic—"resolved that the legal voting age of the United States should be reduced to 18." The affirmative side of this topic was so strong in my mind that along with a high school buddy, Bill Zimmerman, the two of us formed a little grass roots mostly teen-age political action group to work toward achieving this change in the Kansas voting laws. Mostly we worked toward our goal by urging people to write their Kansas State Representatives and Senators to support such legislation. We also worked at writing "Letters to the Editor" to be printed in the Hutchinson News-Herald.

John concurred with us in the idea of Eighteen Year-old Suffrage and was willing to help us in what we were doing. The strongest reason to lower the voting age he felt, as did we, was "if people are old enough to be drafted and go into the defense of their country, they should be considered old enough to vote in their nation's elections." Active in Republican politics, John had a lot more political savvy than did we. He knew we needed to build grassroots support and was quite helpful in making local contacts for us to speak about the merits of 18 year-old voting to civic clubs and church groups. Bill and I, both individually and collectively, made quite a few of these presentations. I'm sure that returning veterans and their friends were doing the same thing in other Kansas communities although I have no recollection of any organized state-wide network to implement our cause. Whether through the efforts of John and/or others, a bill to lower the voting age was introduced for consideration in the 1946 Kansas Legislature.

The Bill got far enough along in the committee process that a public hearing (i.e. public testimony) was set. John offered to drive two or three of us up to Topeka to testify before the Committee. Not only was this tremendously helpful, but it was a great ego boost for this 17 year-old.

Picture this: John Crutcher leading a small entourage of us up the steps of the magnificent State Capital building, through the large heavy entrance doors, along the high, wide, marble floored hallway into a place we'd never been, a small hearing room. We stepped inside the room. It was about 15' x 20' with a small rectangular table in the center. Six or so representatives were sitting around the table. We were almost trembling with a combination of awe and anxiety as we took our seats in the chairs ringing the room along the wall—chairs reserved for the public. Two or three other members of the public are sitting there. We sat quietly. Nothing much seemed to be happening. It was 9:00 o'clock in the morning and the first hearing of the day was about to begin. Most of the Representatives were shuffling their notes, looking at them, or reading their morning newspaper or mail. We felt this was a momentous occasion. Tension built for us.

Suddenly the Committee Chairman walked into the room, took his seat, and called the meeting to order. The number and the title of the Bill before the Committee were read. The Chairman announced, "Mr. John Crutcher and some students from Hutchinson have come to be heard." John thanked the Committee for giving us the opportunity to speak in favor of this Bill and introduced each of us. I was the first to testify. I stood up and began making a statement according to our plan. Only 2 or 3 of the Committee lifted their eyes to look at me, or even seemed to focus on what I have to say. A couple members continued looking at their notes and at least one continued reading his morning newspaper. This seemed a little strange to me, a little rude, but I did the best I could in the face of this response.

When I finish, before either of my colleagues could stand to make their statement, John stood up again to address the members of the Committee in a polite but very forthright way. He told the representatives that it seemed they were making a mockery of the legislative process by inviting people to testify at their hearings, yet not paying attention to what was said. Moreover, he said, "You are setting a terrible example, for these young people, of what government is all about." The representatives seemed a little startled to be called on the carpet. They squirmed ever so little and did sit up a little straighter. They hardly acknowledged John, though, and I recall no verbal response from them.

The experience of seeing this one adult confronting other adults, especially elected officials, in defense of and on behalf of his young teen-age friends made a deep, positive, and lasting impression on me.

The State Affairs Committee did not recommend our bill to the Legislature that year, and I learned that in the legislative process many good bills are killed several times before they ever pass into law. However, within a couple of years, Kansas did vote to lower the voting age to 18.

I deeply appreciated John Crutcher's friendship and encouragement. The time spent with him also gave me an opportunity to quiz John about my teen fantasy, the U. S. Navy. By the end of 1946 which was in the middle of my senior year, I was visiting the Naval Reserve at their Monday night drills. My residual patriotism lingered on from the war as well as my fantasies of enlisting in the Navy after high school graduation. These things combined with my relationship to John so that by 1 January 1947 I enlisted in and was officially part of the U. S. Naval Reserve.

Eventually John ran for the state legislature, was elected and served a few years in it. After this, John threw his hat into the ring for Governor of Kansas. I had a chance during the mid-1960s when I was living in Winfield to work on his behalf in the primary campaign for Governor. When he had a conflict which prevented his participation in an Arkansas City Republican Rally for primary candidates, John asked me to stand in for him and make a speech on his behalf. I was honored and excited to do this. John didn't make it through the primary election, but eventually he was on the Republican gubernatorial ticket and was elected Lieutenant-Governor of Kansas.

John, in my opinion, was always a shining light in the Republican Party. It was probably his influence that caused me to become a registered Republican when I first started voting. I wasn't a dyed-in-the-wool Republican. From the beginning I was always an independent thinker when it came to voting. But since Kansas was a dominantly Republican state I just felt that through voting in the Republican primaries I had more influence in choosing elected officials. I remained a Republican until 1992 when I moved to Wichita. Again having to re-register in order to vote, I finally felt that in terms of where the two parties stood on issues, I was probably two-thirds to 75% Democratic and only a third to 25% Republican and that I would be more honest to register with the party closest to my convictions.

Another person from this same period needs to be mentioned because of the profound influence he ultimately made on my life even though he never knew it. He was the Rev. Dr. Alvin Murray, my pastor at Trinity Methodist Church in Hutchinson. He was not so much a close personal friend but a friend because he was my pastor. His influence came about by a seed he planted in my life.

One Sunday morning Dr. Murray was preaching on the subject of Christian vocations. In the course of his sermon Dr. Murray said words to the effect, "A church the size of Trinity, if it is living faithfully, should be having at least one young person in every generation choosing to become an ordained Methodist Pastor. It has been so long since we have sent a young person into the ministry that we are due for at least two young people to enter the ministry in the near future."

I had never ever given the slightest thought to becoming an ordained minister. While such a thought had *never* crossed my mind, at this particular time in my high school life I was beginning to search vocationally. I had a rather shallow understanding of what it meant to be a pastor. To me, a pastor was primarily a preacher which meant that his main task was public speaking. Since I was active in debate, which obviously meant active in public speaking, two thoughts crossed my mind in response to Dr. Murray's message that morning. One thought I had was, "I could be a minister." The other was, "Is he pointing his finger at me? Does he think *I* should become an ordained minister?"

No overt response was called for. Even if it had been, I would never have made such a response at that moment. I simply wasn't ready in any way shape or form, spiritually or otherwise, to make that kind of commitment. But the seed had been planted! I never forgot his message. Off and on in years to come, the thought would cross my mind, perhaps even haunt me. When I finally came to the time in my life when I made that decision, I was grateful to Dr. Murray for first causing me to think about my calling. He was always interested in young people; in fact at one time he served as President of Southwestern College. For me, all-be-it in a different sense than John Crutcher's friendship, Alvin Murray was that kind of adult whose interest and friendship in relationship to a teenager made a profound difference in my life by lifting up a vision and a possibility.

Chapter 22

THE EXAMINATION

In May of 1947 I walked across the stage of Convention Hall, one of 313 students, to receive my graduation diploma from Hutchinson High School. Our Baccalaureate speaker was Milton Eisenhower, President of Kansas State University and brother of the famous WW II General, Dwight D. "Ike" Eisenhower. Sorry to say I don't remember a thing that our speaker said or anything about our graduation ceremony except Milton Eisenhower's involvement and this only because his brother was to become President of the United States six years later, in 1953.

It was four months before this, in January of 1947, when a string of life-changing events began. Shortly after school resumed following Christmas vacation an announcement was made to the senior boys in my class: "On the last Saturday of this month a scholarship examination will be given for the NROTC (Naval Reserve Officers Training Corp). If you are interested in taking this examination, you need to sign up with Mr. Cole."

This exam was one of many such exams being given nationwide and would lead to the selection of more than a thousand young men from across the country to become Midshipmen in the US Naval Reserve program. The NROTC program was to the US Naval Reserve what the Naval Academy program at Annapolis, Maryland, was to the regular Navy. The scholarships provided tuition, books, fees, and $50/month toward living expenses to enable these midshipmen to attend one of 52 universities (1 in each of the 52 states in the union). Applicants were permitted to list their first six choices of schools but the Navy would still do the assigning of midshipmen to a university. Each of these 52 universities had an NROTC Unit staffed by regular officers from the U. S. Navy. Midshipmen could choose their own major in their university, but each semester they would also be required to take a course in Naval Science which meant in effect that all who receive a NROTC scholarship would have a double major. In addition, each summer they would be required to participate in off-campus training— usually a cruise, or a similar type of naval experience.

Since I had not been planning to go on to college, initially I didn't have a great deal of interest in this announcement. The only thing which perked my interest at all was the fact that the exam related to the Navy and I had been fantasizing that the most exciting and interesting form of military service would be in the Navy. In fact, I thought that enlisting in the Navy and having a 20 year career, followed by retirement at age 38, would be what I might like to do.

That evening at dinner, after the announcement of the upcoming examination, I told Mom and Dad about it. They wondered if I was going to sign up. My reply: "I don't think so." Since there had never been any discussion of college by either my folks or by me while I was growing up, there was no big push to do the exam. Dad, however, did point out to me that taking a big exam such as this might be a great learning experience. He suggested it might be worth the effort just because of what I would learn from taking the exam. This seemed to make sense to me. Without even realizing what I might be getting into, I did sign up.

We were to be at school ready to start the exam by 8:00 a.m. on that last Saturday in January. I don't remember a lot of the details. Perhaps there were 20 or 30 of us who took the exam. The only other specific person I remember taking it was my life-time friend, Jim Jung. We received rather detailed instructions and were spread out so that we weren't sitting next to or directly across from one another. The exam was about four-hours long. I remember getting finished before some of the others. This left time to review and rework some of my answers. Even though we weren't close enough to see each other's work, or to cheat if we wanted to, I recall Jim sitting across from me, down to my right. Somehow one sheet of his paper was close enough that I could see one of his algebra problems. I noticed he had a different answer from mine. This made me keep working with that problem. Eventually I came up with another answer than I'd first put down. I've sometimes wondered in retrospect about the ethics of reworking that problem and whether I had the correct answer either time.

It was many weeks after the examination before I heard anything and I don't really think I expected to hear anything. Then one day when I came home from school there was a letter from the Bureau of Naval Personnel telling me, "on the basis of the exam, you are being considered for NROTC Midshipman status." There was lots of paper work for me to fill out including giving the names of people who could be used for personal references and listing my top six choices for universities. I also had to go to Kansas City to take a physical examination.

The only person I remember naming as a reference was my friend Lt. John Crutcher (US Naval Reserve). I've always felt having John's reference as a USNR officer, especially as Commandant of the local Naval Reserve Unit, plus having joined and served in the Naval Reserve during high school stood me in good stead in the midshipman selection process.

When it came to naming universities that I would like to attend, I had nothing in mind to start with since I had not been planning to go to college. However, since I had always enjoyed the days I'd worked in the soda fountain at the Naval Air Station's Ship's Service and later at Black's Drug Store in town, I began to think that working in an ice cream manufacturing plant or in the dairy industry would be a neat occupation. Going to our public library and spending endless hours pouring over college and university catalogues, I discovered a cluster of Big Ten Universities around the Great Lakes all of which had majors combining studies in the fields of business and dairy technology. On this basis alone I listed as my university choices half a dozen of these schools including the University of Illinois.

A few weeks later I received notification that I had been selected for an NROTC scholarship and was being assigned to the unit at the University of Illinois. As far as I know, that year I was the only one from my high school to be awarded this scholarship. Upon arriving at the U of I and in the process of enrolling for courses I discovered that the major I was contemplating was a five-year program of studies whereas my scholarship allowed me only four years. Having to rethink things, I ended up enrolling in the College of Commerce at the University of Illinois rather than the School of Agriculture.

Chapter 23

"WORKING ON THE RAILROAD"

One of the perks that go with having your father work where he doles out lots of business to others is that they are often willing to return favors. Once we knew that I would be entering the University of Illinois fourteen weeks after I graduated from high school, my dad and I both knew that I needed not just a short part-time or temporary summer type job but a full-time good paying job that would last until I left for school. Dad inquired about such job possibilities with the station agents for each of the three railroads in Hutchinson—Santa Fe, Rock Island, and Missouri Pacific—with which he shipped thousands of cars of wheat and other grain every year. The Santa Fe agent extended an invitation for me to talk to him. Upon completion of an interview and written applications, I ended up with what proved to be a very interesting job for my first four months after graduation—"working on the railroad." These were still the days of steam driven locomotives. I don't recall my starting hourly wage but this was by far the best paying job I knew about for a young high school graduate. What a whole new world this proved to be. I learned so much through practical experience.

Railroads had many categories of employees. Track laborers, doing the rail construction side of things in the days before such work was highly mechanized, were largely unskilled, often migrant laborers, engaging in heavy manual labor out-of-doors in all kinds of remote settings in all seasons of the year. There was no way as a young unathletic man that I could survive that kind of work. At the opposite end of the labor spectrum, there were the operating employees—switchmen, brakemen, firemen, engineers, conductors, etc. Training was by apprenticeship. Those who held these positions worked according to seniority and there were hierarchies with which to contend. One didn't get in to these operating positions quickly or easily. In-between these two categories, another large category of employees were freight handlers, baggage handlers, clerks, etc. My entrance-level job proved to be that of "freight handler."

Box cars filled with freight of all kinds—heavy weight items, light weight items, boxed, unboxed, solids, and liquids in barrels— needed to be unloaded or loaded depending on whether the freight was coming into town or being shipped out. The box cars were parked on tracks along side a freight house, doors slid open, and we used "dollies" to wheel the freight about for storage or movement from rail-car to truck. I remember one time when we opened up a box car only to detect a terrible smell. We discovered some barrels of formaldehyde (a toxic chemical with a suffocating odor) had ruptured. This was long before there were environmental safety agencies or regulations, but common sense dictated that those of us who were freight handlers couldn't be exposed to such a hazard without protection. Gas masks were sent for and when they arrived we had to use them in emptying out the box car and cleaning it up! The fire department loaned them to the railroad and provided the training for their use. Rather "exciting" for a boy not yet quite 18 years old.

A significant early learning for me was about the role of labor unions. Basically all the railroad employees were unionized (except, I think, for the track laborers). A person didn't have to be a union member to get a railroad job, but as I recall after a certain number of months you did have to join the union. No one, of course, really knew that I intended to work only for four months and then quit so I never became a union member even though I benefited from the union. Each local union chose a steward who looked after the welfare of members, looked after union affairs, and served as a union company go-between. After I began work, Jack, our local steward, came by to get acquainted with me and to help me learn the ropes.

Jack was friendly and helpful. He continued touching base with me as a new employee just as he did with all the established union employees. He taught me about the job hierarchy and how seniority worked—how men "bid in" jobs that were open if they thought that would be a better job for them. Seniority meant that the employee with the longest working time in a particular category of work would get the job. For instance, after working a month or more as a freight handler, Jack came by to tell me that the company had posted a job opening for a baggage handler. He didn't know of anybody who intended to "bid in' the job. If no one from within the system bid for it, it would be advertised as an employment opportunity for new hires from outside. He pointed out that since I had one month's seniority as a freight handler, I could get that job before a new hire if I wanted it. Baggage handler was a better job than freight handler so naturally, I wanted to do this. I bid it in and I got the job. Of course I had to go from working days as a freight handler to working nights as a baggage handler, but baggage handlers were better paid, had a little less physically demanding job, and they had more variety of work and more responsibility.

In my role as baggage handler I worked the passenger trains as they traveled through town, stopping just briefly. This included keeping track of the time-tables for arrivals, having our big hand-drawn wagons properly positioned so we could off load and on load with out a moment's delay. Mail was our first priority. Almost all mail was moved from town to town across country and state by train. Mail was carried in special "postal" cars which had a section where postal employees rode and worked sorting letters by their destinations as the trains traveled. Mail was sacked in large waterproof cloth sacks. Filled sacks often weighed 50 to 75 pounds. Once they were ready, they were stacked in the other end of their postal car or in an adjacent car. The minute a train stopped, the postal car door opened and the worker inside started shoving the sacks to be left for Hutchinson and vicinity toward us. We would stack them on our empty wagon. When it was full we would pull it by hand to a waiting truck from the US Post Office and then quickly return to get more mail or to load the waiting outgoing mail into the postal car.

We would at the same time, if we had enough help, or immediately after the mail if we didn't have enough help, unload and load the Railway Express cars. Railway Express was a private company which leased cars, or space, on passenger trains to transport more light weight and/or expedited cargo than would be hauled by freight trains. RX was a precursor of the UPS and FED EX to come several decades later. By far the largest volume of Railway Express cargo which we handled was cream cans. In those days farmers with dairy cattle commonly separated milk into cream and skim milk right on their farms. They kept skim milk for use on the farm but cream was sold to "Cream Stations" as a cash commodity. Cream Stations kept cream as well cooled as possible, consolidating smaller quantities into 25 gallon stainless steel cream cans for storage and transport. Cream cans would be moved from country and small towns to larger cities with creameries (where cream was either made into butter, cheese, or bottled for retail sale, etc.). To prevent cream from souring, these cans needed to be transported as quickly as possible. This was done by Railway Express on the first available train. Cream cans were pretty heavy so working on the railroad also proved to be pretty good body-building exercise.

Even though we were called baggage handlers, we handled very little passenger baggage. Most passengers took their suitcases into the passenger cars with the assistance of a porter. Only if they checked their bags, trunks, or suitcases at the station did they go into a baggage car and only then did we handle this conventional baggage.

Trains came pretty much nonstop throughout the night but sometimes there were delays or natural spacings which gave us breaks to take it easy. I enjoyed this work a great deal. It was interesting to see the city function at night. You also gained a sense of what went on in the entire state. Another task which I had at one point while working as a baggage handler was checking on the icing in refrigerator cars. Refrigerator cars were part of the makeup of freight trains. They usually originated in California and carried head lettuce, other fresh veggies and fruits. There was not much by way of fresh out of season produce in the 1940s. Imported produce was almost non-existent. The utilization of well insulated freight (refrigerator) cars, heavily iced with blocks of ice in both ends of the car, was the main way in-season perishable fruits and vegetables were transported. When freight trains stopped in the rail yards in Hutchinson to add or drop off freight cars, we had to go out to the trains, climb to the top of the cars, open up trap doors, and make sure there was still plenty of ice left. If necessary they could be re-iced while the train was stopped. Today, of course, trains and trucks use mechanical refrigeration to keep fresh and frozen produce cold while being transported.

Five or six weeks after I started working as a Baggage Handler, Jack came by again. This time he was telling me that if I wanted a better job I might want to move into a Clerk position. This would provide better pay, more variety and greater responsibility. To be a Clerk would also give more job security. Once you had established your seniority as a Clerk by taking your first Clerk job you never lost your previously established seniority in other jobs you had held. Even if there wasn't a Clerk job for you (as in slack seasons of the year) you could use your seniority to "bump" someone else who wasn't a clerk out of a Baggage Handler job and thus keep working. If necessary to keep working, you could even bump back into being a Freight Handler.

As before, however, there was a downside to what Jack was telling me. As in any position, Clerks had to start at the bottom and work up. He told me that there was a vacant Clerk job available but it was out in Western Kansas, at Ulysses. "You could bid that in and get it. Nobody seems to want it because no one wants to move out west. Since you're single maybe you wouldn't mind doing this. Besides," he said, "you don't have to stay out there for any required length of time. What you could do would be to go out, work for a couple of weeks, keep your eyes out for a Clerk opening back here in Hutchinson or near here, or maybe a daytime Baggage

Handler job. As soon as one comes open, bid it in. You'll have Clerk's seniority which gives you an opportunity to get the job over some one living here who wasn't willing to go out west and doesn't have any Clerk's seniority." This is exactly what I did and exactly what happened. It was my first time actually living on my own away from home which proved to be a good growing experience and a confidence building preparation for my coming college days.

Whether in the world of industry, business, education, politics, or religion there are many qualities and styles of leadership. As for me, I have come to believe that in any and all of these worlds, better than authoritarian, aristocratic, arbitrary or any other common styles of leadership is what in the world of faith we call servant leadership—leading by helping others and working in a collegial style rather than trying to "lord it over others" or being dictatorial or unilateral. Some people are critical of, opposed to, the movement of organized labor. I know that labor unions are no different from any other human institution. They are imperfect and corruptible and can become overly demanding on behalf of their constituency, but I tend to affirm the ideals of organized labor because I believe this movement represents one of the best and most practical ways of achieving the welfare of all workers and creating a world of economic justice. Reflecting back on my admittedly limited experience while working on the railroad, I feel that Jack, the union steward, was a good leader because he was a servant-leader who helped his "fellow workers" learn how to utilize "the system." He was certainly helpful to me!

Chapter 24

SHIRLEY

I have only one sister and no brothers so I can truly say this makes my only sibling—my sister, Shirley—very special to me. This is not to say that we didn't fight at times when we were kids. Nor is it to say that we've always been extremely close because I was almost 5 ½ years old when Shirley was born. Those five-and-a-half years made a lot of differences. As an only child during those years, I did interesting things with my folks. And, while Shirley was still too young to go places with us, the three of us would have enjoyable experiences that Shirley didn't share. But it was not long until Shirley and I were doing exciting and fun things together.

Beyond remembering that I was excited about the prospect of having a baby sister or brother, and remembering how this led to the move to a new house, my earliest memory in relationship to Shirley is one that goes right back to the time that she was born and came home. I remember Dad taking me up to the hospital. I could hardly wait to see my new baby sister as well as Mom. I was so surprised that she was so tiny. It wasn't that Shirley was abnormally small—I just didn't understand that babies didn't come half grown. Because this occasion seemed very special from the beginning, it seemed to me to deserve a celebration. I'm sure Dad didn't leave me "home alone" while he was at work and they were in the hospital, but I remember going alone—solo and without coaching—in to our kitchen when I knew Mom and Shirley were about to come home. I stirred up and baked my very first cake! It was my gift to Shirley and Mom when they arrived home. I didn't know babies couldn't eat at birth. It probably wasn't much of a cake, but I thought I was being a great help and I was very proud of my cake. I also probably left the kitchen in a mess so Dad had to do a major clean up.

Trips to our grandparents' farm were always exciting and fun. When Shirley was a toddler I took her around the farmyard, just like I owned it, to show her all the animals—pigs and piglets, horses, cows and calves, pups and kittens, chickens and chicks, geese and goslings, ducks and ducklings, etc. I don't specifically remember our folks leaving both of us together with our grandparents at the same time, but I do remember that there were occasions when Shirley had her week for staying at the farm just as I had my times.

I had a variety of pets in our backyard on East Fifteenth Street. These were turtles, garden-snakes, toads and pigeons which I managed to catch around town. Also, inspired by what I saw at the state fair and as well as at the farm, I bought and raised some rabbits. I didn't have and care for all of theses creatures at the same time. They were first one, then another. However I had them all while I was in grade school which meant Shirley was still a preschooler. I enjoyed sharing my "in-town" pets with Shirley just as I enjoyed "showing off the farm animals" to her.

There's another thing Shirley and I share. It is not something we did together but something which was part of both of our childhoods—a memory that we have in common just as we both have memories of family, schools, and of city of Hutchinson. It's the memory of attending Preschool. This Preschool (or Nursery School as many called it in those days) was operated by Mrs. Hook—a wonderful lady and teacher who loved children, and loved nurturing them in their early childhood. She had her school in the basement of her own home and had all kinds of developmental activities and toys that were so much fun. To this day I carry warm feelings and thoughts related to her school. She always had a great reputation in Hutchinson so there was always a waiting list to be in "Mrs. Hook's School." I went half-days for two years before starting kindergarten. When the right time came, Mom enrolled Shirley to share the same preschool experience which had been mine.

I only recall one time when I was really angry with my sister, but I've never forgotten it. Shirley was in grade school; I was junior high. I don't remember what precipitated our fight, but we really got into it. At this period of my life, I had one really big hobby—the building of model airplanes. I would buy kits at a hobby store with the plane's design and building instructions. The kit included pieces of balsam wood (an extremely light wood cut very thin) which was partly pre-carved into wings, fuselages, tails, elevators, struts, landing gears, etc. When I finished the carving, I laid the pieces out on paper with a printed design and then glued them together as they lay there on the design plans. Later when the plane was fully assembled, I took a light weight tissue paper that came in the kit, stretched it out over the wood and glued the two together to make the plane's "skin."

Some kits got quite complicated. Some were powered by a heavy duty rubber band that stretched from the tail to the propeller. When the band was fully twisted, it made the propeller spin. Some kits had battery-powered engines. Later they made gasoline engines for them. All of these were a challenge to construct and took many hours, days and weeks, sometimes even months, to build. I think I especially enjoyed these because sometimes I made models of planes being flown in the war. We had a basement ping-pong table where I laid my planes out while I was working on them. I had one of my most complex creations there at the time. The plane was almost competed when Shirley and I got into our big fight. Shirley got so angry at me that she went rushing to the basement and totally smashed and demolished my plane! I was devastated. I tried to beat-up on her and I've never forgotten this episode. After that I just gave up building model airplanes anymore because it seemed like risking too much time and effort in what might prove to be for naught.

Another family activity which we all did together was something we did weekly throughout the summers. Always an enjoyable treat for us, it was simply going for a ride in the car. Sometimes Dad might take us for a drive in the country, sometimes it was a town drive, and sometimes it might to be to a park, a playground or merry-go-round, or a ride on the miniature train. The best part of this was that it always included a stop at the A & W Root Beer Drive-in where each of us would have a frosty glass of root beer.

Shirley was in Liberty Junior High School when I left for college. I had my four years at the University of Illinois with Midshipman training the three intervening summers. Then I started four years active duty with the US Navy (two of those overseas). I didn't see much of Shirley during these eight years. Before I finished the Navy and my seminary studies and came back to Kansas to serve the Methodist Church, Shirley had graduated from Hutchinson High (1953) and was away from home, training in speech therapy and completing a teaching certificate at Kansas University in Lawrence. After graduation, she began teaching in Salina, Kansas and (for a year) in Japan for the armed services. After this she married an Air Force Officer, Ray Walters, and started her family with a son Russell and a daughter Audrey. This meant both of us, along with our respective families, were pretty much going our own ways. There were not lots of opportunities to get together. Mostly we stayed in touched through Mom and Dad as intermediaries. Of course we corresponded and traded family photos, but not always with the greatest of regularity.

Like most military families, Shirley and Ray and the children, moved a lot. They lived in California, Texas, Arkansas, Michigan, Guam, and Nebraska. After Ray's 20-year Air Force retirement they lived in Springfield, Missouri. Vacation trips were always one of the highlights of my own family. Through our vacations we did manage to visit Shirley and her family at least once everywhere they lived except for California and Guam. Sometimes they visited us. Ben was probably about seven years older than their kids so he was not quite as close, age-wise, to their kids as were Bill and Paul to Russ and Audrey. Still, we always enjoyed these family times when we got together. Warm feelings if not specific memories remain.

The Walters had a cocker-spaniel by the name of Honey. When they moved to Guam for two years, they were not allowed to take Honey with them. We were living in Dodge City at the time. They asked us to take care of Honey for them. We were glad to do so. Our kids were delighted to have Honey join our family, and this made for an enjoyable interaction between our two families. For a year or so Ray was stationed near Vietnam. Shirley and the kids moved back to Hutchinson to be near Mom and Dad and Ray's family. This meant we saw more of them since we were making special efforts to visit my folks.

Overall, in the years following my high school graduation, moving away from home and moving out into new directions, I've always felt that Shirley and I kind of drifted (partly drifted apart) in our relationship. I was mostly to blame for this though I always felt that Shirley was partly at fault. When she and Ray got married, for whatever the reason they just went off to Nebraska and eloped without including any of the family—not even Mom and Dad. Then when they divorced eighteen years later, there was never any advanced warning and communicating, sharing of feelings or talk of strained relationships. Everyone in the family just received a letter one day saying they were divorcing and asking that everyone abstain from any interventions or contacts relative to the divorce.

Following the divorce, however, I tried to be sure that as far as my part of the Kielers went, we would be as supportive as possible. The divorce took place while Shirley was living in Springfield, Mo. We tried to get there at least once or twice a year to be with Shirley. As the years have passed and especially after Shirley's return to Kansas (Lawrence), I feel we've again grown closer and more supportive of one another. Certainly none of our childhood fighting like cats and dogs persisted through the years. The older I've gotten the "gladder" I've become that we have one another as brother and sister. I recall my father-in-law in Kentucky always phoned his brother in Texas every Saturday or Sunday morning just to keep in touch and, in recent years, I've tried to follow a similar pattern of keeping in touch with Shirley. This has been fun.

I have developed great pride and admiration for how well Shirley has coped as a single person. She retired in 2000. I've been really impressed with the new interests and various forms of community service which have emerged in Shirley's life. Shirley has inherited the same gardening genes from dad that I did. She does wonderfully well with flowers and container gardening. I admire her skills. When Lorine and I travel up to Lenexa, Kansas, as we do several times a year to see our kids there, we've enjoyed popping in to see Shirley in Lawrence. I've seen her more often every year since we've both retired than any year since I left home to attend the U of I.

A retirement visit—A walk in the park
Left to right: Shirley Kieler Walters, author, Lorine—author's wife

Chapter 25

"A NEW WORLD"

Picture yourself as a seventeen-year-old, having the experience of being put down by helicopter into a crowd of 20,000 strangers and just left there! This very nearly describes my experience as I arrived at the University of Illinois October 1 for the beginning of the 1947 fall semester. I invite you to come walk with me in my shoes—to experience things through my eyes—that year.

I have never been in the State of Illinois. I've never set foot on *any* college campus. Even arriving here is a challenge. Cars for students are more the exception than the rule. Parking space on and around campus is scarce. Public airlines are only just beginning to emerge as a means of mass transportation. There is no reasonable air connection available between central Kansas and central Illinois. Buses and trains are the only two transportation options available to me for my trip of 600 miles. I choose the latter which requires three stages—taking a Santa Fe train from Hutchinson to Kansas City, Mo., then changing to a Missouri Pacific train to travel to St. Louis, Missouri, and completing my trip on the Illinois Central Railroad going from St. Louis to the twin cities of Champaign-Urbana, home to the University of Illinois.

The GI Bill of Rights enacted by our country just a couple of years earlier gives financial aid to all returning WW II veterans enabling them to receive four years of college in preparation for reintegration into society and the working world. Everywhere I look the campus is literally flooded with returning GIs. Altogether there are 20,000 students. I *do not know a single person on campus!*

The campus itself, at the north end, is approximately a mile wide west to east (much wider as one goes south) and perhaps two or three miles long north to south. The heart of the North Campus is a large beautiful grassy mall surrounded by broad sidewalks lined with tall stately elms. A number of the University's main buildings surround and face inward toward this quadrangle. Beyond "The Quad" other buildings fan out in every direction. North of it is the engineering campus. East and west of "The Quad," on the perimeters of the campus, are older dormitories plus fraternity and sorority houses. Somewhat dividing the North and South campuses is the Library—the biggest library I've ever seen (just one wing of it is a seven-story building). In fact it is one of the 5 largest university libraries in the world. The South Campus is the agricultural campus with cattle and swine, a dairy facility, testing and experimental plots for crops, orchards, fields and more. Today (in 2004) industrial research buildings developed in partnership with private enterprise are also interspersed with the agricultural facilities.

Walking from the Quad to the Southwest, a mile and a half or so, one comes to the Football Stadium—a large U-shaped coliseum. All of the space underneath the bleachers is enclosed. Historically, this voluminous space has only been nominally utilized for storage and much of it has been purely unused empty space. Now, with the postwar flood of students, much of this space has been quickly partitioned into large dormitory rooms each housing 250 men. Each of these huge dorm rooms has a large adjacent study room and also a large room for showering and toileting. Entering the dorm you look up to a ceiling perhaps 25-30 feet high. Looking ahead, and allowing your eyes to sweep form one side of the room to the other, you see rows and rows of double (upper and lower) bunks with large metal storage lockers for clothing and books on each side of the bunks.

I'm always in a throng of chattering students and I feel like I could get lost on this campus. Walking back to the Student Union at the north end of The Quad, I stand in a line to pick up my registration and orientation packet. Thumbing through all the sheets of material in the packet, I quickly discover that the Stadium Dorm is to be my residence this fall! The sheer magnitude of this place is beginning to feel overwhelming. I soon discover walking (or biking if I had a bike, which I don't) to my first class each morning will take about half an hour from Stadium Dorm—rain or snow, sunshine or cloudiness, warm or cold, or whatever—if I don't stop for breakfast. Living conditions at the Stadium aren't exactly ideal, but what I like least about the situation is this walk. (When I returned to visit campus several times in the 1990s and again in the early 2000s, the University or twin cities had a system of buses circling and crisscrossing the campus to provide transportation for students, but no such mass transit system exists while I'm a student.)

I usually spend my entire day in the central part of the campus before making a return to the dorm for the evening. Meanwhile, I eat breakfast, lunch, and supper at any one of a number of places, I walk from building to building between classes, and I spend time relaxing, as well as oftentimes eating, at the Student Union or at the Campus YMCA. I begin to go often to the Wesley Foundation. I spend most of my non-class time studying in the library. Study standards and expectations are entirely different from what I experienced in high school. The variety of courses and viewpoints is something far greater than anything I have previously experienced or thought about. For instance, I experience a lot of distress because my teacher in Freshman English is a committed atheist who delights in ridiculing students of faith—especially those of the Christian faith.

Among the student body of 20,000, I discover not only traditional "just out of high school" students like myself. A majority of the students are ex-GIs. The student body is a microcosm of all the races and religions, the socioeconomic classes and cultures, which make up the United States of America. I also discover that 2,000 of the student body are international students who represent almost every nation in the world. I'm astounded—*this is a whole new world* in which I am living!

The first group of friends I make on campus are my peers in the NROTC Unit. Thanksgiving break that fall will be too short to go home to Kansas so I simply plan to stay on campus. However my best friend from the NROTC Unit is Dave Schmulbach from New Athens, Illinois (not far from St. Louis). Dave and his family invite me to their home for the Thanksgiving break. They also do this a couple of other times while I am in the University of Illinois. They are a warm family and I quickly learn the joy and meaning of receiving hospitality when you are a stranger and alone. Dave isn't the only student from Illinois to befriend me during my U of I days—he's just the first of many. There's also Robin Lahmen who was reared on a farm almost as far north as you could go in Illinois and not be in Wisconsin. Although Robin is from a Church of the Brethren background, while on campus he is active in the Methodist Student Movement, which is where we meet. Robin and his family have me in their home for Easter of my freshman year—another vacation period too short to allow me to return to Kansas. I quickly discover, even in the midst of a crowd of strangers, I can always make friends.

During the fall semester, I apply for a change of dorms in the Spring Semester. I know whatever I get by way of a different dorm has to be closer to my classes and other campus interests. I succeed in getting a new dorm and what I get turns out to be another surprising world. It has several conveniences. For instance, it is right across the street from the Armory. The Armory is a "Quonset Hut"-shaped brick building of enormous size. It covers an entire square block. Its ground floor is mostly a large dirt floor used for indoor track meets. The running track is a quarter of a mile oval. Surrounding it are two stories of classrooms. These were originally used for the Army ROTC and now are also used for the Naval ROTC Unit, which is one of the things that make my new dorm a convenient location. For both units, especially the Army ROTC, the area surrounded by the track doubles as a Parade Ground.

Two things make my next dorm unique. First, it's an Ice Rink! Built a number of years before World War II, it was a very high—ceiling building constructed to be a year-around ice rink for the University's Physical Education Department. As the war began the student body shrank. Given the few students remaining on campus, the rink was an impractical luxury so it was shut down for the duration. Now that the war ended, the flood of students and the need for housing is so overwhelming that it has been temporarily turned in to a dormitory. Secondly, did I think I had lots of roommates in the Stadium Dorm? Well, the rows and rows of double deck bunks and steel lockers are here also, but this time there are no partitions! The Ice Rink Dorm houses 400 students—all in one room! I can't believe it.

Something else, however, is unbelievable and unspeakable for me. Before Pearl Harbor, I had never met a Japanese person or a person of Japanese ancestry. Very quickly a combination of hysteria and prejudice toward all Japanese swept the country after Pearl Harbor. I was caught up in this. In my high school days, I could hardly express my anger enough, my mistrust, my contempt and hatred toward the Japanese. I was quick to verbalize these feelings in the most unreasonable ways. Suddenly, here in the Ice Rink Dorm, directly across the aisle from my row of bunks is a student who appears to be Japanese! Maybe he notices my staring at him and wonders why I don't speak. For several days or weeks I just try to ignore him and give him a cold shoulder. Finally, the influences of my campus church and my conscience begin to work on me. I conclude that from the viewpoint of my Christian faith I'm being very hypocritical not to mention just plain unkind. I decide to change my behavior in relationship to this student who appears Japanese. One afternoon, I screw up my courage, stick out my hand and introduce my self. He responds in a friendly manner saying, "I'm Mac Fukuda, I'm from Hawaii. Where are you from?" We begin to visit. I discover something I haven't learned in school—many Hawaiians are Japanese-Americans. Mac tells me he's a Nisei, a term I don't know. When I ask him the meaning of the term, he explains that a Nisei is a person of Japanese ancestry who has been born and educated in the USA. Mac's father had immigrated to the United States (Hawaii) from Japan. Mac was from Hilo, Hawaii—both the Island of Hawaii and the State of Hawaii. Mac had graduated from high school there before the end of the war and he had been drafted into the US Army. By the time he finished basic training, the war had ended. Mac was assigned to be a member of the United States occupation force in Japan. Interestingly enough, he tells me, he has an uncle who still lives in Japan and he visited him while stationed in Japan. I ask Mac how his uncle feels about all that had transpired during the war. I'm a bit surprised to learn his uncle had not been in favor of Japan's war against United States.

Well, my reader, is this enough to help you understand why I think of going to the University of Illinois as entering a whole new world?

Living conditions in the Ice Rink Dorm are better than the Stadium Dorm in many ways—especially in its proximity to the main part of campus. But 399 roommates are still less than ideal. That spring I again begin searching around for a better dormitory situation. I don't know anything about fraternities. I soon begin to learn about them. They seem to me to be OK for some people, but I decide they don't appeal to me for a combination of reasons— elitism, too much party spirit, and the cost—just to mention a few. Some of my NROTC buddies invite me to rush their fraternities but I decline.

I discover, though, university dorms are still difficult to come by. But I make two other discoveries. There are independent and private dorms. Mac Fukada is also looking for better housing. We team up in our search and we find one of the private dorm possibilities is a Roman Catholic dorm, Newman Hall. It's connected to the Catholic campus church, and it has openings! They are willing to accept Protestants. Newman Hall is a much smaller dorm than either the Stadium or Ice Rink dorms and all its rooms are doubles. Imagine—just two students sharing one room, each with his own study desk! We can also take all of our meals right where we live, and the dorm is very close to campus— just a block from the library. Mac and I agree to share a room and we become roommates for two years—my sophomore and junior years, his junior and senior years. What a welcomed change this is.

Chapter 26

A NEW FAITH

A letter in the mail box perked my interest in late August 1947. The return address on the letter was "University YMCA, Champaign, Illinois." Across the front lower left corner of the envelope was sprawled the phrase "Freshman Orientation Invitation." Midst the onslaught of returning GIs, the university's resources were taxed to the max and the school was not offering any meaningful orientation for new students. Perhaps they never had. As one of its ministries, the Young Men's Christian Association was filling in the gap and offering a 2 or 3 day Freshman Orientation Retreat immediately prior to fall registration. The letter gave me retreat details including an invitation and a sign-up form. This was exactly what I needed and I quickly responded.

Arriving on campus a couple of days before classes began, I checked in with the University, was assigned my housing, unpacked, and then arrived at the campus YMCA building at 1001 S. Wright Street just in time to board a bus for an hour's ride to the camp facility which was to accommodate about 200. The program had a series of speakers both from the university and from among the campus pastors. We learned about the layout of the campus, its facilities and the services it offered students.

Even more interesting to me was learning about the U of I's traditions, campus life and sporting events. Part of the football tradition included a student cheering section called the "Block I." The block was several hundred students in reserved seating shaped like the capital letter "I." They all had matching sweat shirts and colored cards which they held up to make a bright and bold "I" during yells led by the cheer leading squad. Another part of football tradition, was their half-time music. The university had then, and has now, one of the largest marching bands of any university. The band's fame dates back to the 1920s when John Philip Sousa— noted composer of great marching music—directed the U. of I. band.

We learned the story behind the story of their half time program. The Illini Indians were among the early inhabitants of Illinois. Their Chief had been adopted by university students as a campus symbol. Each year one student was chosen to portray "Chief Illiniwek" at football games. This student studied the early Illini culture including their dances. As the half-time program neared its conclusion, Chief Illiniwek sneaked into the mass of band members, hid there until a stirring musical finale when he emerged from the front of the band and performed a wild and dramatic dance on the field just prior to the time when the opposing football team returned to the field. These traditions certainly made me an enthusiastic football fan and Illini.

Coach Ray Elliott, Head Football Coach, was one of our speakers. He told us not only about Illinois' great football tradition but also about the importance of good sportsmanship, teamwork and the qualities of leadership. Leadership skills are something I heard speakers referring to frequently. Counselors and professors stressed the importance of good study habits. I heard them say "a good student should study a minimum of two hours for each hour he or she spends in the class room." I was shocked! Except for debate research, I'd never studied anywhere near this much. I felt both intimidated and challenged for the months ahead. It turned out that two of my eight semesters I made the Dean's Honor Roll. I was excited about the insights I was gaining. I'm still grateful to the University YMCA. Without this Freshman Orientation Program I would never have survived as a student.

Staff members of the Campus Y told us about the facilities, program, and ministries they offered. The student lounge, I soon discovered, was a wonderful place just to sit and rest, or study, on my long days away from my Stadium Residence Hall. The Y was also a place where I could get my lunch. Some of the programs they offered were Bible Studies, a Forum Program for discussion of current world and campus issues, and interfaith dialogues. All of these programs turned out to be contributors to my emerging faith as I discovered many new horizons.

The Forum became just as important to my education as my formal classes. For instance, with the end of WW II and the discovery of Nazi death camps, Jewish Zionists mounted strong efforts for unlimited Jewish immigration to Palestine. Arabs became equally adamant in opposing this. In 1947, midst the confrontations and conflicts, the newly formed UN sent a Commission to the region to seek answers to "the Palestine problem." From this came the founding of the Jewish state of Israel, carved out of the area or nation known as Palestine. Eventually war erupted between the new Jewish nation and its Arab neighbors—the first of their many and continuing armed conflicts and episodes of terrorism.

The Forum featured a moderator and usually four faculty members and/or graduate students discussing the issue for the week. A flashback I have now is of various times when Arabs and Israelis at the same table would become so impassioned in their dialogues they would pound the table, shout at one another, or all talk at the same time much to the moderator's frustration. Even though the animosity rose to the point violence seemed imminent, there was never violence. Almost always the discussion ended with handshakes and goodwill between the participants.

I thought the most unique ministry of the YMCA was its ministry to the 2,000 international students on campus. Virtually every nation of the world was represented in the international student body. A number of the students were refugees. The campus YMCA, even more than the University, sought to relate to and support the international students in terms of their social, emotional, and spiritual lives. One dimension of this support was finding American students who would invite students into their home during university holidays. This helped them during an otherwise lonely time. Transoceanic telephoning was not yet easy, economical or commonplace for the ordinary person.

One of the international students whom I met through the YMCA was Nicholas "Nick" Goncharoff from the Ukraine in the Soviet Union. Nick was drafted into the Russian Army near the end of the War, and then captured by the German Army becoming a prisoner of war. Upon returning home after he was freed, Nick discovered his family had disappeared. He was now homeless. Through one of the international humanitarian programs for refugee resettlement, Nick ended up being brought to the United States and was given an opportunity to attend the University of Illinois.

One of my Christmas vacations I brought Nick home with me. He was bright and personable. Dad invited him to speak to his Sunday School Class on the Sunday after Christmas. Nick told his story to the class and also told of his friend, Alexander Janushevich, who was in the same boat except still back in the Soviet Union in a refugee camp. Nick asked the class if they would be willing to sponsor Alex to come to the United States. Eventually the class decided to do this.

Alex arrived in Hutchinson to spend 1949-51. My parents invited him to live with them. My sister Shirley was still a highschooler living at home so she, too, had a role in helping him learn about America and its schools and customs. Dad's Sunday School class provided the money for him to attend the Hutchinson Junior College. During the two years Alex made Hutchinson his home, he became acclimated to life in the United States, and got started at a beginning level in his higher education journey. On the limited number of occasions when I was home during this time, I enjoyed meeting and becoming a bit acquainted with Alex. When he moved on to complete university studies and graduate work in engineering, I exchanged Christmas cards with him for several years. My folks received Christmas cards and an occasional letter from Alex for many years. After he was married and had young children, he and his family paid a visit to Mom and Dad once or twice. He became successfully employed in Pennsylvania and New Jersey. The last address anyone in our family had for him was 279 Mountain Way, Morris Plain, New Jersey, which may have been his place of retirement.

Nick ended up living and working in Chicago. After Lorine and I married, we visited him once. He took us to his church, not surprisingly, a Russian Orthodox church. This was our first visit to an Orthodox Church and it was a strange new experience with its high liturgy, its two or three hour worship service with people coming and going, and all but the very elderly standing for worship. This was a continuation of the many new vistas of faith which I discovered as a result of my university days. Nick also took us to his apartment where he and his wife treated us to authentic Russian cuisine. Although I lost touch with Nick, I still carry a sense of satisfaction in having played at least some small role in helping him help Alex find "a refuge and a new life" in the United States.

Another discovery I made at the Y's Freshmen Orientation Camp was something I hadn't picked up in my home church—that the Methodist Church, and most major denominations, had campus pastors and facilities focusing on ministry for students. For Methodism, this was found in the Wesley Foundation. I decided to check out the Wesley Foundation and Trinity Methodist Church which were in the same building. I felt my parents might be pleased that I had visited a church by the name of Trinity, and I might find something meaningful to me at the Wesley Foundation. Little did I realize this was to become a faith changing, life changing experience for me!

When I visited the Wesley Foundation I made multiple discoveries:

- The building itself was modeled architecturally after a building in Oxford University where John Wesley studied;
- Sunday morning worship was a rather "high church" liturgy for Methodists and it's order, dignity, and beauty really appealed to me;
- The choir was outstanding not only in its anthems but in introits, responses and hymn leadership which made the worship moving and meaningful;

- The sermons of Dr. Paul Burt (who had been pastor here since 1928*) were both thought-provoking and dealt with the social issues of the day making them as relevant as any sermons I'd heard.

Overall, I discovered that worship could be more exciting and relevant than I had ever previously experienced.

A pair of special Sunday morning classes for students was offered by Wesley Foundation. One was led by Dr. Goodell (known as "Doc" Goodell to students), and one by Bob Trobaugh, a young pastor who was to become a good and life-long friend. Through a special arrangement between the University and the campus ministers certain courses offered by some of the foundations were known as "credit courses." This meant students could actually enroll in them through the university and receive university credit for them. This was something I always wanted to do but could never work into my schedule.

---

* Dr. Burt was the son of a Methodist Bishop who at one-time had been superintendent of the Methodist church in Italy. Dr. Burt was educated in Italy, England and the US; he was scholarly and spoke several languages; he taught at Wesleyan University in Connecticut, served as a WW I Navy Chaplain (and later became a pacifist), and traveled widely before coming to the U of I to succeed Dr. James C. Baker (later Bishop Baker), founder of the Wesley Foundation movement. With this rich background Dr. Burt was a person of great breadth and vision, strong in social conscience and personal commitment. He was reserved, yet always had a smile and a sense of humor. He was cultured, kind and considerate, but he could confront students with the assertion, "What you are going to be you are now becoming" and he could say, "There are many things that we do not know . . . about God. But there are things we *do know* about God . . . man . . . life and death . . . and the hereafter. What are we doing about them? Are we going to live according to the light we have?" No wonder Wesley Foundation was opening new vistas for me!

I did attend Doc Goodell's Sunday morning class. He was a very unusual person and a well trained minister with a PhD from Yale. He had served as a Methodist missionary in the Philippines. When he became deaf as a young missionary, he was forced to take an early departure from Asia. Learning to survive through lip reading, he came to Wesley Foundation to teach. He taught a stimulating Bible class which gave me a whole new insight into the Bible. Though I had not been taught this way growing up, I just assumed that the Bible was literally true in every detail. I did not realize that it was written in a particular social and historical context. Suddenly, through Doc Goodell (as well as Dr. Burt whose sermon spoke to the intellect as well as the heart and soul), I discovered the historical and social context in which the Bible was written. I came to realize *the meaning and message of scripture was not dependent on the* literal *truth of all the events which might be described or pictured in various passages.* Just as all visual art does not have to be a literal representation to express meaning and truth, so it is with the written story. A new faith with great depth of understanding and broader horizons, a faith that could not be shaken by doubt or questions or scholarship, was in the making for me.

I discovered at Wesley on Sunday evenings a Supper Club—a fellowship, a community of faith, a caring for one another, far deeper than anything I'd experienced in the Methodist Youth Fellowship of my youth. *Koinonia* is the Greek New Testament word for this. Each week it began with a gathering time where perhaps 150 of us visited with one another and there was a time for sharing concerns. Then we paused to sing the Wesleyan Grace (something I'd never heard before)—

> "Be present at our table Lord,
> be here, *and everywhere,* adored;
> these mercies bless, and grant
> that we might feast in fellowship
> with Thee."

Following grace, we enjoyed a light meal (something that was not offered on Sunday evenings in either the residence halls or fraternity and sorority houses). After we ate, there might follow any one of a number of things including programs featuring drama, music, film, dance, art, or discussions of the moral issues of the day. This routine became something I looked forward to each week.

A wonderfully young and creative staff and/or adjunct staff worked under the direction of Dr. Burt gave the primary leadership for the Foundations' Student Governing Council and for various Foundation activities. Beyond Sunday activities, Foundation ministries included:

> Wednesday vespers;

> Service activities and work parties directed toward the Trinity Church, the community, and the church at large; packaging boxes of overseas relief supplies, etc.;

> Friday night student parties;

> Married student programs/special activities for graduate students;

> Outreach ministries of many kinds. Students from Wesley provided worship in three rural churches served by the Rev. Glenn Gothard as an extension and laboratory program for the strengthening of students in their faith; and/or sending to other churches upon request various Sunday morning or Sunday evening ministry teams to provide worship, lessons, music, youth events, dramatic productions;

> An annual leadership training retreat for student officers;

An annual Between-the-Semesters Mission Work
Team;

Activities of the U of I Interfaith Council.

I became a sampler of most of these ministries and a regular
participant in several. I discovered new ways of understanding and
living out my faith. I remember going to Chicago my sophomore
year on the Between-Semesters Mission Work Team. This was the
first time that I ever participated in a mission work team. We worked
in the Chicago slums. My assignment was to help paint the kitchen
of an elderly blind black woman who lived alone and could barely
survive on her own. I also helped clean out her flower bed. Her
house was very run down, yet she took a great deal of pride in
being able to live independently. She was gracious and warm toward
the two of us who spent our week-end as her volunteer helpers.
She couldn't stop expressing her thanks to us. This was my first
visit to Chicago, and it was also my first experience in a large slum
or neighborhood of blight. The experience made me much more
sensitive to persons living with handicaps, living in poverty, living
in a segregated culture and it made me much more socially
concerned than I had ever been. Putting faith into action to express
God's love and to help others became very important to me.

Until the University of Illinois I had never met a religious pacifist
or a conscientious objector to war. Through the activities at Wesley
and in the Interfaith Council I came to encounter a number of
pacifists. Meeting and dialoging with them challenged my
culturally-given automatic acceptance of the legitimacy of war.
At first pacifism jolted my way of thinking. With the passage
of time and continued Bible study I began to understand how
their viewpoint could legitimately flow out of the life and
teachings of Christ.

I've often said through the Wesley Foundation I ceased to have
what might be called "an inherited faith" and I developed "a faith
of my own." As my faith evolved, I became very appreciative toward

the staff at the YMCA and at the Wesley Foundation. They were leaders, mentors, companions with me on my spiritual journey. I began to think, "maybe I could do something similar for others. Perhaps I should be an ordained minister." I remembered that sermon of Dr. Alvin Murray back in Hutchinson when I was a high schooler.

As I began struggling with my sense of vocation, I shared this with my mother one vacation while I was visiting back home. When I told her I was beginning to sense a call to ministry, I was startled to hear her shocked reply: "Oh no! Why in the world would you want to do this?" She didn't understand, approve of or support this vocational struggle into which I was entering. This really puzzled me because she was very faithful in worship and in the women's society of our local church. Years later Mom became very proud of me as a minister, but at the time her reaction caused me to think about the difference between religion on the surface of one's life and religion in the depths of one's being. It caused me to realize that there was a price for standing up for one's convictions.

Through the Wesley Foundation I became connected to the Methodist Student Movement at both the state and national levels. During either my first or second Christmas break, the National Methodist Student Movement held its Quadrennial Conference at the U of I. I returned to campus immediately after Christmas Day in order to serve as a student "go-for" or helper for the national leaders who had come to campus to resource this conference. These leaders greatly impressed me by the way they related to all students with openness, patience, gentleness, challenge and support. In particular, Heil Bollinger, senior leader of campus ministries from the General Board of Higher Education, showed special interest in understanding of and support for me. I was deeply touched by him.

In this event I experienced a gathering of 2,000 students from most every college campus in the country. The conference worship was more creative, exciting, artistic, challenging, and relevant than any worship I had previously experienced. The speakers were mind stretching. My life was transformed.

Chapter 27

MIDSHIPMAN TRAINING

The "price tag"—the commitment I made—for my NROTC scholarship included taking one required Naval Science course each semester. The courses I remember were: Introduction to Naval Science; Sea Power and Maritime Affairs; Naval Ship (weapon) Systems; Naval Engineering; Navigation and Naval Operations One and Two; Naval Leadership, etc. The "price" of my scholarship also included spending each of the three summers between my four years of college on midshipmen training cruises—a requirement that I found very interesting.

A midshipman is a student naval officer. These cruises really introduced one to life aboard various ships and various other forms of naval service. I especially remember my first summer's (1948) cruise. It was aboard a west coast battleship—the U.S.S. Missouri, a battleship which had figured prominently in WW II and upon which General Douglas MacArthur had received the Japanese surrender documents September 2, 1945. We boarded ship in San Francisco and almost immediately put out to sea headed for Seattle. As Midshipmen, we were organized into our own battalion; the battalion in turn was organized into a number of companies. Basically this was a freshmen cruise on which midshipmen from advanced classes served as battalion and company officers. Duties of midshipmen officers included such things as: holding morning muster; giving out daily assignments and schedules; supervising midshipmen on such tasks as "policing up" their areas (picking up trash, emptying the trash or GI cans as we called them etc.); swabbing the decks each day, and generally serving as an example and an authority figure for the midshipmen. Because the number of midshipmen dropped so quickly at the close of World War II, our program was in the midst of being redesigned. There were not enough upper-class midshipmen to fill all the "midshipman officer" ranks on this cruise. Accompanying us on this cruise was Lt. Commander Fitzgerald, USN, from our own University of Illinois Midshipman Unit. Lt. Cdr. Fitzgerald drew me aside within hours after we boarded ship, told me about the shortage of midshipmen officers and assigned me to become a "Lieutenant" for one of the midshipmen companies.

As we passed under the Golden Gate Bridge heading out to sea for Seattle, the waters suddenly became very choppy. Battleships are among the largest of Navy ships and usually very stable at sea. However, storms and just plain turbulent waters could still create some rolling and pitching of even the biggest ship. This day the choppiness of the sea created a mild to moderate rocking and rolling motion. I had never been to sea before and had not anticipated the turbulence. Moreover as a youngster I had often been bothered by motion sickness when we traveled. Suddenly I found myself getting very queasy, even to the point of fighting to keep my self from becoming nauseated. I soon realized I would feel better if, instead of staying below deck, I went topside where I could breathe fresh air and see the horizon. Even this didn't alleviate all my queasiness and I still hadn't gotten my sea legs. With all the midshipmen aboard ship in addition to its normally large company of sailors, we had a number of GI cans tied down at various places around the deck. Wanting to avoid standing too close to the rail, I soon propped myself up with one of the GI cans. About then a midshipman from my company, not looking too well himself, came up to me, his company Lieutenant, asking "How do you cope with seasickness?" Just then the heaves hit me so hard that I could no longer contain them. I stood up, turned around, lifted off the lid of the GI can, and puked! Since I was the one who was to be an authority and set an example, embarrassing as it was to me, this seasick midshipman had his answer as to what to do with seasickness. Fortunately, it didn't take me too long to develop both my sea legs and an attitude that would keep me from again becoming seasick.

None of our port visits lasted more than two or three days but I enjoyed every city where we put into port—Seattle, Honolulu, San Diego, Long Beach and finally San Francisco again. Whenever I got shore leave, I used it as would any tourist—to see the sights, the main features and famous places located in that city. A special training event in Hawaii was submarine orientation including a day's cruise on a sub and a dive. This was exciting and also very claustrophobic.

University of Illinois Midshipman buddies
Left to right: Dave Schmulbach, Doug Gregory, Harold Kieler

The summer of 1949 took me to Pensacola, Florida, and to Charleston, South Carolina. Pensacola Naval Air Station was the site of orientation in naval aviation. Midshipmen had one of two choices if they were interested in naval aviation. One choice (soon to be phased out for future classes) was to leave the NOTC program half-way through it and go directly to flight training. The other choice was to opt for pilot training upon graduation and following that training become a Navy pilot.

I had two special U of I Midshipman buddies—Dave Schmulbach from New Athens, Illinois and Doug Gregory of Brighton, Colorado. From the time we first met, Doug told me of his intent to elect the first choice for flight training in order to expedite his becoming a Navy pilot. Returning home from our first summer cruise, we rode the train together from San Francisco to Denver where I would change trains. His mother met him there and I had a chance to become acquainted with her a bit. She impressed me as the youngest, most vivacious, energetic mother I'd ever seen. Following our sophomore year, Doug left the unit for pilot training. When we were bidding each other farewell, Doug whipped a dollar bill out of his pocket, ripped it in two, gave me a half and said "Keep this. When we see each other again, we'll have a dollar we can use to have cokes together." Within the year, Doug was killed in a training crash. For years I kept my half of that dollar in my billfold in memory of Doug. I still have it, and with it I still have a regret—I never got in touch with his mother to express appreciation for her son and share my condolences. The next several times I was in Denver I tried to locate her, but to no avail. Now I suppose she is deceased.

Free time in Pensacola wasn't all that interesting. There just wasn't a lot to do in that town. The Fourth of July week-end turned out to be a four-day weekend. Several of us shared the cost, rented a car, and drove to New Orleans for the holiday. This was my first visit to that city famous for its French Quarter, its jazz, its chicory coffee and Creole cooking, etc. New Orleans certainly proved to be one of the highlights of my summer.

Following my Pensacola assignment I was on to Charleston for the second half of my summer training. At the Charleston Naval Base, I was assigned for three weeks aboard a navy mine layer—a small ship about the same size as a destroyer. Quarters are tight on a ship of this size. The Atlantic is a rougher ocean than either the Pacific Ocean or the Caribbean Sea. Tight quarters and rough seas combined don't make for comfortable cruising. Because of the smallness of these ships and of the Officers' Quarters, the midshipmen were all split up and spread around the whole fleet with only one or two of us assigned to each ship.

While stationed aboard the mine layer, I discovered something that I had not previously known. Officers, aboard ship, have their own "mess" (i.e. dining room, kitchen, and cooks) separate from that of the crew. They are in charge of their own mess. This means they can establish, within in limits, their own menus. They could even decide, and often did, to kick in a monthly allowance of money over and above their allotted funds for food in order to eat "higher on the hog" than otherwise. Officers on this particular ship had decided, among other things, that they would like to have steak and eggs for breakfast each morning! I'd never even heard of having steak and eggs for breakfast, but I soon got into the swing of things and enjoyed this habit so much that, on rare occasions, through the years, when I want to really splurge and treat myself or others, I still have steak and eggs for breakfast. Whenever this happens, I go back in my memories, of course, to my youthful days as a midshipman.

With its sleepy, rundown, atmosphere and its patterns of racial discrimination, I felt Charleston was not a progressive city. It was the most humid place I've ever visited in the summer. My memories of this assignment, at least of Charleston, aren't as pleasant as those of most cities I have visited. Of course, I did get introduced to some of the traditional culture of the deep south and enjoyed visiting some of the old plantation homes.

As the summer of 1950 arrived, it was back to the East Coast for Marine and amphibious training. The first took place in Quantico, Virginia, and the second, at Fort Bragg, North Carolina. Upon graduation we would have the opportunity to express our preference (from among a number of options) for our first duty assignment. Among these options would be serving in the Marine

Corp, technically a branch of the Navy, or to apply for duty on ships like troop transports and amphibious crafts. Quantico was a brief exposure to the Marines so we would have an understanding of how we might relate to the Corps. Fort Bragg was for our orientation into the transportation side of the navy. Here we were assigned to spend a few days on a troop transport along with doing an exercise in a landing craft.

On board our troop transport, we were assigned to a compartment where bunks were stacked five or seven-high. I don't know how many people a troop transport carries but it must be a thousand and more. With very little space between the bunks stacked so high, sleeping was difficult. There were others aboard ship beside midshipmen. Conditions were really crowded. The air was stale and the smells were foul. There was no sign of cultural refinement in this situation—no manners or verbal niceties between people. When we ate, we were in a mess facility with no chairs, tables at a height designed for eating standing up. We were to eat as quickly as we could and get out so others could come in to the mess and eat. I felt like we were a bunch of pigs being slopped. One day the stew was so tasteless I reached in front of the stranger next to me to get salt and pepper. Suddenly I felt a stab of pain. This fellow had literally and intentionally stabbed me with his fork.

"What in the hell are you doing?" I shouted out, as I saw drops of blood coming to the surface of my hand.

"What the hell are you doing? Didn't anyone ever teach you to say, 'Please pass the salt and pepper' instead of just reaching across another person? Don't ever reach in front of me again!"

With conditions like these, I quickly decided I'd never want be on a troop transport whether as a naval officer or a soldier.

For amphibious assaults by the army, as well as by the marines, it is always the navy that provides the transportation. Landing craft, which is what amphibious vessels were called, are medium sized flat bottomed boats (a boat is a vessel small enough that it can be carried on a ship) designed to carry motorized vehicles like trucks, tanks, and jeeps as well as a number of infantry personnel.

They are launched from a ship a few hundred yards off the coast and then head for the beach. When they grounded themselves, the front end ramp of the landing craft would be lowered, becoming sort of a draw bridge over which the vehicles and infantrymen moved ashore. Flat bottomed boats really rock and roll. I never thrilled to the idea of serving in the amphibious branch of the navy any more than on a troop transport.

Two memorable events from the summer of 1950 loom large in my mind—one a very joyous occasion, the other a somber event truly of historic significance. We cruised on a troop transport ship from the Virginia and Carolina areas to New York City for the Fourth of July weekend. This was my first visit to New York. One's first visit to New York is always memorable simply because it's such a famous city—so gigantic, so full of tall buildings and historic places, things you've always heard about all your life. We had only two or three days but this was enough to do a sight-seeing tour, get a smattering of New York history, and take-in a Broadway Musical. It is the latter that provides me with a sense of joy when I recall it. These were the days of many outstanding Broadway musicals a number of which were composed by Richard Rodgers and Oscar Hammerstein. The original production of one of these, "South Pacific", with its full original cast was still running on Broadway. On the spur of the moment all I could purchase for it was a "standing room only" ticket. I just had to see a Broadway musical while I was in "the Big Apple" so I jumped for the "South Pacific" ticket even if it was standing room only.

This was a Broadway adaptation of James A. Michener's Pulitzer Prize-Winning book *Tales of the South Pacific* based on action that takes place on two South Pacific islands during World War II. It opened April 7, 1949, in the Majestic Theater which is where I saw it. I got to hear Mary Martin who was famous as the lead female vocalist and Ezio Pinza who was male lead. Along with the fabulous choreography, and the outstanding songs and soloists, the action focused on native islanders, U.S. sailors and marines. I, of course, could identify with the sailors. Some of the outstanding songs were "A Cockeyed Optimist," "Some Enchanted Evening,"

"Bali Ha'i," "I'm Gonna Wash That Man Right Out-a My Hair," "I'm in Love With a Wonderful Guy," "Younger than Springtime," "Happy Talk," "Carefully Taught," and "This Nearly Was Mine." Some were fun, some were romantic, and I especially found "Carefully Taught" meaningful because of what it says about human nature:

> "You've got to be taught to hate and fear,
> You've got to be taught from year to year,
> It's got to be drummed in your dear little ear.
> You've got to be carefully taught.
>
> You've got to be taught to be afraid of people
> Whose eyes are oddly made,
> And people whose skin is a diff'rent shade.
> You've got to be carefully taught.
>
> You've got to be taught before it's too late
> Before you are six or seven or eight,
> To hate all the people your relatives hate.
> You've got to be carefully taught!"

For me, this song was a marriage of my Christian faith and the arts. It was at one and the same time delightful and filled with insight and meaning. All in all, my three summers of midshipman training were filled with great and growing experiences.

CHAPTER 28

A NEW WAR

"Unfortunately, it is not practical for great nations to
renounce the use of force. There is evil in the world
and sometimes war seems the only remedy.
Perhaps we can cool the rhetoric and count the cost
more fully before we go to war.
We can work to establish an international mechanism
to fight terrorism and tyranny with law rather than war."

A reader's editorial from The Wichita Eagle, November2003
by Glenn W. Fisher author of a recently published war memoirs,
Not to Reason Why: The Story of a One-Eyed Infantryman in WW II.

Although "South Pacific" still lingers as a truly joyful memory
from the summer of 1950, a less joyful but historically more
significant memory remains from the days prior to my New York
visit that summer. Since early in the 20th Century, Japan had
been subjecting Korea to harsh colonial rule. When Japan lost
World War II, Korea became a pawn of the allies. At the Potsdam
Conference in July of 1945, it was stipulated that Japanese forces
in Korea should surrender to the United States if they were South
of the 38th Parallel and to the Soviet Union if they were North of

38th Parallel. Quickly after the end of the war, the Soviets poured 200,000 troops into North Korea to "accept" the surrendering Japanese. Before U. S. troops arrived in the south the Soviets sealed off their zone to make it a "communist" zone. The Cold War face-off had begun in Korea. United States attempted to have the United Nations supervise elections for a unified Korea, but to no avail. The UN did conduct elections in South Korea after which (in 1949) American forces withdrew from the South.

During my last summer of Midshipman Training, on June 25, 1950, the Soviet equipped and trained North Korean Army invaded South Korea sweeping south very rapidly. Immediately the UN Security Council convened an emergency meeting which called on United Nations members to come to the aid of South Korea in defending itself. Without delay, President Truman ordered our army and navy to join in the first ever UN police action. Nineteen other nations joined this police action and the Korean War, an undeclared war for us, began in earnest. The Korean War would last for three years until July 1953. Upon my return to campus for the fall semester of my senior year, all of us who were graduating Midshipmen received this notification:

> "As you begin your obligatory two years of active duty June 1, 1951, your tour of active duty will be extended to a third year. This makes the first year of your required three year Inactive Reserve duty a "call-up" or active duty year."

My teen years were in a world which experienced the horrors of totalitarian rule in Germany and Japan with all its deceit, injustice, and the inhumanity of the holocaust. Now the world's population was exploding. Nations were becoming interdependent to a degree never before known. I had become a firm believer that we needed the United Nations, needed international law and some form of an international (UN) police force even if this should be counterbalanced with nations maintaining a degree of their own sovereignty.

The more I had seen the working of the Methodist Peace Commission and the American Friends Service Committee, the more I met and dialogued with pacifists during my time at the U of I, the more I had questioned whether war is ever justified—whether the ends could justify the means. During my sophomore and junior years, I experienced a great inner struggle over whether I was being called by God to become a pacifist. For a time I became a part of the Fellowship of Reconciliation—a pacifist organization believing that war only breeds more war rather than ending or prevent it.

As I read and studied various theologians I came to realize that in an imperfect world there is no such thing as a perfect or pure moral decision. In the end I came to believe that what was really morally wrong was to just go along with war simply because one's government said to. Popular support or mass hysteria was no justification for war. I came to believe that just as there are those who are conscientious objectors to war, so one should be a participant in war *only* if led by his or her conscience to believe the war was necessary and just. I coined and used the phrase "conscientious participant." I felt the ultimate loyalty in life was not to one's country or countrymen but to God as I had seen God revealed in Jesus.

I knew the totalitarianism and horrors of World War II would have led me to be a "conscientious participant" had I faced that choice. But, had the war not been a "just war" in my thinking, or if my country had been unilaterally engaging in it, I was sure I would have been a conscientious objector. It was this way of thinking which led me to continue on with my NROTC training after I began questioning whether my service in the navy was morally justified.

Now here in my senior year, I was faced not simply with "another" war in the endless chain of humanities' wars. This was A NEW WAR in the sense of being a different war. It was a war where a "council of the nations" (e.g., the UN Security Council) had met and concluded that nations needed to come to the defense of South Korea against an aggressor. True, war often generates more problems than it solves. I could not be happy about the loss of human life and the suffering. But I felt I should be a "conscientious participant." In the end I was truly proud to be participating in an action on behalf of one nation at the request of the United Nations.

Ironically, at the moment I am writing this, United States is once again engaged in a war which is a very controversial war—the 2003 war against Iraq. It seems to me what I struggled with as a student, in considering the morality of war and my personal participation in it, might well be informative to a young person today or for my descendants some time in the distant future.

As I entered my last semester of NROTC training and moved toward graduation and commissioning as an Ensign in the USN Reserve, I was given the chance (no guarantee it would be honored) to express where I would like to serve. Did I want the submarine service? Naval aviation? The marines? The amphibian forces? A mainline fighting ship? None of these really appeal to me. I had no intention of making the Navy career. I had increasingly been sensing a call to ordained ministry. What really appealed to me was a ship assignment where, in my imagination, there was a quiet non-demanding type of duty which left me with lots of time for myself—for reading and contemplation—just to work on whether I should really become a United Methodist pastor.

Somehow I decided that serving on a fleet tanker which shuttled crude oil from the Persian Gulf to our west coast would be such an assignment. There would be long periods at sea, no place to go, nothing to distract me during non-duty hours. I'd really have the time I was seeking. I submitted this request. When my orders to active duty (dated 2 May 1951) came from the Bureau of Naval Personnel, I got basically what I asked for, but not what I fantasized. I was assigned to tanker duty—to the USS Cacapon (AO 52), a tanker or Auxiliary Oilier (AO). It was named after a river in West Virginia (all Navy tankers were named after rivers which had Indian—Native American—names). My tanker was located with the 7th Fleet off the coast of Korea.

The Author was commissioned as a USNR Ensign (effective 1 June 1951). He was later promoted to a Lieutenant (jg). The breast pocket bar was made up of three short bars recognizing service during the Korean War and with United Nations Forces.

The Author served on this ship during
his sea time in the US Navy.

I was a line officer (in contrast to an engineering officer whose
responsibilities would be overseeing the engineering department—
engines, pumps, mechanical operations, etc.). I had two main areas
of responsibilities. The most demanding was serving as "officer of
the deck" four-hours out of every 12-hour period when we were
underway. An officer of the deck (or day) serves on the bridge.
Once a week we rotated watches so in the course of three weeks I
would take turn on watches. First watch was 8 a.m. to 12 noon
and 8 p.m. to midnight; second watch was 12 noon to 4 p.m. and
midnight to 4 a.m.; third watch was 4 p.m. to 8 p.m. and 4 a.m.
to 8 a.m. The Captain was always the commanding officer who
always had the final responsibility for everything at all times. The
Commander was always the Captain's assistant, next in command
to him. Whoever was on duty on the bridge at any given time
acted as the officer in charge for daily and routine decisions, made
first responses to emergency situations, carried out the Captain's
and Navigator's orders, and gave orders to both the helmsman and

engine room in matters of steering and maneuvering the ship and adjusting its speed.

My other area of responsibility was as Gunnery Officer. Ours was not a fighting ship. As a supply vessel, gunnery was not a major thing, but we had to have some defensive capability in case we were attack. We did carry some guns. Our largest gun was on the fantail or stern of the ship and was a 6" (?) gun (meaning that the diameter of the shells it would shoot was 6 inches). We had other 4" guns, two on each side, one forward and one toward the rear. We also had 4 small stationary machine guns. The larger guns were for defense against surface attack. The machine guns were for defense against enemy aircraft. All this weaponry became obsolete before the end of the 20th Century. I'm not sure tankers carry any guns today. We had gunnery drills about once a quarter, but we were never under direct or close attack. We were close enough to Korea at times to hear the firing of large weapons.

Our job was to shuttle back and forth between Sasebo, Japan, and the 7th Fleet in the Sea of Japan. If I recall correctly, when fully loaded we carried 20,000 or 30,000 barrels of aviation gasoline up forward and 100,000 barrels of fuel oil in the rest of the ship. We loaded up in Sasebo; headed into the Sea of Japan rendezvousing with aircraft carriers when they needed gasoline for their planes and with any ships (carriers, battleships, cruisers, destroyers, minesweepers, hospital ships, etc.) when they needed re-fueling.

We refueled ships while underway at sea, traveling about 10 knots/hour parallel with each other. As a ship came along side, we shot a light line to the other ship, which line in turn dragged a heavier line over to it. The heavier line was used to drag a heavy duty hose, 4" in diameter, from our ship to theirs. The hose would then be lifted and held out of the water by use of a high boom on each ship. When the hose was connected up, we were ready to begin pumping fuel oil or aviation gasoline. On occasions we might fuel an aircraft carrier with two lines at a time—one forward refueling with gasoline, one aft refueling with diesel oil. On rare occasions, when time was urgent, we had a ship on each side of us so we could refuel two at once.

Destroyer refueling alongside the USS Cacapon

Not only did we refuel ships of the U. S. 7th Fleet off the coast of Korea, but we refueled ships of all the other countries participating in this UN "police action." It was not uncommon for us to look over at the ship we were refueling and see a Dutch, British, Canadian, or New Zealand flag or the flag of one of the other participating UN members. As I saw those flags, I always had a sense of pride.

Operating at sea we faced three basic dangers—collision, storms, and mines. Keeping our ships on a steady course while refueling, especially when seas were rough, was always a challenge. Any number of factors—the winds, waves, helmsmen steering errors or faulty judgment by the Officer of the Deck on either of our two ships, and the slowness of heavily loaded ships to respond to course corrections—could combine to bring us perilously close together or to pull us apart to the point our hoses would break. Normally our parallel courses would keep our ships about 50 to 75 feet apart. If we were pulled apart too suddenly and a hose broke the result would be spilled fuel oil or the spewing of raw gasoline on the deck or in the sea until its flow could be cut off. Power wenches were used to handle the lines which held the hoses. The personnel manning these wenches had to be constantly vigilant, constantly working to take up slack or let out more line as called by the motions created through the constant changing of circumstances. When refueling operations were underway, as officer of the deck, instead of remaining inside the bridge, I would move out on the wing nearest the ship being refueled. This way I could monitor the situation more closely and quickly shout course corrections back inside to the helmsman.

Ships might be drawn frighteningly close to one another only, at the last moment before what seemed to be impending collision, to have a space open up between us again. During my two years the Cacapon things went awry only one time—one time too often. Fortunately, I wasn't the one on duty at the time. Rough seas and a combination of other factors conspired to create a collision with a huge aircraft carrier which was towering over us. It wasn't a collision where one ship rammed another, but one where we sideswiped each other. Our refueling rigs were torn apart. Elements of our superstructure, railings, and one of our guns were ripped off and some upper steel siding was damaged. Fortunately there was no loss of life, no injuries, and no damage which would cause us to take-on water. Damage was extensive enough, however, that we were sent back to the States to the Naval Shipyard at Vallejo, California, in the San Francisco Bay for repairs. It was about three months before we got back to Japan.

My scariest moment happened one night. We were in a convoy. It was pitch black so we were operating without any visual sightings. We were totally dependent on radar. I was on the bridge, on duty as the Officer of the Deck. I would put my forehead to the hood of the radar and peer at the screen. The hood blocked out any artificial light, so it allowed little white blips to show up where each ship in the convoy was located.

We came to the time when the convoy was to make a 75 degree turn to the starboard. One after another, I saw the blips reflecting the maneuver. The big difficulty came with determining the moment to change course. It took our heavily loaded ship some minutes to react to the helmsman's course change. Timing when to give the command became a judgment call. If I waited too long to give the command, by the time we made our course change we would be completely out of line with the other ships. We would have moved past the direction of our new course. The danger came from reacting to the situation too quickly. If I were really premature in giving the command, we'd end up out of line only on the opposite side of our column of ships. If I were just somewhat premature, it was like taking a short-cut. We could catch up with the ship ahead while they were still maneuvering and our bow might collide into their starboard side. I needed to be precise.

On this occasion I was premature. Suddenly I realized what I'd done. Our blips were approaching each other. We were on a collision course! I immediately gave a command for a small course correction. Nothing happened. The ship's reaction was too slow. I gave another command. Still it looked on the screen as if we were in peril. I stepped out on the port wing and peered through the darkness to determine if I could see anything. Suddenly I saw a dim outline of the ship ahead. The gap between was narrowing. We were on a collision course. I returned quickly to the wheel house and gave the command for a hard right and a reduction in speed. I couldn't slow too much because of the ship behind us. Eventually things evened out. We were just a little out of place in the convoy, but by this time my heart was pounding and my palms were sweaty.

On a clear day when on duty without much happening on the bridge I would intermittently spend time, between other duties, using the binoculars and a telescope to study the mountains and shoreline of North Korea. We were never as close to land as the fighting ships and never in danger of direct attack. The one related danger that we constantly face was that of mines. The North

Koreans had mined the waters off their coast attempting to prevent attacks or landings. UN mine sweepers worked diligently to clear the waters of these mines but it was always possible for them to miss mines. Thus, there was always the possibility of a loose mine drifting into our path. A tanker loaded with aviation gasoline and fuel oil hitting a mine would become an instant fireball. Consequently, we always kept lookouts posted to scan the waters ahead. On one occasion a mine was spotted ahead, just to our starboard. Leaving a respectable distance between us and the mine we used our forward machine gun to open fire on it, exploding it so that it could no longer endanger us or any other ship. This was the only moment during my personal military service that I thought about how close to death we were.

Storms made deep impressions on me. One time as we cruised the Pacific returning to the Far East from our state-side repairs in dry-dock we were plowing the ocean. For a number of days there was an ethos of quiet and powerful beauty—the sun shining by day, the moon shining by night; ocean currents flowing; the wind blowing—sometimes gently, sometimes in strong gusts, occasionally as a strong gale. A relentless rhythm of sea-swells began building up hills of water like the Kansas Flinthills, each followed by valleys dug in the ocean. Overhead white clouds were billowing, playing hide-and-go-seek with sun and moon. Around us by day the waters were changing from bright blue to green to gray and back again. The sea varied from calm to tumultuous and all the way in-between.

One afternoon a storm began to brew. In the Western Hemisphere giant powerful destructive storms with winds over 75 miles per hour are called hurricanes. In the Eastern Hemisphere, especially the Western Pacific, the same storm is known as a typhoon. This was the beginning of a typhoon. It lasted several days. We did our best to stay out of its path but we could not escape it altogether. Giant shifting swells became like mountains. Our ship rose up until it seemed like we were climbing the mountain at a 45 degree angle. Suddenly we would reach the summit. The mountain would drop out from underneath us and we would plunge downward into the valley, into the ocean. We could barely stay on our feet or in a chair. We dared not venture out on deck unless it was absolutely necessary. Our bow would vanish under water. At times water roared over half the length of our ship. Foam and spray covered everything. Water poured over us, then off us, again and again, pummeling us with force beyond description, violently shaking ship and soul. Up and down, up and down, up and down we ceaselessly moved. I still feel the unspeakable sense of awe and sheer power that I experienced—awe and power greater than anything I have personally known before or since—awe and power that belong to nature, to creation, and to nature's God.

Fortunately our ship was skillfully constructed of steel. We had "battened down the hatches." We suffered no serious damage or injury to crew members, but when the storm suddenly ended and things grew quiet again, I was grateful. It was a great relief. This experience remains with all of its emotion, in my mind and feelings as a vivid picture. A favorite hymn of mine is popularly known as *The Navy Hymn.* Written by William Whiting in the Nineteenth Century, its words are:

> "Eternal Father, strong to save,
> Whose arm hath bound the restless wave,
> Who bidd'est the mighty ocean deep
> Its own appointed limits keep;
> O hear us when we cry to Thee
> For those in peril on the sea.

> "O Christ, whose voice the waters heard,
> And hushed their raging at Thy word,
> Who walkedst on the foaming deep,
> And calm amid the storm didst sleep;
> O hear us when we cry to Thee,
> For those imperil on the sea.

"O Holy Spirit, who didst brood
Upon the waters dark and rude,
And bid their angry tumult cease,
And give, for wild confusion, peace;
O hear us when we cry to Thee
For those in peril on the sea.

"O Trinity of love and power,
Our brethren shield in danger's hour;
From rock and tempest, fire and foe,
Protect them where-so-e'er they go:
Thus evermore shall rise to Thee
Glad hymns of praise from land and sea."

These words seem a bit archaic today. The hymn is not sung as often as it used to be. But whenever I hear it or sing it, I still feel it to the depths of my being and with new appreciation ever since my typhoon experience.

It should be obvious. I had a very good time of things during the Korean War in comparison with the Marines and Army infantrymen, the Naval Aviators and Air Force pilots. They fought for three years exposed to almost constant combat and months of freezing weather with Siberian wind-whipped blizzards. We had hundreds of thousands of U.S. service personnel in Korea. The war ended with an uneasy truce. North Korea, even to this day, is still a threat to global peace. 37,000 Americans and countless thousands of others died in Korea. There were 8,100 MIAs—Missing in Action—in the Korean War.

Several years ago, Lorine and I visited Washington D.C. and the newly belatedly created Korean War Memorial. It was a moving experience for me as one who only experienced a bit of that war. Every time anyone visits a war memorial or a military cemetery, they need to realize these are sacred places. Each name represents a real person, some ones friend or relative.

For some reason, war seems like an exciting adventure to men. I'm convinced we Americans too often glorify war. We jump quickly on patriotic bandwagons to promote new wars when our nation is endangered or offended by other nations. Too many Americans view war like they view a spectator sport. We need to learn to fathom the depths of hell which war is, even the so-called "just war," for all participants, for both sides. We must learn the costs of war. And, we must find within ourselves and our nation, ways to join others in establishing international law, nurturing those things which make for peace, justice, and the qualities of physical, mental, and spiritual well-being for all persons—qualities which engender peace and compassion, not envy, hate or anger among peoples. I would affirm the faith which says "there are no outsiders in God's family." We must not think of people as "us" and "them." Any evil diminishes all of us. And any act of compassion, any reconciling gesture of human hospitality uplifts and unifies all of us.

Chapter 29

THE CALL

Prayer for Healing and Intercession

Lord, we can feel pretty overwhelmed as we become more aware of problems and pain around us. We are tempted to run and hide.

But you call us to a different response.
You call us to be grounded in love, not fear.
You call us to be compassionate, not judgmental.
You call us to commitment, not criticism.
You call us to a life of faith, not fear.

Strengthen us, Lord, with your love.
Change our fear to faith.
Open our eyes, our hearts, our spirits
So that we can move beyond fear to love.
Help us to be healers . . . .
In Jesus' name, Amen

(Prayer by Mary Jo Grant)

Ordained ministers are often asked about their "call" to the ministry—when? where?, how did it occur? My answer to these questions is that for me, my call didn't occur in a single moment, at a single place, or in a single or dramatic way. My call to become an ordained minister happened in a process of personal growth and spiritual development through which I understood God to be working. I've already essentially described most of the process though there are stages of the process yet to be described. The process was like links hooked together in a chain.

The first stage of the process, the first link, in my call to the ministry began in my being reared in a Christian family and in a church atmosphere. This created within me the affirmation that I was a child of God—we are all children of God.

The second stage in the process, the second link, in my call to ordained ministry was the seed planted in that sermon preached by Dr. Alvin Murray. It was the question, "Should I consider becoming a Methodist Minister?"

Every facet of the campus ministry which I experienced at the University of Illinois combined to nurture, develop and lead me into a larger higher vision of life. Intellectually, I began to think of scientific and social evolution as a process of creation by which God made the world and human functioning. I didn't think of evolution as some automatic or inevitable process of progress. I thought of it as a means of grace by which God functioned. The moral struggle through which I passed as I debated with myself "Should I continue to pursue a short-term military career or become a conscientious objector?" became in itself a time of real spiritual growth for me. Both my intellectual growth and my moral struggle, led me to start asking in a deeper way than previously, "What should I do with my life?" "What is meant by the term Christian vocation'?" Intellectual growth, moral struggle, and a quest for a sense of vocation, became the third link in the chain that was leading me to a call to ordained ministry.

I used prayer, Bible study, and dialogue with various campus pastors as tools in my quest for a sense of vocation. I developed a new understanding of ministry. Ministry wasn't just preaching. Maybe it wasn't preaching at all. Christian vocation was something which says "in all our interpersonal relationships serve others as

Christ serves you—serve in the spirit of Christ. This is *something to which every Christian is called.*" We're not called to make a living but to make a life; we are not just to go and find a job, but in whatever we do with our life we do it as a form of ministry.

This stage in the process of my developing call was the fourth link in its chain. It was a very intentional decision that as a lay person I would SAY YES TO GOD WITH MY LIFE. I had enrolled in the College of Commerce. Within the majors or career choices offered there, I chose to major in Public Affairs with a technical specialty in Labor-Management Relations because, at that moment, I felt this would give me the greatest opportunity to "apply" my Christian faith to the society in which I lived.

I began feeling a wholeness in my life. I became grateful for what I felt God was doing in and through in my life. I was grateful for the supportive role of the campus ministers in my life. I began coming to a new conclusion. This was the fifth stage, the fifth link, in my call. I should be focusing on a vocation *within* the church. Maybe I could use my major as a lay person working for the Methodist Church in its own personnel relations. Maybe I could find a staff position in our Methodist Board of Church and Society to help the church address issues related to Labor-Management Relations or other social issues of the day. I said YES to this stage in the process of struggling with my career-to-be.

Again, one decision led to another. Perhaps Alvin Murray's seed was growing in me. Perhaps it was the seeds planted by the life and teachings of Wesley Foundation Staff. At any rate, I found myself asking, "If I'm thinking about employment within the church, wouldn't it be better if I were an Ordained Minister? And, campus ministers have had such a life-transforming influence on me, shouldn't I be willing to 'be there' for some other student(s) in this same capacity?" This was the sixth step in my call.

One day I went into the office of Bob Trobaugh, one of the Wesley Foundation campus pastors, to jaw about this possibility. I had been chosen Student President of the Foundation. While I was there, I was asked to attend the Central Illinois Annual Conference of the Methodist Church for a day, and speak on behalf of the Wesley Foundation. That Annual Conference helped support the Foundation financially. Without their support campus ministry at the U of I couldn't exist. I'd never been to a session of any Annual Conference. While I was there I began to realize the funds they had to give in support of Wesley came from local churches. Some of these local churches didn't even know about, understand, or care about campus ministry.

As I left the Annual Conference that day, I left with another question. It seemed like questions were always guiding my personal spiritual growth. I was asking, "If I want to contribute in a significant way to serving others through specialized social action ministries, or campus ministries, why not serve where it all begins— at the grassroots level, in the local church, where people are introduced to Jesus and the Christian life?" This question became the seventh stage, the seventh link in the chain of events leading to my call.

By graduation time, I almost made this final decision relating to my call. But I was still just waiting and wondering. Would I really be able to fulfill the tasks of pastoral ministry? Then came those first orders which put me on the USS Cacapon in the Pacific as part of the Seventh Fleet in the Korean War. I discovered my ship, with a crew of less than 200 men, was too small to have a Chaplain assigned to it. There were no religious services held during the weeks at sea. Once again, questions began to form in mind. "As a lay person, couldn't I volunteer to lead worship when we were at sea?" "Wouldn't this be a good way to test my growing sense of call? If I could prepare services and preach on regular basis, if anyone responded, perhaps this was a sign that I could be— should be—an ordained minister."

I wondered what kind of training and/or credentialing might be available to me. In addition to faithfully seeking to fulfill my naval duties and enjoying the adventures and international sightseeing that came with being in the Navy, I set another major goal for myself. I would seek to be a lay chaplain. If I succeeded, I would go on to seminary and become a United Methodist pastor.

This plan of testing myself became the final step in my call—link number eight in the events leading to the culmination of my call.

On the way to the West Coast, where I was to report for transportation to my ship, I had time to see my family in Hutchinson. I took advantage of this opportunity to visit with my home church pastor about these things. He gave me both encouragement and direction. I could gain a measure of credentialing by seeking a Local Preacher's License through my District Superintendent and the Annual Conference Board of Ministry. The specific requirement was to take and pass a correspondence course of study for the license. This took a number of months since I was able to do my study and work on it while I was at sea.

On one of my many visits in and out of Sasebo, Japan I found a Navy Chaplain to use as an additional consultant. He wrote a letter of recommendation to our Captain, Commander A. D. Kilmartin, USN. I shared this letter with my Captain and visited with him about my proposal to serve as a Lay Chaplain. It was agreed that when we were at sea, I would hold weekly services.

All this was long before my seminary days. The only experience I had was from my Wesley Foundation days. I was green in this role—especially when some of the men began looking to me as a real chaplain and turned to me with some of their more serious problems. I think of the Chief Petty Officer who came to me for help after receiving a letter from his wife back in San Diego who told him she was leaving him. I felt rather embarrassed at my inexperience and incompetence. I hardly knew more than to utter a few platitudes and words of encouragement.

It was challenging and satisfying to prepare my Sunday messages which were kind of a cross between Bible studies and sermons. Attendance at Sunday services ranged from 6 to 12 crew members in the beginning. Services grew to the point where on a couple of major religious holidays we would have attendees numbering in the nineties. I had one crewman who asked to be baptized. I arranged for a Chaplain in Sasebo to do this next time we were in port.

Overall, things went well enough in this lay ministry that I felt I was definitely being led to become an ordained pastor. By the time I finished that tour of duty of nearly two years, I had held weekly services every Sunday we were at sea. This experience was successful and satisfying enough that I felt my "test" had confirmed and validated my call to the pastoral ministry.

Chapter 30

A NEW ASSIGNMENT

I was young, alone, and in a U. S. Naval officer's uniform. As I meandered around, gawking at the Great Buddha, a young Japanese man had no difficulty in identifying me as an American. Venturing up to me, in a very humble and polite fashion, he began a conversation.

"Pardon me. It looks like you are a tourist. Would you like to know more about what you're seeing?"

"Yes, I'd love to."

"I'm a university student studying English and economics. I'm also studying to get my license as a Tourist Guide. If you would allow me to practice my English with you, I would be happy to be your guide for today."

"Oh, that would be wonderful. I'd be happy to speak English with you if you would be so kind as to show me the sights of your city and tell me about them."

Not only did Eiichi Hiratsuka introduce himself to me. He introduced his country and culture. We became fast friends keeping in touch with each other from that day to the present. There in 1951, not only did Eiichi spend a day being my personal guide, he went on to spend several days! His English was good. He was very helpful. We toured Tokyo as well the area around it. He even invited me to his home one evening where I met his parents and enjoyed their hospitality.

As I came to their home that evening, I was invited as per Japanese custom to remove my shoes as I entered. I discovered they did not use chairs in their homes. Everyone sat cross-legged on the rice straw mat floors. I made my self at home following Eiichi's lead. When the time came for dinner, we were given a ceramic soup spoon and a pair of chop sticks. We were served a bowl of clear broth like soup. A delicious meal was then prepared by his mother right at table side. It featured sukiyaki—thinly sliced sirloin steak, vegetables(spinach and bean sprouts) and onions, bean threads (a kind of short Japanese spaghetti or clear rice noodle) with seasonings and soy sauce all fried together. A big bowl of rice to be eaten with the sukiyaki was served along with a beaten raw egg in a shallow bowl. I struggled with my chop sticks but try to follow the family's lead. We picked up the meat with our chop sticks, dipped it the egg mixture, and placed it in our mouth followed by a bite of rice. The basic meal was followed with a piece of fruit. What a great introduction to Japan!

My arrival aboard the USS Cacapon proved to be an interesting process. After graduation and commissioning at the U of I, followed by some days of leave spent at home in Kansas, it was on to San Francisco for an active duty medical exam. Passing the physical, I was put on a chartered Pan Am military flight from the continental U. S. A., via Honolulu, to the Yokosuka Naval Base for transfer to the Cacapon. In Yokosuka the Navy didn't know exactly where my ship was. When they figured it out, they weren't quite sure how to get me there. While they were trying to figure these things out, they put me up in the bachelor officer quarters. My instructions were: check in every morning at 8 a.m.; if we don't have orders for you, you're at liberty to leave the base and do what you want for the rest of the day. It took them a week to figure out what to do with me so July 30 through August 5 of 1951 I had a ball!

Street scene in Sasebo, Japan

This was my first experience being on the loose and alone in a foreign country. I wasn't completely sure about this, but I went out exploring. The first day I explored Yokosuka itself. Just across the peninsula from Yokosuka was Kamakura known as the site of the Great Buddha—a gigantic and world famous outdoor bronze sculpture. Having discovered that it wasn't too difficult to sightsee even though I didn't speak Japanese, the second day I was off to find the Great Buddha. Because Japan was still technically an occupied country, we didn't have to worry about their currency. We used a military script. Here's where I met Eiichi.

By the time the Yokosuka Fleet Activities Center decided what to do with me, I was addicted to international travel and had learned to thoroughly enjoy the adventures of being in the Navy. On August 5, they placed me on a train heading south where I was to report to the Commander of Fleet Activities in Sasebo. This was a great opportunity to see Japan's countryside. Upon arrival I again found myself awaiting transportation. For a couple of days I had a chance to begin exploring this port city where I would visit many times over the next 22 months.

Sasebo was not large enough to keep me thoroughly entertained all the time so I would frequently venture out into the country surrounding the city. Always I enjoyed the countryside's natural beauty, the small picturesque homes and verdant rice fields as well as the gentleness and kindness of these people who had once been enemies of my country.

On August 8, I boarded another Navy tanker (Auxiliary Oiler 24, the USS Platte) for transportation to the Cacapon (AO-25). Two days later we met up with my ship and I was transferred to it at sea. Now a transfer at sea is another *exciting* adventure to say the least. Mail was frequently transferred between ships, but it was not an everyday practice to transfer personnel. I've already described the process of one ship refueling another. A transfer at sea is quite similar except instead of sending across a refueling hose it sends a person on a heavy line stretched between two ships, hanging from a pulley, in a buoy "chair." Should the interaction of ships and wave part the line you'd not only be in the "drink" but you might even be dragged into the ship's wake and propeller. This may not have been the most risky activity of my life, but I'm sure it wasn't the least daring thing I've ever done! Finally on August 10th, 1951, I reported aboard the USS Cacapon for my first tour of duty as a Navy officer. In the months which followed, in the precious few days I had ashore, I saw as much of Japan, Formosa, and Hong Kong as possible.

During the 22 months I served on the USS Cacapon we had a pretty predictable routine.

We regularly had a rotation approximating 4 weeks which went like this: loading aviation gasoline and fuel oil, as well as mail and a few other miscellaneous items, for supplying other ships; steaming out to join the Navy's supply vessels off the coast of Korea; cruising, and being available as needed for refueling operations until we had transferred all our cargo and were empty; returning to Sasebo for reloading, re-supplying and shore leave; and then, starting the routine over again.

Once a quarter we varied the routine by going to supply a small U. S. naval contingent in what was then known as Taipei, Formosa, now known as Taipei, Taiwan, the island-nation which remained as Free China after the take-over of the rest of China by the Chinese Communists.

Once a year we continued from Formosa to Hong Kong (then a British free port on the Southern Coast of Mainland China and now returned to the People's Republic of China) for 4 days of shore leave.

In Formosa we were entertained by Chinese military officers. Many of them were from mainland China. Sometimes we played pickup basketball. In the process I made my first discoveries about China learning that in some provinces people were very tall while in other provinces they were quite short. I learned that most provinces of China spoke different dialects. These officers took us on a couple of very interesting tours. One was a wild boar hunt. Another was a visit to see Aboriginal peoples—peoples whom I didn't even know still existed.

In Hong Kong I found a thriving modern city like many of the large cities of the Western World. It was a British Colony intertwined with Chinese culture. When we ferried from the Victoria "borough" (or however they designated it) on the Island of Hong Kong to the mainland "borough" of Kowloon we got much closer culturally to the "real" China as well as to Communist China. We were told when visiting Kowloon we were not to buy goods originating from Communist China. Shops and flee markets, of course, were full of fascinating goods. Many of these were old and came from various provinces of Southern China. Some of us couldn't resist certain art objects or other good buys even it they were "off limits." Friends and family who have been in my home know that I enjoy a beautiful old mahogany tray inlaid with mother-of-pearl. This is one of those art objects acquired in Hong Kong.

Those who have been entertained for a meal in our home may have been served on Noritake China (featuring pink carnations). This 12-place setting, still largely intact, was one of my purchases in Japan along with a pair of Cloisonné Vases and several figurines of Japanese craftsmen. Beyond sightseeing, shopping was one of my chief pastimes when ashore.

Nineteen months into my Pacific duty tour, I was still operating under the assumption that I had 17 more months to serve in order to complete the active duty portion of my Navy commitment, be discharged into the inactive reserve, and be able to begin seminary. Then one day I received a letter from the Bureau of Naval Personnel. It read in part:

> "You are being considered for assignment to the Staff of a Professor of Naval Science, NROTC Unit, or to the Naval Academy, Annapolis, Maryland, as an instructor . . . .

> "It is necessary that officers so ordered have sufficient obligated service to remain in the assignment through two academic years.

> "Please advise the Bureau . . . by return mail . . . if so assigned . . . whether you will agree to remain on active duty for a period of two years from the time you report to such institution . . .

> "If you do reply in the affirmative . . . , it is requested that you give at least four choices for duty *areas* . . ."

If I replied in the affirmative this letter meant, I would be extending for a fourth year of active duty. Two thoughts crossed my mind—one, that I had probably seen as much of the world as I was going to see in my present duty assignment; the second, several of the universities to which I might be assigned would have seminaries related to them. This latter eventuality would mean such an assignment would give me a chance to start exploring seminaries sooner rather than later. I thought committing to another year on active duty was a good deal.

Without hesitating long, I agreed to extend. As I replied to this effect, I also gave the following responses concerning my preferences for duty assignment:

First *New England*—	Yale University or Harvard University
Second *West North Central*—	Northwestern University or Wisconsin U.
Third *East North Central*—	University of Michigan or Ohio State Univ.
Fourth *Middle Atlantic*—	University of Pennsylvania
Fifth *California*—	University of California at Berkley or Stanford

As is frequently the case in the military, I expressed my preferences but got something different. When my acceptance and new assignment came back to me, I was assigned to the NROTC Unit at Vanderbilt University in Nashville, Tennessee. Actually this assignment turned out to be providential for me.

Those of us being newly assigned to teaching positions were first sent for several weeks to Northwestern University, Evanston, Illinois, where we were given instruction in educational principles, lesson planning, etc. Almost none of us had previous teaching experience. Our Northwestern classes were preparation for what we were about to do. From Northwestern, I was off to my new assignment and preparing lesson plans for my first fall semester of teaching.

Author stands at a chalk board to demonstrate
the plotting of a ship's navigational course.

"A photograph of the night sky representing a 12-hour time exposure
of the North Star with others rotating around it. The photo was in
the 1953 Navigation textbook used in the navigation course I taught.
For me this giant natural halo scientifically demonstrated the
orderliness of creation. It also gave me an opportunity to offer a
faith-statement along with my teaching."
Harold Kieler, Assistant Professor of Naval Science.

Chapter 31

NASHVILLE (AUGUST 1953-MAY 1954)

Springtime is never more beautiful than in Nashville, Tennessee, with subtle colors of dogwoods, redbuds, and magnolias, bold azaleas and bright yellow forsythia blooming everywhere—blanketing the city's gentle rolling hills, accenting its wooded areas. Nashville's curving, mixed-up, non-symmetrical streets drove this mid-western plains boy who determined his directions by straight east, west, north and south crazy. Spring, summer, fall, I loved the beauty of Nashville. Wintertime, with coal smoke and soot, was another matter.

Some people think of Nashville as the country music capitol of the world. Others refer to it as the Mecca of Methodism. Southern Baptists might even speak of it as their Mecca. Take your pick of monikers, but Nashville was and is the location of a number of numerous national boards and agencies of the Methodist Church—the General Boards of Education (including our national youth work), Higher Education (Methodist College and Universities and secular campus ministries), Evangelism, the Commission on Communications, and The Publishing House. In addition, the Methodist Church's Women's Society of Christian Service (called the United Methodist Women today) owned and operated Scarritt College in Nashville—a Senior College with majors in church music, missions, Christian education, etc. Several other denominations had similar national offices in Nashville.

Nashville was also home to twenty or so institutions of higher education, some independent and some sponsored by other denominations. The most famous of these, Vanderbilt University, had its origin in Methodism. Later it became independent. Two seminaries affiliated with Vanderbilt—one Methodist, the other Disciples of Christ—merged in the 19ᵗʰ Century to form an interdenominational seminary. This school was first called the Vanderbilt School of Religion, later the Vanderbilt Divinity School. About the time of my arrival, the seminary was really beginning to be recognized as one of the leading interdenominational seminaries in the U.S. after Yale, Harvard, and the University of Chicago Divinity Schools.

Arriving August 1, 1953, the first time I'd ever been in Nashville, I found it an exciting and stimulating place. I was able to quickly reconnect staff members of the Methodist Board and Agencies, national Methodist leaders, whom I had met in my student days at the Wesley Foundation and in the National Methodist Student Movement. One of these persons, Roger Burgess, helped me find a nice little apartment—Apt. 6, located at 1600 Sixteenth Avenue South—not far from Vanderbilt and many of the Boards and Agencies.

My new apartment made me a back door neighbor to Jamison and Bonnie Jones, another Methodist Student Movement leader. Jamison also attended Seminary while he was in Nashville. When Lorine and I were married, our friendship with them continued to grow. It was about 1954 that their son Scott Jones was born. Today (2004), Scott has become my Bishop in Kansas. Jamison rose in Methodist leadership preaching and teaching nationally, becoming President of Illiff School of Theology in Denver and later, until an untimely death, the President of Duke Divinity School. When I was a District Superintendent we reconnected and he would serve as a resource person for our Annual Conference, our Area, and our Cabinet.

My NROTC teaching duties didn't begin until after Labor Day. I needed to prepare for my teaching, but except for this for about a month following my arrival in Nashville my NROTC responsibilities were minimal. All year long, unlike my days at sea, I had my week-ends totally free. Thus began what was probably one of the most varied, active, non-stop whirlwind series of events during any ten-month period in my entire life.

With all my freedom during August of 1953, I lunch most week days in the Methodist Board of Education cafeteria. This provided a built-in fellowship group for gaining wonderful orientations into Nashville. I was constantly picking up a friend and exploring sights of the city and its environs. This group also introduced me to the campus and student body at Scarritt College.

At that time the Methodist Church had an active short-term mission program. Some young college graduates were volunteering to work in the States for two years as what we called US-2s. They would serve in various Methodist social action, social welfare, or Christian Education ministries anywhere they were assigned in the USA. Young graduates could also volunteer for three-year terms overseas in a variety of ministries (teaching, preaching, health related, social action, administrative). They were known as J-3s (Japan), A-3s (Africa), LA-3s (Latin America), E-3s (Europe), etc. When I had been considering becoming a conscientious objector to war, I had also explored rather seriously with our General Board of Missions in New York the possibility of becoming an A-3 in what was then Southern Rhodesia. Consequently, I had a special interest in these short-term mission programs.

Scarritt College had an orientation and training program for US-2s. It was just concluding that August. I quickly became friends with a number of these students. One of them was being assigned to the Wesley Community Center in Chattanooga, Tennessee. At the close of his training, he needed transportation to his assignment and I volunteered to drive him there one week-end. Two or three of his peers came along for the fun of it. This was a first visit to Chattanooga for all of us. Exploring that city made the trip a neat time.

While spending time around the Scarritt campus, I made friends with one of the relatively few black persons with whom I've had a long term connection. DeLaris Johnson, a scholarship student sponsored by the W.S.C.S. The city of Nashville, the state of Tennessee, like the entirety of the South, was a highly segregated society. Methodism had split over slavery during the Civil War era and the North and South Churches had not reunited until 1939. Even then, in the reuniting, Jurisdictional Conferences were formed. Five Jurisdictions were geographic and a sixth Jurisdiction, called the Central Jurisdiction, was for black churches. From 1939 on there was no segregation at the national church level, even though segregation existed regionally and locally until 1968.

Scarritt had no official policy of racial segregation but there were few if any black students on campus. Dee was a racial pioneer in her student body. She was a neat person, but lonely. I enjoyed becoming acquainted with her. From time to time we would do things together, but since Nashville was segregated it usually had to be either on the campus or at my apartment. I tried to be a source of encouragement and support and I guess I was. In her 2003 Christmas greetings DeLaris (Mrs. Modie Risher for the past five decades) was very gracious in writing,

> "I will never forget your support to me when I was a student at Scarritt. You, Mac and Norma (two other seminarians) were there for me and made it possible for me to survive emotionally. Many days I felt like leaving . . ."

I discovered that Nashville was a city of untold numbers of churches. Three became focal points of interest for me. West End Methodist Church across the street from the west edge of the Vanderbilt campus was the "premier" Methodist Church in Nashville. It had a fine Gothic structure. It seemed almost like a European cathedral. It was served by one of Methodism's leading preachers. His congregation was large and contained a significant portion of the leadership community in Nashville, the Capitol of Tennessee. My first weeks in Nashville found me frequently worshiping there. Eventually, however, I felt a bit like a fish out of water.

I began worshipping at Fisk Chapel because of what I had heard about it from friends. Fisk University, a school of the Congregational Church, was one of the leading black universities of the nation. It had a student body of about a thousand students plus others who were attending Mehary Medical College. Mehary was one of our nation's few black medical schools and probably the most noted. Fisk Chapel, a university church, was part of this educational complex. Fisk Chapel was famous for its preacher, Dean Faulkner, and for its large outstanding choir—the Jubilee Singers. The choir made frequent national tours and was noted for its interpretations of black spirituals. Faulkner's sermons were stimulating; the music was moving. Fisk Church was probably 95% black in its make up, but it did have a smattering of other racial and ethnic groups. Being something of a "boundary crosser," one who often chose not to go with the flow so much as to go against the stream, I became an "affiliate member" of Fisk Chapel and remained so until I was appointed to serve in the Methodist Church.

I worshipped with some regularity at Fisk for a couple of years or more, but I knew I needed to keep my roots in the Methodist Church. Adjacent to Vanderbilt University, on the opposite side of the campus from West End Methodist Church, was another large well-known Methodist Church—Belmont. Belmont was something of a "rival" to West-End except that its congregation was probably more mid-stream in its socio-economic make up. This is where I ended up maintaining my Methodist connection. Realizing that I needed to begin developing my skills for use in the local church, January through May of 1954, I volunteered to help teach fifth grade Sunday School at Belmont.

Soon I wonder why I had volunteered. Teaching the class was more than a bit of a challenge. I had no experience in teaching Sunday School, no experience in relating to kids of that age. Belmont's Director of Christian Education coached me some and I had a regular church member to assist in the teaching. It was a challenge but I really enjoyed it. I tried to be creative.

With my interest in building better understanding between races, I decided to be venturesome. Methodism had an annual

"Race Relations Sunday" to encourage churches to work on issues of race relations in church and community as well as to raise money in support of our denomination's black colleges. I decided to piggy back on this with my fifth graders. I wasn't exactly sure how to go about this. I knew it was easier to talk the talk of good race relations than it was to walk the walk. I came up with the idea that since Nashville had segregated public schools and community activities, the church ought to be setting the right example. It was a touchy thing to do, but I conferred with my assistant teacher and a couple of other key persons. We decided that for a Sunday or two, our fifth graders should meet in Sunday School with fifth graders from one of our black Methodist Churches in Nashville to create an experience of learning together.

One practical problem, with only 15 minutes between Sunday School and Worship, was the logistics of physically getting together since the closest back Methodist congregation was more than 15 minutes away. Another practical problem was the comfort level of parents in both churches in their segregated society. I came up with the idea that Scarritt College was a good half-way point. This wouldn't cause the kids to be late returning to either of their churches. Moreover, Scarritt was what you might call "neutral ground" for the venture.

I found a cooperative black church whose leaders were as excited as I was about engaging in this kind of learning experience for children. Scarritt was receptive in giving us the needed facilities. I'm sure the parents were a little dubious, but there was no adamant resistance. What could have been an explosive situation in some communities or circumstances became a kind of non-event. It went along so smoothly the kids felt fine with each other, no one got offended or up-tight, and we demonstrated that maybe the church could move farther and faster in breaking down barriers than people thought it could.

Within a month of my arrival in Nashville, a big development beyond my NROTC teaching, was the decision to take a plunge into seminary life. I had thought I would only become acquainted with the seminary while I was teaching. That first August, when I went over to Vanderbilt Divinity School to look around and inquire about their programs, I discovered they were still using a quarter system. While many of their required courses conflicted with the hours when I would be teaching, some more specialized or advanced courses were offered later in the day. "We'd be happy to have someone like you come take even just one course per quarter," said Mrs. Abernathy, the Registrar.

I decided to give this a try. The big difficulty was my lack of the prerequisite or background courses. And, of course, I had to keep up with my own teaching. I really struggled with these, but by the time I completed my active duty commitment I had accumulated two academic quarters of credits or the equivalent of two-thirds of a year of seminary. Seminary was three years of study so I had really gotten a qood start.

My first fall in Nashville I met a tall lanky student from Alabama—Ken Bohannon. We seemed to strike it off well with each other. I invited him to share my Apartment. We became good friends and enjoyed being roommates until I found a prettier, nicer apartment mate—Lorine. Ken moved out when we got married although our ties have continued through the years.

Ken was an avid fisherman as well as a hunter. He served a student appointment during seminary—just a small open country congregation housed in an old frame church building. One story from this uninhibited, informal country preacher comes back to me when ever I think of Ken. He told me a pigeon had gotten into his church and become a nuisance. One morning he brought his rifle into the church and laid it on the pulpit. When the pigeon started began flying around in the middle of the service, he simply stopped the service, picked up his rife and shot it. Ken became a career army chaplain and in retirement head of the Chaplaincy Department of the University of Alabama Medical Center.

My initial intent was just to sample seminary life and then transfer to Yale Divinity School when I was out of the navy. I became so excited and thrilled with our VDS faculty that I never once wanted to leave Vanderbilt Divinity School. Beyond the academic work, I found other things lots of fun. When week-ends

came, most students had local church responsibilities and were
out of town. During the week-days, a group of us developed a
custom of having "quicknics." About once a week, someone would
have a sudden urge to take a real break at supper time. They would
spread the word, "we're going to have a 'quicknic'—a quick spur of
the moment picnic. Grab whatever food you can for sharing. Let's
meet at Belle Meade Park (or some other park) at 5:30 pm and
we'll all eat together." These were inexpensive and great times for a
little get-together which really enriched our social life and a sense
of supportive community.

We would also have visitors to campus from such groups as the
Fellowship of Reconciliation (a pacifist organization which was
very creative in also dealing with issues of non-violent resistance to
various forms of evil and violence), and also the Fellowship of
Southern Churchmen (a fellowship of pastors devoted to three
types of issues—issues impacting the rural church, issues of
Christian social concern versus the personal piety only positions of
fundamentalists, and issues of interdenominational cooperation).
I enjoyed being involved in the dialogues that surrounded these
groups and found them to be very stimulating.

CHAPTER 32

WHAT BRAND OF
PATRIOTISM IS YOURS?*

As I've been writing these memoirs, I've come to realize that I was reared to be a dynamic patriot without even knowing it. In the 1930s, grade schools everywhere in America including my North Side school in Hutchinson, Kansas, began each morning with students standing, hand over heart, to pledge allegiance "to the flag . . . and to the republic for which it stands." We followed this with the singing of "America"—

> "My country, 'tis of thee,
> sweet land of liberty, of thee I sing;
> land where my fathers died,
> land of the pilgrim's pride,
> from every mountain-side let freedom ring!
>
> . . . .
>
> Our father's God, to thee, author of liberty,
> to thee we sing;
> long may our land be bright with freedom's holy light . . ."

Weekly visits by our music teacher included our national anthem, "The Star Spangled Banner," and "America the Beautiful" as part of the repertoire we learned. Other lessons included: learning that our cultural heritage derived from many corners of the world; memorizing the Bill of Rights and the Gettysburg Address; having Armistice Day (now Veterans' Day) visits by veterans telling us their stories—helping us understand what it meant to help defend our nation.

Then came the early 1940s, World War II and new lessons of patriotism to be learned in my teen years. Defending this free land did not just mean mass mobilization of Americans for the armed services. All Americans had a job when it came to patriotism—a call to service and sacrifice. War factories needed to be staffed by those never before in the labor force. There were civil defense programs, scrap ("recycling") drives, war bond savings campaigns, and more for all citizens to participate in. There was a new song to be sung—Irving Berlin's "God Bless America."

After the war, graduating from high school into a university flooded with returning WW II veterans, I quickly began to learn still more about patriotism. Not all veterans were the same color; not all veterans thought the same; and not all patriotic Americans were veterans! I was dumbfounded when I met a young pacifist fresh out of prison because his God and his conscience commanded "Thou shall not kill' and he had been willing to go to prison for the sake of his convictions. Yet he wanted to serve—serve God, serve country, serve humanity. To help save our service personnel and generations yet unborn, while in prison he volunteered to be a "medical guinea pig." New medicines would be tested on him and refined until they were safe for others.

1950 and there was a new war to be fought—my war in which to serve, a war against a new totalitarianism, communism. More lessons on patriotism. Americanism is more than rugged individualism. It's learning team work and cooperation. In a world which had become so interdependent, no single nation can go it alone; no one nation can decide for others whether the moment to fight war against the forces of evil has come. June 25 the North Korean People's Army crossed the 38th Parallel driving into the Republic of South Korea. June 27, 1950, the Security Council of the United Nations invited its members to come to the assistance of South Korea. President Truman ordered our armed forces into action. This "first ever UN police action" became the Korean War even though there was never a formal declaration of war. As I stood on the deck of one of the ships of the US 7th Fleet off the coast of Korea, how proud I was not only to see our flag but to see it flying among the flags of 15 other United Nations countries all moving together in the defense of freedom.

Before the 1950s were over, those who had fought in WW II and in Korea began to realize that our racially segregated patterns of society denied freedom right here at home. By 1960 sit-ins began, spreading from city to city, from lunch counters to stores, theaters, and polling places, and nonviolent civil disobedience became a new way of working for liberty and justice for all, a new way of expressing patriotism.

Decade by decade we continue to expand our vision of patriotism without even knowing it some times. I'm proud of my country, proud to sing of a sweet land of liberty, proud to honor those who have died in the cause of freedom for all. I'm proud of our Bill of Rights and of every symbol of these United States of America. I'm especially proud when we are at our best with *all* Americans serving and sacrificing and working together for liberty and justice and the welfare of all. I'm proud when we can respect the right to dissent, proud when we can join as United States of America in a United Nations of the world in strengthening the values for which we stand. I'm proud when we are able to recognize that patriotism is not something fixed and static, but a dynamic creative quality of life that includes service and sacrifice in the Peace Corps and in space exploration as well as in times of war.

As I've been learning patriotism for nearly eight decades, I've concluded that there are two kinds of patriotism. One says "America first and only!" The other, humbly recognizes that we do not have a patent on all that is good and right, knows that our understanding of freedom and the ways we nurture and protect it are forever growing. Which brand of patriotism is yours?

For me, my kind of patriotism is one that sings from Lloyd
Stone's *"This Is My Song":*

"This is my song, O God of all the nations,
a song of peace for lands afar and mine.
This is my home, the country where my heart is;
here are my hopes and dreams, my holy shrine;
but other hearts in other lands are beating
with hopes and dreams as true and high as mine.

My country's skies are bluer than the ocean,
and sunlight beams on clover leaf and pine;
but other lands have sunlight too, and clover,
and skies are everywhere as blue as mine.
O hear my song, thou God of all the nations;
a song of peace for their land and for mine."

---

*   Previously published in *active aging*, July 2003.

CHAPTER 33

A FUNNY THING HAPPENED TO ME
ON MY WAY AROUND THE WORLD

One dream filled my mind from my University of Illinois days right on through my first two or three years in uniform. It was the dream of taking a year, when I got out of the navy, to spend on a tramp steamer bumming around the world in order to see and experience as much of it as possible. To give reality to my dream, I sought to save all the money I could and to save as much leave time and sick leave (both of which I could convert into cash at my discharge from the navy) to be able to finance my around the world trip.

In Nashville I made many friends—peers in my NROTC Unit, within the program staff of the Methodist Board of Education, among the US-2s and students at Scarritt College, and in the Vanderbilt Divinity School student body. I made girl friends as well as male friends, but my girl friends were just that—friends. I'd never fallen in love with any girl, gotten infatuated with or seriously pursued any girl. I always enjoyed feminine company and I guess I assumed that someday I'd find someone who was special enough that I'd want to get married, but I wasn't in any hurry. I was just turning 24 in October of 1953. More importantly I still had to take that 'round the world' trip.

I didn't even have a bonafide date with anyone the first two or three months in Nashville. There was one girl who tried to improve my dancing skills, and I met another girl who was a University of Illinois alumna. She was driving back to her sorority for Homecoming that fall. She offered me a ride in her MG to Champaign-Urbana. Since that would give me a chance to get back to visit Wesley Foundation I took her up on the offer. Still nothing out of the ordinary was happening in terms of my social life until I received a certain intervention.

There were five of us naval officers who made up the teaching staff of our NROTC Unit at Vanderbilt. All were married except for me. One of the five was a Major in the Marine Corp—Major Earl Kirby-Smith. The Major's wife, Joanne, was active in Nashville's Community Theater. Their play that fall was *Cyrano de Bergerac.* Naturally there was to be a cast party at the close of the play's run. Since one of the cast members didn't have a date for the party, Joanne, playing the part of "match maker," had Earl talk to me. "How would you like a blind date next Saturday night?" asked Earl as he told me about this nice young single girl who needed a date. Naturally I was all for that! The ball bounced back to Joanne's court. She proceeded to tell this "nice young single girl" about this "nice young single officer" in her husband's NROTC Unit. "Would you like my husband to set you up with a blind date for the cast party?" And so the date was arranged.

Meanwhile, even though I had the blind date set for Saturday night, I wasn't attached to any one. I'd been noticing this good looking vivacious single secretary at the Divinity School. Deciding that I might as well enjoy the nice fall weather, I dropped by her office midweek to ask if she'd be interested in playing tennis when she got off work Friday. Because I was the only Divinity School Student in a uniform, Lorine was pretty sure that I was her blind date. Thinking that it was nice of me to set up this "tennis date" so that we could get acquainted in advance, Lorine was all for tennis. When I didn't even mention our Saturday night blind date during the course of tennis she thought something (*me* for instance) was a little strange. I didn't have a clue what was going on until Saturday night.

Come Saturday night, I was happy to discover who my date was and the party turned out to be a great cast party! It even included dancing! Not my favorite activity, but since I wanted to further our relationship I decided to act as if I enjoyed dancing. We partied and danced until 4 a.m. I decided I'd like to see more of Miss Martin. Later we attended a Midshipman Ball, and years later we took square dancing lessons in Belle Plaine, but only rarely have we gone dancing since Nashville days. Across the years "Miss Martin" has delighted in telling people that I got her under false pretenses just as she has also enjoyed giving this story of our first dance a different twist. In fact, through the years we've often seen things from different perspectives!

Lt.(jg) Kieler and his new wife at Midshipman's Ball

Through the winter we began going to movies, plays, symphonies, dining out and attending church services together. I think we both were drawn to one another because come spring, Lorine decided it was time for a weekend auto tour to show me Kentucky and in the process stop over for a night with her parents in Owensboro, Kentucky, so they could meet me.

In the Spring of 1954, from a former Ph.D. student at the Divinity School, Lorine received a job offer to work in a Presbyterian Church in the vicinity of Knoxville, Tennessee—200 miles NE of Nashville. She asked me what I thought. My response was, "If it's something you really want to do you'll have to decide—I can't tell you what to do with your life, but if you are really interested in pursuing our relationship, I don't see how that would work out with you 200 miles away." Lorine decided against taking the job.

Meanwhile, I had orders for "temporary additional duty" that summer. I was to take midshipmen aboard the battleship New Jersey for a summer training cruise. This would be a six weeks transatlantic cruise taking us to LeHavre, France and LaCoruna, Spain. Lorine wasn't too happy when I broke this news, but I suggested the short separation might be a good test for our relationship's durability. So it proved to be.

A bit of unplanned social life came up when we got to Spain. A series of social events were planned by the locals to entertain the midshipmen and their officers. In the process of participating in these events I met a beautiful young senorita who happened to be the daughter of an Argentine diplomat. We hit it off pretty well at the arrival reception/mixer. Following this I received a pair of invitations from her. The first invitation was for dinner at her home, with her parents; the second invitation was to be her escort the next night at a Ball for the midshipmen. I accepted both invitations and had a delightful evening at her home, thoroughly enjoying her parents as well as getting better acquainted with her. Her mother had a gourmet dinner that evening. There was just one problem. Unbeknown to me, the topping for the nice fresh dinner salad contained flecks of shrimp. I've always been deathly allergic to shrimp. That night, back at the ship, after I'd gone to bed, I awoke with extreme nausea—so extreme that it continued through the next day—the day of the Ball.

There was no way for me to attend the Ball but some how I did manage to communicate word of my plight. The Senorita's father was gracious enough to come to our ship and check on my well being. He also delivered a note to me from his daughter which included her address so that I could write her and keep in touch. Much as I did enjoy this brief encounter in Spain, and nice as this Senorita and her family were, some how my heart wasn't in a new romantic relationship—my heart was back in Nashville.

Lorine had a brother, Ben, who was also a Navy Officer. Returning to the States from my cruise, we put into the Naval Ship Yards at Norfolk, Virginia. Ben's ship happened to be in harbor there which gave me an opportunity to meet and become acquainted with him. I thoroughly enjoyed Ben, and my positive impressions of the Martin family were further reinforced.

I could hardly wait to take Lorine out to a nice restaurant on West End Avenue when I returned to Nashville. It was a place where we had both enjoyed great steaks together on previous occasions. It was a quiet, intimate little restaurant with a wonderful atmosphere of candlelight and soft music. We were seated in a secluded little niche. I ordered a two-pound sirloin for the two of us to share. This kept us busy enough so we had time to catch-up on each other's summer. Then, I popped the question: "Will you marry me?" I don't remember a lot more details, but I do remember that there was a YES answer and my heart jumped for joy! SO . . . a funny thing happened to me on my way around the world—my dream trip got replaced with a new dream—the dream of sharing the journey of life with Lorine.

Lorine shifted into high gear that fall making wedding plans for a week before Christmas, coinciding with the end of the fall quarter at Vanderbilt. Her family church was the First Presbyterian Church of Owensboro. It was a pioneering congregation uniting two congregations, each from a different denomination—one from the Southern Presbyterians, the other from the Northern (USA) Presbyterians. Together they were building a new facility which would be dedicated by Thanksgiving—a beautiful southern style colonial structure with tall spire and the familiar white columns that accompany this style of architecture. Lorine's father had been chairman of the building committee. Naturally this was the place for our wedding!

Who would officiate? Of course she would want to include her own pastor, the Rev. John McQueen. But Lorine's secretarial position at Vanderbilt Divinity School included serving half time as personal secretary to Dr. Nels Ferre, typing manuscripts for the books he was writing. He was a wonderfully warm person to work for and he also happened to be one of my favorite professors at VDS. Naturally, we wanted both pastors to co-officiate at our wedding. And who would make up the wedding party? I couldn't believe it! Lorine wanted to have the biggest wedding party that I'd ever known. She wanted to have a Matron of Honor plus four Bridesmaids which meant that I should choose an equal number of men to stand up with me plus three ushers. I hardly even knew that many guys to ask!

Anyway, Lorine planned a beautiful wedding in a beautiful church with a beautiful reception featuring some authentic touches from the old south and at a beautiful time of year—beautiful because on that Saturday, December 18, 1954, we began with a cold clear sunny day and as we came out of the church, after the wedding and reception, to leave on our honeymoon, there was a lovely 4 to 6 inch blanket of snow over everything.

Left to right: Ken Bohannon; Waitman Taylor; Dave Schmulbach; Taylor Stevenson; Roy Rauschenberg; Harmon Hoffman; Ben Martin; the Groom; the Bride; Joyce Taylor; Jane Stevenson; Shirley Kieler; Sarah Martin; Mary Hoffman.

Family Photo at the Wedding (December 18, 1954) Left to right: Ben Martin, bride's brother; Shirley Kieler, groom's sister; Fred and Blanche Kieler, groom's parents; groom; bride; Mary Hoffman, bride's sister; Sarah Martin, bride's sister; Mary and Ben Martin, bride's parents.

At this point in our lives Lorine didn't know much about the Midwest or West and I didn't know much about the South. For our honeymoon, I chose to take Lorine on a snowy drive west to the Broadmoor Hotel in Colorado Springs in the foothills of the Rockies. Our first stop on the way was Evansville, Indiana, where I had reservations in a downtown hotel. The bellman helped carry our bags to our room placing them on the bed. As I was fumbling for a tip, Lorine proceeded to open her suitcase. Unbeknown to us, it had been tampered with by her little sister or one of her bridesmaids. Much to our embarrassment, rice came tumbling out everywhere making it obvious to the bellman, if he didn't already know it, that we were newlyweds on a honeymoon. Returning home to Nashville, our next to last stop was just west of either Kansas City or St. Louis, I don't remember which. Shortly before stopping for the evening we were driving up a little incline on a snow packed highway US 50 when all of a sudden our car went into a spin. Fortunately no other car was near us. We did a 360 degree spin and then ended up in the ditch. No damage was done, but we were unable to extricate ourselves from the ditch. Along came a beer truck and fortunately the driver stopped to help, attaching a chain and pulling us back onto the highway. We've never been as appreciative of the Budweiser Brewing Company as we were at that moment.

I must report my two-fold motivation for the Broadmoor honeymoon destination. First, I was eager to show Lorine the Rockies. They were "my" mountains and, I thought, grander and much more impressive than "her" mountains which were the Appalachians. Secondly, this was a time before snowing skiing became a hugely popular sport. The Broadmoor had its summer-time reputation of being *the elite hotel of* Colorado. But in the winter-time it was nearly empty. In its low off-season period, it had dirt cheap rates—rates that even I could afford.

Our Christmas honeymoon was really our official honeymoon, but the following May, 1955, when I was discharged from the navy, I got my expected pay-off for unused leave and sick-leave which I had been saving for my trip around the world. It wouldn't take two of us around the world. We did, however, choose to use it for a summer trip to Europe in order to participate for a month in a World Council of Churches Work Camp in Denmark—a work camp building a playground (a soccer field) at a school for handicapped orphans from World War II. We also were able to travel in Holland, Switzerland, and Germany the month preceding our work camp and in Scandinavia the month following our work camp.

The two of us have been traveling the globe ever since and enjoying every minute of it. I guess I might say that I did get my 'round the world trip after all, only in a slightly modified way. It has been fun. I'm writing this chapter the week of Valentine Day, years after our first Valentine's date (which I don't even remember). December 18, 2004, I will have been married 50 years to this indescribably wonderful, intelligent, beautiful, kind, sensitive, caring, affirming, loving woman of good humor and a contagious laugh, who is a friend to all. She has patiently endured all my many faults helping me become a much better person than I ever could have been without her! How can I ever express my joy and gratitude for the love journey we've been on?

Chapter 34

WINDING IT UP AND
NEW BEGINNINGS

Returning from our European World Council of Churches' Work Camp and our "second honeymoon" in August of 1955, Lorine was quickly back at work at the Divinity School continuing her employment as Secretary to the Faculty. Now, for the first time as full-time student, I was there too. It would take two years plus the summer between to wind up my first professional degree which would be awarded on the 2nd day of June, 1957. At that time, whatever the seminary, whatever the denomination, one's first professional degree was titled a "Bachelor of Divinity" even though it was offered as a professional or graduate degree following completion of traditional undergraduate studies. By 1973 the reality of the degree as a graduate degree was being recognized by many seminaries in the diplomas they awarded. On May 25, 1973, my degree would be reissued as a "Master of Divinity."

To do a respectable job of preparing for parish ministry, I felt I needed to keep my nose to the academic grind-stone. I didn't seek a student church or any other employment during the 1955-56 year. I was fortunate to be able to do this without incurring debt because the GI Bill of Rights for WW II veterans had been reinstated for veterans of the Korean War. Part of the required field work for my degree did involve doing some volunteer pastoral work.

Come back in time with me and relive the setting for my field work. In a rural setting an hour east of Nashville stands a cluster of rather unimaginative two story red brick rectangular buildings nestled in the gently rolling hills of that region. As we approach this setting, we can immediately sense this is the campus of one of those traditional state institutions. As we turn into the grounds we see the simple modest sign reading "Cloverbottom." What strikes us as we approach these buildings is the absence of any human beings on the grounds. We know this isn't a prison. Leaving our car and walking into the first building, there's no security system of any type. Once inside we begin to see people and mental assessment quickly tells us that this is a residential type of facility—something of a cross between a hospital and a dormitory. Observing the residents, we realize they are a little "different" from most people we're associated with throughout our lives.

A few of the people here are in wheel chairs. When we walk down the hall, as we glance into the rooms, we see some people who are immobile and bedfast. However, most residents here are ambulatory. Physically and mentally many of them appear to have some abnormalities. A few have larger than normal heads. Many have thick necks, noses, lips, etc. A lot of them have difficulty coordinating their movements, posture, or balance. In terms of motor activities or skills, many seem to experience involuntary movements and the inability to control muscle activities. Most of these folks are in their twenties, thirties, or forties, they are a very friendly lot even though they frequently have difficulty speaking and expressing themselves. There's a slowness about them. They seem to be limited in their emotional development as well as in their understanding and awareness of their environment.

This is the Tennessee Hospital for the Mentally Retarded. Today these patients would be referred to as the Developmentally Disabled. Returning to the present from this journey that we've taken, this is where I spent Sunday mornings working as a volunteer chaplain doing my field work for my first fulltime semester or two of seminary. My principal task was to conduct a kind of combination Sunday School and Worship for the more advanced patients.

I had to become familiar with this world with which I had little familiarity, and I had to learn to feel comfortable where in the beginning I felt out of place and ill at ease. The additional challenge for me, perhaps the real challenge in this role, was balancing the graduate level study of scriptures with the adaptation of them to the level of those to whom I was ministering. In a sense this is every ministers' problem in every parish setting.

When I arrived on Sunday morning, a cluster of chairs were simply lined up in a corner of the lounge. I greeted people engaging them in a bit of chit-chat. When we were ready to begin the service, I spoke in the simplest vocabulary possible. I read a little scripture but then mostly I had to communicate its meaning with story telling. For the ritual of worship, I could offer a prayer, but about the best we could do as a congregation was to recite the Lord's Prayer. The only hymns I dared to have us sing, or try to sing, were those the patients themselves suggested. After the benediction, I lingered for awhile to visit as people might want to visit and then I would be on my way back to Nashville.

As we approached the summer of 1956, Vanderbilt University was converting all of its courses from the quarter system to the semester system. No summer courses were to be offered. I now had, counting my part-time studies while I'd been teaching NROTC, hours equivalent to one year and two quarters but not equal to two full academic years. I wanted to complete my BD by June of 1957. I had to find a summer school some place else. To make this possible, Lorine requested leave. After researching various possibilities, I came up with plans to study at Garrett Biblical Institute's summer school. Garrett was a Methodist seminary related to Northwestern University, Evanston, Illinois. Located on the beautiful shores of Lake Michigan, just north of Chicago, it turned out to be a wonderful place to spend the summer.

Garrett was great for my purposes. I studied with some wonderful faculty from Garrett and also with a visiting professor from Yale University Divinity School. Week-ends were free. Lorine and I could enjoy jaunts to Wisconsin, Michigan, and the City of Chicago itself.

The summer of 1956 turned out to be even more interesting for Lorine. As I registered for summer school, she read the bulletin board in the registrar's office. She came across this letter: "Mr. Herbert Johnson, President of the Garrett Board of Trustees, an attorney with offices in 'The Loop' in downtown Chicago, has a secretarial position open for the summer. He would be happy to receive an application from the wife of a seminary student." Lorine ended up getting the job. Her new world of law with contracts, wills, trusts, estates, and related billings was a world apart from her Divinity School work but she found it interesting. Her job meant commuting daily on the Elevated Train (the "L" as it was called) from Evanston to the city and back. The commute was relatively easy because we were living in a big old frame house right next to the "L." We lived in what was called co-op housing owned by Garrett and shared the house, cooking and cleaning duties, with John Decker and his wife, also from Kansas, and another couple.

At summer's end, Lorine's brother Ben Martin was marrying Pat Sessions in her hometown of Idabel, Oklahoma. Naturally Lorine wanted to be there. So did I, but the week of the wedding proved to be the week of my final exams. Lorine quit work a week early to join her family for the wedding. After the wedding and my exams were over, we arranged to reconnect with each other. Following a short trip to Colorado and Kansas, it was back to Nashville for the final year of my Bachelor of Divinity studies.

Since graduation was in sight, I really needed to get moving on preparing for ordination, conference membership, and local church ministry. I needed to be serving a student charge. I had been in touch with the appropriate powers in my annual conference as well as with Dr. Speers, a District Superintendent from the Louisville Annual Conference. That fall there was an available student charge in Kentucky, the Adairville-Oakland Charge in the Hopkinsville District. I accepted the offer of this student appointment.

In October I returned to Kansas briefly to attend our Annual Conference at First Methodist Church in Wichita. Its worship sessions were held in an old, yet beautiful, classic Gothic sanctuary. There on October 6, 1956, Bishop Dana Dawson ordained me a Deacon in The Methodist Church. This was another step into parish ministry. Today that sanctuary is long gone, replaced by a beautiful contemporary sanctuary which is where I am once again worshipping.

Before I graduated from seminary, I began feeling I'd only started to scratch the surface of so many subjects. Lorine and I visited about this and made a decision. I would stay on for an additional year of study after graduation. I would enroll in the Graduate School to do a Masters degree in Theology. There was just one problem. A pre-requisite for Graduate study in theology was a reading knowledge of German. I had studied no languages. The summer of 1957 I had to take an intensive crash course in German and pass the examination before I began my theological studies in September. I never worked so hard academically, before or after this summer of German. I just passed. And, the old saying goes, "Use it or lose it." I've never used my German since that time and I've long since lost it.

Two guests came to visit us during my graduate studies. A former pastor from my home church, then District Superintendent, the Rev. A. O. Mulvaney, his wife and their very good friend Vetra Hahn, visited us. They were vacationing, visiting another of our nation's National Parks. Before they finished their traveling life, they would visit every park in our system of National Parks. Dr. Mulvaney stopped by to discuss my first appointment back home. Bishop Dana Dawson was also in Nashville that year. He contacted us in advance making plans to take Lorine and me out for a fine dinner. He was simply seeking to become better acquainted with us. It was his way of providing support and encouragement in my studies and in our returning to serve in my home conference. Both these visits were greatly appreciated and deeply meaningful to us personally.

I thoroughly enjoyed my graduate theological studies. In addition to my year of studies, I had a thesis to do. The topic of my thesis was *Some Theological Contributions of Christianity to Political Democracy as Found in Contemporary Protestant Theologians.* I did my course studies in the Fall and Spring Semesters of 1957-1958 and worked on the thesis the summer of 1958. My fantasy that I might complete my thesis before returning to Kansas proved to be just that—fantasy. Then I thought I'd finish my thesis as soon as I got back to Kansas. Little did I realize how consuming parish ministry and family life would be. It was several years before I again really picked up completing my thesis. It was 1963 before it was finished and accepted. Even though it was a Master thesis in theology, officially the degree awarded to me in June of 1963 was a Master of Arts.

In 1958 our Central Kansas Annual Conference shifted its annual meeting time from October to May so new appointments for pastors would become effective June 1st rather than two months after their children had started school. I was to have been ordained Elder back in Kansas that spring. Remaining in Nashville to work on my thesis meant that I would not have my Elders orders when I returned home in September for my first appointment in Kansas. I had a student connection with the Louisville Annual Conference, and it was meeting in Owensboro, Kentucky, Lorine's home town. Arrangements were made for me to receive a "courtesy ordination" there even though it was neither my home conference nor where I'd be serving. On the 27th day of June, 1958, I was ordained an Elder in The Methodist Church by Bishop William T. Watkins.

This was the final credentialing step of my journey into ordained Methodist ministry and into "full connection (membership)" in a Methodist Annual Conference. I was now truly ready for a new beginning in my life and ministry—ready to return to Kansas that fall to start what would become a challenging, rewarding and satisfying, although at times stressful and overly demanding, career as a parish pastor.

Chapter 35

ADAIRVILLE DAZE

Adairville seemed like a little, sleepy old town with a population of less than a thousand. Driving between Nashville and Owensboro, Kentucky, on US Highway 431, just after you crossed the Tennessee-Kentucky border headed north you passed through it. Many times Lorine and I had driven this road on the way to visit her family in Owensboro, but we'd never stopped there. To the left of Main Street heading north was a small town square. It was neat and nice enough, yet none of the buildings surrounding the square were very new. A few seemed a bit faded with age. Imagine our surprise when we learned from Dr. Speers in the summer, 1956 that the "connecting link" between seminary studies and my first church in Kansas, my student appointment, would be to the Adairville-Oakland charge. This would be the "clinical setting" need to wind up my preparation for parish ministry.

A charge is an assigned place of responsibility for a pastor. It can be "a single point" charge meaning one church. Or, a charge can be a "two point" charge, two places, two churches for which you are responsible. Or, a charge can even have many points. In the frontier days of America when travel was difficult, and small places of worship were scattered through out the country-side, a Methodist charge frequently had multiple points.

In the Eighteenth and Nineteenth Centuries, population was sparse, Preachers were few and far between. A Circuit Rider would sometimes serve so many scattered little churches that riding horseback from place to place took a month to make the rounds of his circuit. Even late into the Twentieth Century, between WW I and WW II, it was not uncommon for a preacher to be appointed to a rural charge with several points—perhaps 4, 5 or 6.

By the time I was beginning ministry, the shrinkage of rural communities, the consolidation of schools and churches, had been underway for a long time. Many of little churches had dwindled to the point they could no longer pay a full-time preacher a living salary or even a full-time Circuit Rider who now "rode the range" in an automobile. Full-time students often served churches on week-ends as part-time pastors. They were commonly appointed to circuits of two or three churches.

The Adairville-Oakland charge consisted of a small Methodist Church of about 150 members located in Adairville, plus the much smaller Oakland Methodist Church of 50 to 70 members located in the open country seven miles to the southwest of Adairville. Having never before served *any* Methodist Church, and having only been a member of large Methodist Churches, you can imagine I was in a daze when I began this student appointment. I found myself responsible for not one but two churches! Both of them were so small that I was the ONLY staff person. There was no secretary to prepare bulletins—that was my job, too. All musical leadership, custodial work, and a variety of other tasks were done by volunteers with whom I wasn't even in touch during the week.

Our arrival in Adairville was late Friday afternoon, the first week-end of September, 1956. We served weekends and school vacation periods through Memorial Day of May, 1958. Having worked and studied all day in Nashville, then hurrying to pack and travel to our new church and parsonage, we were hungry when we arrived. We hadn't moved into the parsonage yet let alone set up for housekeeping. There was only one café in town, a modest little place, typical of any small town café, so there wasn't any choice about where we would eat that night.

Entering the café, we found it fairly full but managed to discover an empty table. It was noisy with a juke box in one corner and people talking loudly to one another, sometimes even shouting over to other tables. Everyone in town knew everyone, but we hadn't met a soul yet. We sensed that all eyes were on us. After we ordered our meal, we were pleased to see one man get up and come over to our table. He introduced himself to us. "Hi. I'm Jimmy Betts. Are you the new Methodist pastor by any chance?" When I answered in the affirmative, he continued, "I'm the undertaker here in town. I'm sure we'll be working together. I always like to be the first to welcome new pastors to Adairville and to let them know that I'll be the last to let them down." With that, he burst out into a loud belly laugh. I thought his sense of humor was great, but Lorine was rather shocked that Jimmy, as a professional funeral director, was seemingly so blasé about death.

Jimmy Betts lived across the street from our parsonage. It was only a week later when, shortly after our afternoon arrival at the parsonage (we called it our "country home," and referred to our Nashville apartment as our "town house"), Jimmy came across the street to tell me Mr. Fort, an elderly member of my congregation, had died. He informed me Mr. Fort's family wanted to have the funeral Sunday afternoon. I was stunned. I hadn't even considered the fact that "doing funerals" would be one of my responsibilities. I'd been to only a handful of funerals in my life. I had no seminary course preparing me for this phase of ministry. I didn't have a clue what to do. After supper that night, I went back across the street to Jimmy Betts' house and made my confession to him. "This is my first funeral. I don't know what to do or how to do it!" Jimmy was helpful in giving me a bit of guidance. I managed to make it through the week-end, through that first funeral, but not with a very high comfort level.

It seems to me in many ways I've lived through the end of one era and the beginning of another. Rural Kentucky wasn't that far removed from the frontier days when people in the U. S. were moving west, settling in undeveloped regions of the country. Frontier funerals could be held almost anywhere and almost at a moment's notice—by the side of a trail, out-of-doors, near a farmhouse, in someone's home, in a little country church, or in a funeral parlor. On the frontier, carpenters and cabinet makers were also the persons who made caskets IF there was to be a casket. The cabinet makers frequently doubled, vocationally, as a furniture maker and furniture store proprietor/undertaker. He could use part of his furniture store as a "funeral parlor" or a "funeral home" for services, if need be.

In the case of my first funeral, Mr. Fort was a member of our church. Jimmy Betts had his own funeral home. Either of these places would normally have been the site for the funeral. But Mr. Fort's only survivors—an out-of-town nephew and niece—wanted the funeral in their uncle's house. I'd never seen this done. Jimmy Betts briefed me on how things would be arranged and how the logistics would work. That was my first and last funeral to conduct in the home of the deceased.

There was another time when I was in a "daze" in Adairville. Throughout my ministry, I always enjoyed conducting confirmation classes. One portion of these classes would be learning about the sacraments—communion and baptism—and another part would be the study of Methodist polity. I enjoyed my own theological studies of baptism and Methodist polity. In the Methodist Church, we practice infant baptism. It's the basic the norm for us. Of course, for those who are not baptized as infants, we also practice adult baptism. Historically, Christians have used three modes of baptism—sprinkling, pouring and immersion. Some denominations hold that only one out of the three ways of baptism is valid. Other denominations, like Methodism, recognize the validity of all three modes and may even practice all three. In explaining these things to my confirmands, I explained the symbolism which went with each mode of baptism, and I told those who had not been baptized they were free to choose their method of baptism. I had a couple of youth who wanted to be baptized by immersion. Since Methodists, in my experience, seldom choose immersion, I was a bit surprised and puzzled until I realized the cultural context of this southern community. In terms of religious denominations, Baptists were the dominant faith group. They claimed, insisted upon and required adult immersion baptism as the only valid form of baptism. My young people were influenced more by their peers and the culture around them than by their own Methodist norms. Though I felt these were rather poor (non-theological) reasons for deciding to be immersed, having made it clear that Methodism recognized the validity of all forms of baptism, I felt compelled to honor their choice.

Once again there were practical problems for me: I had never in my life seen a baptism by immersion; I wasn't familiar with the fine points of actually performing immersions; and, since immersion was not a common custom in the Methodist Church, my church facility was not constructed with an immersion baptistery. Once again, I turned to someone else for assistance. I went to meet the local Baptist minister, asking if it would be possible for us Methodists to borrow the Baptist church for our own service of baptism. I also asked if he would coach me in the technicalities of doing an immersion.

"Brother John" as the Baptist pastor was called by his people, was very gracious. We were able to work out a time when the Methodists could "take over his church building for our service of baptism." He explained to me the way he conducted immersions. While many churches which practice immersion baptism are very sophisticated in the practice of it—using robes for all participants and waders for the pastor so his clothes would not get wet—Brother John pointed out in a small rural town they didn't bother with such niceties. All participants simply wore a set of clothes they didn't mind getting wet and brought an extra set of clothing into which they would change following the immersion. There was a changing room for men and another for women. I figured I could handle this all right. Just one more problem arose. I was the only man involved that day. Following the immersion, while I was changing out of some blue jeans into a suit of dry clothes, I suddenly realized I had failed to bring along a set of dry underwear! "Nothing to do but to just get dressed without underwear. No one will ever know the difference," I said to myself. When the service was over,

I drove home. As I walked in the front door of the parsonage, Lorine said "You're walking kind of funny. What's the matter?" I guess I was feeling a little self conscious which led me to walk a bit differently. At any rate, I told her what had happened. We had a good laugh and this has been one of our favorite stories through the years.

There are always regional differences within the church. One of these differences, within Methodism at least, was the Southern church custom not only to provide a parsonage for their pastor, but also to completely furnish and equip the parsonage. In the rest of the nation, Methodist Churches only provide the parsonage. Pastoral families have their own personal furniture which they moved from parsonage to parsonage as appointments changed.

Unfortunately rural southern churches, often financially strapped, usually simply collected from members used furniture and "cast-offs" to put in their parsonages. Needless to say, parsonage families were not often pleased with the tastes of others or the condition of "hand-me-down" furniture. Aunt Susie's art work or favorite chair was difficult to dispose of if you didn't want it— particularly if she were still a member of the church. This is one of the reasons why I had no difficulty in convincing Lorine we should return to serve my home Conference in Kansas when our seminary days were over. Of course, in our situation in Adairville, it really worked out pretty well for us because we didn't have to try to come up with another set of furniture for our "country home."

Our parsonage, however, was not the most modern which leads to another story about both of us being dazed. I always had a long list of things needing to be done upon our arrival in Adairville on Friday afternoons. About five months into this appointment, we arrived from Nashville one week-end, walked into the parsonage, and discovered a heavy coating of black soot all over the main floor. Our parsonage was heated with a free standing oil burning stove which sat in the middle of the living room. Somehow, during the week, while we were in Nashville, the furnace had malfunctioned and exploded. The explosion was not the type which destroyed things with physical violence, but it was the type which sent smoke and the residue from the burning fuel oil everywhere around the house. What a mess! Obviously, it would take hours to clean everything up. I had only about twenty-four hours to prepare a sermon and service for Sunday and to touch base with people making necessary consultations and visits. After doing a few minimal necessities in helping with our catastrophe, I turned to Lorine and said, "I'm going to have to leave this mess with you to clean up. I've got to get going." I know she's never forgotten this and I'm not sure whether she ever forgave me.

My ministry with the Oakland Methodist Church was largely a Sunday Morning preaching service. One Oakland experience still stands out in my memory. The little white framed church was not air conditioned. During the spring, summer, and fall we had the windows and doors open while we were holding services. This, of course, allowed a variety of winged creatures to enter the sanctuary. As clearly as if it were yesterday, I remember one morning when I was preaching, I felt something! It seemed like a bug or something was crawling up my leg. I continued preaching, saying nothing about this to the congregation. Occasionally I would stand on one foot and shake my other leg hoping to dislodge whatever was there to get it to fall to the floor. Finally, it seemed that the intruder was getting so high that it was just about to invade the close quarters of my private parts. To prevent this, I reached down, in the most inconspicuous way possible, to squash the bug before it crawled any higher. What I thought was a bug turned out to be a yellow jacket wasp. When I sought to squash it, the wasp went into a defensive mode and began stinging me. I could no longer contain myself. Uncontrollable I stepped away from the pulpit and began to do a dance, jumping up and down, stomping my foot, trying to get the wasp out of my trousers. I don't know how long this effort went on. I know by the time the wasp was finished with me and I was finished with it, and with my dance, I had one curious congregation wondering what was going on. I was almost dazed from the sting.

Week-ends in Adairville were always very full. Only minimal amounts of time could be called free-time or recreational time.

Adairville didn't have a theater. The county seat of Logan County was Russellville, ten miles north. We could find a movie and a nice restaurant there but seldom felt we had time to go even that far. What little week-end recreation we indulged in was pretty much homemade recreation. For example, in the early spring, we were often able to go driving in the country and find wild asparagus growing in the ditches and fence rows. It was fun to go out looking for asparagus, harvesting it, and returning home to feast on it. Basically tobacco and corn were the main cash crops of our farmers, but around Adairville there were farmers, and other people with small tracts of land, who raised strawberries by the acres. Adairville's only industry was a plant which froze strawberries for the commercial market. Each spring Adairville had a strawberry festival. In both the spring of 1957 and 1958 we had fun being part of this community celebration and we delighted in picking all the strawberries we could consume.

When weather was nice and time permitted, cruising the countryside in our car was always enjoyable. One unique thing about the Adairville Church was its connection with early American Methodism. A required reading book for my "History of American Denominations" course at Vanderbilt was the *Autobiography of Peter Cartwright*. This is an absolutely fascinating book not only from the point of view of early southern church history, but also because of the way it pictures and dramatizes the western movement of people in early America and their culture. If it can be found, it is still worth the read for present-day readers.

Peter Cartwright was one of the early Methodist circuit riders and among the first to serve in Kentucky, Tennessee, Indiana, Ohio, and Illinois. For over a half century he rode wilderness circuits through heavy forests and shoulder-high prairie grasses, from the Appalachians to the Mississippi River. Not long after Peter Cartwright's birth in Virginia, September 1, 1785, his parents decided to move to Kentucky where they chose a homesite in Logan County. This home site was south of Russellville and near where present-day Adairville is located.

It was in this pioneer environment that Cartwright grew up. Near the turn of the century a remarkable religious awakening, known to historians as the Great Western Revival, began in this very area. One of its prominent features was the gathering of thousands of people in camp meetings, in the forest, for days at a time and often for several weeks at a time. There was constant preaching and hymn singing, lengthy sermons and high emotion. The teen-age Cartwright was converted in this setting. When he was about seventeen, his family moved west a couple of counties. A preacher commissioned him to create a new circuit in this "unchurched wilderness." Taking Cartwright's autobiography, other texts from my American Church History course, plus various local church records, Lorine and I would sometimes go cruising in the country trying to find the places I was reading about. It was a great form of fun.

Ministers often say they gained far more from the churches they served as students than the churches gained from them. I'm sure that was true in my case. I'm forever grateful to the good people of Adairville for tolerating me and allowing me to practice parish ministry skills on them.

I've saved the best of all the memories from this period of time until the last. Lorine and I wanted to start a family. While we were serving Adairville she got pregnant. We were thrilled. Back in Nashville in preparation for our family addition, we moved from our small one-bedroom apartment on Sixteenth Avenue to a much larger two-bedroom duplex at 3703 Rolland Road. We greatly enjoyed the more spacious home and neighborhood. Because we spent most days of the week in Nashville and because Nashville had a stellar medical center, Vanderbilt University Hospital, with excellent obstetricians and pediatricians (Adairville didn't have a single doctor), we planned for our first child to be born in Nashville.

Things went well for Lorine during her pregnancy. She continued her weekend commutes to the country with me. We knew the baby would be born in August (1957). We planned for Lorine to "give her notice" to the Divinity School when the 1956-1957 academic year ended. This would leave her free the rest of the summer to make final preparations for the baby's arrival. Our second bedroom was to be turned into the nursery. This meant getting a crib, painting it, and finding special curtains, etc. I was struggling so that summer taking and trying to successfully pass graduate school German I wasn't much help to Lorine. I was fond of saying, "It's harder to do German than it is to have a baby." To this Lorine was fond of replying, "What do you know about being pregnant and going through child birth?"

Once July came, we began to discuss the wisdom of Lorine being in Adairville on weekends. There seemed to be no urgency to change things along this line. The first week-end in August Lorine's dad brought her mother to spend a week or so with us. By the next weekend we thought the baby's arrival time was drawing near. Lorine's father returned to Nashville so they could stay with Lorine while I went to Adairville to conduct services. This way Lorine could be near the doctor and the hospital. As soon as Sunday services ended on August 11, 1957, I headed back to the city. Once I was there, Lorine's folks returned to Owensboro. Lorine was still feeling fine although a bit restless. We took a walk and had a nice quiet Sunday evening together.

About 5 a.m. the next morning Lorine woke me saying, "I think my water has broken. I'm not feeling all that many contractions, but I think we'd better head for the hospital." We dressed and headed for the hospital as quickly as possible arriving there before 6:00 a.m. I dropped her off at the emergency entrance where the aides took her to the birth care center. I went to park the car. By the time I got to her room, she was having contractions. However, I was told "You need to go downstairs—officially check her in to the hospital. The doctor hasn't arrived yet and it will be a while before the baby comes." Following instructions, I went to check Lorine in but to my amazement by the time I got back upstairs, we had a healthy new baby son—6 pounds, 8 ounces, and 21 inches long. I couldn't believe I'd missed most of the action! While Lorine was still in her predelivery room, she told a nurses' aide that she needed to use the rest room and was accompanied there by the aide. As she was using the toilet she looked down and said, "I see the baby's head!" Everyone really swung into action, but by the time the doctor arrived so had our son.

Like all parents to be, we discussed names but rather easily came up with Benjamin Martin Kieler, mostly because of my admiration for Lorine's dad, Benjamin Martin, not to mention her own appreciation for him and partly because I was aware that Ben was the name of an uncle I never knew due to his early death in the flu epidemic of 1917.

We enjoyed doting over him in ways appropriate to any child—rocking him, talking to him, singing to him, reading to him, taking him for walks in a baby carriage, photographing him, changing diapers (which in this period of history were always cloth diapers that required rinsing out in the toilet stool before depositing them in a soiled diapers pail until laundry time) and bathing him, etc. Strollers were not so common at that time although we had them for our other two boys. Giving Ben baths and taking him for walks were two of my favorite things to do when he first came home.

The 1957 Model baby carriage in which Ben was taken for
walks by his father and mother.

As soon as Lorine and Ben were ready to be dismissed from the hospital, our obstetrician recommended a pediatrician for us—Dr Pennington, a woman doctor. We were impressed with her in a variety of ways. One of these was her "prescription" for sun bathing. She said children needed regular sunlight. She showed Lorine (who usually took Ben to the doctor for his regular appointments) how to protect his eyes. Then she said, just take all his clothes off and lay him on a blanket on the lawn, and give him 15 seconds of sunlight on one side followed by rolling him over and giving him 15 seconds of sunlight on the other side. We were to do this twice daily, once each morning and each afternoon. She gradually increased the length of time and I think before cold weather arrived she had us giving him maybe 2 minutes of a sunbath on each side.

First time parents have a way of panicking when it comes to their child's safety and well being. Dr. Pennington was very understanding and supportive at this point. For instance, all of our children grew up before the days of child-restraints in cars. One day Ben's mom was driving him home from a doctor's appointment. Ben was in a child's seat placed on the front passenger seat of our car. Ben was fussy, and Lorine handed him her wallet to try to entertain him. He dropped it. With one hand on the wheel, she reached down to pick up the wallet and in the process allowed the car to swerve just enough to run into a parked car. The sudden impact jarred Ben out of his seat, to the floor. He began screaming and Lorine was sure the fall must have injured Ben in some way. Turning around, she quickly returned to the doctor's office. Dr. Pennington gave Ben a quick once over, reassured Lorine that babies don't break very easily and said he was OK.

It was Ben's first Christmas that gave us perhaps our greatest fright. We were spending a couple of weeks in Adairville during school break. We went to Owensboro for Christmas. Not only would we get to visit Ben's grandparents, but this would be a chance for him to meet others in the Martin family. His Aunt Mary and Uncle Harmon Hoffman and their three boys, Leslie, John, and Alan, were coming from Alabama to Owensboro for the holidays. We'd all had a day of enjoyment together. At bedtime it was discovered that Alan had chickenpox. We were devastated. How could our little Ben at the tender age of 4 months possibly survive chickenpox? We phoned Dr. Pennington back in Nashville to consult with her. She assured us the situation was not critical, but did say that the longer he was exposed to chickenpox the harder it might hit him. She recommended we leave right away. If Ben got chickenpox, he would probably have a lighter case of it. We were disappointed to have to leave in the middle of our Christmas celebration with all the Martins, but we went back to Adairville for the balance of the holiday. Sure enough, Ben did get chickenpox, but sure enough, he had a fairly light case of it.

We had one big help when we came to Adairville after Ben was born. About the time of Ben's birth, we met a young black woman in her twenties. Landonie was willing to work for us about 4 hours each Friday afternoon plus extra times when we might be coming to Adairville. Landonie's jobs were to come to the parsonage 2 or 3 hours before we arrived, turn up the heat so it would be warm when we arrived, give the place a quick dusting, and prepare a nice hot supper for us! She was great. She also tutored Lorine in a few of the southern ways of cooking—things such as making a pecan pie—things which Lorine had not learned as she grew up. Landonie's pecan pie is one item that all in our family still enjoy to this day.

Ben was baptized in Adairville. One of the executive program secretaries of the Methodist General Board of Higher Education in Nashville was Heil Bollinger. He was at the leadership helm in Methodist student work. I first met Heil when he was on the University of Illinois campus to organize and carry-off the Quadrennial National Methodist Student Movement Conference at Christmas of 1947. The Wesley Foundation asked me to serve as his "go-fer." I came to enjoy Heil a great deal; he seemed to take a great interest in me—even to the point of encouraging me in the direction campus ministry and recommending Yale Divinity School as an excellent place for me to go to seminary. Heil was one of those persons with whom I reconnected when I came to Nashville. It was his encouragement and influence on my life, which caused us to ask Heil to come officiate at Ben's baptism. Ben, of course, never knew him, but for us having someone of Heil's stature baptize our firstborn was pretty special.

**Ben Kieler and his parents in front of his
Adairville parsonage home the day of his baptism.
The Rev. Dr. Heil Bolllinger in center.**

Back to Dr. Pennington once more. In the spring of 1958, after Ben was crawling, Dr. Pennington drew our attention to the fact Ben's feet were both tending to turn inward. "A bit more than normal," she said as she referred us to a pediatric orthopedic specialist. The specialist felt that this was something best corrected sooner rather than later, meaning before Ben started walking. As result, Ben received a metal brace (bar) with his two shoes attached in a manner that kept his feet facing straight forward. For a few months, Ben was to wear this all the time; later, he had to wear this only during his night-time hours. By the time we left Nashville, in August of 1958, Ben's feet seemed to be pretty normal again, but we were to keep using the brace until we could connect with a Kansas specialist who could assess the situation. When that time came, everything was OK again. Certainly being first-time parents can leave you in a daze as well as being a first-time pastor.

Even though I "cut my ministerial teeth" on this parish, I guess I didn't do too badly. Speaking with Dr. Spears, my District Superintendent in Kentucky, about our plans to return to Kansas he was very affirming of my ministry there saying, "I don't want to try to take you away from your home Annual Conference, but we would be pleased to have you stay in the Louisville Annual Conference." I could have enjoyed doing that and I'm sure Lorine would have been happy, but beyond the magnetic pull of home, of Kansas, there was one basic reason why I chose not to stay. I had strong convictions on civil rights. I knew these would always be part of who I was and what I had to say and do. In Kentucky, I would always be an outsider. What I had to say about these things could be discounted and probably resented. In Kansas, I would be speaking as one native to other natives and might have a better hearing.

Chapter 36

OUR FIRST KANSAS APPOINTMENT

If Radio's Slim Fingers

If radio's slim fingers can pluck a melody from night
And toss it over a continent or sea;
If petalled white notes of a violin are blown
Across a mountain or a city's din;

If songs like crimson roses are culled
From thin blue air
Why should mortals wonder
If God hears prayer?

(A poem of unidentified origin used by Dr.Ronald Meredith in
every Sunday morning service at First Methodist Church,
Wichita in the late 1950s and in the 1960s)

It was a beautiful, mild, late summer Sunday afternoon. Lorine and I and one-year old Ben had been to my parents. We were driving from my folks in Hutchinson through Wichita and were now headed south on US Highway 81. Even though I'd been a life long Kansan, I could not remember having ever previously traveled this stretch of road. It seemed like one giant truck garden, like paradise. On both sides of the highway there were roadside stands where farmers were selling their late summer and early fall produce. There were still homegrown tomatoes, squash and all the vegetables of summer gardens adorning the stands plus watermelons, cantaloupes, and a few early pumpkins along with baskets of already picked fruit. We were driving by numerous peach and apple orchards. Peach season was over, but the apple trees were loaded with ripe apples. People were driving to the orchards to "pick and pay." They could go out among the trees and pick tree ripened fresh apples—as many or as few as they wanted. It was a great family activity.

The roads were lined with giant cottonwood trees still largely covered with their shimmering light green leaves now freckled with the fall beginnings of leaves turning yellow. The area was a flood plain so the soil was a rich fertile sandy loam. Picturesque fields of grain were everywhere. After a few miles, to the right of the highway, we could see the Ninnescah River. Out of sight, to our left 4 or 5 miles, was the Arkansas River. The underflow beneath the land was not deep. Unlike many parts of Kansas, this meant easily available water which contributed to the verdant garden-like nature of what we were seeing.

About 15 miles south of Wichita US Highway 81 took a 90 degree turn to the right for a mile or two before continuing south to Wellington, county seat of Sumner County, and the county which normally produces more wheat than any other Kansas county. As the highway turned west, we saw a little green highway sign pointing the other direction, reading "Belle Plaine 3 miles." Belle Plaine is French for "beautiful plain." In the 1870's, pioneers from Belle Plaine, Iowa, had traveled here by covered wagon. Appropriately they brought the name with them to their new town.

We turned left for Belle Plaine—also our destination. Bishop Dawson and his cabinet of seven District Superintendents had chosen the Belle Plaine Methodist Church for our first appointment in the Central Kansas Annual Conference.

The Rev. Paul Gilbert had been serving the church for 5 years. During the spring session of Annual Conference, Paul was appointed to another charge. They knew I was remaining at Vanderbilt for the summer to work on my thesis. Dick and Shirley Robbins were a young couple just graduating from Southwestern College. Dick was a pre-ministerial student and that fall they would be leaving Winfield heading out to Iliff School of Theology in Denver to begin seminary. Arrangements were made for Dick to "cover for me" until I got to Belle Plaine on Labor Day.

I had been given the name of Paul Nelson, Principal of Belle Plaine High School and Chairman of the church's Pastor-Parish Relations Committee, as the person to contact upon our arrival. We were thrilled with this appointment. I had majored in Public Affairs with a Labor-Management Relations specialty at the University of Illinois. Accordingly, I had requested an appointment that might give me a chance to relate to people working in an industrial setting. While Belle Plaine was located in a rural setting, in the midst of "the beautiful garden," it was only 20 miles or less from the Wichita aircraft plants—Boeing, Cessna, and Beech, and related suppliers. Belle Plaine was as much a bedroom community, from which people commuted to work in the city, as it was a rural community.

Arriving in town, we inquired where Paul Nelson lived and found him at home. He reported to us an interesting bit of previously unreceived news. The church's parsonage had been very old, run down, and basically beyond renovation. Since there would not be a resident pastor that summer of 1958, the church had decided to tear it down and build a new parsonage on the same spot, just to the north of the church. This was great news. The bad news, as you might guess: the contractor was running behind schedule. The house wasn't ready. It would be another 30 days before we would be able to move into the new parsonage. However, just across the street from the high school, the committee had found a 3 or 4 room apartment which they had rented for our use during September. By October 1st, the attractive 3 bedroom blond brick parsonage built over a full basement was completed and ready for us. The total cost of this new home was $15,000!

Even though our streets and roads in Central and Western Kansas sometimes had nice trees, basically, we were a treeless state in comparison to forested Kentucky where Lorine grew up. Abundant rain of the south helped trees grow much faster and larger than in Kansas. Missing the trees, Lorine soon found herself a bit homesick. She wondered what she had gotten into, following me to Kansas. But Belle Plaine was full of highlights for us. One of these was "the Arboretum."

The Arboretum in 1910 by Dr. Walter B. Bartlett, a physician from New York State, who had come to practice medicine in Belle Plaine. Avocationally, he was a horticulturalist and arborist. In the southwest corner of town, Dr. Bartlett purchased a little tract with several acres of land with a nice little draw, sometimes creek, running through it. It was there Dr. Bartlett began to develop his own Arboretum. He had two special interests. One was to select species of trees not commonly found in Kansas, some not even native to the USA, seeking to nurture them to maturity in his Arboretum. The other interest was tulips. Each fall he would import bulbs from Holland planting countless varieties in order to produce a splendid show when tulip-time came in the spring.

Dr. Bartlett was succeeded by son, Glenn, trained in horticulture and landscape design. Later they were assisted by their daughters, especially Mary Bartlett Gourlay and her husband, Bob, who eventually became their successors. A paragraph taken from an Arboretum tabloid of the 1980's speaks of its mystique:

> "As they escape from summer's outside heat and wind, visitors, upon entering the Arboretum, have a sudden feeling of stepping into another world. They are enveloped in an air of peace and enchantment. They . . . stroll along quiet paths in the shade of trees native to China, Japan, Africa, Europe and other exotic lands as well as various sections of the United States . . . . Here they discover the charm of plants from other parts of North America and other continents. They may travel far in spirit and

experience a feeling suggesting the atmosphere of the Versailles in Paris, Kew Gardens in London and other renown gardens."

When Lorine discovered the Bartlett Arboretum, this forested little beauty patch, she soon began spending time there and rather quickly overcame her homesickness.

Another highlight of Belle Plaine, for us, was the large number of young couples who lived there. Many were in our church and several soon became good friends. Mary Bartlett Gourlay and her husband, Bob, and their four children were among our friends.

By the first of October we were in the new parsonage. As a personal contribution to the new parsonage, we engaged Glenn Bartlett to make a professional landscaping plan for it. We got some of the plantings that fall. The next spring we finished setting out the shrubs, plants and flowers. Glenn also recommended a new grass, zoysia, for a lawn. It was a warm season grass which flourishes in Kansas summer heat, but like Buffalo grass, its green carpet turned brown with the first touch of cold weather and stayed that way until late spring. However, during the summer it was nice as a golf green. One draw back—it had to be planted in the spring by either placing plugs in holes scattered throughout the newly prepared ground or by pulling sod apart and laying rhizomes in shallow trenches. In the spring of 1959, we spent many days at this planting task.

Lorine's good friend, Jane Stevenson, one of the bridesmaids at our wedding, came to visit in our new home. She got more than she bargained for! We put her to work on her hands and knees helping us plant Zoysia. Jane has never been back to visit us since. Unfortunately, with the passage of years and the coming of other pastors who had different interests than ours, the landscaping plan was never maintained.

Jenny Bell was an older lady who found her niche in life by grand-mothering the children of others. We discovered her to be a wonderful lady with whom to entrust Ben when we needed a baby sitter. On one special occasion, we wanted to go to Wichita for dinner and an evening out at the symphony. We arranged for Mrs. Bell to stay with Ben. As the day wore on, Ben seemed to be getting a cold and began developing some fever. Lorine took Ben down the street to Dr. Y. E. Parkhurst's office to have him checked. The doctor wasn't overly concerned so we left as planned for Wichita. Coming home that night we saw a police car with red light and siren headed north. Naturally we wondered what had happened and to whom. Pulling up to the parsonage, we saw another police car and Mrs. Bell was in tears. Ben's fever had suddenly shot up very high. He'd become nauseated and aspirated vomit into his lungs. Mrs. Bell called Dr. Parkhurst who came to the house. Not wanting to wait for an ambulance to come from Wellington, Dr. Parkhurst called for the local police to take Ben to St. Joseph Hospital in Wichita where he could be seen by a specialist. He even accompanied Ben on the trip. Ben ended up spending several days in the hospital, but by the time he was dismissed he was no worse for it all. We were eternally grateful to Mrs. Bell and Dr. Parkhurst for their prompt and caring responses to the crisis.

Across the years, several impressions, tasks and/or events stand out from our first appointment in Kansas. The first of these is that Belle Plaine seemed to be a very open and progressive congregation. We had a retired Deaconess, Fredda Dudy, who gave excellent lay leadership; we had LaVonta Wagner who was a certified Lab School teacher who conscientiously trained our Sunday School teachers; we had a strong youth program, and a strong choir under Barbara Brummett's direction. Beyond Sunday Morning worship, we frequently had Sunday evening services which varied in form from mission or Bible studies, music and drama, to forums dealing with social issues of the day and vespers for times of quiet.

An example of one of these services comes from the days of rabid and emotional right wing public and political anti-communist tirades sparked by Senator Joseph McCarthy. In the Vietnam War era, our Social Action Commission brought a colleague to help the Sunday evening forum think through a number of these issues. Another time a professor from Wichita

State University helped us, calmly and rationally, think through the issue of whether the United States should recognize Communist China. Always we had time for give and take discussion.

I don't recall that these types of presentations generated conflict, but they certainly had the potential to do so. My own feelings about leadership in such situations were these: make the church a forum for important social issues (using the Karl Barth model of holding the Bible in one hand and the newspaper in the other); be clear in my own convictions and understandings of the faith, but don't avoid conflict just for the sake of maintaining harmony; respect people; and honor their right to differ.

I did not always have annual evangelistic or special services adapted from the days of revivals, but some years I did seek to feature special guest pastors in a series of services. Our first Easter season in Belle Plaine, I arranged for us to have a Sunday, Monday, and Tuesday evening series of services featuring the Dr. Ron Meredith, Wichita First United Methodist Church. Ron was a very popular pastor known beyond his congregation because his Sunday morning services were broadcast on the radio. He was a warm, literate, folksy type preacher. I was always taken by his use of the poem "If Radio's Slim Fingers" before each pastoral prayer.

During these services, I led the entire service except for the preaching. As a young pastor, I greatly appreciated something that Ron did with my permission. He critiqued portions of my public demeanor in leading worship. With a kind and gentle spirit he gave this new pastor suggestions that were quite helpful. As young parents, Lorine and I appreciated something else about Ron. During one of the evening services, our two year old Ben was being very active. He wouldn't sit still and he insisted in crawling on the floor under the pews and generally making a scene. When Lorine came up to Ron at the close of the service to apologize for Ben's behavior, Ron just smiled and chuckled and said, "Don't worry about it. If God didn't want children to be so active, he wouldn't have put so many wiggles in them." It was this spirit, I'm sure, which drew lots of young families to First Church Wichita.

At least three young couples gave dedicated and creative

leadership to our Methodist Youth Fellowship. The names of two of the three couples still pop into my mind—Bud and Maxine Olson and "Duck" and Roscine Downing. Good natured Bud impressed me and was an inspiration for our youth because although he was a one armed man, he managed to do virtually everything any other person could do. All three of these couples had boats and were water skiing enthusiasts. Part of their UMYF activities included an annual summer retreat on the shores of Grand Lake in Oklahoma. A big feature of the retreat was three or four hours of water skiing each day.

I was co-opted to give the content leadership each retreat while we were in Belle Plaine. Neither Lorine nor I water skied, but these couples saw to it that we learned to ski just like each of the kids did. This was no problem for Lorine, but since I'm a non-swimmer I was sure I would drown. I easily panicked. Bud Olson, however, could ski and he insisted he could teach me. He taught me how to lie comfortably on my back before starting, how to use my knees to pull up out of the water, and how to flex my knees to stay up. Bud helped me anticipate the experience by telling me that it was just like standing on an empty hay rack when the horses were trotting. I could relate to that from my childhood days. I've always been grateful to Bud for the coaching and understanding I received, and skiing became something I could enjoy throughout my life.

My skills in working with youth were also honed during these years by a pastor who became an unlikely friend. Rev. Orson Evans had grown up a Nazarene and become a Nazarene pastor. This meant he had a very conservative faith. Several years before I returned from seminary, Orson switched from the Church of the Nazarene to the Methodist Church. One of his strong suits in ministry was youth work. In our Annual Conference's camping program, Orson became well known and appreciated for the leadership he gave for many years to two boys' camps in Colorado—Camp Pike and Camp Sheldon Woods. His leadership was also unique because a rather large number of those young men who worked with him later became pastors themselves.

Camp Pike was a large camp which gave summer pleasure and

inspiration to between 75 and 100 older elementary age boys. For a week, the camp used a Mennonite campground between Divide and Cripple Creek, on the back side of Pike's Peak (14,000+') In addition to good food—both in the mess hall and in daily devotions—and to the emotionally moving setting of the mountains and evening campfires, the camp featured two things. The big feature for the boys was the camp's grand finale—climbing to the top of Pike's Peak after 5 days of conditioning hikes. The other feature was daily Bible study. Everything was done in small groups of about seven boys under the leadership of an older teen-ager. Hikes were also planned from a naturalist's point of view to engender an appreciation of nature and a sense of stewardship in relationship to God's earth. Orson, the Dean of Camp Pike, always had an Assistant Dean who was one of the younger ministers of the Conference.

Camp Sheldon Woods' setting was unique for church camps. Large private rustic ranch style homes, located in a little Mennonite enclave in a valley high above Camp Pike, were rented for the week preceding Camp Pike. This was the training site to prepare older teens who were to be the leadership core for Camp Pike. Many tasks were to be learned. The Pike leaders needed to become familiar with the various trails over which the Camp Pike boys would hike. Flowers and fauna along the way were to be identified. Safety was taught. We needed conditioning hikes plus a trial hike to the summit of Pike's Peak in preparation for the next week. We studied the same Bible study which was to be taught the next week so that each teen was prepared to teach the boys in their small group. The younger minister chosen to be Assistant Dean for Camp Pike was always the Dean of Camp Sheldon Woods, and Orson was the Assistant Dean for Sheldon Woods.

Orson Evans was the unlikely friend because he was older than I and was so much more biblically and theologically conservative than I. Our faith journeys had been very different. I probably would never have singled Orson out to be one of my mentors in ministry. However, about 4 months after my arrival in Belle Plaine,

Orson, then serving as pastor at the Augusta Methodist Church, singled me out, inviting me over for a Coke. Being new in the Conference I was unfamiliar with Camp Pike and Sheldon Woods. Orson told about the two camping programs and said, "I'd like to invite you to work with me this summer, to be my Assistant at Camp Pike and to be the Dean of Sheldon Woods." I quizzed him some more and then replied "Yes." I profited ever so much from that experience the next two or three summers not to mention the thrill of climbing Pike's Peak several times—even those climbs when we were pelted by ice and snow in July.

In later year's Orson's conservative streak (eventually even to the point of seeking to run church members out of the church on moral grounds) led him to become very unhappy with Methodist Church leadership, with his peers and even with me. When we worked together, Orson always accorded me freedom to teach and lead as I felt led, respecting me in the process. We were good friends until he went "off the deep end." Then he became withdrawn and isolated himself form most of his peers. Later as his District Superintendent I tried to reach out to him in several ways, but no avail. I'm not sure what I learned from this experience but there's got be a lesson in it.

An additional highlight of our Belle Plaine years was the satisfaction of working with the congregation in beginning a new church building program. The white frame church, located just to the south of our parsonage, may have been Belle Plaine's original Methodist Church building. Six years after the congregation was founded this church building was erected. A small educational wing was later added. The old frame structure was still used when we arrived in Belle Plaine—nowhere near adequate size for its congregation. The tiny "church office" was located in the furnace room for lack of other space. There were not enough church school classrooms. At least two adult classes had to meet in the sanctuary where there were only fixed pews for seating. The fellowship hall was inadequate for most social occasions.

The author standing in the Belle Plaine pulpit of the
Belle Plaine Methodist Church during his 1958-1963 tenure.

A wedding catastrophe resulted in part because of the inadequate entrance to this old building. Guests and ladies in wedding parties always seemed to have their hair "just right" and to be very fashionable in their dress. It was a summer wedding. The tiny 10' or 12' square foyer, leading from out-of-doors into the sanctuary, was packed with ladies waiting to be seated. All are properly attired. A severe summer thunderstorm suddenly broke loose. A couple, arriving late and running to get out of the downpour, opened the door to enter the foyer. At that moment a huge gust of wind blew a torrent of water into the foyer dousing several of the ladies waiting to be seated, drenching one to the extreme. The material of which the dress was made suddenly began to shrink. Not only was the lady embarrassed because of being soaked. Now she was embarrassed because her slip, which didn't shrink, was two or three inches longer than her dress!

I wasn't in Belle Plaine long enough to see a new church but I started a planning process. A planning committee was established. In those days the structure of the district provided a "Building

and Church Location Committee" and the General Board of
Missions also offered helpful resources. I was able to help our
planning committee draw on these resources to do a study of what
we needed. The site of the old church was very small with little or
no off-street parking. The town of Belle Plaine was growing to the
east and to the north. A couple who were members of our church
lived on a half section of land at the north edge of town. We were
able to negotiate the acquisition of several acres of land from them
for use as a future building site.

At this time a number of new churches were being built
everywhere by almost every denomination. Many congregations
thought they had discovered a way to "save money"—the use of
Pyle Construction Company in McPherson. The owner specialized
in building generic churches. He was a man of faith and integrity
so he was dependable, but he was not from a "mainline church"
tradition. His method of "saving money" was to use an in-house
architect who drew basic building plans with the same formula for
all the churches. This eliminated the expense of employing a regular
architect. The only trouble was the lack of imagination in the plans
coupled with little hint of either the great traditions of church
architecture or of Christian themes.

I wanted Belle Plaine to have a more distinctive church and I
was able to connect our planning committee with an architect
whom I knew in Hutchinson. We were able to come up with a
more creative proposal for the new church, a proposed building which
would make a definite statement of faith and be a work of art. Still, we
were years away from having the money to build. Between the time I
left Belle Plaine and construction actually began, a hybrid combination
of this plan and a Pyle proposal was the end result.

In spite of the resulting compromise, the satisfaction of having
helped the church move from a 19th century facility to a 20th
century facility which presented a progressive witness to the
community has lingered with me throughout my life. Moreover,
we had some great fun in getting started with the fund raising.
Barbara Brumett, our choir director, was an energetic and very
talented musician. Barbara came up with the idea of a community

musical to begin raising funds for the new church. She did a splendid job with this. It was a great success and for several years it became an annual tradition.

Someone else came up with an idea borrowed from several other communities—"let's have a big community pig roast!" This, too, proved to be a source of enjoyment with a unifying effect for the whole community of Belle Plaine.

A large pit several feet deep was actually dug in the church backyard, hickory wood was burned for an entire day to fill the pit with a deep bed of hot coals, and then layers of wet burlap were placed on top of the coals to insulate the aluminum foil wrapped pork from the coals. The pit was sealed with the meat remaining there for almost 24 hours after which the feast was held. This was so successful that it became a community tradition for several years.

My final and probably most significant contribution to the building program was helping lead the church into the use of a Board of Missions professional fund-raising consultant who in turn led them in a successful three or four year pledge program for the building program. At that time this was a relatively new idea for churches and certainly an idea unknown to our congregation. It really proved to be a launching pad that led ultimately to building the new church.

Chapter 37

TWO MORE TALES FROM
BELLE PLAINE

Two important memories from Belle Plaine remain to be shared—a joyful event, personal in nature, and an unhappy event within the congregation and my ministry.

By the time Ben was two years old, we were settled into a comfortable routine in Belle Plaine and were eager to expand our family. Lorine didn't get pregnant quite as quickly or easily as we had hoped, but by April of 1962 she was pregnant. On January 24, 1963, our second son, William Harold Kieler was born. Partly we chose his name just because we liked the sound of it, partly because the names were connections with the Kieler heritage.

Lorine had a pretty easy time of things through these nine months of pregnancy. When I got back from doing my two camps in Colorado the summer of 1962, we turned around and went back out to Colorado to tent camp for our summer vacation. We even did some horseback riding while she was carrying Bill. That fall Lorine did some substitute teaching in the Grade School just across the street from our parsonage.

Belle Plaine was a town of about 1,600. It had two physicians— Dr. Phipps and Dr. Parkhurst. We used both of them on occasion. Sad to say, we can't remember which one delivered Bill. Belle Plaine was too small to have a hospital, but we were surrounded by hospitals. As I made my pastoral rounds to visit the hospitalized, I might go to any one of eleven hospitals. Wellington, 15 minutes to the south had 3 hospitals—an Osteopathic Hospital, the Hatcher Clinic hospital and St. Luke's Hospital, a general community hospital. Wichita, 30 minutes to the north, had 5 hospitals— Wesley, our Methodist hospital, St. Joseph and St. Francis, two Roman Catholic hospitals, a psychiatric hospital, and the VA (Veterans Administration) Hospital. About 30 minutes to the southeast, Winfield had two hospitals—a general community hospital, Newton Memorial, and a Roman Catholic hospital. 15 minutes south of those was the general hospital in Arkansas City, best known for an eye surgeon associated with it. I frequently spent the better part of a day when I went hospital calling because it was not uncommon for us to have parishioners in four, five, or six hospitals in 2 or 3 different communities. There were rare occasions when I had someone in all 11 hospitals!

We anticipated Bill's birth would occur about three weeks into January. In planning for Bill's arrival, we focused on Wellington because our local doctors used St. Luke's Hospital and it was nearest. On January 17, 1962, we headed to the hospital when Lorine began having pains which we interpreted as labor pains. I guess the doctor also thought they were labor pains because he admitted Lorine to the hospital. By the next morning, all was quiet. "False labor" they called it and they sent Lorine home. A week later, January 24, 1963, a snow storm was beginning to move in. Lorine was beginning to feel a few pains again. We debated what to do. We were embarrassed to go through another false alarm but with snow coming, we didn't want to risk getting stranded in Belle Plaine. Playing it safe, we headed once more for Wellington. This time, Bill arrived at 7:17 p.m. that evening.

Bill was a normal, healthy, typical baby boy. Our joy doubled. Since we had practiced our parenting skills on Ben, we handled Bill's first few months, yes the first few years, with a lot less anxiety than with Ben. Within a few weeks we started planning a baptism.

"My boss," so to speak, our District Superintendent Dr. Loyal Miles, was a person whom we greatly appreciated. He had been a banker, a lawyer, and then an FBI agent. Finally, Loyal left the Federal Bureau of Investigation to become a Methodist pastor. He was fond of telling people he "quit practicing and started preaching." He was younger than most DSs, a very open, helpful, friendly, supportive person.

In those days, when Annual Conference met each May, it was the custom for pastors and spouses who had new children arrive during the previous year, to have them baptized at a special service conducted by the bishop.

This was a nice custom and we appreciated our Bishop. But, we felt we'd like to share our special moment with the congregation. Moreover, we wanted to have someone with whom we were personally well acquainted baptize Bill, so we asked Loyal to come to Belle Plaine and baptize him in our Sunday morning worship service. We felt honored to have Loyal accept our invitation and it was a very meaningful occasion for all concerned.

We were almost finished with supper a few weeks later. The phone rang. "Harold, I know you weren't planning on being here tonight, but we've got a crises and we *urgently* need you. Can you come over to our meeting in the church basement for a little while?" I felt I needed to respond. I ended up being there nearly three hours. In the meanwhile, Lorine had no idea what was going on and why I didn't return for my dessert. She was worried.

When I did return, she of course asked, "What was going on over there tonight? Why did it take you so long?" My response was basically an invoking of confidentiality in Clergy-parishioner relationships. Perhaps I was overly concerned to maintain confidentiality on sensitive personal issues. My responses to Lorine's questions were all general. They didn't shed much light on the specifics of the situation. Her frustration about the way I had disappeared on an evening that was to be our personal evening at home weren't really helped much.

The Church's Cub Scout Committee was meeting with an angry father that night. The father of one of the boys in our Cub Scout pack had reported that the male Cub Scoutmaster had taken indecent liberties with his son. The incident hadn't occurred during an actual scouting activity. The Scoutmaster picked the boy up on the way home from school. At any rate, the father was issuing an ultimatum to the committee and to me as a symbol of the church. "Either you get rid of this abuser of children, get him out of this Cub Pack, out of this congregation and out of this community, or I'll go to the county Sheriff and press legal charges against him, and all of you, and the church."

None of us had ever before had any occasion to be related to a case of sexual child molestation. We were totally inexperienced in dealing with "sexual perversion." We had no familiarity with the issue. We hadn't experienced it first hand nor had we heard it discussed in a public way. We spent most of our time that evening discussing, brainstorming, and debating our best strategy in dealing with the situation. We weren't sure what to do but we had to do something. Right or wrong we handled the situation the best we could.

The angry father was an active church member well respected by all of us. We listened to his story never questioning the veracity of his charges or inviting the accused to be heard. Our first decision was the easiest. The Cub Master would be dismissed as Cub Master. From here on we were less sure. Some wanted to bring legal charges against the Cub Master; others wanted to avoid any publicity for fear of it producing a negative image for our scouts and/or our church. Several of us thought of the accused's behavior as a manifestation of mental illness. We assumed that the child's parents could appropriately care for his needs and for their own needs so there was little further focus on the victim or his family. Strangely, I can't recall that we were ever in conversation with the district Boy Scout Council.

In the end, we arrived at a consensus and a "delegation" of two or three including the father was appointed to go and talk to the accused. The jist of the visit was to be mostly an ultimatum. "You have violated the trust that we and our community have had in you. You need to seek counseling for yourself, but you also need to leave this community and, if you don't move, we will press legal charges."

Not long after, the person in question did move to Derby. I do not know whether he was ever again involved in child molestation. Whether he sought help I'm not sure. I do know that he talked to a Methodist Pastor in Derby after which that pastor in turn called to warn me that I could be in danger—that the man harbored ill will and violent feelings toward me and toward our church.

I have pondered this incident from that day to this. I also think of it, and of other things that I have known directly and indirectly, as a pastor, in the light of current events today. In recent years, society has become greatly concerned with the issue of pedophiles. In the past couple of years much publicity has been given to child abuse (seemingly mostly of male children) by priests of the Roman Catholic Church. It has been asserted that the Roman Catholic Church has engaged in a gigantic cover-up of this scandal. I have no doubt about the magnitude and truth of this cover-up. There is no excuse for what has happened. I do know that there have been some abuses and cover-ups by lay and clergy leadership in Protestant churches.

I think of an instance when I was becoming a District Superintendent. I was not yet officially a DS, but for training and orientation purposes I was sitting with the Bishop's cabinet during their annual appointive process (the time when pastoral appointments are reviewed and either renewed or changed for the coming year). We had a pastor whose behavior was not overtly sexually inappropriate but was by innuendo. Reports and questions came to his District Superintendent. No charges were filed by anyone in or out of his congregation. The collective memory of the cabinet was that this had also happened elsewhere. The matter was simply handled by transferring him to a different church.

I remember another case where a woman pastor wrote inappropriate invitations of a lesbian nature to a young girl in her church. Again, no formal charges were filed by the girl's mother or anyone else in the congregation, but the matter was brought by the mother to the DS's attention and through him to the Cabinet. Eventually it was dealt with by transferring the pastor to another Annual Conference. All too often the Church has been guilty of dealing with moral wrongs through secrecy and by passing problems off to some other congregation or denomination.

Fortunately, today the United Methodist Church has policies and procedures in place to appropriately deal with these situations for all concerned—perpetrators, victims and congregations. These provisions may not work perfectly; they may seem too bureaucratic; but, they do try to protect privacy and make a best faith effort to replace cover-up with positive and healing solutions.

Another present day social issue increasingly coming to the forefront of our attention has to do with civil and ecclesiastical rights and rites of persons with a publicly acknowledged homosexual orientation. I do not know exactly how all of these issues will be resolved in a healing and positive way for our church and for our world, but I believe we need to do all we can to protect and ensure the civil rights of all people. I know from Belle Plaine days that one of the reasons this is such a "hot" issue is that people do not distinguish between pedophiles and persons of a homosexual orientation. Not all pedophiles are homosexuals and not all homosexuals are pedophiles. We need to be clear about this. While society has so much to learn on how best to protect children, and how to cope with bonafide pedophiles, society also still has a lot to learn about how to treat persons of a homosexual orientation with dignity and respect. The homosexual individual still needs the same caring and compassion, the same empathy, the same civil rights, which we want for ourselves when others misunderstand us or unjustly blame us for things wrongly done or things left undone.

Chapter 38

SCARED TO DEATH

Have you ever been scared to death when asked by someone to engage in a new venture? When Loyal Miles phoned us in late April or early May, 1963, to inform us the Bishop was asking me to take a new appointment, we were enjoying Belle Plaine and feeling quite comfortable there. We hated to think about moving. When he said the Bishop wanted to appoint me to serve Grace Methodist Church in Winfield, Kansas, I was scared to death!

Winfield was a town of about 12,000, the county seat of Cowley County. It was large enough to have two thriving Methodist Churches—First Methodist Church (founded in 1870 when Winfield was a one-year-old village in Indian country), the downtown church, the oldest and largest of the two, and Grace Methodist Church, known as "the College Church" because it was adjacent to Southwestern College. Of course, the church wasn't exclusively a college church. Its members included entrepreneurs and other business men, bankers, physicians and nurses, public school teachers, blue collar workers, and people employed at the State Hospital for the Mentally Retarded.

Southwestern began in 1886. Almost immediately and inevitably homes began to spring up on or near College Hill. Paraphrasing the words of Blanch Rush, in her history of Grace Church, *A Century of Grace* (p.7), it was a long walk, two miles, to

First Church. Few persons owned horses and buggies. The majority didn't. The mule-drawn streetcar had not yet come into existence. When it was wet the streets were almost impassable and on bad winter days the frozen streets were difficult to negotiate. It was not easy to be actively involved in First Church. By 1888, inhabitants of College Hill established Grace Church. Thus both churches became prestigious in their own respective ways.

Grace Church had within its membership and leadership circle a large number of the college faculty. It was usually filled on Sundays with large numbers of students who came from all over Western Kansas and their guests. Like many college churches it was generally known as a very progressive congregation. Dr. Joe Sims, a former Fulbright Scholar in South America and Professor of Choral Music at Southwestern, was Director of Grace Church's five gifted choirs. Grace Sellers, Professor of Piano at the College, was the organist. The main choir included several faculty members and music majors.

Educational ministries were highly valued so the church's Christian Education and youth programs were strong and effective. The church had a heritage of faith-filled responses to the lean and difficult times through which both the college and congregation had had to struggle. It also possessed a heritage of strong ties with Methodist mission work. Many pastors who had served the congregation through the years had later become Conference leaders, District Superintendents, College President, and/or pastor of some of the largest churches of our Annual Conference.

To me, this was an awesome heritage. To think of all those members who would be sitting out there on Sunday mornings whose education far exceeded mine, with degrees of all sorts and magnitudes, was intimidating. When Loyal Miles phoned me, I protested I didn't have the abilities needed for this appointment. The Cabinet insisted that I did.

When we arrived for our first Sunday at Grace Church, the congregation had an afternoon reception for us. It was by far the nicest, most creative reception we have experienced in our years of

ministry. It was filled with fun and entertainment, a real celebration
with music and the arts, short speeches and good humor.

Later during the reception there was time for people to
introduce themselves and visit with us individually. I particularly
remember the reassurance I received from Bill Moneypenny, former
track coach and Director of Placement. In our conversation I
expressed my awe at serving a college church and my anxiety about
being equal to this challenge. Bill's response was to the effect that
"all the teachers and leaders of Southwestern have the same hopes
and dreams, needs and problems, as any other parishioner in any
church—they all put on their trousers, one leg at a time, same way
as other folk—and you'll do just fine." He, like so many, was so
supportive that our Grace Church years were truly grace-filled years.

The parsonage into which we moved was a well maintained
38-year old home even if a bit dated in some respects. When it was
built the family moving into it, the I. D. Haris family, had a gala
opening celebration (September 18, 1925) described by the
Winfield Courier as "one of the largest and most beautiful affairs
ever held by Grace Methodist Episcopal Church." The parsonage
was, it said, "a stately (white) frame building of six rooms plus a
large sun room and breakfast nook on the first floor and a spacious
sleeping porch on the second floor."

It continued to serve as a parsonage until 1988. From then
until the fall of 2002 it was known as "Grace House" and used in
such capacities as a Halfway House for persons suffering severe and
persistent mental illnesses, a clubhouse for social/vocational
rehabilitation of the mentally ill, and finally a Community Learning
Center for the Winfield High School's Diploma Completion
Program. These uses symbolize something of the missional spirit
of Grace Church. After the fall of 2002 the Ron Gaither family
purchased the old parsonage moving it to a new location near
Oxford, Kansas. As a gift to them, Debra Carr of the congregation,
compiled a booklet entitled *Oh, Tell Me the Stories of Grace
House.*

I shared several of my memories for that booklet. The most
vivid of these pertained to our son Bill, still a toddler, when we

were experiencing our first winter in Winfield. At this time the parsonage had no air conditioning or central forced air heating. Downstairs the house had an old fashioned floor furnace covered with a grate. It was located between the living and dining rooms. One evening as we were putting supper on the table, we called Bill to come. He came running from the living room. Just as he got to the floor furnace, he tripped and fell. Throwing his arms forward to break his fall, one of them came down on that very hot furnace grate. Bill immediately screamed out in pain from the burns he incurred. As I scooped him up, I discovered a nice red set of grid marks on the underside of his arm. Needless to say, he continued screaming for some time and Lorine and I were very distressed. Fortunately, the burns turned out not to be serious and normal first aid took care of things leaving no permanent scars.

The Trustees of the church, typical of most church trustees, had long been discussing the need for parsonage central heating and air conditioning without taking action. This episode became the catalyst causing them to finally make the affirmative decision. Even then they didn't rush into the job. More than a year later Nuel Hinegardner, a faithful Grace Church member who was in the Heating & AC business, finally took the lead in the project by donating a significant part of his labor to get the job done.

Another bright memory from this parsonage is the window count. We were so aware that it was a house of many windows. One day Lorine took it upon herself to count them. There were fifty-five windows—certainly enough to make a home filled with light and sunshine.

Family memories from these years abound. Since Ben was the oldest of our boys, six years old the summer of our arrival, perhaps memories related to him are the most numerous. Ben had been in Kindergarten in Belle Plaine. When it came time that fall for him to start First Grade, we had two options. Discussing the qualities of each school, Stevenson and Irving, with friends, we learned Stevenson had a first grade teacher with a reputation of being "the best teacher around for helping beginning readers gets started." This is where we enrolled Ben. It was a wise decision because Ben developed excellent reading skills which have served him well throughout his life.

By the time Ben was in the third grade, his interests were blossoming. Cub Scouting proved a stimulating activity for Ben since his Cub Master was an archery and fishing enthusiast. Winfield was also blessed to have a lady, Mrs. Foster (Alta Mae) Newland, known for her ability as a violin teacher, who introduced young children to her instrument. Ben began studying violin when he was 8 years old and in the third grade. He may not have been a musical prodigy, but he certainly grew and developed in his skills as a young violinist. He continued playing violin through his Junior High years in Wichita excelling to the point of being part of a quartet which went to the District to the State Music contest in Topeka.

I constantly interacted with the college community—faculty and students—in many ways. On the personal level, we often used students for child care when sitters were needed for our children. Ross Herron, my Junior High science teacher, had a daughter, Shirley Herron, who was a junior at Southwestern. I'm not sure whether we became acquainted through using her as a sitter, because she was a student attending our worship at Grace Methodist Church, or simply because her parents told her about me as a product of Trinity Church, Hutchinson, her home church and hometown.

Southwestern still maintained an old fashioned tradition from its early years—the celebration of May Day. In the spring of 1964, Shirley Herron was elected May Day Queen. The campus was full of flowers and blooming trees. Shirley chose our son Ben to be part of her court and to carry the train of her dress during the Royal Procession. The Queen and her court processed down the seventy-seven steps that led from the Christi Hall, the Administration Building perched on a high hill, to the main level of the campus. The student body, gathered at the foot of the steps, awaited the Queen's arrival. As the trumpets sounded the fanfare, the Queen descended followed by Ben, dressed for the occasion and very serious, bearing her train. At the foot of the steps, the Queen walked to a shady grassy area near the Library and the special social festivities began. These included a coronation of the May Day Queen, music, and the winding of the May Pole with ribbons of all colors. Ben proudly played his part to perfection and, naturally, Lorine and I proudly stood nearby happily involved in this event through Ben.

Bill was only 5 months old when we arrived in Winfield so these years were his pre-school years. One of our Grace Church ladies, Montra Bergdall, operated a preschool. I wanted Bill to have the kind of preschool experience and stimulus which had been mine when I was growing up. As soon as Bill was old enough, we placed him in her school. We still remember with a smile and a laugh one of the sharings he brought home. Christmas was drawing near. Mrs. Bergdall was having a pageant for the children. Bill came home full of excitement reporting to us, 'I'm supposed to be one of three wise-guys!"

We wanted to round out our family with a third child—who knows, maybe even a girl this time? There were no sonograms in those days so we wouldn't know ahead of time. Our "girl" turned out to be a boy! Paul Frederick (Paul for the Apostle and Frederick for my dad, Fred) was due to arrive in mid-December of 1965. It's just about as crazy for pastors to have a child in December as it is to be married in December. Advent and Christmas make such a busy season. Lorine knew she had to have all of her Christmas shopping finished before the baby's arrival in a few days. She went to Arkansas City on the afternoon of December 10th to do her final shopping. I had two Commission meetings—Education (Church School) and Worship—scheduled that night to finish up the church's planning for Christmas.

About four o'clock, Dr. Leland Kaufman, a member of our church and Lorine's doctor, phoned me when he was unable to reach her at the parsonage, saying "The baby is due in about three or four days but I've got a problem. My father is critically ill and not expected to live. I need to go be with him. The baby is so far along there would really be no problem in inducing labor. I could do this yet today, or if you don't want me to I'll need to find another doctor to do the delivery when the time comes." Lorine wasn't where I could consult with her so I had to make a preliminary decision subject to her approval. I said I wasn't sure what time she would be home and I mentioned the evening meetings which had to happen and which, I thought, needed my attendance. "What about 9:30 pm? Would that be too late for you?" I asked. "It's all right with me," he replied. I told him we'd call and verify things as soon as Lorine returned.

When Lorine got home she was dead tired from shopping. When I reported the afternoon's communiqué from Dr. Kauffman, she flipped! Unhappy and upset as she was, she understood Dr. Kauffman's situation. With firmness she asserted, "I don't want a substitute doctor whom I don't even know!" She couldn't believe that I had suggested such a late hour to begin inducing labor, and especially she couldn't believe I thought I needed to attend my church meetings. Nevertheless, the decision was to go ahead as per the preliminary plans. Once things got started it wasn't long before Paul arrived. Once again we were blessed with a healthy baby boy and added joy for us.

From that day until this, Lorine has delighted in telling people about my mixed up priorities. Indeed, this is symbolic of a perennial struggle between church and home which was always one of the dynamics in our marriage as it probably is in the marriages of all clergy. In fact, I insist finding the proper balance between work and family is a tension point in many marriages, not just for clergy, although I've had a hard time convincing Lorine that pastors are not unique.

In the spring of 1966 we were fortunate to have our Bishop, MacFerrin Stowe scheduled as a Sunday morning preacher. Once again we wanted to share our special moment with our congregation. We asked Bishop Stowe if he would be willing for us to make Paul's baptism a part of the worship service that morning. To our delight we received an affirmative response.

It would be hard for me to single out just one church which I enjoyed more than all the other churches which I served. Certainly Grace Church was one of my most enjoyable appointments. It was also a time of true maturing for me in my ministry. I have high standards for what I consider good preaching. In all honesty, I'm not often excited by the preaching I hear. Consequently, I've usually tended to be pretty critical of my own preaching. However, I feel I began "hitting my stride" while I was at Grace Church. For one thing, perhaps because of the college environment, I seemed to do a pretty good job of keeping up with my reading and studying. This is always important for any preacher, for good preaching. It's not easy to do with the multiple demands which a pastor is constantly facing. For another thing, it was while I was at Grace Methodist Church that I learned the importance of continuing education for any profession and certainly for pastors. This was to enrich both my preaching in particular and my ministry in general.

In every period of time, certain teachers, writers, and leaders rise to the top of their profession and catch the imagination of others. They're the ones who are on the cutting edge of things and who become very popular with peers in their field. Among clergy, one of these persons in the nineteen fifties and sixties was Reuel L. Howe, an Episcopal clergyman. Three of his books had great appeal: *Man's Need and God's Action*, *The Creative Years*, and *The Miracle of Dialogue*. Howe was schooled in psychology as well as Bible and theology. Traditional theological studies for centuries stressed "dogmatics" or doctrine. Consequently, the church and its clergy have been all too often dogmatic in relating to people. Howe's gift to the church and clergy was helping develop the realization that dialogue is essential for good communications and for bringing about the miracle and the reality of the redemptive reconciliation which is at the heart of the Gospel. At an Episcopal retreat center in Bloomfield Hills, Michigan, (a small suburb north of Detroit), Reuel Howe offered retreats for clergy.

I attended two of Howe's retreats while I was at Grace Church. The first was on "The Dialogue of Preaching." It was here I really learned the importance of sermons as *two-way communication* and learned to take the risks associated with dialogue in preparation for preaching. Not only did my preaching mature—so also did my skills in dealing with inter-personal relationships. Sensitivity training was growing in popularity in the 1960s. The second seminar I took was a sensitivity training seminar. This helped me in knowing myself and in dealing with my own personal problems, as well as helping me in my communication skills, in counseling parishioners, and in working with small groups.

Following my return from this seminar, I offered a personal growth group to interested persons. Leading this group contributed both to my own personal and professional growth and to my satisfaction in ministry as life-changing experiences resulted for several of its members.

Look in on eight persons gathered in a personal growth group once a week, for several months. In a simple unadorned room they were seated in a circle, spending their time engaging in personal sharing. At first they only knew one another superficially. Early on their leader helped them develop relationships of trust through exercises with one another. Later on they began to feel free to do the sharing to which they had committed themselves. They came to the point where they could strategize with each other about how they could grow and develop in their personal lives and relationships. Each person in the group brought his or her own unique personal needs for fulfillment.

Judy seemed to be much needier than the others—she had an extremely poor self image. If you listened in on the group and observed its activities, you would discover one of the personal growth skills the group was working on was the skill of self-affirmation. Week by week you could discern that Judy (not her real name) was making tremendous personal growth and gaining a better feeling about her self. During the course of the group's life, the members came to use a group hug as a way of closing each session. After a few week of working on the skills of self-affirmation, they added to their closing hug the use of a mantra. The mantra was a chant they repeat several times with increasing intensity and feeling—"I'm a good person; I'm a good person; I'm a good person!" At first, Judy resisted being part of the group hug. Later she began to feel comfortable with this, but she resisted participating in the mantra.

Some weeks into the life of the group, comes a moment when she bursts into a flood of tears and joy, with laughter and crying, squeezing ever so hard in the group hug and joins in chanting the mantra with real feeling. Experiences like this made my efforts all worth while.

Another member of this group was Avenell Elliott, a young widow in our congregation. Avenell, like all of us, profited from being in the group. I know she grew in her own self-confidence, but even more she grew in finding her way into the future. She was an active volunteer leader in our church school program. As a widow with young children, she had continued being what we call a "stay at home" mom while her three sons were moving through the elementary school, but she needed to figure out both how she was going to support them and what she was going to do with her life after they were out of school.

I've already named the church school program as a point of strength at Grace Church. Almost every year we had a Laboratory School of some sort for the training of church school teachers. As a congregation, when we were projecting plans for our future, we set as one of our goals that *every* lead teacher in *each* of our Sunday School classes would become a Certified Laboratory School Teacher. If and when we could reach this goal, our next goal would be that our church school would become an on-going Laboratory School where others from or beyond our community could come to train as church school teachers. We also set a goal of growing our own staff so that we would have a full-time Director of Christian Education.

We worked very diligently at these goals. Avenell became the first of our church school teachers to be a Certified Lab Teacher. Certification was an Annual Conference and national training process for laity as well as clergy. Even for the most conscientious person, it usually required, two years to achieve this status. Avenell attained certification even more quickly.

One day Avenell came to my office for a visit. "Harold, ever since our personal growth group, I've been thinking about the future. I know our church wants to have a full-time Director of Christian Education soon. What would it take for me to qualify for that job?" We talked and strategized. The Methodist Church's educational standard for becoming a DCE was to have a Masters of Christian Education degree. The best place for getting this was Scarritt College in Nashville—750 miles away. With 3 sons still in school it was a big stretch for Avenell to consider going back to graduate school.

Avenell's journey unfolded this way: Because of her certification, Grace Church employed her on half-time basis as a Christian education worker (which also began to improve Avenell's bottom line). This, in turn, allowed her to test her calling. After a year or two, with a promise from Grace Church that she would have a fulltime job upon achieving her degree, by faith she moved her family to Nashville where she gained her Masters of Christian Education degree. She returned to Winfield to become a full-time Director of Christian Education serving Grace Church for ten years although the last few years she divided her time with First United Methodist Church.

Eventually, our Annual Conference tapped Avenell Elliott for their staff in the role of leadership development across the western two-thirds of Kansas. Avenell's role in our Conference was strong and effective. She was greatly appreciated throughout the Church until her life was prematurely cut short in a tragic auto accident. Many people had a role in nurturing Avenell through her life's journey and I must confess that one of the great joys of my ministry was having a part in this.

One of my involvements with our youth was the development of summer retreats and work camps. Twice we went to Texas with youth work camps. Once we worked in a rural migrant labor camp. Living facilities for these workers were woefully inadequate. Our task was restoring the torn, broken and missing screens for the shelters in which these people slept. Part of my philosophy in youth work throughout my ministry has been to open the eyes of our youth to the poor and to those who are victims of the world's injustices, and then to help them learn to respond as Christ would respond—to help them experientially learn the meaning of scriptures such as Matthew 25:31ff.

Another of the youth work camps I led was in Dallas-Ft.Worth, an urban area. We worshiped at Grace Church on a Sunday morning, traveled to Texas that afternoon and spent Monday through Friday working in two Hispanic Methodist congregations. We told these churches we would work by day at whatever they felt needed to be done, but we would hope to have the evenings to spend with their youth. The major task assigned our youth was to go door-to-door blanketing the area around these two churches with evangelistic literature and hand-outs about the churches. In the process, our kids got well exposed to the neighborhood and its culture and to forms of church work with which we were not so familiar. In the evenings, our youth had a great time interacting with their Hispanic counterparts.

For the final 48 hours of the retreat, our group shifted from the Hispanic setting to a black church for an "exposure experience" with those youth and adults. I had to be back at Grace Church to preach and conduct Sunday worship, so I was unable to be with MYF (Methodist Youth Fellowship) for this final exposure, but I had to smile when I heard the report on the last two days. In setting up the plans, I simply made arrangements by phone. I had no familiarity with the black pastor, the church, or its neighborhood. The pastor turned out to be a very dynamic young man who liked to fly airplanes and who had lots of pizzazz. If memory serves me right, he was Zan Holmes who over the years became one of the leading black pastors in Methodism. The neighborhood turned out to be a very affluent black neighborhood. The church, correspondingly, was a very "upper class" black Methodist Church with a rather high church liturgy. Our kids were as guilty of racial stereotyping as any of us. They reported back to our congregation, "We didn't know there were any black people like this."

The word black also conjures up for me an entirely different kind of memory. Southwestern College had its own Chaplain, but as pastor of "the college church," I tried to relate closely to the students and faculty and to facilitate within our congregation a sense of mission to and with the college. As I raised questions relative to our mission, I was able to help in the creation of a "coffee-house ministry" just across the street from the college, only a block away from the church.

Except for a mom and pop grocery, Winfield had no businesses or entertainment near the college. Students always like to exercise their freedom and were always looking for something to do. For students without cars, the campus was doubly confining. We established a task force to explore both how we could better serve and be in dialogue with them. The task force concluded there was a need for something like a coffee house ministry. In July of 1966 Bernice Walker presented this recommendation to the Official Board and gained its approval.

It was highly unlikely the church could make a true coffee house self-sustaining, or afford to subsidize it. It was decided just to operate from 4 p.m. to midnight on Fridays and Saturdays. The owner of an empty little frame storefront building donated its use to us for little or no rent. Grace Church Trustees paid the utilities. Since everyone working there was a volunteer from Grace Church, operating costs were kept to a minimum and dialogue between church and campus would be a given. Additional forms of dialogue were generated through having occasional planned or impromptu folk music jam sessions and/or invited guests to conduct a kind of bully-pulpit on social or religious issues of the day with opportunity for students to quiz the guests or dialogue with them.

In my coffee house memory-room, one recollection relates to the naming of the place. Given our plans for and our desire that this be a form of Christian witness, the recommendation was that we name it "The Black Aye," a name which would reflect a kind of off-beat affirmation of faith. In passing this along verbally to the publicity people, the name got changed to "The Black Eye" which really wasn't so clear or meaningful.

One of my tasks was the procuring of our coffees and teas from several different shops and stores in Wichita during my frequent hospital visits in the city. Until that moment I never knew the world had so many different flavors of coffee and tea.

Lorine and I would get baby sitters in order to take our turn working at The Black Eye. Volunteering at The Black Eye was something we thoroughly enjoyed even when it was a drafty place where we nearly froze when the winter weather was harsh. Volunteers from the church for coffee house staff seemed to be easily forthcoming. This probably indicates the congregation had a true sense of mission about it. Some evenings we would have only a handful of student customers—perhaps giving us almost a one on one ratio between church members and students. Other evenings we would be so crowded that a Fire Marshal would have closed us up if he'd seen the place. One evening Dr. Wallace Gray was exploring a subject related to sexual ethics. Things got so heated you could hardly hear to take orders.

Relating to the larger Winfield community was just as important for Grace Church as relating to the College community. Winfield had no child care facility for working parents at this time. A vision of service and ministry I lifted up to the congregation was the possibility of offering child care for the community all day each week-day. This included serving families of all economic levels with the definitely intent to include the "working poor." In the spirit of Christ, this would be our contribution to what our nation was calling "the war on poverty." Helping set the stage for this was perhaps my last major accomplishment before moving on to a new appointment.

The vision created a lively debate if not controversy in the church. As always, some members were afraid the children would be too hard on our physical facilities. Others felt we would incur too many expenses or the possibility of unlimited liability. Once again, Bernice Walker of our Christian Social Concerns Commission, successfully brought this first to our Official Board and then to the congregation for the approval the Board felt it needed from them.

Meeting governmental licensing requirements, jumping through all the practical and personnel hoops for the start-up of this kind of ministry, is always complicated. These things seem to take forever. These were worked on during my final year at Grace Church. We moved to Wichita at the beginning of the summer of

1968. By the beginning of school that September there were nearly a dozen children enrolled in the Grace Church Child Care Center. Several years later it grew into what became a Winfield Child Care Center and re-located to a building once used as a public school. I feel great satisfaction in this kind of accomplishment. Obviously it's a huge team effort involving many people, but I find great meaning in being part of the team.

Warm feelings abound from the abundance of friends we made while in Winfield. Perhaps we found more friends here than in any other appointment. Lorine was often the key to this. In Grace Church, for instance, I would be busy in numerous ways on Sunday mornings but Lorine was part of a Sunday School class made up chiefly of young parents like ourselves. This quickly generated many bonds and friends too numerous to list, but Don and Betsy Drennan who lived just one block down the street from us had three boys, just as we did, and approximately the same ages. We were constantly back and forth with each other.

One of the most supportive groups of peers we ever had in ministry came about in Winfield through the initiative of our District Superintendent who lived there—Loyal Miles and his wife, Reba Mae. I've previously mentioned his warmth, openness, and supportiveness. Reba Mae possessed these same qualities. About a year into this appointment Loyal and Reba Mae invited Vern and Lois Livengood who served the church in Wellington, Chet and Pat Osborn who served the Oxford Church, Forrest and Betty Jean Robinson who served First Methodist in Winfield, and Lorine and I to join them for dinner at their house. We had a delightful evening together. It was the kind of evening where we could all "let down our hair," enjoying each others' company and sharing our ministerial and family joys and frustrations. This also gave the four couples of us a chance to have very close, personal relationship with our supervisor. Out of this came the custom of getting together several times a year, for several years, and developing a truly supportive, encouraging community with one another.

A final and varied "group" of friends came both from membership in Grace Church and the Southwestern faculty. Often these were overlapping circles. This wasn't a group which got together in total, but persons with whom our lives intersected meaningfully as couples or threesomes or whatever. Some weren't at the college the entire time we were in Winfield. A few who quickly come to mind are: the Don Andersons, the Albert Dimmitts, the Carl Martins, the Lee Dubowskys, the Wallace Grays (with whom we share a wedding anniversary), the Elmer Douglasses and Sassi and Marguerite Hessini. Some had young children, some didn't. We picnicked and/or camped with some; with some we simply shared dinners or evenings of conversation. I can still see us driving out into the Flinthills east of Winfield, picnicking on a sandbar in Grouse Creek, with Sassi and Marguerite Hessini and our small children.

Sassi was a native of Algeria who spent a significant part of his childhood in a Methodist orphanage. Marguerite was a native of France. As a Methodist from Strasbourg, she went to Algeria as a missionary. Somehow they got together. Dr. and Mrs. Douglass had been missionaries in Algeria and knew them. When the Douglass retired, they came to Winfield for a time. Dr. Douglass did translating and Eva Douglass taught French at Southwestern for a few years. When she was ready to retire, Eva recommended to President Orville Strohl that he bring Marguerite to be her successor. The Hessinis came as a young almost newlywed couple. It was our pleasure to befriend them as newcomers to America.

Although Lorine's college majors were History and Religion, from high school on she studied and enjoyed French. Although her life as a young mother of two, then three, was quite busy while we were in Winfield, we discussed the possibility that since we were so close to Southwestern this might be a great opportunity for Lorine to work on additional studies. These studies might provide her with "an insurance policy" in case I were to die prematurely. Or, they could provide a career after our kids were older.

After consulting with friends in Southwestern's teacher training program, Lorine decided to take a number of education courses and go for a teaching certificate. Her focus became secondary education. She already had what she needed to teach history if she were to do that. Because of her love of French, Lorine also took all the courses Eva Douglass and Marguerite had to offer thereby equipping herself to also teach French. Lorine did her practice teaching at Winfield High School. By the time we moved to Wichita for our next appointment, all that remained for Lorine to do was to complete a single educational course for her Kansas teaching certificate.

Kieler family photo from their 1957 Christmas card.
Left to r.—Lorine holding Paul; Ben standing; Bill seated; Harold

Chapter 39

HISTORIC MOMENTS

Eight of us were seated around the table for a late supper that Sunday evening. We had just arrived in town. The room was dimly lit by a single bulb hanging from the ceiling over the table. As my eyes looked around the table, seated nearest the kitchen stove was an older black woman; then, in random fashion, were her children who were all young adults in their twenties, a son and two daughters, and the four of us—four white men, a college professor, two young students from Southwestern College and myself. On the inside, it was a well kept although poor home while its outward appearance was very weather-beaten and run-down.

We really hadn't become acquainted yet. We were late in arriving and were immediately invited to "Please be seated right away. We can visit as we eat." We didn't expect a big banquet; in fact, we didn't know what to expect. We registered at a church in the heart of the community upon our arrival in town. There we had received a brief preliminary orientation with instructions to return the next morning for our full orientation. We were also given our housing assignment which we had paid for in advance and it was explained the people with whom we were staying were living on very marginal incomes. They were hosting us as a way of augmenting their income.

A nice family style meal was placed on the table. There was roast pork, potatoes, cooked greens, a gelatin salad and bread. At each plate there was a fork and spoon. After the food was passed and our hostess offered a prayer, we were ready to eat. It was at that moment that I made my *faux pas*—one of the most humiliating and embarrassing moments of my life.

Wanting to cut the piece of meat I had just placed on my plate from the platter, and not seeing a knife among the pieces of silverware beside my plate, I said, "Excuse me, but I think you forgot to put a knife at my place. May I have one?" Apologetically our hostess replied: "I'm sorry but we don't have any knives. We just share the carving knife on the meat platter." I hadn't realized the family we were staying with was so poor they didn't have even simple things like full table settings which I took for granted.

Where in the world were we? We were not in some third world country (a "less developed nation" as we sometimes say). We were in the United States of America, in Mississippi, in Greenwood, in the heart of the black neighborhood in a town of 17,000. We were there to encourage black citizens to become registered voters—we were part of the civil rights movement in the 1960s during our nation's civil rights struggles. This Voter Registration Mission was an Easter Mission of Grace United Methodist Church.

Following World War II, law suits by returning veterans began this struggle at a greater depth than ever before. Back in my own State of Kansas, in many other states as well, one of the many law suits took place. On May 17, 1954, the US Supreme Court ruled in favor of Linda Brown in the case of Brown vs. The Topeka, Kansas, Board of Education. The court declared that in education (and by implication, in all areas of civil rights) "separate but equal" is inherently unequal. From the Civil War forward in legal history, American courts had upheld "Jim Crow laws" found mainly in the South but also throughout the country. These Jim Crow laws allowed and often required for black and white people, separate facilities ranging from restrooms and drinking fountains to hospitals and schools. They permitted or required, depending on the state, segregation *in every level of life*. Slavery may have been defeated with the defeat of the Confederate States of the South, but its injustice and segregation had been slow to die.

We didn't have segregated education when I was growing up in Hutchinson. For that matter, we didn't have a lot of forced segregation of any type. Kansas law permitted segregation, but did not require it. Out of the twelve largest school districts in Kansas, Hutchinson was the only non-segregated school district. Topeka and the other large districts in Kansas had it. The Supreme Court, overthrowing separate but equal schools in Brown v. The Topeka, Kansas, Board of Education was arguably the most significant civil rights decision in United States history. It launched and inspired new movement to fulfill the vision of civil rights for all people in all of life.

Another spark in the American civil rights movement began in Montgomery, Alabama, just days before my first wedding anniversary on December 1, 1955. I still vividly remember this as it was pictured in the newspaper story. Rosa Parks, a tired domestic worker, at the end of her work day, boarded a bus to ride home. She sank down in the first available seat. Soon a white man boarded the bus but by then it has only a few empty seats at the rear. The driver told Rosa Parks to move to the rear of the bus, but in her stressed-out weariness Rosa refused. She decided she was too tired to give her seat to a white man. The driver stopped the bus, stepped off and summoned a nearby policeman. Rosa was arrested on the spot.

Local black leaders came to her defense. They organized an unprecedented protest with a massive year long boycott of the town's buses. They kept at it despite police harassment and violence. A 26-year old Baptist pastor, Martin Luther King, Jr., educated in a Methodist Graduate School and Seminary—Boston University, and drawing his inspiration from Mahatma Gandhi's movement of non-violent resistance in India, became their inspirational leader. A number of times he was arrested and jailed, but never did King give in to the status quo. He became one of the key leaders of the entire civil rights movement.

One of the greatest victories of the civil rights movement came about a decade later, in 1965, when the U.S. Congress finally passed a Voting Rights Act unequivocally legalizing local as well as national voting rights for all citizens of all races. In the spring of that year, Southwestern College held its annual Religious Emphasis Week. Southwestern featured a Jewish Rabbi as their guest speaker. He addressed the great moral issues of the day.

Piggy-backing on this REW, I invited the Rabbi to preach at Grace Church Sunday morning at the close of Religious Emphasis Week. He continued addressing the day's moral issues giving a powerful sermon based on the Judeo-Christian prophets. Grace Church has a pulpit centered semi-circular sanctuary with a semi-circular balcony above the main floor. Virtually every seat was filled that morning. As the Rabbi finished his sermon and turned to takes his seat, I came to the pulpit expressing my appreciation for his inspired and moving message. I offered a prayer of commitment. And then, spontaneously, I was moved to make a further response to the relevance with which our Jewish brother had spoken. I issued an "altar call" as we sang our closing hymn saying, "I invite all of you who, in the spirit of the prophets and in the spirit of Christ, would wish to participate with me in a mission to the south to assist with voter registration during the college's spring break, to signify this commitment by coming to the altar in prayer."

I was amazed and overwhelmed at the response. All over the sanctuary a sprinkling of people rose and began moving toward the altar. Almost a 100 people came forward forming two or three rows. Most were college students, some were faculty, and a few were townspeople. There were too many people to relate to one on one at that moment. Not being quite sure how to proceed, just before the benediction, I announced that we would gather again at 4 pm that afternoon to discuss this further and formulate plans.

By the time we gathered at 4pm, some parents had been called by their sons or daughters. Many of those parents were fearful or unhappy about their children participating in any civil rights activities, or at least in the south where turmoil, resistance, and sometimes even violence was possible. Some of our group offered apologies for not being able to go on the mission. Some didn't think they could come up with the necessary funds. All of us had questions about how we should organize and prepare for the mission. We wanted to be realistic about what we were getting into, what we were about to embark upon. There were real dangers and the mission needed to be carefully planned. Some, who didn't think they could go, volunteered to help with the planning, the fund-raising, the training and the logistics, of the mission. As might be expected, our numbers began to drop, but in the end 22 of us still made the trip to Mississippi.

This is the story behind the Sunday evening supper in Mississippi. During our week in Mississippi, we gained a new understanding of and appreciation for black culture. We were schooled in the ways of non-violence. We were given training for and then engaged in door to door home visits in the black community explaining to people their right to vote and how they could register to vote. We encouraged them to actually go do it.

Most of us like to think of ourselves as being free of racism, but let me share with you a picture of how subtle racism can be. Four of us were out in the neighborhood visiting homes. There was Sam, at whose home I was rooming and taking my breakfast and dinner, another black man, then Gordon, a Southwestern student, and myself. We worked in teams of two on opposite sides of the street walking door to door. We began our canvassing visits about mid-morning, and by one o'clock we were tired and hungry. The four of us got in my car to go look for a lunch counter somewhere. When we found one and went in to eat, we knew that whether by law or by custom, integrated dining had not been previously allowed in town.

Knowing about violent "red neck" responses to efforts like ours, I felt a bit uneasy as we entered. Would you? But I was committed to what we were doing. I was determined that making this kind of statement was an important part of our whole mission. We found a place to sit. Eventually, after what seemed to be a long wait, the waitress took our order. No sooner had we given our order than Sam asked the waitress where the restroom was located. My heart sank. What was wrong with his request? Absolutely nothing. It was a normal natural thing for people to do. But it was pushing against a cultural pattern that had been in-grained for over a century. We were already rocking the community's boat by being in town, by promoting voter registration, by being an interracial group coming in to eat. I found myself thinking, "Maybe this is enough. Sam, do you really have to ask where their previously all white restroom is? Can't you just wait?" I wonder if my readers share my feelings. I didn't say what I was thinking because I knew the philosophies of "don't rock the boat" and "just wait" were part of the attitudes which perpetuate racism. The waitress told Sam where the restroom was and Sam used it.

*   *   *

Of all the decades in which I've lived, the 1960s represent the decade which I feel has been most filled with historic changes in our nation.

Three months after we moved to Winfield, June 1, 1963, three months before Kennedy's assassination, Martin Luther King Jr., and a number of other civil rights leaders organized the historic March on Washington D.C. to raise American consciousness about racism. I very much wanted to be part of that march. Having just moved to Winfield, I believed family and church responsibilities made it impractical for me to literally participate in the march. A then record 300,000 people of all races, creeds and backgrounds gathered at the Lincoln Memorial to demonstrate for freedom and basic civil and human rights. I was there in spirit. I was glued to the television as we saw people from all over the nation traveling by foot, bike, car, train, and plane to the nation's capital to make a statement. We watched the gathering itself taking place. Throngs of people peacefully and urgently assembled. Most Americans were not in the capitol—some because of valid daily personal reasons and responsibilities; some because they disagreed with holding such a massive demonstration; and some, of course, because they were hate-filled racists opposed to everything for which the civil rights movement stood. Those who gathered and the many of us who were there with them in spirit were truly united.

On August 28, 1963, Martin Luther King, Jr. galvanized those 300,000 people in the Washington March, plus all who were watching or listening via the media, with his now famous "I Have a Dream" speech. Inspired and inspiring, laced with Biblical quotes or inferences, it exemplified the transcendent vision of the movement. It was quoted in thousands of pulpits the following Sunday. It's still a motivating part of my life today. Christians learned in those days to sing "We are one in the Spirit" and all of us in the movement, regardless of our religion, learned to sing "We shall overcome" as we struggled with the world's injustices.

*   *   *

I was home eating lunch with Lorine on Friday, November 22, 1963. We were sharing what was going on with each other, talking about events, when suddenly at 12:30 pm the whole day changed—and our lives were changed forever. Radio and television broadcasting was interrupted, and phones began to ring as people called people, with news of the assassination of John F. Kennedy, the 35th President of the United States of America. John Kennedy had been a young, dynamic and progressive president who had captivated our nation with his idealism. He was riding in a Dallas, Texas, procession in a limousine convertible when Lee Harvey Oswald, a 24-year old employee of the Texas School Depository, standing at a sixth-floor window, fired the shots at the President killing him. We, and everyone we knew, were stunned. It was like the heart and soul of our nation had been suddenly sucked out of us.

Although the Washington March unified and energized our nation as it had only rarely been unified before, the unity was not complete and all the energy was not positive and constructive. In 1966 the movement began to splinter with Stokely Carmichael's abandonment of nonviolence and his cry for "black power." For

Carmichael and others, blacks—or any people for that matter—could not be whole if they were without the power others possessed. I did not agree with much of what Carmichael advocated or did, but I could understand his point.

Five years after the death of JFK in 1968, America, still grieving, was again shaken to the core as assassinations took the lives of two more of our greats. Martin Luther King, Jr. was a preacher and leader with an incomparable oratorical ability, a man of steadfast allegiance to the principles of nonviolent resistance to evil, and perseverance even in the face of police brutality, harassment, arrest, and time spent in jail. He was a mover, a shaker, a doer. He was our country's greatest human rights leader. These qualities earned King a Nobel Peace Prize as well as global admiration. During a garbage worker's strike Martin Luther King, Jr. came to Memphis, Tennessee, to give moral support to the workers. King was almost the same age as I was. On April 4, 1968, at the age of 39 (my age), he was assassinated by James Earl Ray, a white drifter. His death did not bring an end to the movement, but it brought for all of us who had identified with him and appreciated his leadership a deep and profound sense of loss, of tragedy and mourning.

Two months later, June 5, 1968, 43 year old U. S. Senator Robert F. Kennedy, brother of the late president, promising statesman and political leader in his own right, contender for the Democratic Party's nomination as President, was assassinated in California as he celebrated his victory in that state's presidential primary. These two assassinations, overlaying the lingering grief from President Kennedy's assassination, gave us the feeling of shock and being stunned over and over again. Preaching, for me, in the face of it all was tough. These tragedies only forced or reinforced for many of us the belief that there was no other to whom we could really turn than the eternal God as we know him in Jesus Christ. It again felt as if the heart and soul of our nation was being cut from us. Words were not and still are not adequate to express our sense of loss and despair. Today, in 2004, in the first decade of the 21st Century, in the face of so much terrorism and global strife, I find the same kind of pain and feeling of senselessness rekindled in me in what seems a never ending stream of suicide bombings directed toward leadership and often just ordinary and innocent people.

*   *   *

I grew up hearing about the 1918-19 flu pandemic which swept the globe killing more than 22 ½ million people. This was far more death than occurred in World War I. I heard my Dad speak of several of my Uncles and Aunts and other relatives who died "of the flu." Eventually the world learned to control flu epidemics. During my teen-age years the world suffered a polio epidemic and learned to prevent its repetition. AIDS was unknown until two or three decades ago. Today it is an epidemic which has not yet been successfully controlled. I have lived through these traumatic events.

*   *   *

When I was born, the biggest cities in the world were New York, London, Berlin, Paris and Chicago—all in Europe or United States. Today, the world's biggest cities are Tokyo, Mexico City, Sao Paula, Seoul, and New York. I've lived through population shifts from rural to urban, from Western nations to Eastern nations, from the developed nations to the lesser developed nations (and now perhaps back again because of AIDS almost decimating whole populations of nations). I've learned to live in a world of constant change, an ever-changing world not only in terms of population, but of the dominant occupations and life-styles of the populations, and of the natural world in which we live. Whole species of wild life have been destroyed—eradicated from the face of the planet. Some natural resources are being consumed to the point of exhaustion, climate is being changed. I find myself wondering, "Is the human race committing environmental suicide?"

Scientific concern for the health of our planet's atmosphere and ecologies, environmentalism as a global movement, began to emerge in the decade of the 1970s after Rachel Carson's *Silent Spring* sounded an alarm in the 1960s. I remember practical action-

steps and political activity which began with the first Earth Week
in April 1970. As I write these words, we're mid-stream in the
2004 presidential election campaign. One of the big debate issues
is still environmental stewardship and responsibility. Many of us
have grave questions about President Bush's record in this area.

In the 1930's under the administration of President Franklin
D. Roosevelt, I witnessed the development of many social changes
such as the beginning of public works, national conservation
programs, the instituting of Social Security. These were related to
helping people in our nation cope with the economic depression,
but there was also a correlation with technological development
and its effect on our society.

I've spoken of the meaning of "the farm," my grandparents'
farm, for me. I've always tended to romanticize the farm. Look. In
the evening as the sun sets, darkness envelops their house.
Eventually, the interior becomes so dark we have to have light. My
grandparents get their coal oil lamps. When I'm lucky, I'm asked
to help. I get a lamp. I inspect the globe shaped reservoir at the
base to ensure there's enough coal oil for the evening, then I twist
the little knob at the top of the base to adjust the ribbon shaped
wick dangling in the coal oil so the wick will hopefully be just the
right height for the flame to burn bright but not too bright, not
bright enough to be smoky. Then, I remove the clear glass flue,
strike a match, light the wick, adjust the flame, place the flue back
on the lamp, and we have the soft warm glow of light that we need
to overcome the darkness. Occasionally, we may use candles as an
alternative to the coal oil lamps. Either way, the evening ritual of
lighting the farm house for an hour or two before an early retirement
to bed gives a romantic tone or feeling to its atmosphere. If, after
sunset, there's milking still to be done in the barn, the kerosene
lantern is lighted. With its bail, it can be carried anywhere light is
needed for the milking chores. (Coal oil is not a product refined
from crude oil, but a petroleum product obtained through the
destructive distillation of bituminous coal. Kerosene likewise comes
from shale.) Even here in the barn, or around the barnyard and
homestead, the light of the Coleman lantern creates a special
atmosphere. When I was eight or ten years old, I did not understand

how difficult life without electricity was for my grandparents and all the other farmers in Kansas. I was enthralled and excited with the atmosphere produced by these primitive forms of lighting and other primitive way of doing things. I was disappointed, my grandparents thrilled, July 14, 1938, when the Flinthills Electric Cooperative was incorporated under the Rural Electrification Administration program created by a decree of President Roosevelt in May, 1935, and approved by Congress a year later and the word was "electricity is coming to the farms of Kansas." By the time World War II shut down the construction process, Marion County had only 264 miles of energized electric power lines but electricity had gotten to the farm. The rest of the county and farms in the western half of rural Kansas didn't get electricity until after the War. I lived through this change.

*　　*　　*

When I was born, the marriage of man and woman was taken for granted as something stable. It was the norm for family life. Growing up I don't remember knowing anyone who was divorced. Less than 15% of all couples were ever divorced. I've lived through a trend with a growing divorce rate. In the past couple decades, the ratio between lasting marriages and failed marriages has become approximately 50-50. The definitions of marriage and family have increasingly been challenged and changed. I believe persons who are not married should be legally entitled to having a supportive person in their life, a domestic partner of their choice (friend, relative, same sex, opposite sex, who ever) the same as those of us who are married. We all need to live with some supportive companion in our lives. But, I still believe the best environment for raising children is the conventional and the extended family.

*　　*　　*

In the decade of the 1920s, less than two years before I was born, motion pictures were silent films. My first movies were talking films in black and white. Then came "Technicolor." Radio broadcasts in AM (amplitude modulation) were noisy, static-filled when I was a kid. Marvel of marvels, along came FM bands (frequency modulation) which were static-free and of much higher quality.

Television was non-existent when I was growing up. The first time I heard about TV was during my college years. While I was at sea in the navy (1953), word from home told me that the first commercial television station in Kansas, KTVH Channel 12, was beginning broadcasting in my hometown—Hutchinson. Later that year, when I was home visiting my parents, I watched TV for the first time. It seemed to me more a novelty than anything else—mostly just entertainment. I probably could have found television to experience earlier if I'd gone looking for it in clubs, bars, or hotels, but I didn't have the interest. The next year (1954) two more TV stations went on the air in Southcentral Kansas—KAKE and KARD, Channels 10 and 3. Television, like the movies, began in black and white. The TV sets were big and bulky as lots of them still are today, although now we're beginning to see thin flat screens that don't take up nearly the space. They were all very expensive. Lorine and I never had a television set until the late 1950s when my parents gave us a set for Christmas when we were in the new parsonage in Belle Plaine. Today we have one in our den, in our kitchen, and in our basement family room.

The Personal Computer only began to become a family item for the home when we were serving the Augusta United Methodist Church during the years of 1986-1992 when I was in my late 50s and early 60s. A PC is still a bit of a bewilderment to me.

The first recorded music I ever heard was on hard wax records about 12" in diameter played on a handcranked Victrola (trademark for an RCA phonograph) in my grandparents' home. Through the years recorded music evolved through records made in various sizes to be played at various speeds on a variety of instruments. Eventually tapes became more the norm than records, but today CDs (compact disks) are the norm with the disks becoming ever smaller.

Today satellites with a variety of computers and telecommunications devices have created transnational communications crossing traditional boundaries and borders as never before. This has done much to enhance communications and unify our world, but in my judgment it has also created difficulties. The world's cultures are increasingly homogenized to the destruction of folkways and the uniquenesses of ethnic groups. Again, I'm living in the midstream of these historic changes.

Two years before I was born, Charles Lindbergh flew solo and nonstop across the Atlantic from New York to Paris. This was such a spectacular feat that among my early childhood memories is the memory of hearing people talk about this as though it had just happened yesterday. In fact, this small child often thrilled to hearing discussions of the feats of aviation history being made. I remember the name of Wiley Post—the first man to fly solo around the world. In July, 1938, Howard Hughes circled the earth in less than 4 days. This was an historic feat. Until about 1945, world news events were commonly filmed and shown in motion picture theaters when people attend the movies so in a sense I was an eye witness to these events.

Also in 1938, Orson Wells produced a radio drama which nearly created mass panic in the United States. Again, I don't actually remember hearing this radio program, but it created so much stir and talk that as I listened to people discussing what Wells did, it's as if I've heard the program myself. He used a news broadcast format for his drama and reported on a "Martian invasion of the world." Even though an effort was made at the beginning and ending of the program to clarify this as drama or fiction, many people tuned in while the program is in progress, took it for real, and panicked. What I remember is the way public discussion speculates on whether there is life on Mars and whether space travel is possible. Obviously the latter proved true.

As aviation history evolved through the 1930s and World War II, airplanes became bigger, faster, and capable of flying higher than human beings ever had before. By the end of WW II and shortly after, jet planes were the emerging new phenomenon in power and speed. Simultaneously the Cold War between the East and West, especially between the United States and the Soviet Union, began. Our country became almost paranoid over the threat of communism. Suddenly we were surprised—perhaps the word was shocked—on October 4, 1957. I was 28 years old. The Soviets launched for the first time in human history an artificial satellite (an aluminum sphere smaller than a basketball) called Sputnik. It circled the globe every 95 minutes sending signals back to earth.

With humankind's first successful venture into space, the space race between the world's two superpowers began. In 1958, President Eisenhower created a National Aeronautics and Space Administration (NASA). In another year our first seven astronauts were in training to be the first Americans in space. In 1961 President John F. Kennedy established the national goal of putting a man on the Moon before the end of the decade.

On Sunday, July 20th, 1969, after I conducted morning worship at Trinity in Wichita, Lorine, our three sons, and I, piled into our station wagon, pulling a camper, heading northwest on a month's vacation. We were barely underway that day when we turned on the radio and learned our goal of putting a man on the moon had just been achieved. Neil Armstrong was the first man to set foot on the moon. He uttered words which became famous, "One small step for man, one giant leap for mankind." He was followed down the ladder by Buzz Aldrin, Jr. The entire space race is well documented in exhibits at the Cosmosphere in my hometown of Hutchinson. By 2003 and 2004 we had placed unmanned rovers on Mars to explore that planet.

It was in the mid-1940s at the end of World War II when United States dropped two atomic bombs in Japan, one killing 80,000 civilians, one killing 40,000 civilians, giving us a new reputation as the most deadly power on the planet. Soon the Soviet Union tested its own A-bomb, which in turn, accelerated research on a still more powerful weapon of destruction—the Hydrogen Bomb. November 1, 1952, while I was serving on the USS Cacapon, the United States tested our first H Bomb—500 time greater than the atomic bomb which destroyed Hiroshima. It was tested in the Marshall Islands of the South Pacific. One of the islands completely evaporated. The Soviets responded with a test of their own "thermonuclear device" so we did more testing. It was no wonder the nuclear arms race began a "Cold War" in earnest as the Soviets created the Eastern communist block of nations to confront and intimidate the free world. All of this had a chilling effect on international relationships. A blanket of near fatalism and doom covered the world as both sides menaced each other with doomsday weapons.

By August 1961, East German soldiers, part of the communist block nations, were creating the Berlin Wall in an effort to cut off East from West and to separate communism from capitalism (really to prevent East Germans from escaping their repressive government by fleeing to West Germany). For 28 years the Berlin Wall stood as the prime symbol of the Cold War and its brinksmanship. Finally, following verbal confrontations by U. S. President Ronald Regan in the 1980s, and realizing the folly of the Soviet Union's harsh and totalitarian ways, Mikhail Gorbachev began democratic reforms in a modest way. "Glasnost" (meaning openness) became his operative word. This was like opening flood gates. In July of 1989, Gorbachev told Eastern European leaders, the Soviet Union would no longer use its military muscles to enforce conformity and the communist empire began to crumble. On November 9, 1989, the Berlin Wall came tumbling down at the hands of thousands of Germans from both East and West and the Cold War confrontation was virtually at an end. My what a roller coaster ride of international relationships, of hope and despair and new hope, I've experienced in historic moments such as these.

In so many ways, the past century, the century in which most of my life has been lived, seems to me to be the most far-reaching and momentous century in history to date, although who is to overlook or minimize the Great Civilizations of other centuries since the beginning of time? In terms of the sheer explosion of knowledge, the drama of atomic energy, and the era of human flight and space exploration, the 20th Century has been amazing. It's hard to believe—I have lived through all this history and more!

* * *

Interspersed with these and other historic events, I have witnessed an American tug-of-war in foreign policy and popular mind-set. It's the tug-of-war between isolationism's desires to be neutral toward belligerency between nations, and to remain isolated from such problems, vs. internationalism's seeking to build coalitions of cooperation in matters of self-defense and the meeting of humanitarian needs.

Go back to the decade of the 1960's. Can you envision a Protestant and Catholic being able to marry as equals? Can you envision a Catholic mass being conducted in English? Do you know that Protestant Clergy and Roman Catholic Priests sometimes take communion together? If your answers are yes to these questions you were born after 1962. I well remember an event which generated among Christians a hope and vision greater than most had ever imagined.

In the last three months of 1962, Pope John XXIII convened a council known as Vatican Council II made up of Roman Catholic leaders. In contrast to his arch-conservative predecessor, this Pope became innovative to the point of "opening the windows of the church to a breath of fresh air" as people referred to his reign. This was a true recognition of changing times and a genuine welcoming of the 20th Century. The Pope held that it was necessary for the church to serve as a bridge between nations East and West (communist and non—communists), North and South (developed and developing nations), and for there to be reconciliation between the various Christian denominations and among the different world religions. Moreover, he felt the Roman Catholic Church needed to update its language and its ancient traditions.

I invite you again to join a small group with me. A small circle of less than a dozen clergy gathered in quiet secluded room of a large suburban church. I was sitting in that circle at a continuing education/retreat event. Members of the small group were from eight different denominations. One of them was a Catholic priest— one of the few priest with whom I had studied and socialized. I always had been taught that Catholics, with their self-proclaimed superiority in matters of doctrine, faith, and practice, were not permitted to cross denominational boundaries or engage in communion with those of other faith traditions. Imagine my delight, then, when the leader announced that the closing our several days together would be a breaking of bread—a communion service. Without a word or a moment's hesitation, this Catholic priest took his turn in receiving from me the bread, the cup, and the words of communion, and then, turning to the next person, offering the same as the elements of communion as they were pasted around the circle from one participant to another. Imagine my delight a few years later, when I invited another Roman Catholic priest to be a guest worship leader in my congregation and he readily accepted. Not all priests would do these things then or now, but virtually NO priests would have considered them before Vatican II, before the spirit of Pope John XXIII. Nor would there be Catholics singing hymns, especially some hymns which had Protestant origins!

*   *   *

In the fall of 1964, I was leading worship one Sunday morning, when in the middle of my sermon, one of my prominent parishioners seated in an obvious place, stood up and stalked out of the church never to return to that congregation. What triggered this?

August 7, 1964 was another historic moment in that decade. On this day, in response to an attack on 2 U.S. destroyers in Gulf of Tonkin, the U.S. congress passed a resolution authorizing the President to freely intervene and retaliate in Vietnam. By another year we had made this an undeclared war and began escalating it. I was among those who were greatly distressed over our approach to war. The fall of 1964 was a Presidential Election featuring the combative, hawkish and conservative Senator Barry Goldwater (Republican) against Senator Lyndon B. Johnson (Democrat). I would never presume to tell my parishioners for whom they should vote. But in this particular election year, there were ten major moral and spiritual issues which seemed to surface in the debates. After a good bit of personal and prayerful agony, I decided I needed to address these in some way. What I did, was to name these issues which were before our nation, identifying in each case the way in which I understood the scriptures to speak to the issues. For example, one issue was civil rights. After naming and illustrating the issue, I drew on a variety of scriptural concepts and passages that spoke to civil rights. War was another issue. I believed there were scriptural attitudes pertinent to whether we should be moving toward an escalation of hostilities.

At the end of my sermon, I invited my people, in considering how they should vote, to analyze each candidates' stand in relationship to these issues. Sad to say, my sermon's implications could not be as non-partisan as I would want. The stands of the two candidates were very different. From a scriptural point of view one stood much more in harmony with the faith than the other. This is what offended Dr. White as he left the service that Sunday. His candidate did not "fit."

The period of the Vietnam War was one of the most divisive periods of our nation's history. In early 2002, I received from a person doing historical research a "Questionnaire About the Activities and Reactions of Individuals and Local Churches in the Kansas West Conference in Relation to the Vietnam War." Here is a portion of my reply.

What was your attitude toward the involvement of the U.S. in Vietnam?

"Our congregation had been focusing more on the civil rights movement than Vietnam. At first I had ambivalent feelings about the Vietnam protests because I saw them as a distraction which diverted the nation's attention from dealing with civil rights issues."

Did you participate in any activities—protests, policy making, petitions, etc. (describe in detail including people involved, result of action, response of community, etc.) Complete sentences not necessary.

"My attitude toward U.S. involvement was that our national goals were not clear and war was not the basic solution . . . . During my 5 years at Grace UMC, my focus on social issues gradually shifted

from civil rights to the war . . . . Since Grace UMC
had a significant number of students and faculty the
impetus for this shift came largely from identifying
with the needs felt within the college community . . . .
The church itself was not really involved in protests
or demonstrations . . . Grace Church dealt with the
issues in the following ways: DISCUSSION GROUPS
(in Sunday School and through specially planned
forums); PASTORAL COUNSELING (of students
struggling with the personal issue of military service);
SERMONS."

"I have reviewed my sermon notes from this period of time and
found 4 times when my preaching had a heavy focus on Vietnam.
The first of these occurred October 10, 1965 when I preached on
the text of Isaiah 2:2-5. I had a two-fold introduction. I read a
Wichita Eagle letter written home by a young soldier to his mother
telling her about having to kill a woman and her baby for the first
time. I also asked Stu Mossman, a Southwestern student, guitarist,
folk singer, grandson of Southwestern's first President, to sing one
of his compositions, 'Guns and Sharp Swords in the Hands of
Small Children.' The sermon itself focused on the vision of Isaiah
by focusing on 3 affirmations—the work of the UN; the spiritual
foundations of peace; God's love in Christ reconciling all persons
to himself and each other.

"A second sermon was August 28, 1966. It was for an outdoor
Sunday evening community (interdenominational) service in the
park . . . A third sermon was Lenten sermon in 1967 . . . . Its
introduction included reference to sermon being preached in
response to a group of Junior High students who were asked to
suggest a sermon topic.

"Then in the Fall of 1967, I had a sermon series on DILEMMAS
YOUTH FACE. Each was a dialogue sermon with a different
student from Southwestern College. One of these was on the
dilemma of facing military service and involved L. A. Stanton, a

senior from Dodge City who was struggling with this issue. The sermon's 3 foci were: the moral pull between personal plans and public duty; the moral tension between the 'right' and 'wrong' of participation in war; the difference between the way people think about this war and they way they've thought about other wars of our nation. My concluding statement was drawn from my own experience at this age. 'whatever we do, let us do it not in an act of conformity to what the masses are doing, but as an act of conscience in obedience to Christ . . .'."

Bridges span gulfs be they little or large. They enable people to move across a gap from one side to the other. Bridges can serve as symbols of how change takes place, of how human creativity— using the present—can connect the past to the future, or how human differences can be spanned and overcome. In the 50s or 60s, Simon and Garfunkle wrote a song entitled "Bridge Over Troubled Waters." For me that song symbolized the work, the life and teachings, of Jesus Christ in reconciling human differences and those at war with one another. I was born in 1929. I've lived through the entirety of seven decades in the 20th Century. Now I'm well into the first decade of the 21st Century so my life bridges seven or eight decades (even nine if you consider 1929 a different one) depending on how a person looks at it. I guess I feel like a bridge across quite a span of time, across a lot of troubled waters, but overlooking a lot of beautiful scenery and tying together a lot of wonderful relationships. To some extent, my motivation for these memoirs is to interpret the past and the present to future generations. My hope is that in some small but meaningful way my life may have reflected some of the reconciling work of Jesus, that to some extent I may have been a peacemaker.

Chapter 40

TRAVELING WITH ABE LINCOLN

In 1961, Kansas was celebrating its centennial birthday. Many celebratory events of all sorts were planned across the state. In Wichita there was to be a grand historical pageant on the 4th of July. Included in the pageant was a portrayal of the early struggles over the issue of slavery so it was quite natural to feature a part pertaining to Abraham Lincoln's role in the great slavery debates, in the Civil War, and in issuing the Emancipation Proclamation. In January, a friend and colleague of mine, Charles Curtis, who served the Anthony Methodist Church concurrent with our time in Belle Plaine, began growing a "Centennial" beard as did many Kansans. Charles was a true orator, a lanky kind of person—tall, lean, dark haired. He was 6'8." Lincoln was 6'4." Charles styled his beard after Lincoln, and became such a "spitting image" of our 16th President that when he auditioned for the part of Lincoln in the pageant he easily won the role.

Just after Easter our Methodist General Board of Christian Social Concerns was holding a Washington-United Nations Seminar. The Seminar had two foci. One was on the role of Christians, and of congress, in facing the social issues confronting our nation. The other was on the role of the United Nations in facing issues related to world peace. The week long seminar began in New York City. Our Board of Social Concerns owned, and still does, the only non-governmental building in the immediate vicinity of the United Nations building. The Board used its building as a base for ministry to diplomats and other UN personnel, and as an ecumenical place in which to educate church people from across the nation in ways to support the United Nations and the causes of peace and justice.

Charles and I were both serving on our Annual Conference's Board of Christian Social Concerns and related sub-committees. We decided that it would be an appropriate expenditure of time and resources to attend the Washington-UN Seminar as part of our continuing education. We couldn't afford to fly. The best alternative was to drive since we could share the driving and gasoline was cheap. We needed to avoid as many lodging expenses as possible while in transit. In planning with Lorine, we came up with the idea of her joining us for the seminar. We would make a long 650 mile day's drive from Belle Plaine to Owensboro, Kentucky, taking 4-year old Ben with us. We could then leave him in the care of Grandmother and Grandfather Martin. Just "incidentally" this gave us free lodging as well as child care. After a day in Owensboro, we made another long hard day's drive to New York.

The UN seminar proved to be stimulating. Then, for the seminar's second half, we moved on to Washington D.C. Between sessions of the seminar, we squeezed in as much sightseeing as possible. Naturally some of the great monuments of our nation's capitol were on our agenda. Late one afternoon, along with a throng of other tourists, we came to the Lincoln Monument. We stood there at the foot of its steps for a few moments. Then Charles, looking every bit the part of President Lincoln, began to climb the steps up to the statue of the seated Abraham Lincoln. Arriving at the top, he turned to wave to us. Suddenly a hush came over the place. Many of the tourists were surprised and thrilled to discover a living likeness of the President at his monument. Quickly the cameras came out and there was a frenzy of picture taking. Standing in front of the Lincoln Monument has always been an awe-inspiring, sacred kind of moment for me, but this serendipity augmented the occasion.

The real reason I was traveling with "Abe Lincoln," was to equip myself for serving Methodist churches in the western two-thirds of Kansas. Some denominations stress what is called "congregational polity" meaning an emphasis on the autonomy of each of their local churches. Methodism has always stressed "connectionalism"— the idea that each local church is a connected part of the Body of Christ, therefore connected to one another through its Annual Conference. Even the Boards and Agencies of the denomination are considered part of the "connection."

Throughout my ministry I lived with the expectation that all pastors, in addition to serving their local church as their primary responsibility, should invest time and energy in serving the Annual Conference's camping program and serving on one or more of the boards and agencies of the conference. Some pastors considered these connectional responsibilities a distraction from their parish ministries and resisted them. They did add to the load one was carrying, but most pastors looked at connectional service as a means of continuing education for themselves and an enrichment of their ministry.

I always enjoyed working in connectional ministries. For instance, following my Washington DC-UN Seminar trip with "Abe Lincoln," I accepted the responsibility of helping to create a major one-day Conference on International Affairs to be held in Wichita that November. One of those with whom I worked in the planning was Ora Martin, a prominent wheat farmer from Garden City. It was through Ora I first came to know about a young man, Carl Martin, who was preparing for Methodist ministry. Carl and his wife, Mary Lou, would become some of our closest friends and colleagues across the years.

The featured speaker of the all day International Affairs event was from the National Council of Churches' Department of International Affairs. Participants also spent a significant portion of the day in two smaller workshops, selected from many, dealing with facets of the major peace issues. For our workshop leaders, we drew upon such people as U.S. Senator Frank Carlson, a founder of the U.S. Peace Corps, the President of the Kansas NAACP

(National Association for the Advancement of Colored People), the President of St. Paul Theological Seminary, state leaders in various fields of agriculture, leaders from academia, etc. More than 500 Methodists from the western half of Kansas attended and returned home inspired to help members of their home churches become peacemakers.

Early in my ministry I began serving as a Methodist representative to the Kansas Council of Churches. I continued in this ecumenical responsibility for perhaps a dozen and a half years. I was involved in numerous other connectional ministries at various times. I served on the Winfield District Committee on Ministry for several years. I served as a Trustee of Camp Lakeside at Scott City for six years and served an equal number of years as a Trustee of Methodist Youthville in Newton. I served two different terms as a Trustee of Southwestern College—one term while I was pastor of Grace Methodist Church and another term while Superintendent of the Dodge City District. While I was a DS, I served six years on the Annual Conference Council on Ministries with an equal number of years on the Dodge City District Committee on the Ordained Ministry and the DC Council on Ministries.

Only a handful of the several hundred active and retired ministers in any United Methodist Annual Conference are ever privileged to be elected a member of (a delegate to) our General and Jurisdictional Conferences. General Conference convenes once every four years as the legislative body in the Methodist Church. I was honored to be elected as first alternate to the Jurisdictional Conference in 1976. The single most important business of Jurisdictional Conference is the election of our Episcopal leaders and of those persons, lay and clergy, who make up our General (National) Boards and Agencies

In the summer of 1976, Jurisdictional Conference met in Lincoln, Nebraska. My sister and brother-in-law and their two children lived in Omaha, Nebraska. We decided to make my attendance at the Jurisdictional Conference the occasion of a mini-vacation for the family. We drove to Omaha a couple of days early to spend time with the Walters family. I left Lorine and the boys with Shirley's family and drove back to Lincoln for Jurisdictional Conference. We planned for me to return to pick up the family as soon as Jurisdictional Conference ended and hurry home non-stop to Dodge City.

In the process of the hurry, I failed to gas up the car. Sometime after dark, after we had driven beyond Salina, I realized my omission. As I watched the reading on my gas gage drop, we looked for gas at every town. Unfortunately, small town gas stations aren't open in the evenings. We kept thinking "surely the next town will have a station that's open." Not so.

About 1 a.m. we arrived at Kinsley, less than an hour from Dodge City. By now the gas gage was showing EMPTY! With lots of truck traffic on the highway, I had been confident Kinsley would have an open station. Again, no luck. This time we couldn't chance going on. We knew it was just a matter of minutes before we'd run out of gas. We looked for a motel. No luck on this score, either. The few motel rooms in Kinsley were all filled for the night. All we could think of was going to the town park and stopping for the balance of the night. We would have to sleep with all 5 of us sitting up! By daybreak, the gas station was open. We filled up and headed for home arriving about five or six hours later than planned.

While I was serving my El Dorado appointment, I also served 8 years on the Annual Conference Board of Ordained Ministry where I was privileged to help screen and nurture prospective United Methodist pastors preparing for ordination and membership in the Annual Conference. This certainly was one of my most challenging and significant forms of connectional ministry. It is not easy to make decisions about another person's future.

One of the most controversial events in the life of our Annual Conference occurred in 1985. For the better part of a century, the Conference created and helped support health ministries in the form of hospitals from Wichita and Salina west across Kansas. In the beginning, this was a pioneering Christian ministry which filled a real gap in Kansas. Gradually, health care became more widely available. Local churches could no longer contribute significant support to the six or seven Methodist hospitals in our connectional system.

One by one, these hospitals closed until by 1985 only two or three remained. The largest and most prominent of these was Wesley Medical Center in Wichita. It was difficult for the hospitals to continue financially supporting or underwriting millions of dollars worth of annual care to the poor and uninsured. Faith based charitable hospitals were closing everywhere and/or selling out to the newly emerging for-profit hospital chains. With the changing dynamics of health care, plus projected changes to come, the Trustees of Wesley Medical Center panicked. With no notification to the Annual Conference which had elected them, the Trustees began to negotiate a sale of the hospital to the Hospital Corporation of America (HCA). Suddenly the sale was announced as a "done deal." This was the first sale of a major tertiary care hospital in United States to a for-profit corporation. The hospital had been sold for $265 million which was to be placed in a health care foundation previously created by Wesley.

In the founding of Wesley and through the years, significant portions of its capital had come by way of charitable donations from Methodism. Immediately surprise, shock, and anger swept across the Annual Conference. Because of the secrecy in which decisions had been made, debate, rancor and threats of lawsuits were the order of the day at Annual Conference. Eventually litigation was avoided and a compromise was worked out. The Annual Conference received compensation in the amount of $33 million.

In 1986 the Annual Conference created a not-for-profit Foundation named the United Methodist Health Ministry Fund which was to keep the $33 million as an endowment and use its earnings for grants in support of unspecified health ministries. A 22-member Board of Trustees was elected to breathe life into the Foundation. Our Bishop, Bishop Hicks, was one of these Trustees and at least two came from each of our seven districts to ensure that we represented all geographical parts of the Annual Conference. All but five Trustees were from the laity. I was honored and pleased to be one of the five clergy, one of the 22 charter Trustees. It was our task to develop a mission statement, create by-laws, develop all the foundation's polices and procedures pertaining both to our investments and our grant-making, to select a city and a building for our offices, to choose the one who was to be employed as our president and main staff person, and finally, to make the actual grants. I served from 1986 to 1997 when our trustee tenure rule rotated me off.

Of all the connectional ministries in which I engaged during my forty years of active ministry, this was by far the most unique, the most involved, and the most significant ministry. As of this writing, former and present Trustees have grown the fund to $60 million even with all the ups (which hit $72 million at one point) and downs of the stock market. The Fund has responded to countless grant requests approving 1,235 grants. It has given away $34 million dollars to both semi-traditional health care ministries and to new and/or innovative ways of doing health ministries. The smallest of these grants was $482; the largest was $550,000 which was to establish a Kansas Telepsychiatry Network that is saving millions of dollars and man-hours in the field of mental health.

I give God thanks for all those who have been part of this United Methodist Health Ministry Fund and for all church and community organizations which have received grants and carried on the Methodist tradition of healing ministries. Of course there have been failed programs that we supported, but we learn from our mistakes as well as our successes. I can't reflect on all our hours of weighted discussion and decisions, but I am proud to have had a part in such things as:

— establishing and maintaining health care clinics including a clinic developed by the UMWKMexican-American Ministries to serve the underserved within the Hispanic community ($1.7 million given over 18 years); a clinic developed by the UM Urban Ministries, now functioning separately in Wichita as GraceMed ($1.2 million given), and a number of other low income clinics;
— pioneering care on behalf of children and youth through underwriting the opening of 5,000 new child care opportunities;

— expanding CASA, a program of Court Appointed Special Advocates who serve as the eyes and ears of judges and as makers of recommendations when children are in need of court care (usually through no fault of their own);

— assisting many programs addressing issues of substance abuse;

— establishing a computer Network of Medical Hospice programs to serve every county of Kansas, an effort for which the Fund was given national recognition;

— assisting in the development of two nursing education programs, one at Southwestern College; one at Kansas Wesleyan University;

— partnering with the Robert Wood Johnson Foundation in helping a Wichita organization, Higher Ground, expand their "Learning the Rope" program for youth with addictions (an 85% success rate).

— helping establish various youth mentor program and also to help create 30 Big Brother/Big Sister programs throughout Kansas.

The last vote I cast before retiring as a UMHM Fund trustee was to begin an Oral Health initiative in Kansas. This was to give preventive care, aimed at children, through application of a "teeth sealant" to more than 8,000 children and also through financially assisting communities to fluoridate their water. At the time this initiative actually got underway two years after I left the Trustees, the UM Health Ministry Fund was the lone voice in Kansas preaching the gospel of Oral Health. Today the state and our society are beginning to recognize its importance and the linkage between oral health and physical health.

Unless and until people have had a chance to be immersed in the connectional ministries of United Methodism they can hardly appreciate the breadth and the depth of these ministries.

Chapter 41

MY TOUGHEST APPOINTMENT

Trinity had once been a thriving church filled with prosperous people who lived in grand and beautiful homes built on the fringes of Delano just across the river west from downtown Wichita.

In the spring of 1870, a Methodist circuit rider arrived in Wichita to preach to a small Methodist congregation in a hall above the town's livery stable. Within two years, a Methodist Church stood where the First United Methodist Church stands today. For decades Wichita grew steadily and Trinity—founded in the 1880s—grew steadily. Trinity peaked in 1946 or 1947 as a congregation of 1,850 people. For whatever combination of reasons, immediately after its peak, Trinity began a sharp straight-line decline. Certainly one reason was the new rings of suburban growth which followed World War II. Also, blight began to affect the core area of the city. Inner-city decline was a phenomenon common to many cities—something with which all denominations struggled.

In the spring of 1968, I received another one of those telephone calls every Methodist pastor knows about. Coming two or three months prior to Annual Conference, when the Bishop and his Cabinet are meeting to plan appointments for the coming year, it often means a move to a new appointment. This call was from Paul Matthaei, Superintendent of the Wichita District. "Have I got a wonderful opportunity for you," he said.

I was asked to accept an appointment to Trinity Methodist Church in Wichita, at the intersection of Maple and Martinson (catty-corner across from St. Mary Orthodox Church, home of the best Lebanese food and annual church dinner in the city).

In the 1960's, the Rev. Dean Gleason led Trinity in using a consultant in planning for urban ministry. The congregation faced a decision. On the one hand it could remodel and update its facilities in an effort to revitalize and minister relevantly to its neighborhood. On the other hand, it could abandon its inner city location and follow the move of many young families to the suburbs. The church chose to stay put and remodel by going heavily into debt. When the remodeling was finished, Dean Gleason moved on.

Trinity United Methodist Church as it appeared in 1968

This wonderful opportunity turned into the toughest appointment that I ever served. I inherited a strong church of about 950 members, half what its size had once been with membership almost stabilized by the remodeling. But the membership was still slowly declining and the large indebtedness still needed to be dealt with. I had the "opportunity" to reverse the decline as well as to help lead the congregation toward paying off its loan.

On top of this, Wichita was just beginning another of its periodic economic downswings ("bust" cycles some would say) following a time of high prosperity. For more than a half century, Wichita's economy has been dominated by the presence of four major aircraft manufacturers—the Boeing Company, Beechcraft (later, Raytheon), Cessna, and Learjet (later Bombardier). In 1969 the bottom fell out of the aviation industry. Many people lost their jobs. Church finances suffered. Trinity struggled to meet its mortgage payments.

Another of the tough challenges was preaching weekly in the midst of the great social unrest prevalent throughout American society at that time. Seven weeks before I came to Trinity the Rev. Dr. Martin Luther King, Jr., America's prophet of nonviolence and racial brotherhood, had been gunned down in Memphis, Tenn. Less than two months later, five days after my arrival at Trinity, Senator Robert F. Kennedy, following his winning of the California primary in his quest for nomination as the Democratic presidential candidate, was shot and mortally wounded in Los Angeles. Our nation was stunned and in shock over these assassinations.

The nation was divided over the Vietnam War in a way that it has seldom been divided. Anti-war demonstrations intensified the division. The Civil Rights struggle continued in full sway. After gains made through the legislative process, the struggle shifted to the implementation of the Civil Rights legislation. We were being forced to confront both our institutional and personal racism. The busing of school children for the purpose of integrating schools was a hot button issue for Wichita. Wichita was divided over all these things.

Trinity's neighborhood had become a blue collar neighborhood. This began to change the congregation and its relationship to the neighborhood. To be faithful to the scriptures, I felt my preaching should not, could not, be mere platitudes. The issues of our day were also spiritual issues. I needed to be addressing them. An early reaction of my congregation illustrates what I faced.

In mid-July an issue affecting the near west side of Wichita became a major source of controversy in the city. I had eased into my preaching at Trinity preaching with two series of sermons—

one on the Great Commandments and the second on personal life crises. Now I felt compelled to interrupt my sermon series to address the issue facing the city.

"Meeting Christ in Wichita in 1968" was the title of a sermon I preached as the controversy reached its peak. After an exegesis of my text (Matthew 25:31-46), I said, "Christ comes into our world incognito—in ways which are not always obvious, in disguise so to speak." Then I shifted to the issue at hand for Wichita and especially for the West Side—our part of the city.

An order of Catholic sisters had abandoned their use of a square block or two of land at Douglas and St. Paul (a mile or two from Trinity, even nearer to some of our members' homes). They made the land available for sale. The Tabernacle Baptist Church focused boldly and forthrightly on the presence and call of Christ in the city's pockets of poverty and in Wichita's black ghetto. Tabernacle Baptist was proposing to purchase this land and develop new housing available to those from poor ghettos. This became a zoning issue before the City Council. It was greatly opposed by many. TV news portrayed Council meetings with overflowing numbers of citizens in attendance. To determine the true root of these objections was difficult. Were objections grounded in pure prejudice toward persons of color or those of low income? Were they grounded in a desire to maintain property values in a white middle class neighborhood? Which was the transcendent concern? Human values or property values?

The answer to these questions, of course, is "Yes" to all of them. I acknowledged issues are never clear cut. I included both sides of the argument in my sermon. I also said, "Where great need exists and nothing better is being proposed to meet it, we need to live by our faith, not our fears." I said, "We need to ask ourselves, can we accept the persons about whom we are speaking into our personal lives?, into our neighborhoods? We need to recognize Christ standing in the slum and ghetto, among the poor and minorities of our city, calling to us."

Before the benediction that morning, I invited those who might like to pursue the subject further or carry on a dialogue, to stop by the church library after the service. We could visit more. I finished greeting people at the sanctuary door, and went to the library on the way to my office. I was dumbfounded. It was full to overflowing. People were angry—it was a hornet's nest!

I tried to hear people out, to carry on dialogue the best I could. Perhaps this had been too soon in my ministry at Trinity to deal with such a hot issue, but it was then or never so far as that issue was concerned. The City Council was making its decision that week. A call for citizen input had gone out.

This sermon immediately colored the response of some members to my ministry for all four years I was at Trinity. Maybe I could have been wiser in the way I approached this issue, but overall I've never regretted that sermon. Certainly other members were quick to give an "Amen" to what had been said. Overall, more people were supportive of me than not.

With sons Ben 11, Bill 5, and Paul 3, Lorine and I were still in the "young adult" category. Trinity had a strong, vital, committed and fairly large group of young adults with children of similar ages. Lorine joined their Sunday School class. We became friends with many, shared children's activities, and worked together in church programs. They were a joy and a sustaining force for us through our four years at Trinity.

Over the next couple of years, Wichita schools were debating the issue of bussing children from one part of town to achieve racial integration in all public schools. Again, there were loud vocal opponents to what they called "forced bussing." In an effort to build public support, the Wichita Board of Education decided to begin a one year voluntary bussing program. This would give the District a chance to work out kinks before bussing became a mandatory tool of integration and education. Following this, they would use a "lottery" selection of student birthdays to determine who would be bussed for a year.

Bill's Kindergarten and First Grade classes were at our neighborhood Franklin Elementary School and Bill was having a ball. Midst all the controversy over bussing and with our strong convictions relating to racial equality of opportunity, Lorine and I felt volunteering Bill for the 1970 pilot project would be an appropriate thing to do. But we also wanted to involve Bill in the decision. We explained to him the best we could the what's and why's of bussing and how we felt about it, asking him if this was something he might like to do. How much he really understood what he might be getting into I don't know, but he responded in the affirmative. The die was cast.

There were five white kids, all boys, in Bill's Second Grade class at L'Ouverture School, 1539 Ohio. Four of the boys were Steve Witherspoon, Paul McCord, David Knudson and Bill. The name of the fifth escapes me. They were all sons of people of faith. The unnamed one was son of the James Donnells, a Catholic physician, city council member, and Wichita's mayor in 1973-74; Paul's father was also a pastor (Disciple's Church); and David's father was the Director of Lutheran Social Services I'm not sure of the occupation of Steve's father. The experience really worked out quite well for all concerned although their teacher in the Second Grade may have erred a bit in favoring "her white boys."

The boys learned much more than "reading, 'riting, and 'rithmetic." We still remember the day when the school phoned Lorine at home telling her Bill was running a fever and asking her to come get him. Paul was home with his mother so she took him along as she went to pick up Bill. Returning home, the school's neighborhood was strange to Paul. As Lorine made a wrong turn Paul became fearful they were lost, anxious because some of the buildings were run down, and alarmed that everyone was black. Bill sought to reassure him saying, "You don't have to worry, we're just in an economically deprived neighborhood." By the time the second year for bussing came around, Bill was eager to return to L'Ouveture for his third grade year.

In addition to the difficulty of repaying the church's loan and the social turmoil, another factor made this a difficult appointment. 1968 was also the year The Methodist Church and the Evangelical United Brethren Church merged into one new single denomination called The United Methodist Church. People often resist change. There was need for doing lots of educating of ourselves in the heritage of both former denominations as well as learning about our new united church. The uniting meant implementing new structures. This consumed much time and energy. Organizing the bureaucracy is never as exciting as actual hands on ministry and mission.

Something important to me personally as well as for the church hierarchy, was the full annual payment of what we Methodists called "our apportionments." An apportionment is an assigned contribution from the local church to support all kinds of Annual Conference benevolences (our colleges, hospitals, youth camps, a children's home, retirement homes, etc.) and ministerial pensions, plus administrative expenses at all levels of the church from bottom to top plus missionary work at home and abroad, etc. The size of each church's apportionments was related to its membership, its worship attendance, and its historical giving record. Sometimes the size of apportionments was great enough to really stretch and challenge a congregation in meeting the goal of fully paying them. Also, members who were not sympathetic to one or more of the causes in the apportionment package sometimes became vocal and generally create resistance to paying our portion fully.

Some pastors work more diligently than others in interpreting these to the congregation and in encouraging their payment. I had always prided myself in successfully enabling my churches to fully pay their apportionments. One of the changes which came about as a result of the merger of the two denominations was a changing fiscal year from beginning June 1 to beginning January 1. This meant in my first year at Trinity we had a seven-month fiscal year. We were able to fully pay our apportionments during this period. But as Wichita's recession set in and as we faced the pressure of meeting our loan payments, we failed to fully pay apportionments during the remaining three years of my appointment to Trinity, Wichita. In fact, Trinity from that time on to the present has never been successful in fully paying *all* apportionments. This was a great personal disappointment for me—another thing which made this appointment "tough."

Among the changes of the sixties, society was beginning to experience was what was called "the counterculture" or the "Hippie Generation"—young people experimenting with drugs, breaking with traditional norms of society, shifting from traditional life styles and music, and sometimes even moving into communal living situations. The Church tried to minister to these young people in a variety of ways. Our Annual Conference created the Wichita Urban Ministries to serve both the "down and outs" and the "counterculture dropouts" of society. The Rev. Gene Seeley, one of my friends and peers, was appointed to develop our Urban Ministry. His ministry became controversial and so did Gene. It disturbed many traditionalists. In my opinion, we needed the Urban Ministry and it was dependant upon the support of local congregations. My support of the Wichita Urban Ministry and of Gene managed to upset my critics.

Many new forms of worship were beginning to emerge among churches in the late sixties and early seventies. Foremost among the changes were music and liturgy. Worship sometimes included such things as "dialogue preaching" with two people conversing with one another in the course of the sermon. Once more, I felt innovation was important. I experimented with some of new things as a way to continue reaching youth and young people on and beyond the fringes of the church. I enjoyed including contemporary music and liturgy in worship and I frequently utilized film clips in worship.

I tried to involve several "different voices" in worship each year. For instance, Protestant Churches still recognized a "Reformation Sunday" each fall as part of the church year. Historically this had been a theological teaching tool in many major denominations, but for some pastors and some denominations it degenerated into a time for "Catholic bashing." I wanted to recognize this special Sunday making it something positive and creative. I was able on one occasion to have our neighborhood Catholic Priest share the pulpit with me—something innovative both for him and for us. On several occasions I involved one of the Catholic sisters from Newman College. Most of these occasions involved doing dialogue sermons. As our Methodism worked toward developing ecumenical relationships between several major Protestant denominations, pulpit exchanges with the neighboring Presbyterian Church just down the block took place. Westside Ministerial Association also became a tool of fellowship between pastors and cooperation between congregations. A dialogue sermon with an unwed mother and another with an alcoholic were among my efforts at dealing with contemporary and personal issues.

Sometimes these efforts were well received by the congregation. Sometimes there were those who preferred not to recognize such problems. The latter individuals added to the stressful nature of my Trinity years. Overall I've felt that if one word was to sum up or describe the thrust of my ministry at Trinity it would be "reconciling." Always my aim was to build bridges where there was separation or estrangement in church and society.

A special joy in this appointment was having an Associate Pastor with which to work—actually a series of associates. A year before I came, Duane Dyer was appointed Associate Pastor to serve with Dean Gleason. Duane proved to be a very popular young associate. He was not eager to move after just one year. I liked the idea of staff continuity and having an energetic young associate to help carry the load. We agreed to continue this relationship and it worked well. Duane was strong and effective. He possessed good leadership skills. By the end of his second year at Trinity Duane was eager to be appointed to a church of his own.

I felt, as did the Staff-Parish Relations Committee, that Trinity needed to replace Duane. We asked for the appointment of another associate. Fortunately, Tom Sheldon, a very fine young pastor was just coming out of seminary. He was married to Barbara (Cottle), a student whom I knew from Southwestern days when she had been very active in the Christian education ministry of Grace Church. Barbara was finishing graduate work in Christian Education at Perkins School of Theology, SMU, in Dallas, where Tom did his seminary work. She was hoping for a job as they returned to Kansas. There was a Director of Christian Education opening at Valley Center. The two positions, ours and Valley Center's, made an attractive situation for Tom and Barbara. I thoroughly enjoyed working with Tom. I believe we both felt we made a good team, but once again as is almost always the case when young pastors just out of seminary take an appointment as an Associate, within a couple of years Tom was eager to have his own appointment. Moreover, the financial crunch was now hitting Trinity so hard we no longer could sustain a fulltime second pastor.

The crunch was hitting other churches—not just Trinity. First United Methodist Church downtown had three associate pastors. Two of the three were a clergy couple, Tom and Sharon Emswiler. First Church was unable to continue supporting a senior pastor plus three associates. After appointments had been finalized at Annual Conference, they decided to cut a position. Sharon was the pastor left hanging without an appointment even though our covenant between pastors and the Annual Conference is supposed to guarantee "every church a pastor and every pastor a church".

That summer, after we were without Tom Sheldon, I discovered what had happened to Sharon. We ended up developing a halftime pastoral associate position filled with Sharon Emswiler. This was for the 1971-1972 appointive year. Sharon proved to be a wonderful asset. She was extremely creative. However, this was before women clergy had become common place and accepted in our Annual Conference. Not only did her creativity stir the waters for some of our members as creativity frequently does in any profession; having a "pioneering" woman clergyperson upset some people.

By the end of the 1971-72 appointive year, I was beginning to grow weary of what seemed to be a complex, underlying and never ending struggle at Trinity. We enjoyed most of our church members but we did not enjoy the constant nit-picking of a few, or the struggle for economic survival. We enjoyed Wichita for all it offered culturally, educationally, and recreationally. It was a fine city for our kids. Lorine was able to complete her teaching certificate which was virtually finished when we left Winfield. She enjoyed taking additional courses in French, linguistics, and education at both Friends University and Wichita State University.

Our son Ben grew long hair as did many of the city's kids in that era. This bothered us some, but we felt Ben needed freedom to do his "own thing." Ben did well in drama, violin, and in his academic subjects at Allison Middle School, only about four blocks from home. This was what really counted. He had friends both at church and at school. Bill also did well in the schools he attended. There were a number of kids for him to enjoy at the church. The parents of the little cluster of five white boys at L'Ouverture got them together to celebrate birthdays and special occasions so they became little group of supportive friends. Paul had neighborhood and church kids his age to play with and Lorine was able, when the time was right, to enroll him for a couple of years in the well-thought-of Woodland United Methodist Church's Preschool.

Our kids were at an age when they were exploring every thing and we had great family fun. Beyond the ordinary things that families do and our family travels, one special family activity for us while we were in Wichita was Cheney Lake. This reservoir was completed about a year before we got to Wichita and was only about 30-40 minutes west of the city. Our interest in the lake evolved while we were in Belle Plaine and Winfield. We often drove by it on trips to visit my mom and dad in Hutchinson. We watched its construction develop and come to fruition.

As we were moving to Wichita, on the way out of Winfield on our final trip, we drove by a nice aluminum motorboat parked on the street with a "for sale" sign on it. We stopped to look at it, and then knocked at the door to inquire, "How old is the boat? How well does it run? How much do you want for it?" The lady at the door told us, "It's not really my boat. My son's gone to Vietnam and thought the boat would only deteriorate while he was overseas. He asked me to sell it for him for whatever I could get for it. It's about 8 or 10 years old. He said it runs real well." I forget the exact price but it seemed like a bargain. We jumped for it on the spur of the moment.

As soon as we got settled in Wichita we began trying out the boat at Cheney. Boating became a favorite family activity. Twelve years later in El Dorado, after another reservoir was built there, we traded the aluminum boat for a yellow fiberglass motorboat. After eight years, we traded that motorboat on a brand new motorboat. Altogether we've had thirty-six years of boating fun while the kids were at home, after they had flown the coop and when they come home in the summer. This isn't the end of the boating story though.

A year after we got the motorboat, Ben came home all excited after a week's campout with his Boy Scout troop at the Quivira Scout Ranch in Chautauqua County. He'd learned to sail and nothing would do but that we needed to have a sailboat. Some of our friends—the Bob Eades and Ken Shorts—were beginning to get into sailing. We were a bit dubious, but we went shopping, found a boat on an end-of-the season sale, and ended up with a 12' or 14' Starfish sailboat. This also proved to be a source of great family fun. When we moved to Western Kansas, we were able to take the sailboat with us for use on some of the small lakes in Ford County, Clark County, and Seward County. This was nice because we had to leave our motorboat behind until we returned to Central Kansas.

We've got a variety of family stories we like to tell from sailing days. One is from Cheney Lake itself early in our sailing days. There was usually a pretty good breeze there. We had purchased the boat in August and were trying to stretch the season by sailing anytime in September or October when it was warm and breezy. One Saturday the wind was up. We decided to try it. We shoved out from a beach on the south end of the lake with all five of us aboard.

In no time the wind whisked us quite a way up the lake. We knew we'd be going against the wind on the return so we didn't linger at the north end—we just headed right back. We soon learned there was no way to sail directly into the wind. We had little experience tacking (running a course obliquely against the wind). Tacking is not always easy for the experienced sailor, and it was really difficult for the inexperienced person. You can be flipped over rather easily unless you're very careful. The going was difficult. Progress was *extremely* slow. After an hour or more we were still a long way from being back where we started. The kids were beginning to get cold. Our Starfish was one of those little boats that are more like a surfboard skimming the water than a boat in which you ride deep inside. The norm for us, and the fun of it, was being splashed and wet all the time you were sailing. The fact that the kids were wet didn't help when the weather was beginning to get colder and we were all getting hungrier.

Eventually we began to despair of getting back in any reasonable time at all. We strategized on what to do. I finally decided we just needed to beach the boat on the western shore which was not so far away and was easy to get to. I reasoned the kids could quickly get out of the water, I could either hike or catch a ride back to where our car was and then come get them. This is what we did. We drove a station wagon which had a luggage rack on it. Our sailboat was small and light enough that with all of us working together we could turn it upside down and hoist it on top of the station wagon whenever we went sailing. Eventually I got back with the station wagon and was able to retrieve not only the kids but also the boat. From then on we were very careful not to get into that situation again, since we might not always be where our 'beach and retrieve' procedure would work.

Another of our stories comes from being on a strange lake for the first time. We were all on board—the kids sitting on the deck up forward, Lorine and I with our feet in the little well to the rear. The stability of the boat came from its "dagger board"—a smooth sculpted board about 10 or 12 inches wide, and an inch thick— inserted down into the water for about 3feet through a slit in the bottom of the boat. We were unfamiliar with the terrain of the lake, but the water looked good and we were scooting along in great fashion. All of a sudden the dagger board hit an immovable object—a large boulder—under the water's surface where we couldn't see it. We were stopped instantly resulting in all three boys being unexpectedly catapulted through the air, over the bow of the boat, out into the lake without a moment's notice. They were no worse for the wear and fortunately the only damage to the boat was a big nick which permanently remained in our dagger board.

Although I was growing weary with the constant stress during the spring of 1972, I was not in despair. Beyond the comfort and power of God's Spirit, and the comfort and support we found with one another in our family, there was "the bridge group"—a wonderfully sustaining force that we experienced during these four years at Trinity. I'm not sure when, where or how this group began. I still see it clearly in my mind's eye—a group of us, pastors and spouses, who liked to play bridge frequently sitting around our parsonage dining room table at 1327 University enjoying dinner together and then adjourning to our living room to spend the evening playing bridge and visiting. The whole evening was one of relaxation. We could just let our hair down, share our joys and woes in ministry and be ourselves whether we were commiserating or laughing with one another or both.

The main criteria of "belonging" to this group was to enjoy bridge, and to live in Wichita or to be close enough to come play regularly on the first Friday evening of each month. Through the thirty-five years a number of couples have been part of the Wichita Bridge Club—some only for awhile, some in and out of the group as their appointments changed. These have included the Coopers, Eades, Wayne Findleys, Gants, Iwigs, Osborns, Robbins, Rosses, Ken and Mel Shorts, Smoots, Staplefords, and Wingets and others. Lorine and I have been part of it all this time except for the six years we were appointed in Western Kansas. Everyone needs a group like this in their life where they unwind and share life and feel acceptance no matter what. These friends kept us going through this "toughest appointment" of my career.

Chapter 42

THE APPOINTMENT I NEVER WANTED

Some pastors are eager to "climb the ladder of success," what ever that may mean. For some, it means going to a bigger church; for some it means getting bigger salaries; and, for others it means having a higher office within the denomination—especially to go from being the pastor of a local church to becoming a District Superintendent. My dream for ministry never included the hope of being appointed to a large church or to "a district" as this goal is called. For me professional success meant faithfulness to my Lord and to my appointment, wherever or whatever the appointment might be, not to mention having a good family life and personal integrity even though some people would not equate these latter things as part of professional success. I simply was not locked into "ladder climbing."

In the early days of American Methodism pastoral appointments were seldom renewed more than once. This is to say the typical length of a pastor's service to his congregation was only a year or two, almost never more than three years at most. Then there would be a new appointment. I'm not sure of the reasons for these short pastorates. Pastoral folklore often says with the time and distance involved in traveling the circuit, there wasn't time to prepare sermons so when a pastor had used up his sermons at one church he needed to move on to another. Gradually across the years, the length of stay for pastors with their congregation lengthened. Even though appointments were one year at a time, subject to annual renewal or reappointment, *never, with the* exception of District Superintendents was there any fixed limit to the length of time that a pastor could be appointed to serve the same church. *The Discipline of the United Methodist Church*, our governing rules, did limit the length of time a DS could serve to six years. By the time I became an ordained minister, I suppose the average length of a pastoral appointment, following one's initial appointment, may have run from 4 to 6 years. I seemed to be on a 5-year plan if one were to judge by my stay at Belle Plaine and Grace Church.

Even though Trinity was a struggle and I sometimes grew weary with the struggle, I had not asked for a move nor had the church, to my knowledge, asked for a change of pastors. Toward the end of February or early in March of my fourth year at Trinity Wichita, late one evening the phone rang at the parsonage. It was the bishop—Bishop McFerrin Stowe. I was genuinely surprised. I had never before had a phone call from a bishop. I couldn't imagine why he would be calling me.

"As you know," he proceeded to say after opening pleasantries, "the Cabinet and I will soon meet to begin making appointments for the next appointive year (June 1 to May 31). This next year there will be two districts open for new Superintendents—the Dodge City and the Hutchinson District. I'd like to invite you to become one of my District Superintendents. At the moment, the choice is yours as to which district you might like to serve."

Most District Superintendents were older men. I was young for the job. I was dumbfounded. I'd never thought about being a District Superintendent. This was not an office to which I aspired. There were moments when I questioned in my mind what some of our District Superintendents did, or the way they did it. Many times I'd said to myself, and sometimes to other people, "I would never be a DS!"

There was an awkward silence before I said or asked anything. Eventually, I stammered something to the effect, "I'd like to think and pray about it and I'd like to talk it over with Lorine. When would you need to receive an answer?"

"I'd need to know tomorrow, preferable early in the morning," replied the Bishop.

Somewhere during our relatively brief conversation I did find out that my main training would be a kind of apprenticeship gleaned through sitting with the cabinet whenever and wherever it met during the next three months. Also I learned, for the first time ever the General Conference would be offering an orientation course for new District Superintendents. This pilot course for new Superintendents from across the nation would be held in Iowa, in June.

Needless to say, Lorine and I spent the balance of the evening discussing this sudden turn of events which would be life-altering for us and the family. As usual, Lorine was supportive. She simply said, "You need to do whatever you think is best." My invitation surprised me. I was flattered, honored. I felt God had to have a hand in this and that I needed to be responsive to Him. The appointment would be a tremendous responsibility—overseeing 52 churches, shepherding 42 pastors, participating in the making of all of the appointments in the Annual Conference, and helping to enable the total ministries of the United Methodist Church. There was little comprehension of what I'd be getting into. Little did I realize that I would be driving 35,000 miles a year for 6 years while carrying out all my responsibilities. While I had many mixed feelings, I hesitated to say to the Bishop "You're offering me an appointment I don't want."

In the end, I decided that my covenant was to serve where appointed by the Bishop. The next morning I called to say "yes" to the invitation. At that time, I also learned that the other person being asked to serve as a DS was Harold Nelson. By then, Harold had spoken for the Hutchinson District which really made the decision for me as to where I would be appointed. Through the next six years, there were a number of times when people would mix up the two of us thinking that I was Harold Nelson or that he was Harold Kieler. This was just one of many things that were to make these six years interesting. In terms of my feelings, even though

I never sought or wanted this appointment my excitement and anticipation over it grew.

I would never have said "it stinks!" But in one literal way, this appointment did sometime stink. As the moving van was unloading our furniture at the District Parsonage at 504 Annette in Dodge City, we detected the most awful smell. Upon inquiry, we discovered less than two miles to our southeast were large feedlots where cattle were being fattened for market. Such feedlots dotted Western Kansas because the area normally raises an abundance of milo providing the grain and forage needed for fattening cattle. The cattle industry is something for which this corner of the state is famous. At any one time, there are millions of cattle being fed in Southwest Kansas. They, in turn, produced mounds, some would say mountains, of manure. When it rains, fresh manure generates a stink that drifts downwind for miles, for days. In Dodge, people said, "Don't knock it; it's the smell of money." Fortunately the prevailing wind in Kansas is from the southwest. We were able to tolerate the stink because southeast winds blew only occasionally, but this smell remains one of our strong memories.

Overall I had a great time in this appointment. I had much greater freedom and control over my calendar than in the local parish. Especially around holidays, I was able to spend more uninterrupted time with my family.

One thing I gained by serving as a DS was a much greater vision of our overall connectional church and of the larger Church. I enjoyed the sense of participating in this larger ministry. On the district level, I enjoyed the many pastors and laity with whom I worked. Crossing and criss-crossing my native state time and again, I always thrilled to its rolling hills and undulating prairies, its ever changing seasonal textures with broad vistas uninterrupted by trees or skyscrapers. Occasional grain elevators are the only skyscrapers in Western Kansas. But one of the things I missed was the more in-depth thrill of relating to people in just one single local church as I had done when I was a parish pastor. In the end, when my six years were finished and I had traveled 210,000 miles, I was ready to return to ministry in the local parish.

Chapter 43

GUNSMOKE

A chill was setting in. The wind was coming up. As I walked briskly from the church to my car, I pondered the sky. I'd been in Salina for two days of Cabinet meetings. As always, when my meetings were finished, I was eager to get back home. I pulled on to State Highway 140 driving west southwest from Salina. Showers had begun about mid-afternoon just a couple of hours before the meeting adjourned. Seemingly, this was just a developing rainstorm.

At Ellsworth I turned straight southwest on US Highway 156. Now the rain seemed to be getting heavier and the clouds darker. Night was coming on earlier than usual. Near Great Bend the road joined US Highway 56 heading straight west for a few miles. At this point I noticed a few snowflakes smacking my windshield, mixed in with the rain. As the road turned to the southwest again, the ratio between rain and snow began shifting dramatically. Before I reached Larned I was no longer in any rain—I was in a full-blown snowstorm. Between Larned and Kinsley the highway became snow packed and the wind picked up to a howling pitch.

By the time I reached Kinsley, I knew I was in one of those infamous Western Kansas blizzards. It was obvious. This was a dangerous storm—the kind where people become stranded on roads, slide into ditches, and lose their lives if they leave their cars to seek help. But staying in their car, stranded people sometimes die either from carbon monoxide poisoning if their tailpipe gets blocked with snow while their engine is running, or freeze to death if they run out of gas. This is why everyone in Western Kansas is always schooled to carry blizzard gear in their trunk from November through March. Blizzard gear means at least a heavy duty sleeping bag for each person, foods like dried fruit and nuts, chocolate and water, candles which could be burned if you opened your window just a crack to allow for fresh oxygen-filled air, plus a little shovel and sand which might be used to dig traction for the car.

At Kinsley I began debating with my self about the wisdom of continuing on. "Maybe I should spend the night here. Maybe I should see if there is a motel room available. On the other hand, Kinsley is only 40 miles away from home. I can usually drive this in a lot less than an hour and it's only about 8:30 p.m. I'll be careful." This was decades before cell phones were in common use. "Lorine shouldn't have to worry about me because I can be home before 10 p.m. even with slow going. I'll push on."

By the time I reached Offerle, eight miles down the road, it was clear that I'd probably made the wrong decision, but Offerle was a tiny town. No public services were available this hour of night. I hated to knock after dark on some Methodist door asking for shelter. I stopped just long enough to move my blizzard gear from my trunk to my back seat. If I ended up stranded I didn't want to have to get out of the car.

Just after I pulled back on the highway and started out of town, I realized the blizzard was becoming a "white out"—the type of storm where the wind is blowing a blinding snow sideways across one's windshield in such a fashion as to block any view of what lies ahead. There's nothing but a white sheet in front of you. It's enough to make you become dizzy and disoriented. What bad luck! But then, what good luck! One of the many eighteen wheelers which crisscross the highways of Western Kansas passed me. The truck's cab was high enough above the highway the driver could look down on the road and see well enough to keep going. Not only that—the back-end of the truck was well marked with a combination of many tail lights and much reflecting tape. This made it easy to follow him since my headlights lit up the tape. Instead of slowing down, I sped up to keep the truck in view and allow him to be my eyes.

For 11 miles I moved right along through the storm almost feeling safe and comfortable. As we came to Spearville, another town of perhaps 250 people, my guiding trucker didn't even slow down. I felt compelled to slow up a bit as we went through town. I lost sight of him. What bad luck! Emerging from Spearville with only 15 miles to home, only 10 miles to Wright, the final little community before Dodge, I once again found myself in the midst of a white out. And the snow was getting deeper all the time. The only way I could maintain any orientation was to roll down my window every minute or so to look sideways to catch a glimpse of where the edge of the road was. I couldn't keep my window down because the driving snow blew in so fiercely. Soon I was unable to see even the edge of the highway. I could see nothing and I was down to driving only 5 or 10 miles per hour. I saw no other cars. I had no idea whether I was in the right lane, the left lane, the middle of the highway or perhaps on shoulder on the verge of dropping off into the ditch. It was terrifying. Finally, I knew I simply had to stop, which in itself was a dangerous thing to do. For at least 5 or 10 minutes, it seemed like an eternity, I sat there in panic never knowing when another vehicle might plow into me.

Then, what good luck! A National Guard jeep with 4-wheel drive and a two-way radio appeared out of no where. They stopped to notify me that the highway had been closed for the duration of the storm. They were bringing in any stranded travelers they could find. Just before I would reach Wright, Kansas, now 5 miles ahead, there was a fertilizer plant with a large parking lot. The Guard was using it as a command post and a place to park abandoned cars. Stranded travelers were being ordered into the jeep while a guardsman would take over their car and drive it to the plant. It could be retrieved there another day. As I crawled into the jeep, I discovered it was crowded with six persons.

By 10:30 p.m. they had driven their passengers the remaining three miles from Wright to their homes in Dodge City. How grateful

I was for the National Guard. What a relief to arrive home safe and sound! Fortunately almost none of my continual road trips as District Superintendent were this dramatic.

A prime reason I didn't want to be a District Superintendent was the reputation so many DSs, especially the old-timers, of being authoritarian and autocratic. There was a difference for me between management and authoritarianism. Consequently, once we arrived in Dodge City, I devoted much of my first summer to making the rounds of the district in a listening tour. I was on the road visiting all my churches that summer. I had a somewhat set pattern for each visit. Upon arrival, I asked the pastor to give me a quick tour of the community, church and, if convenient, to introduce me to the parsonage family and their home. I tried to spend a minimum of an hour with each pastor. During my time with him or her, I asked them to tell me about themselves (because I did not know many of the pastors in the district) and to tell me the way they saw their ministry in their present appointment. I'd also requested in advance of my visit, that each pastor would have the Lay Leader or the Staff/Parish Relations Chairperson and/or one or two other lay persons available to give me a short orientation into their community and church from their point of view.

I asked one final question of each pastor and of the lay persons with whom I visited: "If you were to single out the one greatest unmet social need of your community, which the church could or should address, what would that be?" Amazingly, even though more than one need might be singled out, the most common reference was to the unmet needs of migrant laborers. Many of the migrants were seasonal agricultural laborers although more and more they were beginning to settle in and live year around in the Kansas communities where they worked. Some were even taking other forms of employment. Most migrant laborers were of Mexican origin. Some were what are now called "undocumented workers" although the common term at that time was "illegal aliens." In Finney County, there was a large Hispanic population with a heritage of at least three resident generations. Garden City had also had a Methodist Mission for Mexican people which had been abandoned some years before, but which left a residual of Methodist

Mexicans. Language, poverty and discrimination were the chief ingredients in naming this unmet need.

By the end of the summer one thing was clear to me. United Methodism needed to be involved in a ministry to Mexican-Americans in Western Kansas. I convened a task force consisting of pastors and lay persons whom I selected from among those who had expressed the greatest interest in this unmet need. For the next year we met approximately monthly for research, brainstorming and the planning process to begin such a ministry. Somewhere between a dozen and a dozen-and-a half of us worked diligently to create what we came to call "The United Methodist Western Kansas Mexican American Ministries."

We launched the UMWKMAM late in 1973 or early 1974. We centered it in Garden City, housing it, to begin with, in the First United Methodist Church. We secured an Executive Pastor from the Rio Grande Conference of the United Methodist Church. The task force became the Board of Directors. Members were all United Methodists. Those whom I can quickly recall as giving vital leadership were Wayne Findley, pastor at Johnson; Pearl and Bill Dial, spouse and pastor at Ulysses, Lupie Lopez and Bob Dennis, lay persons from Garden City and Dodge City respectively. Among several early goals was the attempt to expand the number of Mexican American members on the Board of Directors, and to extend the ministry into Dodge City and Ulysses. Early on we discovered and succeeded in employing as our first Community Organizer Jose Olivas, son-in-law of a United Methodist pastor in the Annual Conference.

The ministry continued to expand. Today it has staff and centers of operation in Liberal, Ulysses-Sublette, Garden City and Dodge City. The ministry included a broad spectrum of social services, Bible Schools and various forms of spiritual nurture, and most of all, a medical clinic to help the medically unserved or underserved. Jose, especially, and all of our community developers, generally, contributed wonderfully to the ministry's development.

For years, Pearle functioned as our Board Chairperson in an exceptional way. Later she was employed as our Executive Director. I never held any office except that of an *ex officio board member.* I continued to be supportive and actively involved throughout my superintendency. As of this writing UMWKMAM is, in my opinion and that of many, one of the premier social service agencies of the state of Kansas. Without seeking to brag, I do believe that Wayne, Pearl and I were among the key persons who birthed this ministry into life. My wife, Lorine, was also tremendously supportive in this as in all my ministries. She personally engaged in helping many people learn English as a second language. I believe for my District Superintendency and through all my days of my ministry, this was probably my most significant contribution to my church and society.

Less than six months after I was invited to become a DS, Bishop Stowe was transferred to Texas. A newly elected Bishop, Ernie Dixon, a black Bishop, was assigned to the Kansas Area. Ernie, as those of us on the Cabinet called him, was the Bishop under whom I served the balance of my six years as a Superintendent. To me he was a wonderful person and a wonderful Bishop. Bishop Stowe had a strong Cabinet in place. There were no "yes" men in it. Bishop Dixon brought his own heritage plus his own gifts and graces to the job, but as a person who had never been a District Superintendent, who was new to Kansas and new to the episcopacy, he was open to our input and coaching. A couple or three months after his arrival, he was eager to make a listening tour of his new Episcopal area. Each of the seven District Superintendents in the Kansas West Annual Conference was responsible for setting up the Bishop's tour in our District.

With all the Bishop's many connectional responsibilities, his time for the listening tour had to be limited. To maximize his one on one time with people and to minimize the time which would be required to travel the 21 counties of my District (20% of the geographical area of Kansas); I came up with a wild idea. Bill Dial, our Pastor at Ulysses, was a veteran World War II pilot who had kept his license and skills current. The bank in Ulysses had its own plane which it used not only for business purposes but also for civic and charitable purposes. When there was a need for mercy flights out of Ulysses, they frequently used Bill as a volunteer pilot. I asked Bill if he thought he could get the bank to allow him to use their plane to give the Bishop a tour of the district. They agreed.

Bill and I flew to Hays to pick the Bishop up early the morning following his tour of the Hays District. Bill flew low over most of the towns of our district so the Bishop could see the land, the communities, and the churches from the air. We landed at a number of county seat towns where clusters of pastors were convened for conversation with the Bishop. This proved to be a productive time as well as a time of fun and excitement both for the Bishop and for me.

Speaking of the fun and excitement of air travel, I remember two other experiences. Wayne Findley, my good friend and pastor at the Johnson UMC in Stanton County, took flying lessons while he was there and got his pilot's license. Both of us were members of the Annual Conference Council on Ministries. Usually, whenever I had a chance to be in Hutchinson, I would capitalize on it because I could kill two birds with one stone—I could drop in and pay a visit to my parents at the same time I was there, as well as passing through, on business. For Wayne, to drive to Hutchinson from Johnson was something like a 4+ hour drive each way. This meant a minimum of a full day of his time even to attend a meeting lasting only a couple of hours. Council meetings usually took 6 to 8 hours which compounded Wayne's situation. My driving time was only about half as much. One time Wayne phoned me about a meeting of the Council which was being held in Hutchinson. He said he was going to fly this time and asked if I wanted to meet him at the Dodge City Airport. He could drop by and pick me up. That sounded like a fun offer. I said "sure."

Wayne was in a little Cessna. He was navigating visually—that is by eye contact with the ground as opposed to using instruments. The flight would be just over an hour. We were chatting away when Wayne rather casually remarked that he hadn't been paying much attention to things. "I'm not right sure where we are," he said. That kind of perked my interest so I asked how he was going to figure it out. "Oh," he said, "see that water over there to the right? I'll just drop down and circle it. The name of the town should be on the tower." This is what he did and when he found out where he was it wasn't hard to finish finding the way to Hutchinson.

Another time I had driven to Hutchinson for a specially called meeting of the Cabinet. Since it hadn't been pre-planned, it turned out that I had a conflict with an evening meeting in Ulysses. Both meetings were pretty essential. With over four hours drive time between the two places and only two hours between the two meetings, how was I to do both? I inquired about the cost of a charter from a flight service in Hutchinson; then, I checked with our Annual Conference Treasurer. When we computed all the factors involved, it didn't seem like the extra expense was unwarranted. I simply left my Hutchinson meeting, flew out to my Ulysses meeting and then back to Hutchinson to be there for the next day's business. Business people do this kind of thing all the time. It was atypical for a DS to do it, but it worked for me.

The travel required of me by this appointment put some extra stress and strain on the family. Most of the time, if I needed to be out in the District for an evening meeting, I would be able drive back to Dodge to spend the night. I usually arrived back after the kids, even Lorine, were in bed but I was able to be up early and present for breakfast with them before they went to school. Often I had to be on the road again before they got home from school in the afternoon. This didn't leave lots of time for togetherness and conversation. Lorine was at home and my office was in the District Parsonage so the two of us had quite a bit of time together, but Lorine ended up with more than her share of parenting. Normally I was able to keep Saturdays free. This became our family day.

Dodge City was a time during which Ben really began to spread his wings. He was entering senior high school when we moved to Dodge City and all the adolescent struggles that go with these years. On top of this, Ben's long hair, which he insisted on maintaining in the move from Wichita to Dodge, didn't fit in too well with the Western Kansas culture where most kids had conventional haircuts. The kids who tended to related quickest to Ben, and vice versa, were often the most free-wheeling kids or those on the fringes of experimenting with drugs or at odds with the law. We had a number of confrontations over issues of discipline.

I didn't want to be the absentee father who came home just to be the disciplinarian. Once when Ben was at odds with us and we with him, I had an evening meeting at the Plains United Methodist Church—about an hour southwest of Dodge. In order to have time just to visit with Ben, and also time to talk about the issues, I insisted on an early supper followed by Ben riding in the car with me to Plains. This would give us a couple hours together. Ben protested. I told him to bring his homework along and we'd find a place in the church were he would be able to study while I had my meeting. By the end of the evening, I felt it had been a helpful time together and a good way to dove-tail parental and church responsibility.

On another occasion I learned one of the farmers with whom I worked had fish (mostly bull-heads, though) in his irrigation ponds. He was willing for me to take my kids fishing there. This gave me the opportunity to combine a family fishing trip for the boys with business.

When I was a kid, my parents drove through Dodge City a couple of times on the way to Colorado. We would see the old run down original Dodge City Front Street which faced the railroad, and we would stop to look at Boot Hill. Dodge City was full of the lore of the Wild West days—pioneering days of cowboys and Indians on which every American grows up. Boot Hill was the cemetery. Supposedly, when there were gunfights between "the good guys and the bad guys" and people were killed, they were brought there for burial in shallow graves—burial with their boots on so the toe of the boot stuck out of the ground and could be seen by all forever.

When our family came to Dodge City in 1972, there was a famous TV series called "GUNSMOKE." We didn't watch it much, but many people did. The setting for "GUNSMOKE" was Dodge City. The era was that of the Wild West. Dodge City became a major tourist attraction for cross country travelers although by the time we arrived there, in typical American fashion, the original frontier frame buildings had been torn down and replaced with new and slightly relocated buildings. Supposedly they replicated what they were replacing. Front Street wasn't so authentic, but it was a popular place. They staged a gunfight each evening to show tourists how it used to be, and the "saloon" had a show with

sarsaparilla and "the dancing girls of the 1880s." Our family enjoyed
visiting Front Street several times each summer. Another form of
entertainment brought a sense of western pleasure for the family:
each year Dodge City had several days of Rodeo.

The district parsonage at Dodge City was built by the Annual
Conference 12 or 15 years before we came. It was a well—
maintained spacious two story home with a three-quarters
basement. We used the basement essentially as a recreation room
with a foldout couch in one corner which doubled as a spare
bedroom. Lorine called it her favorite parsonage.

Our family Christmas card photo: 1974
Left to right: Paul; Lorine; Bill; the author; Ben

We tried to have lots of things to keep the boys interested around
home. Back in Belle Plaine, Roy Smith, the shop teacher at high

school, helped me build a nice electric train table for Ben. Through the years the train had gotten upgraded. It was handed down from Ben to Bill to Paul as it was "outgrown" by first one and then another. The basement was home to the train table. As we left Trinity, the church took up a "love offering" to give us as a farewell gift. Lorine and I chose to invest that in a pool table for our boys. This too was placed in the rec room and was a source of endless pleasure for all of us—the guys especially. I always enjoyed playing ping pong as a kid. A hand-me-down collapsible ping pond table from dad found its way into our basement.

During our Dodge City time, one new game Ben learned and became quite skilled in playing was Foosball or Table Soccer. Eventually one Christmas before we left Dodge, we also added a Foosball Table to our family recreation equipment. Between trains, pool, ping pong, and foosball we had quite three ring circus in our basement for the kids and their friends.

Apart from family vacations, the other family thing we frequently did during the summertime was sail boating. Usually we used the two closest lakes—Ford County Lake or Clark County Lake. Sometime we drove farther to Scott County Lake State Park and Mead State Park. They were relatively small lakes but we could picnic, sail, fish and have great fun.

Ben graduated from high school midway through our time in Dodge. City. He chose to attend Kansas State University but after a year he was disillusioned with KSU. Not having a clear sense of direction, he came back to Dodge to attend Dodge City Community College. After a semester at DCCC Ben decided DCCC just didn't compare with a four year school. He ended up attending and graduating from Wichita State University before going on the graduate school. Lorine and I gradually began to have a foretaste of the "empty nest" syndrome.

Several points of tension stand out in my memory concerning my role as Superintendent.

First, there is the perennial tension in a position where one is thought of and charged with the responsibility of being both a shepherd and a supervisor. It's not easy to combine these two roles. While I may have thought I was hitting the proper balance and doing OK, those for whom I was responsible may have looked at it differently. As shepherd, I needed to be supportive to my pastors and their families in difficult personal and professional times. I still look back and shake my head about the time when we returned from vacation to find out the wife of one of my pastors had moved out. Somehow either I had overlooked cries for help from one or both of them, or they had been hesitant or fearful in seeking help from me. I felt I'd let them down.

As a supervisor, I needed to be an "evaluator" of each pastor's professional performance. Our Annual Conference had a formal annual evaluation form and process in which we were trained. Inevitably this fed to the appointive process so it was threatening to some pastors. I tried always to be very affirming of each pastor's ministry, but this was easier said than done. For instance, the Annual Evaluation was based on three inputs—a self evaluation by the pastor, an evaluation of pastor prepared by the Staff/Parish Relations Committee, and an evaluation by me as his or her District Superintendent. One of the areas for evaluation was "Continuing Education." A pastor, a committee, and a superintendent could look at this section of the tool in two different ways. One way would be to think about what a pastor's greatest strength was and how s/he could find and do continuing education to build on and accentuate this strength. Another way would be to identify a pastor's greatest weakness in his or her general practice of ministry and seek to use continuing education as a means of shoring up or strengthening that area. I tended to think both approaches were needed. Some pastors had a "pet hobby horse" which they wanted to ride to the neglect of other areas of ministry. But some pastors had a very fragile ego so to explore an area of "needed professional growth" was painful to the point they would completely resist such exploration.

Annual pastoral evaluation sessions could take place out in the district or in my office. My office was a room incorporated into but really separate from the district parsonage since anyone coming to it didn't enter our residence. However, sometimes a pastor would bring their spouse, so before or afterward they could do other things.

A funny thing happened at one of my pastoral evaluations. Wilbur Rothfus was coming in from Tribune, the northwest corner of the district—almost from the Colorado border. He had phoned a day ahead to say his wife would be coming along. Lorine often functioned as a gracious hostess. She invited Ethel to have coffee with her while Wilbur was with me.

The evening before they were to arrive, Lorine received a phone call reporting that her cousin, Fred Stirman, in Oklahoma City, had died. She was the closest surviving relative and needed to go to make arrangements for and attend the funeral. I had a string of evaluation appointments set up. It wasn't easy to cancel and reschedule them all. We decided I would watch after the kids; Lorine would drive to Oklahoma on her own. When Ethel walked in for the coffee, Lorine was loading her car. She explained what had happened and proceeded to apologize about having to leave before Wilbur's consultation would be finished.

"Oh," Ethyl said, "I have a daughter who lives in Oklahoma City. I haven't seen her for a long time. I've got a tooth brush in my purse. Can I go with you?"

What a neat thing! Lorine wouldn't have to make the long drive through Western Oklahoma by herself.

Another tension point had to do with the question "to set goals or not to set goals." Again, as a District Superintendent I tended to encourage pastors in their professional life to set goals for themselves and likewise, to encourage congregations to set goals for themselves. These could become the criteria by which the pastor and/or the people could evaluate themselves, their faithfulness, their growth, their "success" in the coming year. Some pastors, some churches, thrived on this. Some resisted setting goals for themselves. Some could not realize that to be meaningful, such goals needed to meet the SAM test—to be specific, attainable, and measurable. They either frustrated themselves and/or frustrated me by dealing in generalities.

Without a doubt, the point of greatest tension for me as a District Superintendent during my term was a point of tension shared with a number of my colleagues. It was working with some clergy and laity who were caught up in the charismatic movement. The charismatic movement was the theological and spiritual movement which emphasizes speaking in tongues. I can't write a history or critique of this movement in my memoirs. Suffice it to say, it's a movement which begins by taking a few "tongues speaking" Biblical passages and making them normative for the faith. It surfaces periodically in church history. It was re-emerging again in the 1960s and 70s. There are charismatic denominations (like the Assemblies of God), but this particular time the charismatic movement centered in and was active in mainline denominations— Catholic and Protestant. It was a movement across and within most denominations. It tended to *equate* speaking in tongues, and other emotional manifestations of worship, with being filled with the Holy Spirit. It became very judgmental and divisive in the non-charismatic denominations because it resisted or put down rational approaches to Christianity. It insisted on the sole "rightness" of its own approach to Christian spirituality. Because of this "I'm right, you're wrong" attitude, "I've got the Spirit you don't have the Spirit" tendency, and because the majority of Methodists were not of this persuasion, those who prided themselves as charismatics were very difficult to work with. They often tended to undermine or lead people outside of mainstream Methodism.

I prefer to find ways to de-stress and resolve tensions whenever and wherever possible rather than to simply live with them. The old saying is "Not to decide is to decide." I believe this. When life is difficult or it's a tangled mess, not to decide is to let circumstances decide for us. So even though things may not be clear cut, I'd rather think things through and make the best decision I can, rather than to do nothing. The way I found to work through the stresses and tensions of life was to focus on the good things that were happening, or could happen, in the District rather than on what might be difficult or wrong. I can't rest telling a few more stories.

When pastors moved from one appointment to another, 98% of the time the move was in the last week of May or the first week of June. Moving is usually a disruptive time in the life of most families. Lorine and I both were committed to doing what we could to help be supportive of our clergy and families. Each summer, about six weeks after moving time, we had a big get-together for all our pastors, spouses, and children. We usually planned it to be at one of the lakes. It was not simply a giant covered dish meal. It was a mixer or get acquainted program enabling the "old" and the "new" families to get to know each other. It was a time of activities for children and youth. We encouraged people to bring fishing gear and go fish. We encouraged anyone who had a boat to bring it. Rides were given to everyone who wanted them. Horseshoes and volleyball would be part of the activities. Because we encouraged people to make a day of it, and bring their easy yard chairs, there was plenty of time just for visiting.

On other occasions we had open houses at the District Parsonage and/or invited in small dinner groups. When we moved into the parsonage, one bedroom needed to be repapered—the room that was to be Ben's. The District Trustees gave us freedom to choose our own wallpaper so, in turn, we gave him the chance to participate in selecting his paper. Much to our chagrin Ben came up with some rather wild ideas and settled on some black and white paper that looked like contemporary or abstract art. We weren't too thrilled with it, but we felt since it was his room and he would have to live with it for the next three to six years, he should be able to have his choice. When clergy and spouses of the district were in our home for open houses, and other occasions, they were always taken by Ben's room. It amazed them and I think made a statement in a world where pastors often felt they had to endure the parsonage choices of other people. Ben's room and the DS's house tended to give other parsonage families the kind of permission they needed to seek some choices of their own for their parsonages and children.

Every year we, like most District Superintendents, also had a Thanksgiving, Christmas, or after-Christmas district "Pastors and Spouses Party." Rather than putting the burden of planning and executing it on a committee of already busy pastors and spouses, Lorine and I, mostly Lorine, tried to make this a treat—a gift—by carrying most of the load related to the annual party. Several times we had the party at First UMC Dodge City, but on other occasions we shifted it to a more westerly church to save driving time for those who lived in that direction.

For one of the parties, Lorine thought it would be nice to feature a Mexican-American theme. She worked in one of the Dodge City elementary schools helping mothers of Hispanic children learn English as a second language and developed a friendship with several of these women. Dora Falcon, who for years was the Mexican American Ministries' Community Developer in Dodge also sometimes assisted Lorine. For this party, Lorine drew on these resources and came up with homemade enchiladas and other Mexican food and fiesta decorations. With piñata and all we had a real fiesta.

There were people from the Area and Conference Staff who would be in and out of our District working with pastors and churches to facilitate ministry and support them. If I knew one of these persons would be around at the time of our party, we would invite them also. One of them whom we had for a couple of parties was the Rev. George Olmquest, Area Director of (Larger) Parish Development. George had a beautiful voice. Both times George was with us, we managed to prevail on him, as a little serendipity for the group, to sing—"The Impossible Dream"—a moving song which we heard him sing in another context. People were always thrilled and moved by his performance of this number. At the Annual Conference following the second time George was with us, he was walking between his motel and the church one evening when he was shot to death by an unknown assailant. George was a wonderful leader. I still feel his loss, as do a number of other pastors—especially whenever I hear that song.

One year to supply the church at Kismet with a pastor, we had to use what we called a Local Supply Pastor. This was a person who had some training, but was neither ordained nor fully trained. This meant when the sacraments were called for, an Elder (ordained pastor) had to administer them. Serving in this capacity as his back-up was one of my responsibilities.

One of the most unusual services I experienced while on the District, was one for which he called me to assist. Kismet's pastor was an energetic enthusiastic young man. He worked diligently in reaching a number of people who had not previously committed themselves to the Christian faith. On this occasion he had a large number of people who wanted to be baptized and received as members of the church. In instructing them, when he named and discussed the modes of baptism which Methodists recognize, he ended up with people who wanted to be baptized by immersion, pouring, and sprinkling. I was to perform the baptisms. There was no problem performing the latter two. We could baptize by sprinkling and pouring indoors in the context of the morning worship. But the church had no immersion baptistry. Our Local Supply Pastor arranged for a couple of farmers to place a livestock watering tank, one that had not been used, on the church lawn and fill it with water. We progressed from one mode baptism to another in our worship service which included processing from in doors to the out-of-doors for the immersion. In all ways, it was an unusual and an impressive service, well done. It's not often that we witness a United Methodist baptismal service which includes all three modes of baptism in the same service. You, gentle reader, can be sure of one thing—that morning I didn't forget to bring an extra set of dry underwear!

The importance, in my view, of each church of fully paying its World Service (General Conference) and Annual Conference Benevolence apportionments has been previously addressed. Many factors influenced how successful each local church was in doing this and how successful each District was in reaching its total apportionment goal. I was determined to do all within my power to be sure that the Dodge City District paid all of its apportionments in full. To this end, after our Annual Conference Treasurer calculated the amounts each church should be apportioned using the weight factors involved, I invited a lay steward from each local church in the District to meet with me as a group.

We reviewed these figures, and developed our own apportionments to help cover shortages from churches which might be too weak or distressed to pay apportionments in full. The details don't need to be spelled out, but I still feel a bit of pride that in my six years as a District Superintendent, we essentially paid all of our major apportionments 100%.

As I came on the District, I inherited a legacy in which the District paid toward the salary support of an overseas missionary. That missionary was now retired or retiring. It was my hope to build on this legacy. Within my first year, using the assistance of our General Board of Missions, I was able to sponsor a District Missionary conference to challenge our local churches to work on giving Advance Specials over and beyond what we gave in apportionments. We were able to have present for that conference a medical doctor (a surgeon) and his wife (who was a nurse) who were medical missionaries—Dr. and Mrs. Marvin Piburn. They were back in the states for additional education and about to return to Africa. Out of this meeting we were able to gain within the District enough commitment toward an Advance Special to pay a very significant portion of their salary.

These high points helped me feel very good about my six year term as District Superintendent. While I was superintendent, we elected the Annual Conferences first female District Lay Leader. I also sought to encourage a sense of unity and commitment within the District. People in western Kansas often had a feeling of being overlooked or ignored by others in the eastern half of the state. This was, perhaps still is, felt by people in many fields of endeavor. I became a bit political at one point. At a District Conference prior to the Annual Conference when we were to elect delegates to our United Methodist General and Jurisdictional Conferences, I pointed out that each church had a lay member of annual conference who had a vote. Votes were cast without any nominations. People simply voted for those who came to mind as persons of ability and talent. It was kind of a free wheeling spirit-led process, but inevitably those who were best known tended to get votes. The voting cycle was repeated as long as need be to elect the proper number of lay and clergy representatives. I reminded the group that it had been years, if ever, since people from the Dodge City District had been among those elected to go to Jurisdictional and General Conference. If they felt a bit resentment in their church life because of feeling underrepresented, I suggested they should try voting for those within in our District whom they felt might best represent them. As an upshot of it, that year, and almost every year since, they have been represented to at least some extent in the delegations elected. It was good to be part of an enabling and visioning process.

During this six-year appointment, our cabinet met monthly and, when appointments were being made we even met weekly. The collegiality and camaraderie of the cabinet and our working relationship with Bishop Dixon was one of the most supportive team relationships which I've ever experienced. The qualities of this relationship, the nurture and encouragement which came from it, still wells up in my spirit to this day.

Chapter 44

TRAVELS AND MORE TRAVELS

Growing up as a kid in the 1930s I was filled with excitement about the things I was learning in school. One of the things we learned in geography was that many nations had overseas colonies. We learned what a colony was, and that in Africa most nations were colonies of other nations, not independent nations. It wasn't until after college, after my time in the navy, even after seminary, it wasn't until 1957 that Ghana became independent. Ghana was the *first* African nation south of the Sahara Desert to become independent. Three years later, in 1960 alone, 17 African countries ceased being colonies.

For many people around the world, this seemed like a movement toward democracy, a liberating of people from oppression, a time of hope. Many of these seeds of hope had been planted by missionaries from Europe and United States. Many of the missionaries had been United Methodists or their predecessors. Mission schools had nurtured indigenous leadership. Needs were still great and Methodism was still committed to the continent of Africa.

By the 1970s Africa began experiencing a new darkness. Two of the major nations of Africa, Rhodesia and South Africa, were still not free. They were no longer colonies, but they were in the grip of white settlers who were fully committed to an oppressive apartheid way of life. In the face of indigenous black Africans struggling for independence, these nations were moving toward civil war. Even the newly independent nations were beginning to experience internal revolts and coups d'etat.

As a District Superintendent seeking to build support and understanding for our mission work in Africa, in 1976 I planned a Mission Study Tour of Africa. My focus was on five nations— Nigeria, Zambia, South Africa, Rhodesia (soon to be renamed Zimbabwe) and Kenya in the order of our travels.

In Nigeria the focus was at Jos, Bambur (a remote rural community with a mission hospital) and Lagos. *In Zambia* we made an historical visit to Livingston (with sightseeing to Victoria Falls) plus a study visit to ecumenical work at Kitwe. *Johannesburg, South Africa,* was included in our itinerary for several reasons. Methodists had mission work in the city; we were concerned for what was transpiring in the black struggle for independence; and, since United States and most of Africa was boycotting Rhodesia there was no way to enter Rhodesia except through South Africa. It was the one remaining country allowing travel and trade with Rhodesia. The *Kenya* emphasis was three fold—sightseeing with recreation and rest, the work of the United Nations in Africa, and church work.

Rhodesia (soon to be renamed Zimbabwe) was our primary focus—especially the Methodist rural mission station of Nyadiri 80 miles out in "the bush." Nyadiri had a cluster of missionaries and Methodist church workers. It included a K-12 school, a church, and the 220 bed hospital and nurse training school where Dr. and Mrs. Piburn were working.

Because the tour's focus was mission study, we stayed in mission facilities for the most part. Missionaries, plus those with whom they worked, were our teachers. Little land transportation was available so most of our travel was by air. Altogether we flew 25,555 miles, half of them in Africa. I personally few 27 flights—3 more than most of our group. Because airplanes in Africa were small to medium sized and everyone traveled by air, of necessity our group was limited to a dozen people. Lorine was my co-leader. We left

Paul, too young for this kind of travel, with my parents. Ben chose not to join us, deferring what we would have spent on him for use on later travels. Working that summer in Dodge City following his first year of college, Ben took care of the house for us. Bill, our middle schooler, said he would like to come along.

Six people from our Dodge City District joined Lorine, Bill and me. They were Rev. Merton Zeisset and wife Ina from Satanta; Mr. and Mrs. Carl Warner of Garden City; Ida Nonamaker, Dodge City and Ms. Mavis Hughes, Larned. A young student from Southwestern College took the tour for college credit. She was Miss Carolyn Gebhardt, From Nashville, Kansas. Avenel Elliott, of the Annual Conference staff in Wichita and her Kansas University son, Roger, rounded out the group. It was nice for Bill to have Roger, another "young" male student, traveling in the group.

Lagos, Nigeria in Africa 1976
The whites are our Mission Study Group. Left to R they are:
Mrs. Warner; Mavis Hughes; Ina Zeisset; Carolyn Gebhardt;
Merton Zeiset; Avenell Elliott; Ida Nonamaker; Carl Warner;
the author; Bill and Lorine Kieler; Roger Elliott.

We had advance study preparation and orientation for all members of our group. With a great deal of excitement and anticipation, we gathered August 1 at the Wichita Airport to depart for an additional day of orientation at our Global Board of Missions in New York City. Then it was on to Rome. On Pam Am Flight 747, we flew the Atlantic all night. None of us had been to Rome. We wanted to make the most of our monetary investment and of our time as we passed this way. We engaged in a four—hour sightseeing tour of the landmarks of this ancient city. Then, tired and sleepy from a 30+ hour day, we spent the afternoon and early evening resting and sleeping in rooms at the YMCA.

As per instructions, we arrived at 11: OO p.m. at the Rome International Airport for a midnight departure to Kano, Nigeria, on Nigerian Airways. It was at this point that our early mood of elation quickly began to dissipate in the midst of the realities and riddles of our journey.

I had already learned to expedite things for everyone by gathering up all of the tickets and passports for presentation to the gate attendant as a single group rather than 12 individuals. As the attendant pulled the tickets and reviewed our documents, he seemed puzzled. After some delay, he told me, "One of your tickets for this leg of the flight is missing—Lorine Kieler's."

Without relating all the details of the story, we discovered the gate-keeper at New York had not only pulled Lorine's ticket for the transatlantic flight but also her ticket for this Rome to Kano leg of the flight. The only way the airline would allow Lorine to proceed with our group was if she purchased a new, individual (therefore expensive), one-way ticket to take the place of her missing group-fare ticket. This required Lorine to use up virtually all of her travelers checks which left her feeling vulnerable.

The next morning when we arrived at Kano, Mavis discovered that the flight crew had ripped off her luggage. A few days later, in Lagos, Roger Elliott went through the agony of an hour standoff with local police as they attempted to confiscate his expensive new camera acquired for the dual use of this trip and of his photo journalism major at KU. Days later, in Zambia, Bill and I were forced to stay behind when our group was departing the capital city, Lusaka, for Johannesburg, South Africa. It was all because our connecting flight to Lusaka arrived late due to a flap between a local passenger and flight officials. I knew Lorine was capable of carrying on, but having the group split, sending Lorine ahead on her own, created a great deal of anxiety for both of us. Bill and I didn't catch up with the group until Salisbury, Rhodesia (Zimbabwe) two days later.

Lorine assumed full leadership of our study group in Johannesburg, but after hearing the evening's presentation by native South Africans and missionaries, she was sure that the revolution, the civil war, was going to begin that night right at the hotel where they were staying.

In Zimbabwe, as I preferred to call it in anticipation of its future new name, we were hosted by Dr. and Mrs. Piburn, our medical missionaries whom the Dodge City District was supporting. Marvin and Carolyn hosted us wonderfully both in the capitol, Salisbury (now known as Harare), and at the Nyadiri Hospital (where Dr. Piburn was the only surgeon for a large region) and Mission Center.

As they escorted us between Salisbury and Nyadiri, Dr. Piburn stopped briefly at another clinic to touch base with a colleague. He received a report that armed gangs had shot up the town the previous night and a land mine had killed two persons 2 nights before that. This kept us mindful, as did the shells of bombed out buildings, that we were traveling in a nation which was in the midst of civil war.

High ancient stonewalls and buildings made without benefit of mortar were the most impressive of our sightseeing ventures. These were the mysterious ruins of the 11th-15th century pre-white civilization named Zimbabwe.

Marvin Piburn and his late wife, Carolyn, gave many years of their lives to mission work in Nigeria, Vietnam, and Zimbabwe and finally Wichita. They seemed greatly encouraged and supported, beyond our District's monetary support, by a constant series of varied contacts from within our district. Marvin was an avid baseball fan but through most of his mission service he was out of contact with baseball news. I used to mail him a weekly summertime packet of baseball news to help him keep in touch with the outside world of home. They seemed to doubly appreciate our visit coming as we did, as a group, to be with them and learn from them for a few days even in the midst of a difficult and dangerous time. They dubbed me "their fearless leader" and have called me that ever since. Always, we were mindful of, and had some uneasiness about, the civil war situation in Rhodesia, but this is not to suggest that our study was dominated by fear or misgiving.

Wherever we traveled in Africa, we found the cities and towns to have similarities with which we were familiar as well as differences. Outside the cities and towns, cross country roads, certainly paved roads, were rare. More often what we saw were trails and paths crossing the savanna or bush. Usually, it seemed to be the women who would be carrying the burdens of life on their head—water, food (sacks of grain, yams, vegetables), fruit, firewood, and/or children on their backs. Everywhere we would see an abundance of barefooted children. Outside the urban areas, people lived largely in the open air. Often their shelters, schools, churches were without windows or doors and almost always without utilities. What we would call roadside stands or "mom and pop" stores were the norm in contrast to anything like the business districts we westerners knew.

People for the most part were very friendly. They were pleased when you were interested in them. If you were in a marketplace where tourists had been before, then they might seek in a little more aggressive fashion to sell anything they had. Throughout the continent, and especially in Zimbabwe, it was emotionally stirring to hear people sing, often spontaneously and with wonderful harmony, the unofficial anthem of the continent—"My Africa."

We did a safari in Kenya. Seeing zebra, wildebeests, gazelle, lions, elephants, rhinoceros, hyena, giraffe, ostrich, hawks and vultures at close range in the Amboseli game preserve was by far the most exciting sightseeing highpoint in our journey to Africa. Experiencing a lion kill was the kind of drama which really made our adrenalin flow. Neither the safari, nor our two nights of plush hotel accommodations in Nairobi, took the place of our purpose of discovering the United Nations, the World Council of Churches, and the Methodists and Presbyterians at work in Kenya.

Our meals in much of Africa were usually modest and without a great deal of variety. The most memorable dish, for me, was most abundant and served at each meal. It looked something like American cream of wheat, but it was made of ground millet or milo or what African's called guinea corn or durra. In Zimbabwe the dish was called Sazda. It had a different name in Nigeria. It was served by itself with no butter, milk, or gravy. When I started to eat it, it was like eating sand. It was ground very coarsely and it either couldn't be or wasn't cooked to the point of being soft. Not all food was quite as unimpressive. Rice covered with gravy and served with vegetables like chard, cabbage, cauliflower, and carrots was a typical menu along with bread and, often, fresh fruit. What an enjoyable contrast we experienced when we dined in urban settings and especially during the three nights of luxury accommodations which we inserted (one in the middle, two at the end) into our journey of twenty one African nights.

Overall, this was one of the most momentous and meaningful trips I've ever taken. I came back to the states not only with a better understanding of the church and its missions, but of what we often call "the developing world." I came back with recognition and a conviction that "over development is as much a problem here in the states as underdevelopment is in other parts of the world."

MORE TRAVELS

Throughout my lifetime, I've traveled on trips beyond counting. I've been in nearly three dozen countries and in all states in the U.S. except for one or two. During the fifty years Lorine and I have been married, we've taken numerous trips. Many were family trips (with the kids or just the two of us). Some trips, like the Africa trip, were a combination of professional and family travel. Some were exclusively professional travel, perhaps related only to continuing education. Most of our trips have been personal and family trips.

We had a memorable tent camping trip in *July of 1963*. Bill who was only six months old was left in the hands of his Hutchinson grandparents. Ben, six years old, was with us as we drove to Jackson Hole, Wyoming, the Grand Teton National Park, and Yellowstone National Park. Our spirits were moved by the beauty and the grandeur of the mountains. Ben was excited by wildlife of all sorts—bears, buffaloes, antelope, deer, moose, chipmunks, and birds.

In 1964 we left both Ben and Bill with their grandparents while Lorine and I flew to a Christian Social Concerns Conference in Washington D. C. and then to New York for a United Nations Seminar and the World's Fair (theme: "A Great Big Beautiful Tomorrow"). Later in the summer, we took the children to make one of our annual to semi-annual journeys to Kentucky.

The Ben and Mary Martin Extended Family Group
1989 Photo, taken at the funeral of Ben C. Martin, typical of
those present at the many family reunions. The entire family
is present here except for Mary & Harmon Hoffman who
were in Russia at this time.

Five or six times while we were rearing our children, Lorine's parents hosted all their children and grandchildren simultaneously at one of the wonderful Kentucky State Parks. Usually these gatherings were at Kentucky Dam Village State Resort. Sometimes they gathered the clan at other state parks. One of the wonderful things about the Kentucky Dam and Barkley Dam outings was exploring the Land Between the Lakes Park. It's an area of 140 square miles which lay between Kentucky Lake (formed by the damming of the Tennessee River) and Lake Barkley (formed by the damming of the Cumberland River). When these dams were built, all the Land Between the Lakes land was purchased and allowed to revert to native wilderness.

In addition to time for family reuniting and visiting, tennis, golf, fishing, sailing, and other activities were all available to us. These gatherings made for great bonding between members of the Martin family. They were a wonderful part of our family travel adventures and forever part of our family memories. Just a month following one of these occasions, Lorine's mother died, but the sense of family which she bequeathed to us made her passing easier.

In the *summer of 1965* we took Ben and Bill to the Mesa Verde National Park in Southwest Colorado, to explore both the mountains and the remains left behind by the cliff dwelling Pueblo Indians. The week after *Christmas of 1966*, Paul was left with my parents and the rest of us went to Houston and a week on the Gulf Coast at Galveston, Texas.

Another memorable pair of travel adventures were the summers of 1969 and 1970. Both involved camping with our Starcraft camping trailer. The *1970* trip was to Chicago and Michigan. In Chicago we camped in the yard of Mac and Aya Fukuda. Mac was my college roommate. Our kids got acquainted with their kids—kids of another racial background, Asian, and of a different culture, Nisei. We also did the museums of the city. These were good experiences for our children.

The second half of this trip was a visit with my sister, Shirley, and her family at the K. I. Sawyer Air Base on the Upper Peninsula of Michigan. Picking wild blueberries and giving cousins time to play together were neat experiences. A big memory relates to our visit to Isle Royale National Park located 51 miles out in Lake Superior. Paul was a kindergartner. We left our camper on Keweenaw Peninsula while we ferried out to Isle Royale to spend a night in the lodge there. The second day's activities included fishing from the shore. One of the boys got a lake trout big enough to feed the five of us. In the excitement of landing the fish, Paul fell into the icy cold lake. We managed to retrieve him safely, but he did end up with a cold and tonsillitis.

Arriving back at the mainland that evening, there wasn't time left for cooking. We found a restaurant which would prepare our fish dinner for us. It was totally dark when we finished eating. We put up the camper in the dark. As we crawled into our sleeping bags, we realized mosquitoes by the thousands were swarming INSIDE the camper. Apparently we hadn't capped off a drain tube for our camper sink. We fought mosquitoes all night. We heard their quiet buzz and felt them as they lighted on us and bit us. It turned into one of the worst nights we ever had in the camper. To add to our misery, somewhere in the midst of all of this, Paul's fever from his tonsillitis got so high that we had to make a run for emergency medical care for him.

Our "most memorable" family trip was perhaps in 1969, when we planned a Northwestern adventure in our camper that—a trip that required all 4 weeks of our annual vacation. Places which we included along the way were a visit to two sets of my Uncles and Aunts, our children's Great Uncles and Aunts in Fort Collins, Colorado,; a visit to Casper and Cody, Wyoming and the headwaters of the Missouri River in Montana along with the nearby site of Custer's last stand. From here we drove a skyline drive through the Rocky Mountain between Glacier National Park and the International Peace Park on the US-Canadian border. We continued on to Lake Louise in Canada; Banff and Jasper National Parks, and the Columbia Glaciers and Ice Field between the two parks. Following this was a three hundred miles journey southwest across British Columbia to Vancouver and Victoria. Arriving in Seattle we visited our friends, Jim and Phyllis Jung (Jim, being my boyhood friend and classmate for 13 years in Hutchinson). Finally we headed home via Mt. Rainer; Portland, Oregon; the Columbia River Drive, and the Great Salt Lake and Salt Lake City, Utah.

The total mileage according to our odometer was 5,943 miles. My Dad always kept careful notes on the expenses of trips he took. This inspired my wife to do the same on occasions. Her notes for this trip reflect the following: The total gasoline for the trip cost us $ 203; the rest of our other expenses totaled $ 394.

Lorine thought a month of nights in the camper (less one for a motel) with three active boys, plus travel time in the station wagon were enough for one summer. I still get weary when I think of our hike and climb from Lake Louise up the mountain to the Japanese Tea House. Everyone was eager in the beginning. Before long, Paul was "tuckered out." He was a few months shy of being 4-years-old. I ended up carrying him on my shoulders, for what seemed like an eternity (perhaps just an hour or two). At the top, the Japanese Tea House was cozy and warm and gave us the chance to rest and absorb the beauty of the Canadian Rockies. All the boys, especially Paul were excited to watch and feed a myriad of chipmunks as they scampered over the rocks. To this day, our three sons usually name this trip first when they reminisce about great vacations.

Somewhere around *1974 or '75* we included Yosemite National Park as part of a summer vacation to California. National parks are a great part of our American heritage and also of our family heritage. In the years we visited national parks with our children, knowledgeable Park Rangers were part of the wonderful atmosphere which complemented mother nature's handiwork. Rangers led hikes and programs that were educational as well as fun.

Sad to say, today there are those who advocate privatizing park personnel and functions. They are part of a movement which wants to make national park recreational activities a commercial endeavor with no particular emphasis on maintaining the pristine condition of the park. Their movement would exploit, if not sell or give away, natural resources in our parks and would contract out park functions and work to the "lowest bidder." The privatization movement has little regard for maintaining quality experiences for visiting citizens and tourists who otherwise might never be able to experience the natural wonders of the land.

Our Yosemite Park vacation memories moved me to writing this letter to my sons:

"Dear Ben, Bill, and Paul,

What do you remember about bears and our family? We could tell a few bear stories, couldn't we?

I remember, and hope you do, the endless times both your mother and I read or told each of you, when you very tiny, the story of Goldie Locks and the three bears . . . . , and I hope you remember some of the times I gave you bear hugs. Right now, though, I think of at least three literal bear stories.

Ben, do you remember the time when we were tent camping in Yellowstone National Park? This was before national parks required advanced reservations for camping spots. We arrived late afternoon and managed to find ourselves a camp site not far from the banks of the Yellowstone River. The campground was long and narrow, with tents strung out from one end to the other in a single row. We were in the middle. We were tired and hungry. After supper, following ranger instructions, we stowed our food in the ice chests and returned them to our station wagon so as not to attract bears. We turned in right away and were soon asleep.

In the middle of the night, we were aroused by a clanging noise at the far end of the campground. It kept getting louder. Then, we heard people talking. Suddenly we realized, the bears were making the rounds of the trash cans looking for food. The prowling bears drew nearer. Eventually, they were just outside our tent rummaging in the can nearest to us. We held our breath, quivered a bit and hung on to each other. What a relief when we realized they were moving on.

Do all of you remember our Jasper National Park visit in Canada? Supposedly there were grizzlies around. We tried to teach you caution. Bill, like all of you, was always slipping away from us. It was nearly dark and he decided to head over to the restroom area by himself. When we realized it, we started after him and caught up with him as he was passing the big trash dumpsters. Just at that moment, to our horror, a large bear climbed out of one of the dumpsters. We grabbed Bill and quickly headed in a direction opposite what seemed to be the bear's route of travel.

And then, do you all remember our Yosemite trip? We set up our little Starcraft pop-up camper in a little pocket campground with just a few other campers. We did some preliminary hiking and exploring the day we arrived. We were excited about the majestic beauty. The next morning, we left the camper to drive a loop road through other parts of the park. We took our food with us so we could picnic for lunch and supper and have a leisurely day trip of hiking and sight seeing. We had a great day. It was dark by the time we got back. We didn't take time for a campfire or lighting the lantern. We just hopped into our bedrolls.

Before I got to sleep, I felt an usual draft blowing on my head. I got up, turned on my flashlight, and discovered a huge area of the canvas just beside my head was shredded! There was nothing we could do about it for the moment. Thinking it was vandalism, I reported it to the Ranger the next morning. His response? "I'm sure it was a bear. Yesterday we had reports of a bear prowling that campground. He probably smelled something and was trying to get into the camper.'

Maybe you have some other bear stories you remember. There's always a minute risk with bears when you are camping in wild areas, but in all our travels to national parks and to zoos, bears have always been part of the attraction. Things would never be the same without them. Love, Dad"

In *1983*, Lorine and I vacationed in Abe Lincoln country in Illinois and Kentucky. In 1984 Paul joined us in a trip to Quebec. In August of *1987*, we followed Bill to Oregon where he was in summer school, then traveled north along the coastal highway (U.S. 101) to Washington State and ferried to Vancouver Island for two days of chartered salmon fishing. We caught salmon and brought them home on ice. In *1988* we followed Bill to Chinatown in New York City where he was doing an internship. At the *end of 1989 and the beginning of 1990*, we took a 35th Wedding Anniversary trip to Hawaii. After Bill moved to Europe in 1989, we began almost *yearly visits to see Bill and Paula and various areas of Europe.*

In July of *1990* we visited a Methodist Church in Ciudad Juarez, Mexico, on behalf of the Augusta United Methodist Church.

In 1991 we attended Paula's graduation from the University of Leiden. In 1992, we made another Martin family reunion near the Land Between the Lakes introducing Bill's Paula Sastrowijoto from Holland to the United States and to the Martin family.

In September of *1993* we spent a month in Asia—two weeks in Japan, visiting friends and missionaries; and two weeks in Thailand visiting friends from there. In *1994*, I led a First United Methodist Church mission work team to Costa Rica. In the fall of that year, Lorine and I made another of our many trips to Europe and during the trip joined Chuck and Donna Cupit for a week in the French Alps.

My travels, of course, have included many *professional trips*. Each year I served as a District Superintendent, our Area Cabinet (the Bishop, the Area Superintendents of Ministries, and of Parish Development, the seven DSs from the Kansas West Conference and the five DSs from the Kansas East Conference) had a continuing education retreat. These were designed to be in a comfortable and relaxing setting as well as learning environment which would be intellectually, spiritually, and practically stimulating.

Twice our continuing education retreats were held at the Menningers' Clinic in Topeka under the leadership of their staff, and twice at a resort at Gravois Mills on the Lake of the Ozarks in Missouri with guest resource leaders. Once we were at Murray Lake State Park in Oklahoma and once we simply used the conference facilities of a Kansas motel. Our first time at Gravois Mills three of us, my colleagues and friends, Clarence Borger and Harold Nelson, and I, came a day early and got in a wonderful successful day of Crappie fishing. The other time we were at Gravois Mills our guest leader was the noted Methodist scholar from Perkins School of Theology, Albert Outler. We felt these lectures would be of interest to our wives so we invited them to be part of this retreat. Our final retreat was held at the Lake Murray State Park Resort in Oklahoma with Jameson Jones as our resource leader. Some of the presentation was intended for DSs only, but other presentations were for spouses too. We also chose to make this a total family retreat for those who wished to bring their children. A couple of us brought our sailboats and there was enough free time built-in to enable us to do things with our children. This turned out to be a wonderful fun time together with families as well as a productive learning time.

In the spring of *1978*, I was involved with the Bishop's study and sightseeing tour to Israel. This was, for me, a time of preparation for re-entry into parish preaching.

The camaraderie and collegiality of the members of the Kansas West Conference cabinet had been stimulated by the initial retreats we had at the Menningers' Clinic. Their staff helped us become insightful and sensitive about our working relationships with one another and with others. Never have I been part of any group, certainly any group of leaders, which was a greater support group to one another than this group.

Chapter 45

THE OIL PATCH

In 1978 as the movers were unloading our furniture, this time at 502 South Denver, in El Dorado, we detected a terrible smell, but it wasn't the smell we'd become familiar with in Dodge City. It turned out it was from the two oil or gasoline refineries in El Dorado. Still, people in El Dorado used the same phrase as people in Dodge City. "Don't knock it," they said, "it's the smell of money."

Oil was discovered in abundance near El Dorado at the time of World War I and it made the city boom. All around Butler County and beyond, oil wells were drilled. Communities of little shacks sprang up providing housing for oil field workers and their families. These clusters of housing were referred to as "the oil patch." They were usually rather primitive communities with no paved roads, perhaps out in the middle of a field, dusty and grimy, with few if any public services except perhaps a one room elementary school and maybe a small grocery. Workers in the oil field were rough and tough. Sometimes the term "the oil patch" was applied to its residents in a pejorative way; sometimes people applied it to themselves with a sense of pride. El Dorado was the center of this oil field and refining activity. This was June 1, 1978, and for better or for worse we were "moving to the oil patch."

Moving always evokes lots of deep feelings. This move evoked more feelings than usual for Lornie. Her greatest pain was over leaving the District parsonage which was probably the nicest, biggest, most well planned and best maintained parsonage we'd ever had. The El Dorado parsonage, in contrast, was not only smaller, but undoubtedly the least well-cared-for parsonage into which we'd ever moved. It was dimly lighted. Kitchen appliances were on the verge of wearing out. The paint was shabby. There was literally a hole about the size of a basketball in the dining room ceiling. The parsonage was built about 25 years before we came as a replacement for one that had burned. I suspect people always thought of it as "our new parsonage" and forgot that it would need maintenance. Fortunately, we found responsive trustees when we called the problems to their attention. Parsonage repairs and redecorating were soon underway.

El Dorado First United Methodist Church was a church of 1,300 members on paper at least. As often the case, membership rolls were not really up-to-date. In reality the church was much smaller. But it was a strong, vital congregation and blessed with many young adults and young families.

We arrived during the final stages of a church remodeling and modernization program which included the addition of an elevator. During the remodeling, many of the Christian education ministries were temporarily moved to what was called the Wesley Center, an old historic house now owned by the church and just a stone's throw from the church. The church itself was in the kind of mess that usually goes with any major remodeling. But the remodeling had stirred new energy and enthusiasm.

The congregation really needed an Associate Pastor; however it was blessed with three retired ministers one of whom, Merle Nutter, was employed as a part-time Minister of Visitation. It had an excellent church secretary, Jackie Brazill, and a talented, even if not formally trained, Christian Education worker, Linda Nonken. The church also had wonderful leadership in music—Fred Wolfe, Organist, and Marge Marsh, Choir Director plus lots of fine leadership among its laity for other areas of church life. A young couple, Dave and Kim Matthews, among the strongest of those in lay leadership, served as UMYF sponsors.

Dave and Kim Mathews did a great job with the United Methodist Youth Fellowship not only week by week throughout the year, but they also came up with interesting and significant summer youth retreats each summer. As we arrived June 1st of 1978, they had a UMYF trip already planned to an Indian Mission in Oklahoma, to Eureka Springs, Arkansas (called "Little Switzerland"), and the Missouri Ozarks. They quickly invited and involved Bill and Paul in this. I, too, was quickly recruited for the retreat which was to begin at the end of the month.

Now I have a question for all of my male readers. "How many of you know how it feels to have a baby?" If you don't know, then you don't understand why I never made the retreat that year. No, I didn't have a baby! Here's what happened. A week before the retreat was to start, my Sunday morning alarm went off. I jumped out of bed to beginning looking over sermon notes and getting dressed. Suddenly, I felt a tremendous back pain. It almost knocked me off my feet. It was sharp and shooting, deep and persistent. I lay down again for a few minutes in an effort to get comfortable. No luck. I writhed in pain, rolled on the floor. My knuckles turned white as I clenched my fist in pain. Thinking the problem was my back, I tried lying there motionless and flat. I couldn't do it. I could only cry out in pain to Lorine, "Call the Doctor." We didn't even have a family doctor yet, but I had already met Dr. Proctor, a member of the congregation.

When Lorine got the doctor on the phone for me, I told him what was happening. He immediately said, "It sounds like an attack of kidney stones. We have a new urologist in town, Dr. Jacobs. Have your wife take you to the Susan B. Allen Hospital's emergency room and I'll have him meet you there."

I phoned the Chairman of our Pastor—Parish Committee to tell him what was happening and inform him there was no way I would be able to preach that morning. At the emergency room, Dr. Jacobs confirmed Dr. Proctor's preliminary diagnosis and admitted me to the hospital. Everyone proceeded to inform me that having a kidney stone attack was extremely painful so I wasn't unique in the suffering I was undergoing. They also told me, "Women who have experienced both child birth and kidney stone attacks commonly say the kidney stones are at least as painful, and often more so, than labor pains."

An X-ray pinpointed the stone. I was to remain in the hospital until I passed the stone or until the Doctor decided to surgically remove it. It was six days before I passed the stone which turn out to be only the size of a grain of wheat. This happened the day before the departure of those going on retreat, but the doctor didn't allow me to make the trip. I rested and convalesced at home for a couple of days and was back to normal.

Strange as it may seem, this happened my first month in El Dorado and eight years later, the last month I was there, I had another kidney stone attack. Once again I experienced the intense pain without delivering "the baby". This time Dr. Jacobs only waited about 24 hours and then went after the stone with a "basketing" procedure.

One of the strangest happenings which ever occurred during my pastoral ministries happened even before the kidney stone episode—in fact, during my first week in El Dorado. I was in old blue jeans, working in my study, unpacking my library and shelving the books. Suddenly a man whom I had never met came rushing through my door. "Quick," he said, "can you come across the street and conduct a funeral?"

Who was he? Why me? Why the urgency?

The stranger turned out to be Gene Carlson, one of the town's funeral directors. The funeral of a well-known Presbyterian lady had been scheduled at that hour for their church, just across the street from ours. The Presbyterians were between pastors. The family told Gene they would make arrangements with a personal friend, Dr. Joe Riley Burns, one of our retired ministers, to do the service. There had been confusion in the communications. The church was full. Everyone was waiting for Joe Riley to arrive, but he hadn't shown up. He wasn't even in town. What were they to do? Gene Carlson needed my help in the worst way.

I needed to respond affirmatively but I didn't want the townspeople to think the new pastor in town was in the habit of arriving late for funerals he was conducting or that he wore "old grodies" (grubby old jeans) to funerals. We quickly agreed I would perform the funeral if Gene would explained the situation to the people there, including an explanation that I'd never known of nor met the deceased or her family. Furthermore, Gene was to give me time to run home and change clothes.

I phoned Lorine asking her to lay out a dress shirt and my suit and to look for the obituary in yesterday's newspaper. I dressed as she read the obituary to me and I managed to get to the funeral in just over ten minutes. I winged things the best I could. In the end, the service worked out well for all concerned and I became something of a community hero for the week.

Reflecting back on my eight years in El Dorado, I feel this was one of my most satisfying appointments. The church thrived and was responsive to my ministry there. I brought gifts and graces which seemed helpful. We made lots of friends, enjoyed the community and the congregation, and our boys enjoyed their schools and friends. Among other professional achievements was the development of a child care center—a ministry to preschoolers and their families with some before and after school child care.

Bill played football on the sophomore or Junior Varsity Team his first year and even a bit on the High School Varsity Team. He proceeded to make the varsity team his junior and senior years. In 1981 he graduated from High School. He entered Southwestern College that fall with the encouragement of, and some help from, a small track scholarship and graduated from college in 1985.

Paul learned the French Horn and played 7th Grade, 8th Grade and Junior Varsity football teams while he was in Junior High. He excelled in varsity football while in High School. He graduated in 1984 and then enrolled at Kansas University with a major in Environmental Sciences.

Marcia Hinegardner Burlakof, one of our kids from Grace Church days, was teaching French and Spanish in El Dorado High School when we arrived in town. At the end of the 1978-79 school year, Marcia and her husband moved away. She enticed Lorine to apply for the job. Lorine had taken Spanish at St. Mary's of the Plains College in Dodge City, and gained additional proficiency in Spanish through her work with the Spanish speaking mothers of Dodge. She was able to teach Spanish as well as French. In 1979 Lorine began teaching foreign languages at high school. She taught 5 years, mostly full time. After we moved from El Dorado, in 1986, Lorine shifted to teaching French as an adjunct instructor for Butler County Community College. She continued this until I retired in 1995.

Ben was living in Wichita, studying at Wichita State University. This meant he was able to be in and out of our home quite a bit for our first year in El Dorado which was nice for all of us. Ben graduated from WSU in 1979 with a major in Urban Studies.

Two weeks later, on June 2, 1979, Ben married Angela Hardee of Parlin, New Jersey. He met Angela the summer he was studying at Goddard College in Vermont. Later she came to Emporia State College, in Kansas, to do a Masters degree in Art Therapy. Since she was in school in Kansas and they would be living in Kansas, they wanted to be married in First United Methodist Church, El Dorado. They asked if I would perform the ceremony.

2002 Photo of Ben Kieler and his family—wife Angela, son Michael, daughter Alison on her 16th birthday.

I was honored to be invited to tie the knot, but usually pastors are "up front" in worship rather than sitting in the pew with their spouse and family. I mentioned this to Ben and Angela and asked if they might want to consider having another pastor celebrate most of the service allowing me to be with the family. Then I could step up front to officiate at the moment they actually exchanged their vows and said "I do." They chose to ask Ben's uncle, Ben Martin, a Presbyterian Pastor, to be the co-celebrant. Perhaps this was wise. I was so very pleased, excited, and psyched up over the marriage of our first son that by the time the service was finished and we were all involved in picture taking I keeled over in a dead faint. I rather quickly "came to." Since the hospital was just two blocks away and some of the family were very concerned, I was taken over to the emergency room to be checked out. Not only was I OK, but the personnel there managed to be responsive to the situation and got me back to the church in time for the reception line.

When I reflect back on youth work across my years of ministry, one event which stands out vividly comes from El Dorado. At our youth retreat in Colorado in 1979, we were brainstorming and planning for the future when we came up with a goal of going to Europe in 1981. This seemed like a far if not impossible reach. But we had two years to get ready. Dave Matthew and I both felt if we really set our hearts and minds on this goal it could be achieved. I was excited about it because I felt it was a wonderful way to teach our spiritual heritage and Methodist roots. Dave began developing a series of major fundraisers on which the youth could work. We also provided a system of advanced monthly and/or quarterly deposits of money by the individual youths and their families. All monies were kept well invested so as to draw the maximum of interest and compound it. What really helped the group was that this was a period of time when interest rates were at an all time high. In fact, for one year our monies were placed with a local broker in a money market account that was earning between 18 and 20%!

Dave and I worked very closely together in the planning. He worked with an El Dorado travel agent to get the best group air fare and bus tour rates possible. I worked on the itinerary and program design researching and corresponding with overseas contacts. Two other things made the event achievable. All the youth and sponsors (including Lorine and I) took sleeping bags so we could sleep on the floor of churches along the way thus avoiding lodging costs. When final commitments by youth and sponsors were made, we had about six or eight empty spots left on the bus. We found that a number of interested members of the congregation would like to go on this kind of tour, supporting their youth at the same time. We were able to sell them a package tour (including hotel accommodations for them) at pretty much full commercial value. This ended up becoming a real money maker toward the youth expenses because filling those six or eight empty seats on the bus cost us nothing extra.

The trip ended up as a 16 day UMYF trip with 25 kids, including Bill and Paul, plus sponsors and a half dozen or more tag along adults from the church.

We landed in England to spend time exploring the 18th Century haunts of John Wesley. In London, we stayed at Wesley Chapel, visited St. Paul's Cathedral and the burial place of John Wesley, and explored the sights of the city. We traveled to Bristol to see the chapel where Wesley commissioned missionaries for the States. We then headed northeast to Epworth where Wesley's parents served an Anglican Church and where, as a young boy, his life was saved in a dramatic rescue from the burning Rectory. On the way back to London we visited Oxford University, the school which John Wesley entered at age 17 to study for the priesthood and where the Holy Club met and ministered. Along the way we visited historic cathedrals.

In one town, we stayed overnight in British homes. We were able to arrange this with assistance from my friend and Annual Conference colleague, Rev. Harold Cooper who had done a pulpit exchange with the Methodist Church in England. We received a gracious and affirmative response there. It was an excellent way for our group to experience how ordinary people in England lived.

This also turned out to be the night before the marriage of Prince Charles and Princess Diane. The homes where we were staying were all watching the pre-wedding events on television. Not only did we get to see these TV programs, but conversation with our hosts and hostesses helped us see the royal wedding through *their* eyes.

From England we ferried the English Channel, traveled through the French countryside, and spent two nights in a Protestant Church in Paris with a sightseeing day, before moving on to Switzerland. Mostly our Paris stop was to see the famous places of that city. It included the sacred and the secular. In the latter vein, most of our group went to see the Follies Bergere. At least one of our tag-along couples chose to abstain from this trip. The next morning this lady, in shock over the group's destination the previous evening, quizzed Lorine. "Did you and Harold go with our youth to see the follies last night?"

To this Lorine replied, "Oh, I just love the beauty of feathers."

In Switzerland we viewed the Reformation monument, studied the Reformers, visited the World Council of Churches headquarters, and the United Nations. Then we went on to Luzern to experience something of the beauty of that place and of the Alps. Has any UMYF group ever had a finer trip? I still feel gratitude and appreciation for all the hard work and investment in the lives of young people made by lay persons who work with youth in all churches. Especially this goes for Dave and Kim.

Gratitude is also a feeling I possess for all the wonderful musicians with whom I've worked in my ministry. They're too numerous to be named, but Kim was also a wonderful example of dedication and devotion on this score. El Dorado was the first church I served with an extensive English Handbell Choir program. Kim led it. I can see the Bell Choir Tables spread out across the front of our Sanctuary; I can hear the music of those choirs which took turns playing every Sunday—a young children's bell choir, an older children's bell choir, the Junior High Choir, the Senior High Choir, and two adult Bell Choirs.

We couldn't believe our ears, when in November or December of 1983, following the move of Ben and Angela to Garden City, Ben phoned us with the news they were expecting a baby. It was great. Young married couples do these things, but I had always kept thinking and feeling I was as young as ever. My first inward response to the news "You're going to be a grandfather" was "I'm too young to be a grandfather!" The idea grew on me. By the time the summer of 1984 rolled around, I was quite excited about the prospect of my first grandchild's arrival.

Friday morning, July 6, 1984, Ben telephoned us to announce that we had a grandson, Benjamin Martin Kieler, Jr. "What wonderful news. That's great." Then, since in the last half of the Twentieth Century in the USA the arrival of healthy newborn children had become practically routine, it was almost as an after thought I asked, "Is everything going all right with everyone?" Ben's response stunned me. "Angela had a C-section and she's doing OK, but there are some problems with the baby." Some problems. What did Ben mean? He went on to indicate a bit of what had happened. More would come out later. In the birthing process, the umbilical cord had gotten twisted around the baby's neck or throat. In some ways the baby wasn't responding quite as normally as he should have. By Friday afternoon, we received a second call from Ben. "Little Ben," as Lorine and I soon began to call him, was being transferred by air ambulance from the hospital in Garden City to Wesley Medical Center's Prenatal Infant Intensive Care unit. Ben suggested that if we'd like to go see him we could. He and Angela would be coming as soon as she was dismissed from the hospital and able to travel—probably in a day or two.

Lorine and I went to visit little Ben one, two, three times a day. We were still dumbfounded. When Ben and Angela were able to come to Wichita, they asked me to baptize him which I was honored to do. Every baptism is always a moment filled with awe at the potential in the new born child, but in this case there was a dark cloud hanging overhead, and I had a profound sadness even as I baptized him.

"Little Ben" was critically injured and severely oxygen deprived in the birth process because of medical malpractice. After a diagnostic stay in ICU, followed by an uncertain prognosis, Ben and Angela cared for "Little Ben" 24 hours a day, 7 days a week, at home in Garden City. He was constantly subject to seizures. He never developed like normal children develop. He was a beautiful child, but he never uttered a sound, never cried, never laughed, never developed any motor skills. Except for a near smile, he never showed or responded to emotion. For most of his life, Ben had to be fed with a feeding tube inserted in his stomach. Ben and Angela were hopeful that things would change. After months of one crisis following another and little, if any, improvement, they were exhausted.

All they could really do, was find custodial care for "Little Ben." The nearest and best possibility for this seemed to be at Winfield State Hospital. Little Ben was there for over 5 years. Eventually Ben and Angela moved to the Kansas City Area. Both before and after their move, because Lorine and I lived so much closer to Winfield we were able to visit him far more often than were they.

Gradually Ben grew some physically. He became big enough that for the staff to move him about, he had to be in a specially made wheel chair. When any of us went to visit, we could take him for a "walk" in the wheel chair. He continued to be a beautiful child, to appear healthy. Eventually the time came when he made a kind of clicking sound with his teeth but no other sound. There were times when the therapists thought he responded to a little to sound or music, but it was never clear that he really did. He was cared for by the hospital staff with love and sensitivity. I still vividly picture Ben plucking some fragrant honeysuckle flowers at our house one day. He and Angela were going to visit "Little Ben" and Big Ben was hoping somehow the aroma might get through to him or become a means of communication.

My own feeling was always that somehow here was an aware and sensitive soul trapped, imprisoned, in a body which was unable to give or receive communications from those in the outside world.

In April of 1990, "Little Ben's" parents moved him to the Harry S. Truman Children's Neurological Center in Kansas City so they could be near him. Again the staff treated him with utmost care, love and respect. He died February 18, 1992, having lived about seven and a half years. To me, this was a release for him.

The birth, life, and death of "Little Ben" were the most profound grief that I've ever experienced. It was even more difficult for Lorine. This grief to some degree will remain with both of us forever. I was deeply moved that although none of them knew "Little Ben", 113 of our friends sent us cards of sympathy. One of the staff members who cared for him during his final two years of life, wrote and shared with his parents these words:

Ben
For such a small boy and a
Life of short length
The time he was with us
He brought us such strength
We'll always remember
His smile and his face
And can now rest assured he's
In a much better place
Though the feelings of sadness
And sorrow will part
The memories of Ben will
Forever remain in our heart.

I continued throughout these El Dorado years, as always in my ministry, to seek to keep myself professionally alive and vital through Continuing Education. Several of these memories still strengthen me and remain important.

In the summer of 1982 two of us, Kay Ott and I, went to Saint Louis to attend a two week Stephen's Ministry training course preparing us to inaugurate this relatively new and growing ecumenical lay "pastoral care" program for our congregation. Lorine actually traveled there with us, went on to visit family in Kentucky, and then returned to take us home when the course was finished. To this day I feel this was probably the best program I've seen or been involved with when it comes to the local church responding to the sick, the bereaved, the divorcing, the lonely, the addicted, and others afflicted in any one of a multitude of ways. Upon returning, the two of us gathered a dozen members of our church for a year's training, organization, and the development of ongoing supervision of the individual Stephen Ministers. For some years beyond my time as pastor in El Dorado, this program continued as a strong and vital caring ministry.

In July of 1983 one of the quadrennial United Methodist Convocations on "Preaching, Liturgy, Music and the Other Arts" was held at Southern Methodist University and Highland Park United Methodist Church in Dallas, Texas. Because of its proximity, it seemed this was my best chance to participate in one of those convocations. Lorine joined me in attending this week-long event. It was creative and a great event, but what really made it special was being able to share it with Lorine. This wasn't true for many of my continuing education opportunities. It certainly enriched my understanding of liturgy and my use of newer music in worship.

In the fall of 1985, I enrolled in one of my longest and most enjoyable continuing education events—a seminar on Spiritual Formation. This was offered by Perkins School of Theology, Southern Methodist University and took place on their campus in Dallas. It was anchored by three one-week seminars, one in September 1985, another in January of 1986, and the final week in May of 1986. There was a full day or day-and-a half seminar each month in between the week-long seminars plus many reading, journaling, and teaching assignments. The focus was on historical and personal spiritual growth practices, and training to become Spiritual Directors. I'd discovered that throughout my ministry I'd given so much time, energy and effort to teaching, preaching, pastoral care, and administration that I'd shorted my own personal, private spiritual life. I needed something like this. In addition to the Spiritual Formation Seminar, several times that year and the next, I made 24-hour retreats at the Manna House of Prayer, a retreat center operated by an order of Roman Catholic nuns in Concordia, Kansas.

These two events tied together. They did much to nurture me and prevent what otherwise could have been a developing burnout in ministry. Twice, perhaps three times, during my trips to Texas, I managed to take Lorine along so we could enjoy our time together on the road and have a little time for dining out, a movie, and soaking up the beauty of the SMU campus before and after my work on campus. This doubled the pleasure from my continuing education.

In April 1986, the final time Lorine came with me to Dallas, we planned an extended 3 or 4 day trip on to San Antonio for a time of fun together there. The river walk, especially in the spring, is so picturesque. Neither of us had been there before. But something else very special happened while we were there. The summer previous to our San Antonio trip Angela had become pregnant again. While we were in San Antonio, we received a call from Ben that another grandchild had been born April 9th—Alison Marie Kieler. This time everything was fine. What a joy, what a relief, to receive this word.

When we heard this word, immediately we dropped further vacation plans and headed for Kansas City. It was our pleasure to get there in time to visit Angela and our granddaughter in the hospital and to be among those who escorted them from the hospital and welcomed them home.

During the years we served the El Dorado church, I had the pleasure of working of with three associate pastors. Before I came to El Dorado, the church had employed a young student pastor, Don Swender who was in his last year at St. Paul School of Theology in Kansas City. Don was midstream in a career change from being a Debate Coach at Wichita State University to becoming a United Methodist minister. When Don graduated from St. Paul School of Theology, El Dorado FUMC was ready and waiting for an Associate Pastor. We requested Don be appointed to our church and were fortunate to receive him. Don was an extremely capable pastor with a fine family, wife Sue and daughter Shari. He was especially effective in working with young adults. We worked well together and I enjoyed our relationship. During Don's final year with us he was distressed and challenged by serious health problems.

As we sought a replacement for Don following his appointment to Harper, the cabinet presented me with another challenge. Pastors had, for a time, been somewhat immune to the rising divorce rate. Now this was changing. Divorce among clergy was more frequent and when it occurred, congregations tended to be judgmental in their responses. Certainly it was not easy for the Bishop to appoint a divorced pastor. My District Superintendent explained a situation where they were "stuck" in making an appointment. Rev. LeRoy Smoot had been serving at Haysville for some years, doing a good job, but he had just gone through a divorce. I was asked, "Would you be willing to accept LeRoy as your Associate and recommend him to your Staff/Parish Relations Committee?"

I had known LeRoy. I felt he was strong and effective. I was glad to recommend him. I'm sure it was difficult for LeRoy to take a salary reduction and move from being the Senior Pastor of a strong church to becoming an Associate Pastor. Things worked out well for LeRoy, for me, and for our congregation. Seven months later, I had the privilege and pleasure of officiating at his marriage to Joan. LeRoy was strong and effective enough that he was really just being "parked" temporarily by the Cabinet until a more appropriate appointment for him opened. A year and a half later, in the middle of the appointive year, there was an unexpected vacancy at Larned. LeRoy proved to be the pastor they needed. Once again El Dorado was without an Associate Pastor.

While I was in El Dorado, one of my connectional responsibilities was serving on BOOM (the Board of Ordained Ministries). In conjunction with this, I served as a mentor for a young pastor newly out of seminary—Dottie Fornish Knetch, who was serving the Methodist Church in Mentor, Kansas. You could say, I was mentor for the pastor at Mentor! During our monthly sessions together, Dottie impressed me. She had served Mentor as a student charge and stayed on there following her seminary graduation. At the end of that year, she was ready to move on to new challenges and a larger church. I asked both Dottie and the Cabinet about the possibility that she might become El Dorado's new Associate Pastor. By this time we had a growing number of women in ordained ministry in our Annual Conference, yet many churches were still reluctant to accept them as their pastor. I was enthusiastic about Dottie. I also felt it would be a good and a growing experience for the congregation to have a woman pastor. In my humble judgment, I believe since congregations are usually half men, half women, the ideal mix in a church large enough to have two ordained ministers is one male, one female pastor. The dynamics are always a bit more challenging, but Dottie and I worked well in our relationship.

Some pastors are so involved in their parish they neglect to be involved in the community. Others are so involved in the community they neglect their parish. I always tried to strike a good balance. In Belle Plaine, I was active in the Chamber of Commerce and was its secretary for one year. Previous to El Dorado the one thing I had not done was to belong to a "civic club." That just wasn't my thing. Upon my arrival in El Dorado, I was invited to visit various civic clubs and I felt it was probably time for me to belong to one. My Junior High and Senior High friend from Hutchinson and from my home church, Wayne Livingston, lived in El Dorado. He encouraged me to become a Rotarian. I ended up doing that.

I thoroughly enjoyed the club. On the basis of my experience for eight years, I can give a strong recommendation to anyone debating the merits of civic clubs. What most caught my imagination in the Rotary International movement was all of its scholarships and international exchanges. I ended up serving two or three years as District Secretary for RI Youth Exchanges. I was happy to be able to promote this program by encouraging the clubs all the way from El Dorado to Liberal, Kansas, to apply for and sponsor in their local high school a young person from another country. Promoting this, I naturally felt my own club should be doing it. At first I found it difficult to generate much interest in El Dorado. The problem seemed to be finding host homes.

Finally, I talked with Lorine and the boys. As teen-agers, the boys were only so-so about the idea but in the end we volunteered to host the first student who would come if our club agreed to be a sponsor. We agreed to host him for a year if necessary, but we encouraged other members to consider being his host family in the spring so the student could experience more than one American family. The club ended up with Jose Yamuni, a young man from Los Mochis, Mexico. He shared Bill's room. The boys got along pretty well, but Bill still had his friends and his interests. I think Bill was relieved when another family asked to host Jose in the Spring.

Over all, our year went along so well that the next year Jose's family inquired if his brother, Jorge, might be able to come. The club agreed to host a second student and took Jorge. We had no problem finding two other families to step up to the plate as host families. Lorine even had Jorge in one of her high school Spanish classes. This gave him one "easy" class since he struggled with English a bit more than his brother. It also was a very enriching experience for the students in Lorine's class to have a native speaker in their midst. For several years we kept track of the boys. Eventually we lost touch with them which I've always regretted. Before we lost touch we had a wonderful experience with the Yamuni family during a memorable visit to Mexico.

In the Spring of 1984, for spring break Lorine and I planned a trip to Mexico. We focused on a visit to Mexico City, but we thought it would be nice to meet the parents of Jose and Jorge if possible. We contacted the Yumunis and ended up with an invitation to visit in their home. Bill went with us since his Southwestern College spring break coincided with Lorine's. We flew into an airport some 60 or 100 miles north of Los Mochis. Mr. Yamuni picked us up and personally drove us to Los Mochis. I remember that drive because he wanted so much to reassure us. He said there was considerable unrest and lawlessness along that highway and he wanted to care for us. At one point, police did stop us, asked us to step out of the car and proceeded to search for drugs or contraband.

Los Mochis is on the Pacific Ocean. The area there is warm and the vegetation tropical. Like so much of Mexico, there are two kinds of homes—those of the very poor and those of the well-to-do. The Yamuni home was a big two-story Spanish type home, white stucco with red tile trimming, attractively maintained. From our upstairs bedroom, we had a beautiful view of the ocean in the distance. In their home they treated us like royalty. They had a massive backyard beef barbeque with friends and relatives to celebrate our visit. They treated us to a fine seafood restaurant including a calamari feast.

In Mexico City, spring was at its height. Our travel agent had us booked in a fine old downtown hotel in the heart of the city. We were just across the street from the large central municipal park. Flowers were everywhere. The city was quiet and not overly crowded. It was delightful just to stroll and soak in the beauty. We visited the big museums of culture, anthropology and natural history. Every spring when the weather warms and the flowers begin to bloom, my mind and spirit still go back to that spring in Mexico City.

Chapter 46

THE LOFT

Rays of the bright sunlight filtered through the pine trees scattered in clusters around those five acres. The pines dominated the hackberry, ash, redbud, locust and other trees and shrubs, even the cedars, which ringed the perimeter of this small expanse of native prairie grasses.

The lane wound its way up to the northeast corner where "the loft" had been built in 1980. Here the Austrian Pines, even some of the Scotch Pines, hid the building from the north and the east sides of the loft. They were taller than its peak. How was it possible that the gallon-sized holes we'd dug and the spindly twigs we'd purchased from the Kansas State Forester as windbreak plantings twenty years earlier could have produced such wonderful trees?

The initial idea of the loft was to build a large garage where we could store our camper, motorboat, and sailboat, have a little shop, and a half bath for cleaning up after a trip to the lake or spending several hours in the garden. But the idea grew. Why not make this a two-story garage? The upper level could be made into a large one-room efficiency apartment—a kitchen in one corner, a living room area in another corner, a divider where the stairway came up from the garage, then a bed in another corner and a multi-purpose area in the fourth corner. We made the garage 30' x 40' so upstairs we could have two balconies with sliding patio doors leading to each one—the north balcony and the south balcony.

THE LOFT: JULY 4, 2002

Michael Kieler (above) practices his casting at one of the family gatherings at the loft as Ben and Harold Kieler (below) enjoy the north balcony.

From these balconies you could "see forever." The south balcony overlooked the garden (a 35' x 100' area for growing vegetables with an asparagus patch in one corner), the orchard of 20 apple trees, our five acres as well as the neighbors' acreages. You could see for a mile or more. The north balcony overlooked the boundary area of the El Dorado State Park which butted up to our property line and parts of the El Dorado Reservoir with its marina. The lake was near enough we could pull out of our lane with the boat and be on the main boat ramp, getting on the lake, within a five minute span of time. We soon started calling these living quarters our "loft." When the wind was not blowing too hard, we could open both patio doors and have a nice breeze all the way through it. If we needed a windbreak, we could keep the windward door closed and use the leeward balcony. We would choose which balcony to use depending on our preferences for sun or shade, for wind or shelter, for one view or the other.

For years we didn't have a phone or television. We used this place as a get away, a quiet retreat, as well as a base for recreation on the lake and for my hobby of gardening. It was also a great place for family gatherings and entertaining friends. If there was an honest to goodness emergency, some one from El Dorado could drive out in 5 to 10 minutes to get hold of me. Later, after my parents were gone, we brought their old television to the loft so we had some contact with the outside world if we were spending several consecutive days out there. Still later, when we moved to Augusta, 30 minutes away, we found it helpful to have a phone, but we never made that fact or number broadly known to people.

Lorine and I often said, "When our world gets chaotic, it is the loft which helps us keep our sanity." For more than twenty years we enjoyed this place. We enjoyed, more than words can ever express, our closeness to nature—the constantly changing wildflowers, the constantly varying hues of the native grasses, the many kinds of birds and the wildlife. It broke my heart when we finally decided to let it go. I still shed inward tears and long for that place again. If any of my children or grandchildren had been close enough to regularly use and enjoy it, I would have tried to hang on to it. But ten years after moving to Wichita, it became too much to keep up a town place and a country place. Yet, I still go there in my imagination.

Cabins had been part of my family's heritage—Uncle Floyd's cabin, and Dad's Cow Creek cabin. We had friends who had cabins. These created within me a certain pre-disposition for a place like the loft. When we were living in Wichita the first time, while I served Trinity UMC (1968-1972), Mother knew how much we enjoyed Cheney Lake. When she learned that we had found building lots available for as little as $1,200 to $2,500 near that lake, she gave us a gift which made it possible for us to acquire one of these. The property taxes for this undeveloped little plot of rural land were only $10 a year. We even planted small trees there so they could be growing and provide shade by the time we could build a cabin.

A Cheney Lake neighbor family allowed us to run water from their house just two lots away to water our trees. But a very dumb thing happened when we moved to Dodge City. There was no way to keep watering our trees or using our lake lot. We just put it on hold in our minds. After six months, the post office no longer forwarded mail to us so we didn't get our annual property tax statements. The taxes had been so inconsequential, we were so busy with other things, that we lost track of the fact we weren't paying the taxes. Six years later when we came back to South-Central Kansas, we thought we'd pick up with our development plans for the lot. We discovered it had been "sold for taxes" at a Sheriff's auction. We hadn't received any notification because Wichita mail was no longer being forwarded. Our Cheney Lake neighbors knew I was a United Methodist Pastor, but they didn't seek to track us down to tell us about the sale. Instead, they bought our lot for $30 or $50 back taxes and it became theirs!

While mourning the loss of our Cheney Lake cabin site, we became intrigued by the new El Dorado Lake Reservoir being constructed at the time we moved to El Dorado. When we had free time, we'd cruise around, watch them build the lake and look at where people were planning housing developments. Lorine thought I put in too many hours working and didn't take enough time off for myself or the family. She proposed we buy this site where we built our loft. As we discussed it, one of the possibilities we considered was that it could also later become the building site of a retirement home. With this in mind I finally consented. It did seem like a great idea.

We spent a year or more, with the help of friends, doing some landscape plantings. Then I began to draw my own plans for the loft. When we were ready to build, I became my own contractor, taking bids from plumbers, carpenters, electricians, and H & AC contractors and others and putting together the best price configuration. As the basic construction was finished, once more friends helped us and we did our painting.

Many of our neighbors kept manicured lawns like those of town folk, but it was always our intent to keep a natural rustic look similar to the original flinthills. Neighbors may not have appreciated our look but we enjoyed it. Immediately around the loft, we planted buffalo grass. It was slow growing and I did mow it several times each summer. I also mowed close around the trees. Everywhere else, where the prairie grasses were, I left things to grow. Once in early August and again in March, I used my tractor with its brushhog mower to cut the prairie grass. It needed to be grazed, or mowed, or burned in early spring to remain vital.

I had an old horse-drawn hay rake adapted for a tractor. Lorine would help me. One of us, after the mowing, drove the tractor and the other rode the rake. It was a trip-rake. When it had rolled up enough hay that it needed dumping, we pulled a lever which raised the rake and dumped the hay. We then dropped the rake again, and continued repeating the process. When our raking was finished, using a pitchfork to load the hay into either our very small wagon or our yard cart, I would haul the hay to build a giant haystack. This provided mulch throughout the year.

One time this turned out to be a risky experience. Lorine was helping me. I wore a long sleeve denim shirt. Occasionally, for whatever reason, I'd reach down and pick up an arm load of hay by hand instead of using the pitchfork. I did this one time; then the next time, I took up my pitchfork and stabbed up a big fork full of hay. As I turned toward my wagon, I was startled to discover that one of the tines of the pitchfork had speared a huge rattlesnake. Had I picked up another arm load by hand, I might very well have picked up that rattlesnake pulling him in toward my body! As it was, it scared the daylights out of me. I was afraid the rattler would slip off the tine and either get away or turn on me.

I hollered at Lorine, "Quick, run to the garage. Bring me a shovel."

While she was doing that, I turned the tines ground-ward and stabbed them into the earth so the rattlesnake couldn't get off. Still excited, when Lorine got back with the shovel, I shouted, "Hold the pitchfork where it is, while I chop the rattler's head off with the shovel!"

She wasn't very happy with that job, but someone had to hold the fork down for me. This was my closest encounter with a rattlesnake, but one time Lorine just about took hold of one as she reached into the strawberry bed. Neither of us was ever comfortable with the rattle snakes. We killed quite a few at the loft. Eventually we exterminated them from our environment.

In 1990, I suggested to Lorine that since we were only five years away from retirement, we should begin drawing up the plans for our retirement home at the loft. At this point, Lorine balked. She pointed out that most women outlive their husbands. She did not want me to die and leave her to live alone in the country. She felt we needed to plan in a different direction for our retirement home. Her idea was that I could spend time at the loft, commuting there from wherever we chose to live in retirement. She would join me part of the time. This never turned out to be practical.

Lorine had more interests in town than in the country. She wasn't with me enough for the loft to be as satisfying and enjoyable as it had been. The loft continued to be work, but not much play. Ten years after we moved to Wichita, seven years after I retired, I was stretched out and stressed out trying to maintain two properties in two different locations. One of several factors contributing to this was our wildlife friends. Deer became so abundant they used my garden for grazing—for their personal pantry. Many times, when I arrived at the loft, most of the garden would be ravaged.

October 1, 2002, we sold the loft. By then, instead of a rural PO Box number, the loft had a specific rural address—3720 NE 4th, El Dorado. Civilization was beginning to encroach on it more and more. The Acklins, from in town, purchased it from us. They had their own plans for the place and today it's entirely different in appearance. It's been tripled in size, changed in color, and those who enjoyed parties or family-time with us there might not even recognize the loft.

Chapter 47

THE GARDEN

"When the world wearies,
and society ceases to satisfy,
there is always the Garden." Minnie Aumonier

An elderly parishioner was dying. The parents of a young child faced the boy's critical surgery. A woman came to me in tears to talk about her failing marriage. A teen-ager was in trouble with the law. After months of unemployment, the man across the desk from me was saying, "I'm on the verge of despair—I don't know how long I can go on like this; I don't know what to do." We had a personnel crisis relating to the church's custodian. I'd had a funeral that Saturday morning, and now that evening I was to officiate at a wedding. And it was all occurring within the span of seven days!

This wasn't a typical week for me, fortunately, but when you are a parish pastor you do often find yourself carrying a heavy load as you empathize morally, spiritually, and physically with your parishioners. On top of this, I had my own personal family relationships, my own joys and sorrows, which drew upon my inner strength. And how was I to refresh my self in body, mind, and spirit? It might be easy to give a pious or a glib answer, but I'm not prone to do that.

Through the years, I've often answered that question of self—refreshment by saying, "My garden is my therapy." Dad taught me a lot about gardening and so did my grandmother. I always enjoyed both the physical work of the garden and seeing things grow and come to fruition. One of the first things I wanted to do every place I ever lived was to create a garden. I especially liked vegetable gardening because I so enjoyed eating the fresh produce of the garden. Besides, vegetables seem easier to grow than flowers. But, I also enjoyed planting and tending flowers. Their beauty contributed to the beauty and joy of life for others as well as for myself. Seldom was I fortunate enough to have space to fully satisfy my passion for gardening. Wherever I have lived, I planted as large a garden as room permitted whether it was a couple of tomato plants in Nashville, or a nice strawberry pyramid plus a row of red raspberries and a fair sized plot for lettuce, radishes, onions, green beans and tomatoes in Dodge City.

If I may paraphrase Ralph Waldo Emerson's words about the woods, in the garden I always seemed to return to reason and faith. There I felt nothing could befall me in life which nature and her God could not repair. From some other source unknown, there is a little verse which I first discovered through the Soil Conservation Service. It has also often been used as a blessing. It goes like this:

> "Behind the loaf is the flower;
> Behind the flower is the
> Sun, the wind and shower;
> And our Creator's Will."

What I've always liked about these words is the way they connect our human nourishment, our sustenance, with everything that produces the loaf of bread, the wheat—the flower, sun, wind and shower—with the Divine Creator—with God's will, with God's love. These words are an affirmation, as is the garden itself, of the inter-relationship of all things.

It was not until we bought the loft that I had a garden big enough to be thoroughly challenging and fully satisfying. I could spend hours and even days on end in that garden. I could till the soil, rake the clods, hoe the weeds until I was physically weary and all without taxing my mind! On hands and knees, I could plant seeds and seedlings moving the earth with my fingers, getting out all my frustrations. It was really "The Garden" for me. As I worked in it, I could hear the birds sing. It was music to my ears. As I saw a bluebird flying with sunlight illuminating its rosy breast, there was beauty for my eyes. The feel of the sun and wind, the fresh smell from the shower added to my sensory satisfaction. The surrounding prairie grass waved at me in the winds and our perimeter pine trees inspired me to stand and lift up my head toward the sky, to the heavens.

This was a place of prayer for me. To quote Helen Steiner Rice,

> You ask me how I know it's true
> that there is a living God —
> A God who rules the universe,
> the sky . . . the sea . . . the sod . . . .
> A God who holds all creatures
> in the hollow of His hand,
> A God who put infinity
> in one tiny grain of sand . . . .
> A God who made the seasons—
> Winter, summer, fall and spring,
> And put His flawless rhythm
> into each created thing . . . .
> What better answers are there
> to prove His Holy Being
> Than the wonders all around us
> that are ours just for the seeing!

Whether I'm in my garden, or someone else's garden, whether I'm at home or traveling in America the beautiful, or seeing the wonders of the natural world in some far and distant land, I always feel at one with the Native American prayer which goes like this:

O' GREAT SPIRIT,
Whose voice I hear in the winds,
And whose breath gives life to all the world,
hear me! I am small and weak, I need
your strength and wisdom.

LET ME WALK IN BEAUTY, and make my eyes
ever behold the red and purple sunset.

MAKE MY HANDS RESPECT the things you have
made and my ears sharp to hear your voice.

MAKE ME WISE SO that I may understand the
things you have taught my people.

LET ME LEARN the lessons you have hidden
in every leaf and rock.

I SEEK STRENGTH, not to be greater than my
brother, but to fight my greatest enemy—myself.

MAKE ME ALWAYS READY to come to you with
clean hands and straight eyes.

SO WHEN LIFE FADES, as the fading sunset,
my spirit may come to you without shame.

Chapter 48

LOOKING FOR ANCESTORS

There was a knock on the door. I ran to see who it was. He was a stranger. I'd never seen him before. He was showing up at our house unexpectedly, at least as far as I knew. Of course, I was just a young child. Perhaps he did come by prior arrangement with my parents. He introduced himself to me. "Hello, I'm Lloyd Walter from Oklahoma City," he said.

Later I was to learn that he was my dad's first cousin, a Presbyterian minister, and something of a family historian. He was a friendly man and I enjoyed his presence with us. However, he was elderly; I was young. He was mostly conversing with my parents, especially my dad, and I didn't pay much attention. During the next few years, he wrote several letters about their relatives back in Pennsylvania. Dad read them to us as a family but I don't think they were ever saved. I doubt that I saw Dr. Lloyd C. Walter over half a dozen times in my life but I was drawn to him. In retrospect, I wish I'd paid more attention to him, asked more questions, saved more of the family information he possessed.

Doing genealogy is like doing detective work.

Dad did not know a lot about his eastern relatives, but Lloyd Walter and the three "Kieler girls" (Annah, Jennie, and Margaret) in Peabody knew more than did he. Lloyd died before I ever got interested in Kieler genealogy. By the time I was interested enough in my family roots to seriously explore them, Annah was also dead. Margaret, custodian of the papers, pictures, and oral tradition the Kieler sisters possessed, freely shared with me what she knew.

I began digging seriously for my family roots in the early to mid 1980s. Using Margaret's information, I established contact with two Kieler descendants in Pennsylvania. July 24 to August 8, 1984 my wife, Lorine, joined me in a trip to meet Leona Bieber and Helen Menges, two sisters, living in Turbotsville, Pa. The three of us were great-grandchildren of Jacob (1821-1915) and Lydia Kieler. Leona and Helen in turn helped us meet still more Kieler descendents who lived in Williamsport and Montoursvillle, Pa. I gleaned from all of these relatives still more information and more intriguing questions which pertained to possible relationships between our great-grandfather and a Jacob Kieler who immigrated to the Untied States in 1754.

That fall of 1984 I put together a first draft of information which I had gleaned about my paternal heritage. This became a gift to my father, my sons, and other relatives for Christmas that year. In particular, it thrilled my Dad. Because that turned out to be father's last Christmas before he died, I'm ever grateful that I finished that gift. I've kept somewhat in touch with many of these Kieler descendents from other states and it is my hope within in the next few years to search for more of my ancestors and to dig deeper into my family roots. The "case" of the Jacob Kielers has not yet been solved; the detective work is not completed.

People are sometimes asked, "What is your oldest possession?" and invited to tell about it. The first time I visited them, Helen and Leona each showed me an item they inherited which had been hand crafted for their mother, when she was a child, by her grand-father, our great-grandfather. Neither Helen nor Leona has living children. Because I was the only male heir who they knew who still bore the Kieler name, they indicated they might be willing to pass these objects on to me someday. I was delighted. The last time I visited them, they were in failing health. They felt the time to pass on these items had come.

CHILD'S PLAY FURNITURE MADE BY AUTHOR'S GREAT-GRANDFATHER JACOB KIELER

Naomi Kieler (above) holds doll in summer of 2003, Anika Kieler (below) prepares to "pour tea" in spring of 2004, while playing with furniture made by their great-great-great grandfather almost 125 years earlier.

I received from Leona a cabinet for a child's tea set made by our Great-grand father, and from Helen a cradle for a child's doll. How blessed I felt! Since that time, two of my grand-children—Naomi Kieler, Bill's daughter, and Anika Kieler, Paul's daughter—have visited our home and been thrilled to play with these pieces of furniture made about 1880-1885 by their great-great-great grandfather. Looking for ancestors does pay off even if I never had something like this in mind when I began my search.

Sometimes looking for ancestors may also cost something. About the same time I began in earnest to work on Kieler genealogy, I also began looking for my maternal ancestors. I have yet to put together a first draft of the information I've gleaned about my maternal heritage. It's been fun gleaning this information and gathering clues which remain to be investigated. About fifteen years ago, I began searching for my grandmother Taylor's Wurtzel roots. I discovered her parents, my great-grandparents, Nicholas (b. Aug. 26, 1831-d. July 14, 1896) and Elizabeth Arett Wurtzel (b. Oct. 29, 1848-d. Nov. 30,1917) were buried in an unmarked grave at West Point, Nebraska. That discovery led me to solicit donations from others in the family who were their descendents so together we could place a gravestone to mark their burial place.

Looking for my ancestors has been for me a way to discover and honor my heritage and preserve the record of those who have gone before me. I have endless unfinished tasks, "miles to go before I sleep," in the words of Robert Frost. Completing my search for ancestors and completing a final draft of the story of the Kieler family heritage, both paternal and maternal, remains part of my unfinished agenda.

Chapter 49

BUILDING ANEW

In 1986 the time had come for us to move from the church at El Dorado to a new assignment. The Bishop and his Cabinet had two possibilities in mind for us—an appointment to First UMC Winfield or to First UMC Augusta. Winfield was their first choice. It was a larger community. Like El Dorado, it was a county seat town. The church was a bigger church with a larger salary. But, the Bishop and Cabinet, after conferring with me and receiving my acquiescence, were in for a surprise. They knew we had previously served Grace UMC. I wondered out loud with them about this. Because it had been 18 years since we served in Winfield, they felt this wasn't a problem. When they proposed sending us to Winfield First Church, its Staff-Parish Relations Committee balked. The S/PR Committee thought the appointment might lead to ill feelings between the two congregations should any of the Grace Church people "follow me" downtown. Just generally they felt it wasn't wise to have the same person serve both churches. Perhaps they felt the model of a college pastor, or my social activism, was not what they needed though they did not say this.

Naturally a pastor feels a certain sense of hurt and disappointment when he or she is turned down in a proposed appointment. This was also true for me. Like every Methodist and United Methodist pastor, I knew full well the rejection of a proposed appointment is something which can and does happen within our system from time to time. The hurt didn't last long, however.

The Bishop quickly appointed me to Augusta, just 15 or 20 miles east of Wichita, not far to the southwest of El Dorado. An Augusta Circuit, formed in 1870, had five points. The Augusta Church began in a log cabin hall still standing today, at 305 State Street, in what is now the Augusta Historical Museum. In 1874, a site was acquired at Sixth and School streets where a handsome stone church was built for less than $2,500. By 1906 this first church building was outgrown and replaced with a new $10,000 frame church on the same site. Eighteen years later, in 1924, the congregation had again outgrown its building. In that boom time the church was again replaced by building on the same site. They considered this new church "a very modern church" for its time. During its construction, worship was held in the Iris Theater courtesy of members Dave and Alene Bisagno. This third church building was the large brick building being used when I was appointed Pastor in Augusta. Not only was it 63-years-old and located on a flood plain. It was of a most unusual, if not strange, design which by 1986 seemed antiquated. Without going into details, the interior was built on multiple levels none of which were easily accessible to anyone leave alone a person with handicapping conditions.

I was appointed in response to a request from the church for "a person experienced enough to lead the congregation through a planning process, funding raising and building program to either redesign and renovate the existing structure or replace it." Some planning had been begun by Bob Brooks, my predecessor. The church was unable to develop any consensus about what to do. Part of my role included consensus building in so far as practical. A most unusual request came as part of the appointment process. Even though the appointment would not be effective until June 1, 1986, I was asked to start meeting and working with the Planning Committee as soon as the appointment was agreed upon—in early March. With Bob's consent, I did this. Of course the total planning and development process was a long term undertaking, but this was the only time in 40 years of ministry I've ever known a pastor to become so significantly involved over a several month period in the life of a church he was going to be serving but was not yet serving!

Three immediate tasks needed to be addressed—money, decision making about what needed to be done, and creating the needed architectural plans. When I was appointed to Augusta, the only building fund was a $250,000 estate gift. No effort to raise additional funds had been undertaken. It seemed as though the church hadn't really come to grips with the need for the congregation to fiscally underwrite the bulk of its dreams. We had to start with planning what became the first of a series of professionally assisted fund raising drives. Even deciding to invest in the use of a professional fund-raising consultant's services was not easy.

We also had to address the decision-making issue of remodeling vs. building anew. Many old-timers remained deeply tied, emotionally, to the old building. Closely related to the issue of "to remodel or not to remodel?" was the question of where to build IF we were to relocate and build new. Could we find a proper site? We were already in the heart of the old downtown. In a brainstorming process, people identified 14 potential building sites although there was no guaranteed availability of any of them. There were endless pros and cons related to each site. No clear or easy consensus emerged. Since Augusta was growing north along Ohio Street, logic seemed to argue for something in this direction, but people were convinced the most favorable site was impossible to acquire. This site was on the "Bisagno land"—about a half section of land, beginning at 2420 Ohio, running north along the eastside of the street.

The Bisagno family, Italian immigrants, came to the Augusta area in the late 1800s or early 1900s. They acquired a number of acres of land, at least two different sections, north of the town. Dave Bisagno maintained this as largely agricultural land throughout his life until his death in 1965. His wife, and their son Bob, kept it this way into the 1990s. It was generally assumed that Dave's widow wanted it to be undeveloped and that Bob was honoring her wishes so long as she lived. This is why it would be "impossible for the church to acquire it."

Alene Karnes, born in Illinois in 1899, educated at Forest Park University in St. Louis where she trained to be a concert pianist, made a transition in 1922 from her intended career to become a pianist for silent movies. That same year her first job playing for a movie theater brought her to Augusta where she worked for Dave Bisagno in the Iris Theater which Dave owned. They struck it off so well that they married in 1923.

After her marriage, Alene no longer played for the movies. She continued playing for her own pleasure and that of the community, the church and civic groups, and at weddings and funerals. In 1935 in the heart of the depression, the Bisagnos built and operated "the finest deco art theater west of the Mississippi." Dave was the CEO and projectionist; Alene ran the Box Office; their son Bob grew up in the theater and later succeeded his father as "king of the movies" in Augusta until changing times forced the closing of their downtown theater and the abandonment of their Drive-In Theater. By the time I came to Augusta, Alene was still a sharp vibrant almost 90 year old widow, basically homebound in her home, cared for by Bob.

I always considered myself a general practitioner in parish ministry. Involvement in every dimension of parish ministry, without limiting my self to one or two specialties, gave me a great sense of satisfaction and fulfillment. Managerial or administrative skills were probably my over all greatest gift or strength, but one of my greatest joys was visitation—an old-fashioned dimension of ministry now almost totally unpracticed by most pastors. Within this facet of ministry, it was my custom to take Holy Communion to shut-ins each quarter of the year either on the first Sunday of the quarter or around church holidays. I always tried, to the best of my ability, to include the homebound on the day of our Christmas Eve communion. This meant Alene Bisagno was one of those homebound persons whom I visited with considerable regularity.

Visits with Alene were always special for me, and from the feedback I received, special for her. Sometimes we'd begin with a general chit-chat about the community, or the world today and/or the world of yesterday. I enjoyed hearing her tell me about the silent movie days and about her now adult children—Bob of Augusta and June of Oklahoma. She was always clear of mind and warm-of-heart. Sooner or later, before I could ask "Would you like to receive communion today?" Alene would ask, "How are things going with the church?" and "What's the latest on the building plans?" We would speak of these things.

Occasionally I would take quarterly communion to some of the homebound after worship—on my way home for Sunday lunch. I always remember a Sunday less than a year after we arrived in Augusta. When Alene asked, "What's the latest on the building plans?" I responded with candor, "You know, we're kind of high-centered right now on the site issue." I enumerated the different possible sites we'd been discussing. I told her what seemed to be wrong with each site. Then, I said, "Truthfully the most ideal answer to our problem would be to obtain a plot of land in the area where you own land. The virtues of this location are these . . . People say that you wouldn't be willing for this to happen. I'm sure we probably couldn't afford it. Is there any chance you'd be willing to think about, to consider giving the church, an acreage fronting on Ohio Street?" I don't remember Alene's specific response. All I remember was, she wasn't offended at my boldness and she didn't slam the door shut.

An hour later, Lorine and I were almost finished with Sunday dinner when the phone rang. I sighed. Another of those unwanted phone interruptions in the middle of our meal. These were pre-answering machine days. Dutifully, I went to answer the phone. Alene was on the line.

> "I've been thinking about what you said. You know,
> the southwest corner of my land there on Ohio Street
> has a pipeline which goes through part of it, but would
> the church be willing to accept six acres there?"

Wow! It was so usable, so right for us, an answer to prayer!

A year and half of hard work followed. I worked on a proposed theological statement relative to the new building. A Building Committee replaced the Planning Committee. It chewed on my statement, hired an architect, debated first one design plan, then another. Even though some argued for the cheapest "box shaped" building, we ended up designing a much more "idealistic" building, fully handicapped accessible.

Costs were projected. The committee concluded "There's no way we can we afford to build the whole thing at once," and asked "What about building in two phases?"

> "OK, as long as we build the sanctuary first," said the older members. "NO! We have to build Christian education facilities first, for our children," said the younger families.
>
> "Well, then, let's vote to see if the congregation wants do it all at once, wants to go that far in debt," the committee responded. The resulting vote: "NO."

In light of this, the committee decided, "We're going to vote again. We will vote on building a Phase I—a gymnasium tied together to the Educational Wing by a large gathering area for use by the community (both church community and the community-at-large). The gym can be designed as a multi-purpose room. Using the altar from the old sanctuary and moveable chairs instead of pews, it can serve as a temporary sanctuary; including a kitchen, it can be used as a fellowship hall; installing showers in the restrooms, it can be used as a gym. When we get Phase I paid off, we will build Phase II—the Sanctuary, running eastward from the Gathering Room."

This time the vote was 60% YES, 40% NO. Only one family left the church over the decision.

Before we could break grounded we needed another crash effort in fund raising. During this second fund raising effort, an amazing gift came from an inactive member living in El Dorado. Ramon Criss, who owned a redi-mix concrete company, pledged to donate all the concrete needed for the new facility and its large parking lot even trucking the concrete all the way to Augusta. I knew from my El Dorado days that honor prisoners at the El Dorado Honor Camp were sometimes permitted to be in work details which did community service type work. We succeeded in gaining a commitment for volunteer laborers from this state minimum security prison, men who had some construction experience in their background, to be permited to do the work of building the parking lot. Factoring in these two commitments, the new funding campaign was successful enough to enable an October 2, 1988, ground-breaking for Augusta FUMC's fourth building.

Phase I of the new facility was completed by October 22, 1989. For three years it was my pleasure and joy to engage in ministry in and through this new facility. Some indebtedness remained to be retired, but the stage was set for Phase II which was completed during my successor's tenure. On Palm Sunday, April 4, 2004, it was my joy and privilege to be invited back to participate in the mortgage burning and dedication of the final phase—the new Sanctuary. Augusta was unique among the seven appointments of my active ministry in that it was the only one in which I was involved in a major building program from the beginning well into its completion. Seeing the end result, I must admit a real sense of satisfaction in what I feel to be one of the nicest church facilities in the Annual Conference.

Just behind the old church which we left behind, stood a two story white frame house constructed in 1917 as the Methodist parsonage. Eventually it ceased to be used as a parsonage and became a church annex. The upstairs was a youth center; the main floor was dedicated to use as a Community Caring Center sponsored by the Augusta Ministerial Alliance. The Caring Center was primarily a place to receive and distribute used clothing for those in need.

When we finished using our old church building, it was sold to the Church of the Nazarene which had also outgrown its old church. The former parsonage with its lot was part of the sale.

Both the priest at St. James Catholic Church and I were active members of the Ministerial Alliance. He volunteered an old unused rectory of theirs to be the new site for the Community Caring Center providing we all understood this would be limited to a two year period after which they had other plans for their old rectory.

I'd been involved in the leadership of the Ministerial Alliance, and had a deep conviction about the importance of the Community Caring Center. It did too much good for those who most needed it to allow it to die for lack of a permanent home. The Alliance scoured the community to no avail for a suitable empty building which could be used as a CCC home. Through the years Augusta was ravaged by a number of floods. In a run down area in the southwest corner of town, near the old abandoned Mobil refinery, the city owned several lots where empty houses had been condemned and razed.

I made a proposal to the Alliance. "Let go to the City Council and ask for a donation of one of these lots. If they don't want to give it to us outright, maybe they would lease into perpetuity at a dollar a year. The Ministerial Alliance can build a modest new caring center on that site."

We were successful in getting the land, but how could the Ministerial Alliance ever afford to build such a building? I had another proposal.

"Let's use the model of rural Kansas Mennonites who are known for coming to the aid of a neighbor in distress. If a lighting strike burns a barn, or a home, they have a 'barn raising.' They all come together in one mighty effort on a single day and build a new barn with their volunteer labor. Can't we solicit donations of the needed materials and funds from businesses and individuals throughout the larger Augusta area to build a simple frame building? Can't we solicit funds from our own congregations to purchase the needed materials that aren't donated? Let's set a Saturday when most of the members of our congregations could gather at the site from early morning until late in the evening and in one mighty effort build a new Community Caring Center!"

This proposal seemed to strike people's imagination and spark enthusiasm for the project. The community's architect donated his labor in creating blue prints for our center. Fortunately, a contractor in a church represented in the Ministerial Alliance offered to be the lead contractor. A number of other contractors in town joined in volunteering to do segments of the work—plumbing, electrical, roofing, etc. Augusta's redi-mix concrete plant donated the cement needed to build the foundation and slab floor in advance of our "B" (for build) Day. Hundreds of volunteers turned out. Church women's groups and restaurants provided meals and refreshments for the workers. First-aid and other things needed to support the volunteers were donated. Miraculously the Augusta Ministerial Alliance's Community Caring Center had a fine facility built all in one day, thanks to proper planning and preparation, wonderful cooperation from the faith community and the secular community, hundreds of faithful deeds of individuals, groups and businesses generously giving of their time, skills, and resources. This transpired just before Lorine and I left Augusta to move to Wichita. Because of the nature of this mission, I think perhaps this building project was even more satisfying for me than my part in building a new church in Augusta.

Among the memories which go unverbalized, remains a memory that is contained in the memory bank of many United Methodist pastors. Dick and Julie Wilke, friends and colleagues of ours, are well known for developing the Disciples' Bible Study program. *Disciples* is an in-depth, small group, non-dogmatic Bible study and discussion which includes daily scripture reading over a year long period that covers about 90% of the Scripture and aims at personal transformation as well as information. In a time when it's easy for pastors and churches to be superficial in their studies, this was a helpful antidote. While at Augusta, I introduced this progam to the church and was involved with others in its leadership for several years. Disciples gave a needed balance to my ministry beyond building programs and administration. And, for those who participated in it, I believe it provided new personal growth and commitment in their faith.

Chapter 50

ANTICIPATING RETIREMENT

What do you do when your plans go awry? You go to Plan B. One day five years before retirement, I said to Lorine, "We need to get started planning our retirement house."

We'd been looking forward to the day when we would live in our own house. We had always lived in church-owned parsonages. We were ready to become *bonified* homeowners. We'd saved money for years for a home of our own when we retired. In fact, I thought we would build it. We'd talked of using the loft acreage as a building site. It would take time for us to plan the lay out, to put our pencil to the paper, to have an architect draw our plans. It would also take time to find the right builder, to let a contract, to get our dream house built.

I said, "It would be nice to have the house finished so we could move into it gradually during the months preceding our actual retirement date."

With retirement time beginning to come into view, I was suggesting getting started with the process. Lorine balked. She was rethinking things and had decided she really didn't want to live in the country.

We began to develop Plan B.

Where would we go to retire? We spent a couple of years talking. We decided we wanted to stay near our friends. We didn't want to move to some distant state or land. We gave ourselves good reasons for living in any number of communities where we had previously served. In the end, we decided Wichita was the hub of our interests and activities. It was where the largest number of our friends lived. The arts were alive and well in Wichita. There were many educational and cultural opportunities. Wichita had good medical facilities, and it was a good transportation hub.

We had to have some trees and green space around us. We didn't want to look at homes in brand new barren (treeless) housing additions. Lorine came to Wichita regularly for her Masters studies at Wichita State University. I came regularly to make hospital calls. When either of us was in town, we began looking at various neighborhoods and studying the "For Sale" signs. Since we were now talking about acquiring an existing home rather than building our own, we thought of ourselves as being in the dreaming and researching stage. There was no hurry to find a house—it would probably be premature to do so.

Once or twice in the spring of 1992, three years before we intended to retire, we began to cruise neighborhoods together. Once when Lorine was on her own, she saw something she wanted to show me and we looked at it. One time on my way home from visiting a parishioner in Wesley Medical Center, I turned into the Rockwood neighborhood. I saw a house that intrigued me. I had a little extra time that day, so I decided to find a phone and call the realtor. I was lucky enough to find her in her office and she was able to meet me at the house right then and show it. I was taken by the house enough that I wanted Lorine to see it. When we came back and saw it together and talked more, we had some doubts about it. There wasn't a spot for Lorine's grand piano, and there was no basement so it was really short on storage space. No problem. We were just looking anyway; we weren't in the market at the moment.

But the realtor said, "If you will tell me what you really want in a house, and what areas of town you like, I can make a profile of what you are interested in. I can put this in my computer. When something like it comes on the market I can tell you."

Our reply was, "Well, we're really not in the market yet, but if you don't mind the time and effort, and there's no obligation on our part, you can do that. It might be a good learning experience for us."

You might know that within a couple of weeks she phoned saying she'd found four different houses we might be interested in—all in or very close to the Rockwood community. The long and the short of it was, only one proved to be of interest. That one, however, had been on the market several months. Now the family was ready to finish their move to Texas—a move they'd already started the previous fall. They were willing to come down on their price. The more we looked at the house, the more we were drawn to it. We decided the thing to do was to buy it while it was available and priced right. We could rent it for three years and then move into it when we retired.

Lorine was thrilled that at age 62 she was able to own her own home. What thrills Lorine usually thrills me. Since that time, home values in Rockwood, specifically, and in Wichita generally have increased significantly. Our first house has proven to be a good investment and, more importantly, it has proven to be a source of joy and satisfaction for us. I'll never believe that Plan B was better than Plan A but it's been great!

Before we could even think of renting our new house which had been purchased three years in advance, Jerry Vogt, District Superintendent of the Wichita District, phoned me. There were special needs which had arisen at First United Methodist Church. Their new Senior Pastor wanted an Executive Pastor. The Bishop, his Cabinet, and Kelly Bender, the new Senior Pastor, had conferred. They were asking me to fill the position. I was flattered with the invitation, but I told them that I was planning on retiring in three years.

"I don't think you want some one to come for just three years. It wouldn't be fair to you. I'll have to decline," I said.

To this, Jerry replied, "We'll talk about this and get back to you."

The phone soon rang again. It was Jerry. "We've discussed this and we feel you have the gifts and grace that we need at First UMC now. If you will say yes, we will use you for the three years and then you can retire."

I said yes. Kelly and I, and our wives, got together for a consultation and we both thought this was good match-up. Then there was an introductory meeting with the Staff Parish Relations Committee. In the course of this visit, the church said, "We're sorry but we don't have a parsonage available for you. We will have to give you a housing allowance. Will that be OK?"

They didn't even know that we had just purchased a house in Wichita. There was no need for us to rent that to some one. We'd use it ourselves! We'd use it ourselves. Hallelujah!

We left Augusta in mid-September 1992. Within two weeks we were settled into our new house. Lorine was not only thrilled to own her own home at age 62—she was thrilled to be living in it. By October 1, I was on the job in Wichita.

Chapter 51

WICHITA

You look familiar. Don't I know you? Haven't I seen you somewhere before?" Everyone has had someone say this to them. By the time 1993 began, I was hearing this rather often. It's still not uncommon for me to hear it even though I retired nine years ago.

One of the unique ministries of First United Methodist Church, Wichita, (there has been something unique or special about each one of my appointments) is its television ministry. National television networks are known for programs that feature high profile, usually independent, evangelists. Television programs are expensive to produce and of course these independent evangelists have not normally been financially underwritten by an organization. They've become masters at appealing to their viewers for money and many of them have ended up disgracing the Christian faith and themselves either out of greed or through moral corruption.

The television ministry of Wichita First United Methodist Church is nothing like this. It has been expensive enough that the church had to invite viewers to help support it but unlike the network "shows" it hasn't been a money maker—it's been more a financial strain.

This ministry began in 1975 and 1976 as a ministry to homebound people and an outreach to the community. It was simply a televising of what the church regularly did for worship each Sunday morning—just letting people look in, see and experience us "just as we are" *faux pas* and all. The congregation had three appointed pastors while I served it so all three of us shared in conducting each service. That meant I was on weekly television and this is why people were always thinking I looked familiar or that they had seen or known me from somewhere.

I came to First UMC, Wichita, through rather unusual circumstances. In the early 1990s rumors were circulating within the congregation that the Senior Pastor was involved in some moral indiscretions. The procedures of the United Methodist Church for dealing with such situations moved too slowly to satisfy some members. People began to leave the church. Naturally the pastor in question had his supporters as well as his critics. In 1992, after appointments had already been announced by the Bishop at Annual Conference, the pastor resigned and left our Annual Conference. His departure was much to the chagrin of his supporters. This resulted in many of them moving their membership from the church. Financial and spiritual chaos began to reign.

Three new pastors were appointed—Dr. Kelly Bender, a pastor skilled in conflict management and resolution; Nancy Goddard; and, myself. Each of us served in specialized ways. Kelley Bender was our Senior Pastor. He had three foci—preaching, teaching, and resolving the conflict and rebuilding relationships in the staff and congregation. Nancy Goddard's focus was on pastoral care. My title was Executive Pastor. I was to focus on business and property matters along with program planning and execution of programs. None of us were limited to these foci. Nancy and I, for instance, would each preach a couple of times a year when Kelly was on vacation which made us "television preachers" as well as weekly liturgists. Each of us had supervisory responsibilities for about one third of the staff members.

There were so many difficulties to be dealt with that I have never put in so many hours or so much agony as I did with this congregation. One imperative that we had to deal with was an overgrown staff and declining revenues. We had a very large staff with many fine people working for the church. We had perhaps twenty-five or more paid professional and program staff members plus an equal or larger number of support staff (secretarial, custodial, vocalists). One of the most painful experiences of my 40 years of ministry was having to terminate about a third of the church staff.

First United Methodist Church was the largest church in our Annual Conference. Its television ministry was a one-of-a kind in Kansas. It had what we called a Religious Nurture Center which may also have been a one-of-a-kind in the state. The Nurture Center was a specialized ministry which focused on the religious nurture of the developmentally delayed or disabled. We had a missions emphasis which included sending out ten or twenty or more volunteer work teams annually to engage in United Methodist mission work.

Our volunteers in mission teams might go anywhere in the United States or anywhere in the world. In addition to these teams, there is a local Spring Fling each year with 20-40 teams giving a half-day of labor to worthy agencies or causes in Wichita. I led one of the overseas teams to Costa Rica during my three years on the staff. Twenty of us helped in the renovation and expansion of a Methodist Church in Costa Rica. We labored at using sledge hammers to remove concrete walls, did new concrete work, laid title floors, painted, etc.

We have been noted for a strong musical heritage of fine choirs and directors and fine organs and organists as well as other musicians. Other congregations also have fine youth choirs and youth programs, but The Free—our high school youth choir— was outstanding and known for their annual tour in early June. They might travel to the east, west or south coast of the United States or even to Canada. The only musical and dramatic experience of my life came when The Free performed the musical "South Pacific" as a fund raiser. At their request, I played the part of the Naval Officer.

All the good qualities of First Church, only a few of which have been hinted at, far outweighed the troubles or problems I inherited when I came to the church. Nevertheless, I grew weary with the struggles. At the end of my three year commitment, I was ready "to hang it up." Lorine and I had so many deferred personal and family interests that when I retired, as planned, at the end of June 1995, I decided to completely retire. I didn't want to be like many of my peers who in retirement simply took a smaller church or another church related job. But I have tried to be "a good layman." I wanted to redirect my energies and efforts into some other channels.

Since Lorine had followed me all the years of my professional ministry, I wanted to follow her lead and have her choose the congregation where we would make our church home. She had already found a church home in First United Methodist, Wichita. She wanted to stay there. I didn't intend to do anything that would distract from any of the ministries of succeeding pastors, so this was fine with me. Even with its warts and all, FUMC Wichita is a great church.

Chapter 52

THE VALUE OF A DOLLAR

Pulling up memories from my earliest years, I can remember when a penny would buy two pieces of candy or a piece of bubble gum. You could send a one cent post card anywhere in the USA, which means a dollar would buy up to 200 pieces of candy, 100 pieces of bubble gum or you could send 100 postcards for a "buck."

A nickel would buy an ice cream cone, a soft drink, a hamburger, a ticket for a carnival ride, a couple of pencils, a city bus ride, a bag of popcorn! Think about it. This means a dollar would buy 20 ice cream cones, or cokes or root beers, or it would buy 20 hamburgers at the little restaurant on the ground floor of the Wiley Building in Hutchinson, Kansas (where Dad used to take me for lunch occasionally), or it would provide 4 weeks with a daily bus ride, Monday through Friday, or 20 bags of popcorn!

I was nine years old when congress enacted the first federal legal minimum wage. It was 1938 and the hourly rate was 25 cents. When I was a full-time student in seminary I was paid $135 per month on the GI Bill of Rights, and my monthly salary as a student pastor was $200. Lorine's semi-monthly earning as Divinity School secretary was $145. On our combined income of $625 we were able to live quite comfortably, furnishing our own apartment in Nashville and living week-ends in the furnished parsonage in Kentucky.

But the truth is, *the value of a dollar is not in what it can buy but it's in what you can do with a dollar.* Lorine and I have always tried to think of money as an extension of our personalities, of our life together, of our faith and relationships, our desire to grow in mind and spirit. It's a means to an end—to loving others as ourselves.

You can save a dollar or you can spend it. The Great Depression taught us to conserve and preserve the material resources of life. "If you don't waste things, you won't want for things" was an attitude of life engendered in my growing up years and subsequent experiences. It may not be entirely true, but there's a basic truth in this idea. Another old saying is "If you save a dollar it's worth more than if you spend it." Again, this may not be entirely true (inflation can eat it up if it isn't well invested) but there's truth in this saying. Thrift was an important value of life that is still part of whom I am.

If you save a dollar, you can save it in a sock or under a pillow or the bed. That's what people in my grandparents' generation often did.

Or, you can save a dollar where it draws interest—a place such as an interest bearing savings account at a bank or in a savings bond. This is part of what my parents did. There's a miracle in compounding interest. At 3% interest, a $100 with nothing more than its earnings plowed back into it will double in value in 23 years. At 6% interest it will become $200 in 11 years, 7 months; at 9%, it doubles in 7 and ¾ years. This is why my parents always saw to it that my sister Shirley and I each literally had a piggy bank in which we were enticed to put our extra change. As soon as we got two or three dollars, we put them in a real bank savings account to start drawing interest. Through the years, whenever I got a pay raise, I treated it as "extra change." I immediately did two things with it even before I adjusted our living budget. In consultation with Lorine, I increased our giving to church and charity and I increased our savings.

For me, the miracle of compounding interest teaches another valuable lesson which in reverse, may work to my detriment. If I borrow money to make purchases, and pay someone else interest, instead of multiplying my money I'm giving someone else a huge percentage of that purchase price on top of the price itself. When I first realized this, I began the practice of "paying myself interest." I decided to create a "New Car" fund. I bought a used car which I could afford with the money I had on hand in my savings. Then, each succeeding month, I put aside in savings an amount equal to what a new car payment would be. When the time came to buy a new car, I bought it with cash from this fund instead of borrowing the money and paying a large sum of interest on it to some one else. We have had, and still have, many other funds for vacations, furniture, Christmas and so on that work the same way.

Dad also taught me that if I might not need my savings for the next 5, 10, or 15 years, I could save (at least part of it) in a different way—by investing in equities (land, real estate, stocks or shares of ownership in businesses). The growth of this money would far exceed even the interest rate. It's interesting for me to reflect on this fact—if someone would have invested $100 in the stock market for me when I was born (just before the great crash) today that $100 would be worth $115,000. A $1,000 would have become $1,115,000!

Yes, we can save money, or we can spend it. When we receive it, we can spend it as fast as we get it. Or, we can save it for a while and end up with a larger chunk to spend for something bigger and more significant. Or, we can "spend" our money by investing and accumulating our dollars for a longer period of time. Then we are able to spend it on something big and much cherished like an education, a home, a major trip. There's even another way to use money. "Spend" it by creating for one's self a "rainy day fund" to care for ourselves in old age or poor health.

There is at least one more way of spending money. It's called GIVING IT AWAY! I'm talking about the regular weekly or monthly giving of money to church and charity. More than donating pocket money, Lorine and I believe that tithing, and the giving of gifts beyond tithing, should be part of each dollar, each check, we receive. This way we are investing in people.

One of my great joys, one of our great joys, has been to seek a happy balance between all the different ways of valuing a dollar. *Throughout my life, throughout our life together, we've really tried to "live beneath our means" so we could be able to save and to give, so as to have a sense of security and of generosity.* We've tried not to be stingy, miserly, tight, but we've tried to spend less and save more of our money.

I still remember quitting smoking, in the spring of my freshman year in college, long before most people thought using tobacco was a health issue. I did it because I figured it was burning up money. I wanted to do some other things with my money—to be more generous with it. I decided I'd better not spend it smoking and I started budgeting, like my Dad had shown me, in order to control impulse spending and manage my money better.

This philosophy of money management gave me a chance to prioritize how I would spend and save my money. Through the years this has enabled us to have the joy of spending money on fine dining and entertainment, travel and recreation, but also to limit these joys so that we could have the greater joys of spending money for a nice home, for our children and grandchildren. Within the past few years, through the joy of estate planning, we've been able to project leaving what we feel is a helpful and appropriate amount to our children and grandchildren plus having the joy of creating a charitable remainder trust to benefit, upon our deaths, one of our church colleges as well as other Christian missions and ministries in our local church.

I hope these memories are not misunderstood. It may sound like we're rich. By global standards probably we are, By American standards we're probably no more than "upper middle class" at best. But the value of a dollar for me, at least, is the meaning of life which that dollar can convey—the way it is used to affirm just and loving relationships.

I have tried, with my life, to embody the philosophy of John Wesley, father of the Methodist movement within the Christian faith:

> "Earn all you can;
> Save all you can;
> Give all you can."

Chapter 53

THE VALUE OF A FRIEND

"And we shall walk through all our days
with love remembered and love renewed."
Anonymous

With a mixture of puzzlement and alarm, Eunice quizzed our daughter-in-law, "What's going on? Have your in-laws been drinking? Are they drunk?" She had come to our house to visit because the two of them were fellow teacher friends and Angela was in town for the week-end. Lorine and I were having a get-together so they'd gone down the hall to visit in our back den. They couldn't see us—just hear us. The Nircles, our group of friends, had come for dinner. Now we were all seated in a circle in our living room visiting. Our laughter was making such a ruckus that it was disturbing their conversation. We hadn't realized how noisy and uninhibited we were. We didn't have a drink in the house and hadn't for years but, from the noise and the carrying on, Angela's guest thought maybe we'd had too much to drink.

Whenever we got together, we enjoyed each other and laughed so much that our gatherings had become primarily just a time for fun and laughter. We'd play off each other's jokes or stories in our conversations; we'd exaggerate, and do nonsensical things. If it's true that "laughter is the best medicine" and that "it's the sound of freedom," we were free in spirit and should have been well in body and mind.

The Nircles are a group that emerged early during my El Dorado ministry. One of the adult Sunday School classes had an annual Halloween party. It was the kind of party where you have to find the party. There was a starting time and place in the invitation. When you arrived, everyone was teamed up so there were six people per car. Each car load of people received two items—a clue about how to find the party and a sealed PANIC envelope. Each clue was in the form of riddle or rhyme to help the group to figure out where to go next. After discussion and speculation, you would go looking for the next clue. After finding about half a dozen clues, you were eventually led to the party. Clues might be located in public parks, at a street corner, in a newspaper or wherever; they might be in plain sight or they might be hidden under a rock or taped to a light pole. If your group got absolutely stuck and was unable to find the party after 30 minutes of trying, they could open the PANIC envelope which gave them the exact location to the party. No one was to get left out.

Lorine and I were invited to this Sunday School party. We knew the Fowlers, the Grants, the Lawrences and the Peaces. These were the people who helped us with the painting when we built the loft. After the party, the next time this group was together at the loft, we raved about what a great party the Halloween party had been. Mary Jo had helped make up the clues and determine the hiding places for them. We decided to replicate the party with the five couples of us each inviting two non-Methodist couples.

We invited them to the loft. After finding all the clues we ended up at the Grant's cabin. Once again we raved about what fun we had and about how silly and nonsensical some of the clues had been. The hardest clue to find had been one put in a circular hole in a rock in front of a veterinarian's office. Somehow, we turned this into a crazy statement that nothing goes in circles and abbreviated it into the name we started calling ourselves—the Nircles.

For the past 25 years we've been getting together just for fun although there has developed a real caring for one another. A bonus for me was being in a group of laity. True, they were all churchmen, but church was never the agenda. You might say our motto was and is "Have fun together and you'll make the world a better place." What great friends.

The Nircles and our Wichita Bridge Club, to which we have previously referred, are two very long-running groups of friends who, in the midst of itinerant ministry, have given continuity and support to our lives. People are sometimes asked, "When you are desperate and need to talk to someone or find help, do you have someone to whom you can turn?" Or, "If it's the middle of the night, and there is trouble, and you've got to call some one, do you have a friend you can call?" In these two groups, I can find an affirmative answer.

For many years my friend the Rev. Bob Eades, former Director of Chaplaincy Services at Wesley Medical Center, led a number of support groups for various categories of professionals. One of these was made up of former District Superintendents who were back in the pastoral ministry serving a local parish. It too was a quite meaningful group.

"THE GOOD OLD BOYS AND GOOD OLD GIRLS"
Front row (l to r.) Mary Lou Martin, Gloria Short,
Mel Short, Marshall Stanton
Second row: Carl Martin, Harold Kieler, Lorine Kieler,
Willa Mae Borger, Esther Bott,Bob Eades, Charles Curtis;
Back two rows: Clarence Borger, Jack Harris, Dee Eades,
Dick Wilke, Janice Stanton, Julia Wilke, LeRoy Bott,
Evelyn & Harold Nelson, Betty Curtis

With the passage of time this group, "the good old boys" as we sometimes referred to ourselves, dwindled away as a formal group although every year or so we still get together for a "bean bash" or steak fry.

Three couples of us continue to spend an evening a month together. We have a simple meal followed by conversation which focuses mostly on how things are going in our personal and family lives. Sometimes we also try to analyze the woes of the world and the response we and others are making to societal crises. For 15 or 20 years the six of us have shared our lives more deeply, more intimately than we have with almost any other friends. Here, too, I can say we experience invaluable friendship.

Of course beyond such groups as these three groups, any number of individuals have blessed me, and us as a couple, in ways that only a true friend blesses. Last Christmas, my oldest cousin, Garfaye Kieler Carpenter Reher, enclosed for me a poem with her Christmas card. I can't credit it because there's no author to acknowledged. As I've been working on these memoirs, so many people have come to my mind. Many are in our address book. Some are not. I've lost touch with many. A number are deceased. Even though the words of Garfaye's poem are a little corny, and speak in Christmas terms, the thoughts and feelings expressed are those I've experienced throughout this writing.

CHRISTMAS

"I have a list of folks I know, all written in a book
And every year when Christmas comes, I go and take a look
And that is when I realize that these names are a part
Not of the book they're written in, but of my very heart.

For each name stands for someone
Who has crossed my path sometime
And in that meeting they've become the rhythm in each rhyme
And while it sounds fantastic for me to make this claim
I really feel that I'm composed of each remembered name.

And while you may not be aware of any 'special link'
Just meeting you had changed my life a lot more than you think
For once I've met somebody, the years cannot erase
The memory of a pleasant word or of a friendly face.

So never think my Christmas cards are just a mere routine
Of names upon a Christmas list, forgotten in between
For when I send a Christmas card that is addressed to you
It's because you are on a list of folks I'm indebted to.

For I am but the total of the many folks I've met
And you happen to be one of those I prefer not to forget
And whether I have known you for many years or few
In some way you have had a part in shaping things I do.

And every year when Christmas comes, I realize anew
The best gift life can offer is meeting folks like you
And may the spirit of Christmas that forever endures
Leave its richest blessings in the hearts of you and yours.

Chapter 54

NEW HORIZONS

"For all that has been, thanks.
For all that will be, yes."
Dag Hammarskjöld

"Don't think of it as retirement—just think of it as a permanent vacation" were the words on a retirement card I received in June 1995. Retirement was and is great as far as I am concerned. To some extent it has been like a permanent vacation.

Lorine and I have done much more traveling than we were able to in our pre-retirement years. We've been able to participate in at least six domestic and international Elderhostels and numerous other trips to Europe and within the US.

We included in our first year of retirement a six-weeks New England fall foliage driving trip which also allowed us to visit family, friends, and our former colleges along the way. In addition, we included in that first year a four-week winter vacation part of which was a cruise on the SS Crystal Harmony. We boarded at Acapulco, Mexico, visited three other countries, traveled through the Panama Canal, and ended up in New Orleans.

One of our most enjoyable and fabulous trips was to Europe in 1996. The happy occasion was the marriage of our son Bill to Paula Sastrowijoto in the Netherlands.

Preceding the wedding we spent a week touring Gardens of the English National Trust. Following the wedding, the bride and groom treated the wedding party to a week-end in Orvelta, a Dutch village which is a living historical museum.

Bill and Paula Kieler holding their daughter, Naomi.

July 15, 1998, Naomi was born in Bonn, Germany. We first visited Naomi that September and since then she has been like a magnet drawing us to wherever she lived.

For me, part of what it means to live, is to see and experience as much of my home, the Planet Earth, as I can. One of our special times in the USA was being in the Colorado Rockies in June of 2000 when our son Paul married Janet Schaper at Snow Mountain YMCA Ranch in a fabulous outdoor setting. Janet's father, Ed Shaper, and I, had the privilege of being co-celebrants at the wedding. June 30, 2002, Anika was born in Denver, Colorado, and she also serves as a magnet drawing Lorine and me to the mile high city. If all goes well, praise be to God, Anika will soon have a baby brother or sister.

Paul, Solomon (born August 8, 2004), Janet and Anika

Along with the retirement cards came a piece of advice from a friend who said, "Don't retire—just re-direct your life." In a lot of ways, this is also what I've done. I have built two ponds and done some landscaping and gardening around my home, but landscaping and gardening are unfinished art forms. Lorine and I both wanted to be more involved in the Wichita Sister Cities program which has ties with Orleans, France; Kaifeng City, China; and Cancun and Tlalnepantla in Mexico. We were actively involved with the French committee for several years and are still members of the Sister Cities program.

I've sampled a variety of the many opportunities for adult education. I didn't use the computer at all when I retired. Now I'm using it a lot more although I still have a lot of learning to do. We wanted to do more traveling and spend more time with our grandchildren and children and we've been able to do this. But we aren't finished yet with our list of "things we want to do."

Who was it who asked, "What is a horizon but the limit of your sight?" To me this means, if I keep journeying toward my horizons, my horizons will continue to expand and include more new things. I've always thought of life as a journey—a journey with others and a journey with God.

Everyone is religious. Everyone, in my understanding, even the atheist and the agnostic, believes in God. How so? My seminary professor of theology, Dr. Nels F. S. Ferre used as his working definition of religion the phrase "our normally necessary whole-response to what is considered to be most important and most real." To live is to keep on deciding emotionally and intellectually, unconsciously if not consciously, what is most important and therefore most real to us. In looking at the puzzle of life and sorting out what is of supreme value, we are deciding.

What we decide is most important and most real, what we bind ourselves to as supreme in our lives, becomes our God and our religion. For some, this may be self; for some, secular humanism may be their religion. For me, personally, there was a Jewish fellow by the name of Jesus, who lived in the old Arabic-Semitic world, in ancient Israel, who portrayed and still does portray God better and more fully than any other. He taught that God is love and love is God. He's a healer. For me, this God is a very personal God, a god who cannot be limited or contained within static dogmas or ancient creeds, or for that matter cannot be contained within the limit of our minds or the mind of today. For me, God is creative and creating, is love and loving, is a healing force and a dynamic spirit, a God of shalom—peace and wholeness.

I suspect, I hope, my readers have detected in these pages the story of a life that has been molded and motivated by Jesus. I'm grateful for life. A year or two ago, I was in a class was led by a gentleman by the name of Ira "Hat" Hatfield—a man who is now approaching 105 years of age. He closed the class with this prayer he'd learned as a boy and recited everyday at school as he was growing up:

> Father, we thank you for the night,
> And for the pleasant morning light.
> For rest and food and loving care,
> and all that make the world so fair.
>
> Help us to do the things we should,
> To be to others kind and good.
> For all we do and all we say,
> To grow more like Christ every day.
> Amen

As I remember the past, reflect on the present and rejoice in time and oppurtunities left for me to live, as I journey into the future, I hope to keep tweaking and perfecting my life. I don't want to just relive the past, or sit around and watch the world unravel and decay. I've tried, albeit fallibly, to journey in a way that would make me a good citizen of the world, touching one person at a time, doing something positive and good along the way. My prayer is that I'll be able to discover new interests, new ways of serving humanity, new horizons. I have five living grandchildren. I want to leave a legacy for them and for all my descendants.

I want to leave a legacy of peace, a natural environment less spoiled than it is now, a world that runs more on renewable energy than by depleting non-renewable energy. I want to leave a world where a fuller measure of justice prevails. I want to leave a world where every child is wanted and has a chance to grow to his or her full potential. I still hope to contribute, as I hope I already have in some small measure, to a world where every person—no matter his or her status of life, regardless of religion or culture or color or sexual identity or politics—will live respecting and caring for every other person!

I'm not naïve nor am I a Pollyanna-type person. It is an imperfect world in which we live. In the words of the Apostle Paul, "All have sinned and fallen short of the glory of God." There is evil—gross evil in our world—but I do believe grace shall overcome, light dominates darkness. I remember the words of a brother in the faith (far more poetic than I), Charles James "Jim" Matthews. Last year Jim penned and shared this poem with me and others. With his permission, I use these words, which include words from the Psalmist (118:24), as my closing affirmation and my closing memory:

From Darkness to Light
by Charles James "Jim" Matthews

Light of day crept over my soul,
awakening me to voice of ancient times:
"This is the day that the Lord has made.
I shall rejoice and be glad in it."

Too soon those words faded as heavy clouds
raced across horizon, changing day to cavernous night.
Storms of trauma, terror, torture were punctuated
by lightning jags of fear, chaos, hopelessness
while acid rains of illness, starvation, death
fell with ubiquitous, unrelenting destruction,
flooding mind, soul and body with loneliness and despair.

Piercing the tempestuous darkness came a sound—
the song of a bird awakening to the dawn.
There, perched on tiniest of fragile limbs,
swaying in winds that would topple her,
she sang the song of ancient times:
"This is the day that the Lord has made.
I shall rejoice and be glad in it."

A beam of light shone through dark clouds,
and in that light was the figure of One
who bore scars on hands and feet and side.
With fiery eyes and commanding voice
this lonely figure swept storm clouds away,
and gathered up the frightened, hurting, dying souls
into arms of love, gently speaking word of old:
"I will never leave you or forsake you."
"I will go with you wherever you go."

There was a hush and then a bursting forth in song
as all creation welcomed Light that overcame darkness.
Shadows were behind us as we faced the Light
who called forth words of ancient times:
"This is the day that the Lord has made.
I shall rejoice and be glad in it."